3

FOCUS ON GRAMMAR

AN INTEGRATED SKILLS APPROACH

THIRD EDITION

MARJORIE FUCHS
MARGARET BONNER
MIRIAM WESTHEIMER

PEARSON
Longman

To the memory of my parents, Edith and Joseph Fuchs—MF
To my parents, Marie and Joseph Maus, and to my son, Luke Frances—MB
To my husband, Joel Einleger, and my children, Ari and Leora—MW

FOCUS ON GRAMMAR 3: An Integrated Skills Approach, Third Edition

Pearson Education, 10 Bank Street, White Plains, NY 10606

Vice president, multimedia and skills: Sherry Preiss
Executive editor: Laura Le Dréan
Senior development editor: Françoise Leffler
Vice president, director of design and production: Rhea Banker
Director of editorial production: Linda Moser
Production supervisor: Christine Edmonds
Senior production editor: Kathleen Silloway
Art director: Ann France
Senior manufacturing buyer: Nancy Flaggman
Photo research: Aerin Csigay
Cover design: Rhea Banker
Cover images: (background) Comstock Images (#comks76622) RF, (background center) Nick
   Koudis (#AA010649) RF; (center) Harald Sund (#200131667-001) RM
Text design: Quorum Creative Services, Rhea Banker
Text composition: ElectraGraphics, Inc.
Illustrators: Steve Attoe pp. 2, 58, 59, 135, 163, 356; Bumar Technical Corporation p. 172; Moffitt Cecil pp. 19,
   21, 240, 406; Ronald Chironna pp. 28, 419; Chi Chung pp. 249, 250; Chris Gash pp. 8, 9, 212, 217; Brian
   Hughes pp. 16, 139, 210, 229, 230, 281, 285; Jock MacRae pp. 42, 103; Tom Newsom pp. 41, 49, 50, 99,
   100, 208; PC&F pp. 259, 261; Dusan Petrici pp. 17, 65, 149, 150, 256; Steve Schulman pp. 226, 352, 354,
   364, 366, 420 (left); Susan Scott p. 34; Gary Torrisi pp. 199, 201, 295, 420 (right); Meryl Treatner pp. 73, 113.
Text credits: See p. x.
Photo credits: See p. x.

Library of Congress Cataloging-in-Publication Data

Focus on grammar. An integrated skills approach.— 3rd ed.
    p. cm.
   ISBN 0-13-147466-9 (v. 1 : student book : alk. paper) — ISBN 0-13-189971-6 (v. 2 :
student book : alk. paper) — ISBN 0-13-189984-8 (v. 3 : student book : alk. paper) —
ISBN 0-13-190008-0 (v. 4 : student book : alk. paper) — ISBN 0-13-191273-9 (v. 5 :
student book : alk. paper)
   1. English language—Textbooks for foreign speakers. 2. English language—Grammar—
Problems, exercises, etc.
PE1128.F555 2005
428.2'4—dc22

                                                            2005007655

ISBNs: 0-13-189984-8 (Student Book)
         11 12 13 14 15 V064 14 13 12 11 10

         0-13-189985-6 (Student Book with Audio CD)
         11 12 13 14 15 V064 14 13 12 11 10

Printed in The United States of America

CONTENTS

PART VIII   MORE MODALS AND SIMILAR EXPRESSIONS

APPENDICES

ABOUT THE AUTHORS

Marjorie Fuchs has taught ESL at New York City Technical College and LaGuardia Community College of the City University of New York and EFL at the Sprach Studio Lingua Nova in Munich, Germany. She has a master's degree in Applied English Linguistics and a Certificate in TESOL from the University of Wisconsin—Madison. She has authored and co-authored many widely used books and multimedia materials, notably *Crossroads, Top Twenty ESL Word Games: Beginning Vocabulary Development, Families: Ten Card Games for Language Learners, Focus on Grammar 4: An Integrated Skills Approach, Focus on Grammar 3 CD-ROM, Focus on Grammar 4 CD-ROM, Longman English Interactive 3* and *4, Grammar Express Basic, Grammar Express Basic CD-ROM, Grammar Express Intermediate,* and the workbooks to the *Longman Dictionary of American English, the Longman Photo Dictionary, The Oxford Picture Dictionary, Focus on Grammar 3* and *4,* and *Grammar Express Basic.*

Margaret Bonner has taught ESL at Hunter College and the Borough of Manhattan Community College of the City University of New York, at Taiwan National University in Taipei, and at Virginia Commonwealth University in Richmond. She holds a master's degree in Library Science from Columbia University, and she has done work toward a Ph.D. in English Literature at the Graduate Center of the City University of New York. She has authored and co-authored numerous ESL and EFL print and multimedia materials, including textbooks for the national school system of Oman, *Step into Writing: A Basic Writing Text, Focus on Grammar 4: An Integrated Skills Approach, Focus on Grammar 4 Workbook, Grammar Express Basic, Grammar Express Basic CD-ROM, Grammar Express Basic Workbook, Grammar Express Intermediate, Focus on Grammar 3 CD-ROM, Focus on Grammar 4 CD-ROM, Longman English Interactive 4,* and *The Oxford Picture Dictionary Intermediate Workbook.*

Miriam Westheimer taught EFL at all levels of instruction in Haifa, Israel, for a period of six years. She has also taught ESL at Queens College, at LaGuardia Community College, and in the American Language Program of Columbia University. She holds a master's degree in TESOL and a doctorate in Curriculum and Teaching from Teachers College of Columbia University. She is the co-author of a communicative grammar program developed and widely used in Israel.

TEXT AND PHOTO CREDITS

INTRODUCTION

The *Focus on Grammar* series

Written by ELT professionals, *Focus on Grammar: An Integrated Skills Approach* helps students to understand and practice English grammar. The primary aim of the course is for students to gain confidence in their ability to speak and write English accurately and fluently.

The **third edition** retains the series' focus on English grammar through lively listening, speaking, reading, and writing activities. The new *Focus on Grammar* also maintains the same five-level progression as the second edition:

- Level 1 (Beginning, formerly Introductory)
- Level 2 (High-Beginning, formerly Basic)
- Level 3 (Intermediate)
- Level 4 (High-Intermediate)
- Level 5 (Advanced)

What is the *Focus on Grammar* methodology?

Both controlled and communicative practice

While students expect and need to learn the formal rules of a language, it is crucial that they also practice new structures in a variety of contexts in order to internalize and master them. To this end, *Focus on Grammar* provides an abundance of both controlled and communicative exercises so that students can bridge the gap between knowing grammatical structures and using them. The many communicative activities in each Student Book unit provide opportunity for critical thinking while enabling students to personalize what they have learned in order to talk to one another with ease about hundreds of everyday issues.

A unique four-step approach

The series follows a four-step approach:

Step 1: Grammar in Context shows the new structures in natural contexts, such as articles and conversations.

Step 2: Grammar Presentation presents the structures in clear and accessible grammar charts, notes, and examples.

Step 3: Focused Practice of both form and meaning of the new structures is provided in numerous and varied controlled exercises.

Step 4: Communication Practice allows students to use the new structures freely and creatively in motivating, open-ended activities.

Thorough recycling

Underpinning the scope and sequence of the *Focus on Grammar* series is the belief that students need to use target structures many times, in different contexts, and at increasing levels of difficulty. For this reason, new grammar is constantly recycled throughout the book so that students have maximum exposure to the target forms and become comfortable using them in speech and in writing.

A complete classroom text and reference guide

A major goal in the development of *Focus on Grammar* has been to provide students with books that serve not only as vehicles for classroom instruction but also as resources for reference and self-study. In each Student Book, the combination of grammar charts, grammar notes, a glossary of grammar terms, and extensive appendices provides a complete and invaluable reference guide for students.

Ongoing assessment

Review Tests at the end of each part of the Student Book allow for continual self-assessment. In addition, the tests in the new *Focus on Grammar* Assessment Package provide teachers with a valid, reliable, and practical means of determining students' appropriate levels of placement in the course and of assessing students' achievement throughout the course. At Levels 4 (High-Intermediate) and 5 (Advanced), Proficiency Tests give teachers an overview of their students' general grammar knowledge.

What are the components of each level of *Focus on Grammar*?

Student Book

The Student Book is divided into eight or more parts, depending on the level. Each part contains grammatically related units, with each unit focusing on specific grammatical structures; where appropriate, units present contrasting forms. The exercises in each unit are thematically related to one another, and all units have the same clear, easy-to-follow format.

Teacher's Manual

The Teacher's Manual contains a variety of suggestions and information to enrich the material in the Student Book. It includes general teaching suggestions for each section of a typical unit, answers to frequently asked questions, unit-by-unit teaching tips with ideas for further communicative practice, and a supplementary activity section. Answers to the Student Book exercises and audioscripts of the listening activities are found at the back of the Teacher's Manual. Also included in the Teacher's Manual is a CD-ROM of teaching tools, including PowerPoint presentations that offer alternative ways of presenting selected grammar structures.

Workbook

The Workbook accompanying each level of *Focus on Grammar* provides additional exercises appropriate for self-study of the target grammar for each Student Book unit. Tests included in each Workbook provide students with additional opportunities for self-assessment.

Audio Program

All of the listening exercises from the Student Book, as well as the Grammar in Context passages and other appropriate exercises, are included on the program's CDs. In the book, the symbol ⌒ appears next to the listening exercises. Another symbol ⌒, indicating that listening is optional, appears next to the Grammar in Context passages and some exercises. All of these scripts appear in the Teacher's Manual and may be used as an alternative way of presenting the activities.

Some Student Books are packaged with a separate Student Audio CD. This CD includes the listening exercise from each unit.

CD-ROM

The *Focus on Grammar* CD-ROM provides students with individualized practice and immediate feedback. Fully contextualized and interactive, the activities broaden and extend practice of the grammatical structures in the reading, writing, listening, and speaking skills areas. The CD-ROM includes grammar review, review tests, score-based remedial practice, games, and all relevant reference material from the Student Book. It can also be used in conjunction with the *Longman Interactive American Dictionary* CD-ROM.

Assessment Package (NEW)

An extensive, comprehensive Assessment Package has been developed for each level of the third edition of *Focus on Grammar*. The components of the Assessment Package are:

1. Placement, Diagnostic, and Achievement Tests

- a Placement Test to screen students and place them into the correct level
- Diagnostic Tests for each part of the Student Book
- Unit Achievement Tests for each unit of the Student Book
- Part Achievement Tests for each part of the Student Book

2. General Proficiency Tests

- two Proficiency Tests at Level 4 (High-Intermediate)
- two Proficiency Tests at Level 5 (Advanced)

These tests can be administered at any point in the course.

3. Audio CD

The listening portions of the Placement, Diagnostic, and Achievement Tests are recorded on CDs. The scripts appear in the Assessment Package.

4. Test-Generating Software

The test-bank software provides thousands of questions from which teachers can create class-appropriate tests. All items are labeled according to the grammar structure they are testing, so teachers can easily select relevant items; they can also design their own items to add to the tests.

Transparencies (NEW)

Transparencies of all the grammar charts in the Student Book are also available. These transparencies are a classroom visual aid that will help instructors point out important patterns and structures of grammar.

Companion Website

The companion website contains a wealth of information and activities for both teachers and students. In addition to general information about the course pedagogy, the website provides extensive practice exercises for the classroom, a language lab, or at home.

What's new in the third edition of the Student Book?

In response to users' requests, this edition has:

- a new four-color design
- easy-to-read color coding for the four steps
- new and updated reading texts for Grammar in Context
- post-reading activities (in addition to the pre-reading questions)
- more exercise items
- an editing (error analysis) exercise in each unit
- an Internet activity in each unit
- a Glossary of Grammar Terms
- expanded Appendices

References

Alexander, L. G. (1988). *Longman English Grammar*. White Plains: Longman.

Biber, D., S. Conrad, E. Finegan, S. Johansson, and G. Leech (1999). *Longman Grammar of Spoken and Written English*. White Plains: Longman.

Celce-Murcia, M., and D. Freeman (1999). *The Grammar Book*. Boston: Heinle and Heinle.

Celce-Murcia, M., and S. Hilles (1988). *Techniques and Resources in Teaching Grammar*. New York: Oxford University Press.

Firsten, R. (2002). *The ELT Grammar Book*. Burlingame, CA: Alta Book Center Publishers.

Garner, B. (2003). *Garner's Modern American Usage*. New York: Oxford University Press.

Greenbaum, S. (1996). *The Oxford English Grammar*. New York: Oxford University Press.

Leech, G. (2004). *Meaning and the English Verb*. Harlow, UK: Pearson.

Lewis, M. (1997). *Implementing the Lexical Approach*. Hove East Sussex, UK: Language Teaching Publications.

Longman (2002). *Longman Dictionary of English Language and Culture*. Harlow, UK: Longman.

Willis, D. (2003). *Rules, Patterns and Words*. New York: Cambridge University Press.

TOUR OF A UNIT

Each unit in the *Focus on Grammar* Series presents a specific grammar structure (or two, in case of a contrast) and develops a major theme, which is set by the opening text. All units follow the same unique **four-step approach.**

Step 1: Grammar in Context

The **conversation** or **reading** in this section shows the grammar structure in a natural context. The high-interest text presents authentic language in a variety of real-life formats: magazine articles, web pages, questionnaires, and more. Students can listen to the text on an audio CD to get accustomed to the sound of the grammar structure in a natural context.

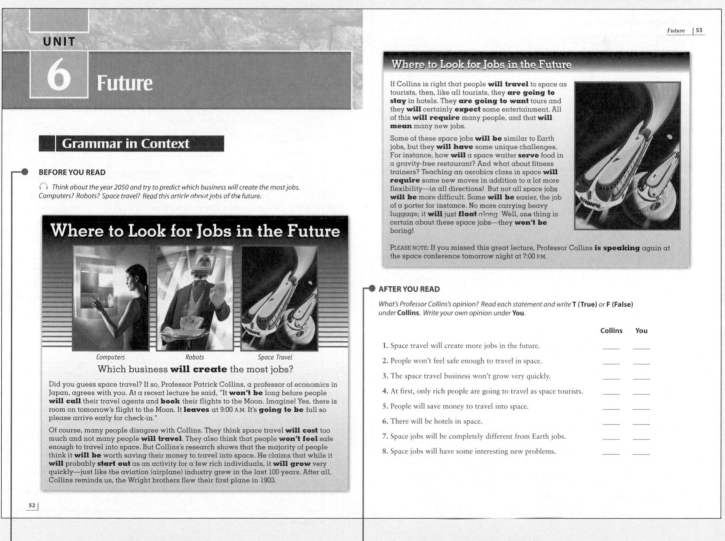

Step 2: Grammar Presentation

This section is made up of grammar charts, notes, and examples. The **grammar charts** focus on the forms of the grammar structure. The **grammar notes** and **examples** focus on the meanings and uses of the structure.

Clear and easy-to-read **grammar charts** present the grammar structure in all its forms and combinations.

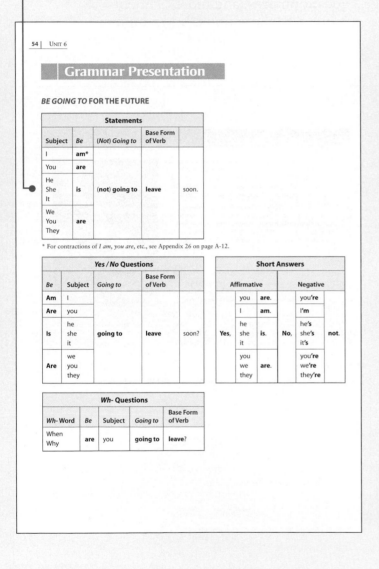

Each **grammar note** gives a short, simple explanation of one use of the structure. The accompanying **examples** ensure students' understanding of the point.

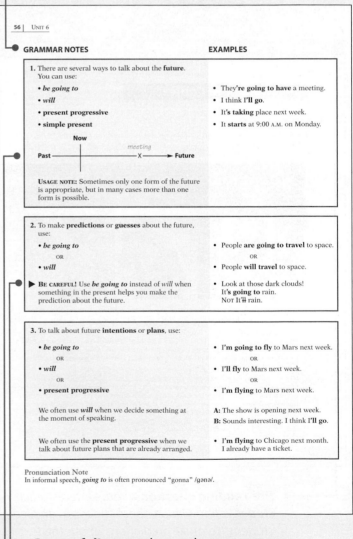

Be careful! notes alert students to common errors made by students of English.

Time lines clarify the meaning of verb forms.

Step 3: Focused Practice

This section provides students with a variety of contextualized **controlled exercises** to practice both the forms and the uses of the grammar structure.

Focused Practice *always begins with a "for recognition only" exercise called* **Discover the Grammar**.

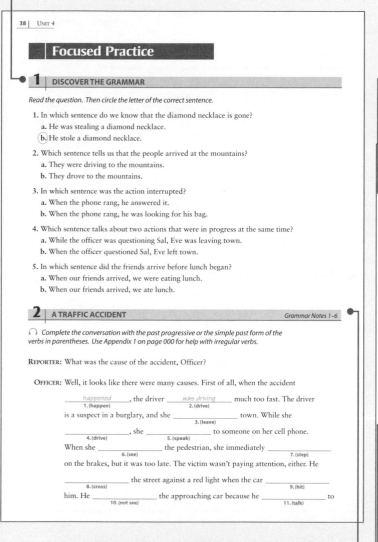

38 | UNIT 4

Focused Practice

1 | DISCOVER THE GRAMMAR

Read the question. Then circle the letter of the correct sentence.

1. In which sentence do we know that the diamond necklace is gone?
   a. He was stealing a diamond necklace.
   b. He stole a diamond necklace.

2. Which sentence tells us that the people arrived at the mountains?
   a. They were driving to the mountains.
   b. They drove to the mountains.

3. In which sentence was the action interrupted?
   a. When the phone rang, he answered it.
   b. When the phone rang, he was looking for his bag.

4. Which sentence talks about two actions that were in progress at the same time?
   a. While the officer was questioning Sal, Eve was leaving town.
   b. When the officer questioned Sal, Eve left town.

5. In which sentence did the friends arrive before lunch began?
   a. When our friends arrived, we were eating lunch.
   b. When our friends arrived, we ate lunch.

2 | A TRAFFIC ACCIDENT   *Grammar Notes 1–6*

🎧 *Complete the conversation with the past progressive or the simple past form of the verbs in parentheses. Use Appendix 1 on page 000 for help with irregular verbs.*

REPORTER: What was the cause of the accident, Officer?

OFFICER: Well, it looks like there were many causes. First of all, when the accident
_____happened_____, the driver _____was driving_____ much too fast. The driver
         1.(happen)   2.(drive)
is a suspect in a burglary, and she _____ town. While she
                                        3.(leave)
_____, she _____ to someone on her cell phone.
    4.(drive)   5.(speak)
When she _____ the pedestrian, she immediately _____
              6.(see)   7.(step)
on the brakes, but it was too late. The victim wasn't paying attention, either. He
_____ the street against a red light when the car _____
    8.(cross)   9.(hit)
him. He _____ the approaching car because he _____ to
          10.(not see)   11.(talk)

Exercises are **cross-referenced** to the appropriate grammar notes to provide a quick review.

A **variety of exercise types** *guide students from recognition to accurate production of the grammar structure.*

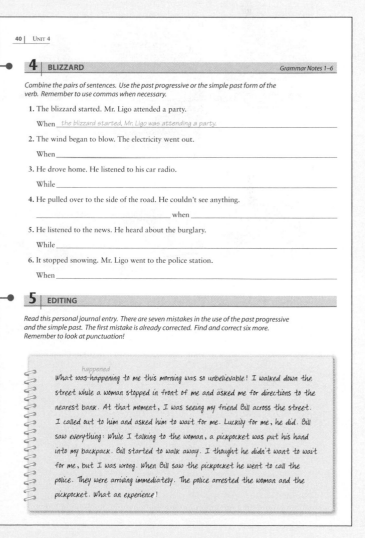

40 | UNIT 4

4 | BLIZZARD   *Grammar Notes 1–6*

Combine the pairs of sentences. Use the past progressive or the simple past form of the verb. Remember to use commas when necessary.

1. The blizzard started. Mr. Ligo attended a party.
   When _the blizzard started, Mr. Ligo was attending a party._

2. The wind began to blow. The electricity went out.
   When _____

3. He drove home. He listened to his car radio.
   While _____

4. He pulled over to the side of the road. He couldn't see anything.
   _____ when _____

5. He listened to the news. He heard about the burglary.
   While _____

6. It stopped snowing. Mr. Ligo went to the police station.
   When _____

5 | EDITING

Read this personal journal entry. There are seven mistakes in the use of the past progressive and the simple past. The first mistake is already corrected. Find and correct six more. Remember to look at punctuation!

                                    happened
What ~~was happening~~ to me this morning was so unbelievable! I walked down the
street while a woman stopped in front of me and asked me for directions to the
nearest bank. At that moment, I was seeing my friend Bill across the street.
I called out to him and asked him to wait for me. Luckily for me, he did. Bill
saw everything: While I talking to the woman, a pickpocket was put his hand
into my backpack. Bill started to walk away. I thought he didn't want to wait
for me, but I was wrong. When Bill saw the pickpocket he went to call the
police. They were arriving immediately. The police arrested the woman and the
pickpocket. What an experience!

Focused Practice *always ends with an **editing** exercise to teach students to find and correct typical mistakes.*

Step 4: Communication Practice

This section provides open-ended **communicative activities** giving students the opportunity to use the grammar structure appropriately and fluently.

*A **listening** activity gives students the opportunity to check their aural comprehension.*

*A **writing** activity allows students to use the grammar structure in a variety of formats.*

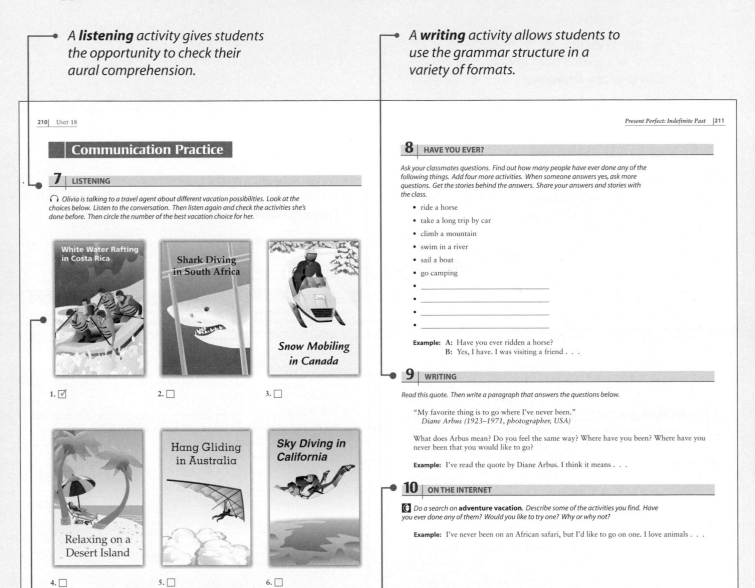

Communication Practice

7 | LISTENING

🎧 *Olivia is talking to a travel agent about different vacation possibilities. Look at the choices below. Listen to the conversation. Then listen again and check the activities she's done before. Then circle the number of the best vacation choice for her.*

White Water Rafting in Costa Rica

Shark Diving in South Africa

Snow Mobiling in Canada

1. ☑   2. ☐   3. ☐

Relaxing on a Desert Island

Hang Gliding in Australia

Sky Diving in California

4. ☐   5. ☐   6. ☐

8 | HAVE YOU EVER?

Ask your classmates questions. Find out how many people have ever done any of the following things. Add four more activities. When someone answers yes, ask more questions. Get the stories behind the answers. Share your answers and stories with the class.

- ride a horse
- take a long trip by car
- climb a mountain
- swim in a river
- sail a boat
- go camping
- _____
- _____
- _____
- _____

Example: A: Have you ever ridden a horse?
            B: Yes, I have. I was visiting a friend . . .

9 | WRITING

Read this quote. Then write a paragraph that answers the questions below.

"My favorite thing is to go where I've never been."
   Diane Arbus (1923–1971, photographer, USA)

What does Arbus mean? Do you feel the same way? Where have you been? Where have you never been that you would like to go?

Example: I've read the quote by Diane Arbus. I think it means . . .

10 | ON THE INTERNET

🌐 *Do a search on **adventure vacation**. Describe some of the activities you find. Have you ever done any of them? Would you like to try one? Why or why not?*

Example: I've never been on an African safari, but I'd like to go on one. I love animals . . .

*Many exercises and activities are **art based** to provide visual cues and an interesting context and springboard for meaningful conversations.*

*An **Internet** activity gives students the opportunity to expand on the content of the unit and interact with their classmates creatively and fluently.*

TOUR BEYOND THE UNIT

In the *Focus on Grammar* series, the grammatically related units are grouped into parts, and each part concludes with a section called **From Grammar to Writing** and a **Review Test** section.

From Grammar to Writing

This section presents a point which applies specifically to writing, for example, using descriptive adjectives to develop a paragraph. Students are guided to practice the point in a **piece of extended writing.**

An **introduction** relates the grammar point to the writing focus.

Students practice **pre-writing strategies** such as word-mapping, tree-diagramming, and outlining.

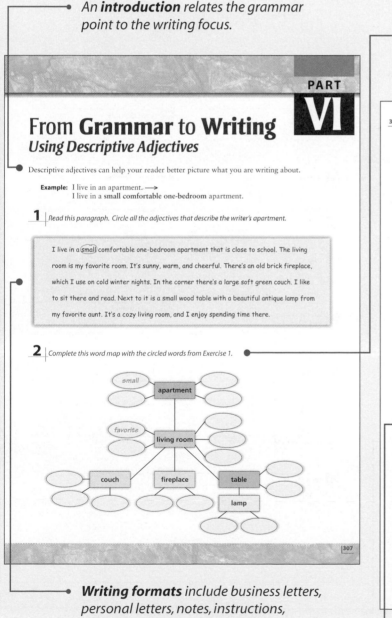

PART VI

From **Grammar** to **Writing**
Using Descriptive Adjectives

Descriptive adjectives can help your reader better picture what you are writing about.

Example: I live in an apartment. →
I live in a **small comfortable one-bedroom** apartment.

1 | Read this paragraph. Circle all the adjectives that describe the writer's apartment.

I live in a small comfortable one-bedroom apartment that is close to school. The living room is my favorite room. It's sunny, warm, and cheerful. There's an old brick fireplace, which I use on cold winter nights. In the corner there's a large soft green couch. I like to sit there and read. Next to it is a small wood table with a beautiful antique lamp from my favorite aunt. It's a cozy living room, and I enjoy spending time there.

2 | Complete this word map with the circled words from Exercise 1.

307

308 | PART VI

3 | Before you write . . .

1. Work in small groups. Put the adjectives from the box into the correct categories. Brainstorm other adjectives for each category. You can use a dictionary for help.

attractive	coarse	comfortable	cozy	cute	enormous
gorgeous	hard	hideous	huge	large	little
lovely	rough	run-down	soft	tiny	ugly

a. things that are big: _large,_

b. things that are small: _little,_

c. things that look good: _attractive,_

d. things that look bad: _run-down,_

e. things that feel good: _soft,_

f. things that feel bad: _hard,_

2. Think about a room you know. On a separate piece of paper, draw a word map like the one in Exercise 2. Use some of the adjectives in the box above.

3. Discuss your map with a partner. Do you want to add or change any adjectives?

Example: A: How small is the kitchen?
B: Oh, it's tiny.

4 | Write a paragraph about the room from Exercise 3. Use your word map.

5 | Exchange paragraphs with a different partner. Complete the chart.

Did the writer use adjectives that describe how things _____?			
	Yes	No	Example(s)
look	☐	☐	_____
feel	☐	☐	_____
smell	☐	☐	_____
sound	☐	☐	_____
What would you like more information about?			_____

6 | Work with your partner. Discuss each other's editing questions from Exercise 5. Then rewrite your own paragraph. Answer any questions your partner asked.

Writing formats include business letters, personal letters, notes, instructions, paragraphs, reports, and essays.

The section includes **peer review** and **editing** of the students' writing.

Review Test

This review section, covering all the grammar structures presented in the part, can be used as a test. An **Answer Key** is provided at the back of the book.

PART VI

Review Test

I *Complete the advertisements by choosing the correct words in parentheses.*

1. FOR RENT. Live _____*comfortably*_____ in this _____ studio
   a. (comfortable / comfortably)   b. (cozy / cozily)
   apartment. _____ rent makes it a _____
   c. (Cheap / Cheaply)   d. (perfect / perfectly)
   home for one student.

2. FOR SALE. Woman's bicycle. I'm asking the _____ low price of $65
   a. (incredible / incredibly)
   for this _____ five-speed bike. I've _____
   b. (new / newly)   c. (hard / hardly)
   used it at all. Don't miss this _____ bargain.
   d. (terrific / terrifically)

3. FREE to a _____ family. Skipper is a _____
   a. (good / well)   b. (beautiful / beautifully)
   and friendly puppy. He behaves _____ with children, and he is very
   c. (good / well)
   _____. We are moving very soon, so if you want Skipper, please act
   d. (obedient / obediently)
   _____.
   e. (quick / quickly)

II *Circle the letter of the correct answer to complete each sentence.*

1. I passed my driver's test. It seemed much _____ this time.   A Ⓑ C D
   (A) easy   (C) easiest
   (B) easier   (D) easily

2. Our team didn't play _____ I expected. I was disappointed.   A B C D
   (A) as well as   (C) as badly as
   (B) well   (D) better

3. The faster Tranh walks, _____.   A B C D
   (A) more tired   (C) the more tired he gets
   (B) he gets tired   (D) he gets more tired

(continued)

|309|

The Review Tests *include **multiple-choice questions** in standardized test formats, giving students practice in test taking.*

The Review Tests Answer Key *provides **cross-references** to the appropriate unit(s) for easy review.*

(Unit 21)
2. enough   8. How many
3. a lot of   9. any
4. How much   10. much
5. a little   11. a lot of
6. a few   12. a few
7. some

III **(Unit 22)**
2. a, a, an   6. the
3. the   7. an
4. The   8. a
5. the, the   9. the, an

IV **(Unit 22)**
3. the   6. The
4. Money   7. Vegetables
5. Travel, Staying

V **(Unit 22)**
1. b. some   2. a. some
   c. a   b. some
   d. an   c. the
   e. The   d. some
   f. The   e. The
                    f. the

VI **(Units 21 and 22)**
2. B   4. A   6. C
3. C   5. A   7. A

PART VI

I **(Unit 23)**
1. b. cozy   3. a. good
   c. Cheap   b. beautiful
   d. perfect   c. well
2. a. incredibly   d. obedient
   b. new   e. quickly
   c. hardly
   d. terrific

II **(Units 25 and 26)**
2. A   5. B   8. B   11. D
3. C   6. C   9. A   12. B
4. A   7. D   10. C   13. D

III **(Unit 23)**
2. C   5. C   8. B   11. C
3. D   6. B   9. B   12. B
4. B   7. A   10. C

IV **(Units 25 and 26)**
2. faster, more confused
3. later, sillier
4. harder, more fluently
5. more often, bigger
6. louder, faster
7. more frequently, worse

V **(Units 24 and 26)**
2. is as large as Apartment 22-G.
3. isn't as far (away) as Tony's pizzeria.
4. is as expensive as Tony's pizza.
5. play (OR are playing OR have played) as
   well as the Shock.
6. doesn't run as fast as (OR isn't as fast as)
   Jennifer.

VI **(Units 25 and 26)**
1. b. longest   2. a. big
   c. hardest   b. than
   d. the   c. much
   e. of   d. exciting
   f. best   e. Sooner
                     f. as

VII **(Units 23–26)**
                                      worst
I think today has been the ~~bad~~ day of my life.
My car broke down on the expressway during rush
                               the
hour this morning—a busiest time of day. I sat
there for an hour waiting for a tow truck. The
              more
~~longer~~ I waited, the ~~nervous~~ I became. I was a
wreck when I got to work. Of course, this was the
day we
         the
were closing ~~biggest~~ deal of the year. My boss
called me five times about one letter. And ~~more~~
                                             the
frequently he called, the worse I typed. My next
worry is the repair bill for the car. I hope it isn't as
        as
high ~~the~~ last time.
   I'm going to try to relax now. There's an
interesting
~~interested~~ movie on cable TV tonight. Jan saw it
                                best
last week and says it's the ~~better~~ film she's seen in a
                               hot
long time. After the movie, I'll take a ~~hotter~~ bath
and go to bed. I'm looking forward to tomorrow.
        bad
It can't be as ~~badly~~ as today!

RT-4|

ACKNOWLEDGMENTS

Before acknowledging the many people who have contributed to the third edition of *Focus on Grammar*, we wish to express our gratitude to those who worked on the first and second editions, and whose influence is still present in the new work. Our continuing thanks to:

- Joanne Dresner, who initiated the project and helped conceptualize the general approach of *Focus on Grammar*.

- Nancy Perry, Penny Laporte, Louisa Hellegers, and Joan Saslow, our editors for the first edition, and Françoise Leffler, our editor for the second edition, for helping to bring the books to fruition.

- Sharon Hilles, our grammar consultant, for her insight and advice on the first edition.

In the third edition, *Focus on Grammar* has continued to evolve as we update materials and respond to the valuable feedback from teachers and students who have been using the series. We are grateful to the following editors and colleagues:

- Laura Le Dréan, Executive Editor, for her dedication and commitment. In spite of an incredibly full schedule, she looked at every page of manuscript and offered excellent suggestions. In addition, she was always available and responsive to authors' concerns.

- Françoise Leffler, Senior Development Editor, for her continued dedication to the series and to improving *Focus on Grammar* with each new edition. As in the previous edition, we relied on her unflagging attention to detail and her wonderful sense of style.

- Kathleen Silloway, Senior Production Editor, for piloting the book through its many stages of production and for always giving us a heads up when more *FOG* was about to roll in.

- Irene Schoenberg, for generously sharing her experience in teaching our first two editions and for her enthusiastic support.

Finally, we are grateful, as always, to Rick Smith and Luke Frances, for their helpful input and for standing by and supporting us as we navigated our way through our third *FOG*.

We also wish to acknowledge the many reviewers for reading the manuscript and offering many useful suggestions.

Aileen Allison, Golden Gate Language School, Campbell, CA; **Larisa Álvarez Ávila,** Centro Educativo Renacimiento, Mérida, Yucatán, Mexico; **Jaime Bolaños,** Colegio Ker Liber, Guadalajara, Mexico; **Vahania Carvajal García,** Instituto Cultural Regina Teresiano, Hermosillo, Sonora, Mexico; **Julie Charland,** Ateliers de Langues CSCG, Québec City, Québec, Canada; **Amelia Chávez Ruiz,** Lake Forest School, Mexico State, Mexico; **Elisa Laura Chavira,** Instituto Cumbre del Noroeste, Ciudad

Obregón, Mexico; **Ronald Clark,** Boston University, Boston, MA; **Judy Cleek,** University of Tennessee at Martin, Martin, TN; **Elizabeth Clemente,** Instituto Tecnológico de Estudios Superiores de Monterrey, Atizapan, Mexico State, Mexico; **Sharon Cliff,** Richmond College, Richmond, TX; **Marilyn De Liro Álvarez,** Instituto "Las Brisas," Nuevo León, Mexico; **Susanna Eguren,** Instituto Cultural Peruano Norteamericano, Lima, Peru; **Marcia Gethin-Jones,** University of Connecticut, Stamford, CT; **Monica Hilding,** Central Community School, Salt Lake City, UT; **Sue Hynes,** Daley College, Chicago, IL; **Silvia Icela Espinoza Galvez,** Colegio Lux, Hermosillo, Sonora, Mexico; **Elizabeth Kelley,** University of California, San Diego, CA; **Anik Low,** Collège Jean-de-Brébeuf, Montréal, Québec, Canada; **Hank Mantell,** International Education Programs, University of California, Riverside, CA; **Javier Martínez García,** Instituto Las Américas, Mexico City, D. F., Mexico; **Darlene Mitchell,** International English Center, Boulder, CO; **Norma Morales Sánchez,** Instituto Carlos Gracido, Oaxaca, Mexico; **Robin Persiani,** Sierra College, Grass Valley, CA; **Mary Lou Price,** University of Texas at Austin, Austin, TX; **Mary Kay Purcell,** University of Evansville, Evansville, IN; **Graciela Ramírez Hernández,** Instituto Hispano Inglés de México, Mexico City, Mexico; **Mark Rau,** American River College, Sacramento, CA; **Nicholas Renton,** American Culture and Language Program, Los Angeles, CA; **Ernesto Romo,** Lake Forest School, Mexico State, Mexico; **René Sandoval,** Martin Luther King, Jr. School, Guadalajara, Jalisco, Mexico; **Allen Sellers,** Oregon State University, Corvallis, OR; **Nicola Teague,** San Diego State University, San Diego, CA; **Elena O. Torres González,** Instituto Tecnológico de Estudios Superiores de Monterrey, Atizapan, Mexico State, Mexico; **María Elena Vera de la Rosa,** Lake Forest School, Mexico State, Mexico; **Magneli Villanueva Morales,** Universidad Regiomontana, Monterrey, Nuevo León, Mexico; **Elaine Wilson,** Culture Works, London, Ontario, Canada; **Essio Zamora,** Instituto Carlos Gracido, Oaxaca, Mexico; **Ian Zapp,** Colegio México Irlandés, Guadalajara, Jalisco, Mexico.

Present, Past, and Future: Review and Expansion

Present Progressive and Simple Present

Grammar in Context

BEFORE YOU READ

🎧 *Look at the cartoons. What are the people doing? How do they feel? Read this article about cross-cultural communication.*

WHAT'S YOUR CROSS-CULTURAL IQ?

Are you **living** in your native country or in another country? **Do** you ever **travel** abroad? **Do** you **understand** the misunderstandings below?

*Why **does** he **look** so surprised? I just **want** to say hello.*

*What **is** he **doing** here? We **don't have** an appointment.*

SITUATION 1

Tomás **is visiting** Claude. Claude **looks** very surprised. In Tomás's culture, people **often visit** without calling first. But in Claude's culture, people **don't do** that. They **always check** with their friends before they **come over**.

What's wrong? I'm just saying hello.

*What **is** she **doing**? Why **is** she **kissing** me again?*

SITUATION 2

Nicole and Sheila **are saying** hello and **kissing**. They **are** both **feeling** very uncomfortable. In Nicole's culture, people **usually kiss** twice, once on each cheek. In Sheila's culture, people **don't kiss** more than once.

AFTER YOU READ

Complete each sentence with the correct name.

1. _____ is visiting without calling first.

2. _____ is surprised to have a visitor.

3. _____ is kissing the other woman twice.

4. _____ doesn't expect a second kiss.

Now circle the correct answer for your own culture.

In my culture . . .

5. People usually <u>call / don't call</u> before visiting.

6. When people say hello, they <u>don't kiss / kiss</u>.

Grammar Presentation

PRESENT PROGRESSIVE

Affirmative Statements

Subject	*Be*	Base Form of Verb + *-ing*	
I	**am***		
You	**are**		
He She It	**is**	**traveling**	now.
We You They	**are**		

*For contractions of *I am, you are*, etc., see Appendix 26 on page A-12.

Negative Statements

Subject	*Be*	*Not*	Base Form of Verb + *-ing*	
I	**am**			
He	**is**	**not**	**traveling**	now.
We	**are**			

SIMPLE PRESENT

Affirmative Statements

Subject		Verb
I You		**travel.**
He She It	often	**travels.**
We You They		**travel.**

Negative Statements

Subject	*Do*	*Not*	Base Form of Verb	
I	**do**			
He	**does**	**not**	**travel**	often.
We	**do**			

(continued)

Yes / No Questions			
Be	Subject	Base Form of Verb + *-ing*	
Is	he	**traveling**	now?

Short Answers		
Yes,	he	is.
No,		isn't.

Yes / No Questions			
Do	Subject	Base Form of Verb	
Does	he	**travel**	often?

Short Answers		
Yes,	he	does.
No,		doesn't.

Wh- Questions				
Wh- Word	*Be*	Subject	Base Form of Verb + *-ing*	
Where	**are**	you	**traveling**	now?

Wh- Questions				
Wh- Word	*Do*	Subject		Base Form of Verb
Where	**do**	you	usually	**travel**?

GRAMMAR NOTES

EXAMPLES

1. Use the **present progressive** to describe something that is happening <u>right now</u> (for example, *now, at the moment*).

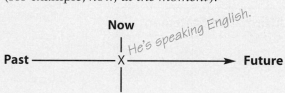

The present progressive is often used to show that the action is <u>temporary</u>.

- Tomás **is visiting** Claude.
- He **'s speaking** English *right now*.

- **I'm staying** with friends *at the moment*, but I plan to leave soon.

2. Use the **simple present** to describe what <u>regularly</u> happens (for example, *every day, usually, always*).

Use the simple present to talk about <u>scientific facts</u>.

- Tomás **talks** to Claude *every day*.
- He *usually* **wears** jeans.
- He *always* **speaks** Spanish at home.

- Stress **causes** high blood pressure.
- Water **boils** at 212°F (100°C).

3. Use the **present progressive** to describe something that is happening in the <u>extended present</u> time (for example, *nowadays, these days, this month, this year*), even if it's not happening at the moment of speaking.

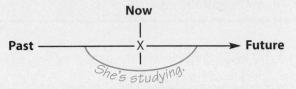

- We**'re studying** U.S. customs *this month*.
- Laura**'s studying** in France *this year*.
- **Are** you **studying** hard *these days*?

4. Use the **simple present** with <u>adverbs of frequency</u> to express how often something happens.

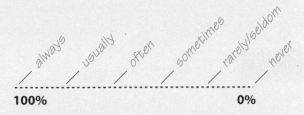

▶ **BE CAREFUL!** Adverbs of frequency usually go <u>before</u> the main verb, but they go <u>after</u> the verb *be*.

- In Spain women *always* **kiss** on both cheeks.
- In France women *often* **kiss** on both cheeks.
- We *rarely* **stand** very close to each other.
- In China children *never* **call** adults by their first names.

- They *never* **come** late.
- They **are** *never* late.

5. Use the **simple present** with most <u>non-action verbs</u>. Do not use the present progressive—even when the verb describes a situation that exists at the moment of speaking.

Non-action verbs usually describe <u>states</u> or <u>situations</u> but not actions. They are used to:

a. express **emotions** (*hate, like, love, want, feel, fear, trust*)

   USAGE NOTE: Unlike other verbs that express emotion, *feel* is often used in the progressive form.

b. describe **mental states** (*know, remember, believe, think [= believe], understand*)

c. show **possession** (*have, own, possess, belong*)

d. describe **senses** and **perceptions** (*hear, see, smell, taste, feel, notice, seem, look [= seem], be, appear, sound*)

- Jane **wants** to go home *now*.
  NOT Jane ~~is wanting~~ to go home now.

- We **like** Claude a lot.
- Ricki **feels** homesick. OR
- Ricki **is feeling** homesick.

- I **know** a lot of U.S. customs now.
- Ari **remembers** your number.

- Cesar **has** two brothers.
- Some students **own** cars.

- I **hear** the telephone.
- Dina **seems** tired.

(continued)

6. BE CAREFUL! Some verbs that describe senses and perceptions such as *taste, smell, feel,* and *look* can have both a non-action and an action meaning.

NON-ACTION

- The soup **tastes** good. Try some.

ACTION

- She**'s tasting** the soup to see if it needs more salt.

Reference Notes

For definitions and examples of **grammar terms,** see Glossary on page G-1.

For **spelling rules** on forming the **present progressive,** see Appendix 21 on page A-10.

For **spelling rules** on forming the third person singular of the **simple present,** see Appendix 20 on page A-9.

For **pronunciation rules** for the **simple present,** see Appendix 29 on page A-14.

For a list of **non-action verbs,** see Appendix 2 on page A-2.

For use of the **present progressive** and the **simple present** to talk about the **future,** see Unit 6.

Focused Practice

1 | DISCOVER THE GRAMMAR

Read these journal entries by Brian, a Canadian summer exchange student studying in Argentina. Circle all the verbs that describe what is happening **now**. *Underline the verbs that describe what* **regularly** *happens.*

JUNE 28: I'm sitting in a seat 30,000 feet above the Earth en route to Argentina! I usually have dinner at this time, but right now I have an awful headache from all the excitement. My seatmate is eating my food. I guess it's good. She looks happy.

JUNE 30: It's 7:30 P.M. My host parents are still working. Carlos, my father, works at home. My little brother, Ricardo, is cute. He looks (and acts) a lot like Bobby. Right now, he's looking over my shoulder and trying to read my journal.

JULY 4: The weather is cold here. I usually spend the first weekend of July at the beach. Today I'm walking around in a heavy sweater.

AUGUST 6: I usually feel great in the evening because we take long naps in the afternoon, but tonight I feel really tired.

AUGUST 25: I'm feeling very comfortable here now—but it's almost time to go home! My host parents usually cook a light dinner, but tonight they're cooking a special dinner for me. I miss them already!

2 | SCHEDULE CHANGES   *Grammar Notes 1–2*

Look at Brian's schedule in Argentina. He usually has a regular schedule but today is different. Complete the sentences below. Use the present progressive or the simple present. Choose between affirmative and negative forms.

```
7:00-8:00      run in the park    get ready for a field trip
8:30-12:30     attend class       go on a field trip to the museum
1:00-2:00      eat lunch
2:00-3:00      take a nap          work on the family web page
3:00-5:00      work in the cafeteria
5:00-6:30      do homework         call home at 5:00 sharp today!
6:30-8:30      play tennis         watch a video with Eva
8:30           have dinner
9:30-10:00     write letters       take a walk with the family
10:00-10:30    take a shower       do homework
```

1. Brian always ___runs in the park___ early in the morning,

   but today he ___is getting ready for a field trip___.

2. Brian usually _____ between 8:30 and 12:30,

   but today he _____.

3. He always _____ between 1:00 and 2:00.

4. It's 1:30. He _____.

5. He normally _____ after lunch,

   but today he _____.

6. Every day from 3:00 to 5:00, he _____.

7. It's 5:00, but he _____ now.

   He _____ instead.

8. It's 6:45, but he _____.

   He _____.

9. It's 8:30. Brian _____.

10. He always _____ at 8:30.

11. After dinner, Brian usually _____,

    but tonight he _____.

12. It's 10:15, but he _____.

    He _____.

3 | CULTURAL DIFFERENCES

Some students are talking outside of a classroom. Complete their conversations. Choose between the simple present and the present progressive forms of the verbs in parentheses.

A. **LI-WU:** Hi, Paulo. What _____*are you doing*_____?
1. (do you do / are you doing)

PAULO: Oh, I _____ for class to begin.
2. (wait / 'm waiting)

LI-WU: How are you? You _____
3. (seem / 're seeming)

a little down.

PAULO: I'm just tired. I _____ evenings
4. (work / 'm working)

this semester. Hey, is that your teacher over there?

LI-WU: Yes. She _____ to one of my
5. (talks / 's talking)

classmates.

PAULO: What's wrong? He _____
6. (doesn't look / 's not looking)

at her. He _____ uncomfortable.
7. (seems / 's seeming)

LI-WU: Oh. That _____ anything. In Taiwan it's not respectful to
8. (doesn't mean / isn't meaning)

look directly at your teacher.

B. **TARO:** There's Miguel. He _____ to Luisa.
1. (talks / 's talking)

MARISA: Yes. They _____ a class together
2. (take / 're taking)

this semester.

TARO: They _____ very close to each
3. (stand / 're standing)

other. _____ they
4. (Do you think / Are you thinking)

_____?
5. (date / 're dating)

MARISA: No. I _____ it
6. (don't think / 'm not thinking)

_____ anything special. I
7. (means / 's meaning)

_____ from Costa Rica, and people
8. (come / 'm coming)

_____ that close to each other.
9. (usually stand / are usually standing)

4 | MORE CULTURAL DIFFERENCES

Grammar Notes 1–6

Other students are talking outside of a classroom. Complete their conversations. Use the simple present or the present progressive form of the verbs in parentheses.

A. RASHA: There's Hans. Why ___is___ he ___walking___
1. (walk)

so fast? Class _____ at 9:00.
2. (start)

He still _____ 10 minutes!
3. (have)

CLAUDE: He always _____ fast. I think Swiss
4. (walk)

people often _____ to be in a hurry.
5. (appear)

B. YOKO: Isn't that Sergio and Luis? Why _____

they _____ hands? They already
1. (shake)

_____ each other!
2. (know)

LI-JING: In Brazil, men _____ hands every time
3. (shake)

they _____.
4. (meet)

YOKO: _____ women _____ hands too?
5. (shake)

5 | CULTURE SHOCK!

Grammar Notes 1–6

Complete the following paragraph. Use the correct form of the verbs in the box.

| cause | feel | go | live | ~~make~~ | travel |

New food, new customs, new routines—they all ___make___ international travel
1.

interesting. But they also _____ culture shock for many travelers. _____ you
2.

now _____ or _____ in a culture different from your own? If so, why
3.   4.

_____ you _____ so good (or so bad)? Some experts say that we often
5.

_____ through four stages of culture shock:
6.

Honeymoon Stage:	In the first weeks everything seems great.
Rejection Stage:	You have negative feelings about the new culture.
Adjustment Stage:	Things are getting better these days.
Adaptation Stage:	You are finally comfortable in the new culture.

Take the quiz in Exercise 6 and see what stage you are in.

6 | QUIZ

*Complete the following statements using the correct form of the verbs in the box. Then
check the statements that are true for you* **now.**

annoy	feel	improve	live	~~love~~
make	think	treat	understand	want

☐ 1. I _____ *love* _____ it here!

☐ 2. People always _____ me very kindly.

☐ 3. The customs here often _____ me.

☐ 4. I _____ here now, but I _____ I'll stay.
     (negative)

☐ 5. I _____ to go home!

☐ 6. My language skills _____ a lot each month.

☐ 7. I _____ a lot of new friends these days.

☐ 8. I still _____ everything, but I _____ at home here.
     (negative)

To check your Quiz results, go to page 92.

7 | EDITING

*Read this student's journal. There are eleven mistakes in the use of the present progressive
or simple present. The first mistake is already corrected. Find and correct ten more.*

> I'm sitting
> It's 12:30 and ~~I sit~~ in the library right now. My classmates are eating lunch
> together, but I'm not hungry yet. At home, we eat never this early. Today our journal
> topic is culture shock. It's a good topic for me right now because I'm being pretty
> homesick. I miss my old routine. At home we always are eating a big meal at 2:00 in
> the afternoon. Then we rest. But here in Toronto I'm having a 3:00 conversation class.
> Every day I almost fall asleep in class, and my teacher ask me, "Are you bored?"
> Of course I'm not bored. I just need my afternoon nap! This class always is fun. This
> semester we work on a project with video cameras. My team is filming groups of
> people from different cultures. We are analyze "social distance." That means how close
> to each other these people stand. According to my new watch, it's 12:55, so I leave
> now for my 1:00 class. Teachers here really aren't liking tardiness!

Communication Practice

8 | LISTENING

∩ *Listen to an interview with a new foreign student. Then listen again and check the things the student usually does and the things she is doing now or these days.*

	Usually	Now or These Days
1. speak English	☐	☑
2. speak Spanish	☐	☐
3. live in a small town	☐	☐
4. live in a big city	☐	☐
5. walk slowly	☐	☐
6. wear a watch	☐	☐
7. study computer science	☐	☐

9 | GETTING TO KNOW YOU

Walk around your classroom. Ask your classmates questions. Find someone who . . .

Name(s)

- likes visiting foreign countries   _____

- isn't wearing a watch   _____

- speaks more than two languages   _____

- is studying something besides English   _____

- doesn't watch sports on TV   _____

- is planning to travel this year   _____

- _____   _____
  (add your own)

Example: **A:** Do you like visiting foreign countries?
       B: Yes, I do. What about you?

Report back to the class.

  Example: Tania and José like visiting foreign countries.

10 | WHAT'S HAPPENING?

Work in pairs. Look at the photographs. Describe them. What's happening? Discuss possible explanations for each situation. Compare your answers with those of your classmates.

> **Example:** **A:** He's pointing. He looks angry.
> **B:** Maybe he's just explaining something.

11 | QUESTIONABLE QUESTIONS?

Work in small groups. Look at the questions. In your culture, which questions are appropriate to ask someone you just met? Which are not appropriate? Compare your choices with those of your classmates.

- How old are you?
- What do you do?
- How much rent do you pay?
- What are you studying?
- Are you married?
- Where do you live?

12 | WRITING

Write a paragraph about a new experience you are having. Maybe you are living in a new country, taking a new class, or working at a new job. Describe the situation. How is it different from what you usually do? How do you feel in the situation?

> **Example:** I usually live at home with my parents, but this month I'm living with my aunt and uncle. Everything seems different. My aunt . . .

13 | ON THE INTERNET

*Weather often affects what people in different cultures do. Do a search on **weather** for a place you know well. Find out what the weather is now. Then compare it to what the weather usually is this time of year. Tell your classmates about the weather and what people usually do in this weather.*

> **Example:** In Haiti it usually rains this time of year, but today it's not raining. It rains so often in Haiti that people usually ignore it. Children often play outside in the rain.

Imperative

Grammar in Context

BEFORE YOU READ

Look at the pictures. What is the woman doing? What do you do to stay fit? Read part of an exercise routine presented in a fitness magazine.

The Warrior Workout

Having a bad day? **Don't let** it get you down. **Try** our kickboxing workout instead. You'll feel better *and* build your strength. **Do** it three times a week for fast results.

THE JAB

Get into the basic position: **Bend** your knees and **place** your right foot in front. **Raise** your fists with your right hand in front. Now **punch** with your right fist. **Don't stand** straight as you punch. Instead, **lean** forward for more power. **Bring** your fist back immediately. Then **change** sides.

THE POWER KICK

Get into the basic position and **move** your weight onto your right foot. **Bend** your elbows and **bring** your left knee as high as your hip. Then **kick** to the side. **Don't point** your toes as you kick.

AFTER YOU READ

*Read the following instructions. Check **Jab** if it is for the Jab, or **Power Kick** if it is for the Power Kick. Check **Both** if it's for both.*

	Jab	Power Kick	Both
1. Start in the basic position.	☐	☐	☐
2. Punch with one fist.	☐	☐	☐
3. Don't lean back.	☐	☐	☐
4. Bend both elbows.	☐	☐	☐
5. Put your weight on one foot.	☐	☐	☐
6. Don't point your toes.	☐	☐	☐

Grammar Presentation

IMPERATIVE

Affirmative	
Base Form of Verb	
Bend	your knees.
Raise	your fists.

Negative		
Don't	**Base Form of Verb**	
Don't	**bend**	your knees.
	raise	your fists.

GRAMMAR NOTES

EXAMPLES

1. Use the **imperative** to:	
a. give **directions** and **instructions**	• **Turn** left at the light. • **Get** into the basic position.
b. give **orders** or **commands**	• **Get up!** • **Don't move!**
c. give **advice** or make **suggestions**	• Always **warm up** first. • **Don't exercise** when you're sick.
d. give **warnings**	• **Be** careful! • **Don't fall!**

2. Use the **imperative** also to:

a. make **requests** (use *please* in addition to the imperative)

b. make **informal invitations**

USAGE NOTE: When using the imperative in a formal situation, add *please*.

- *Please* **read** this article.
- **Read** this article, *please*.

- **Have** lunch with us tomorrow.
- **Bring** a friend.

- *Please* **join** us, Mrs. Rivera.
  NOT ~~Join~~ us, Mrs. Rivera.

3. Note that the **subject** of an imperative statement is *you*. However, do not say or write *you*.

▶ **BE CAREFUL!** The imperative form is the same in both the singular and the plural.

- **Stand up** straight!
  NOT ~~You~~ stand up straight!
- **Don't hold** your breath!
  NOT ~~You~~ don't hold your breath!

- John, **point** your toes.
- John and Susan, **point** your toes.

Focused Practice

1 | DISCOVER THE GRAMMAR

Match an imperative in column A with a situation in column B.

Column A

 1. Don't touch that!

_____ 2. Buckle your seat belt.

_____ 3. Look both ways!

_____ 4. Dress warmly!

_____ 5. Don't bend your knees.

_____ 6. Mark each answer *true* or *false*.

_____ 7. Come in! Make yourself at home.

_____ 8. Try a little more pepper.

_____ 9. Walk two blocks on First Street.

Column B

a. Someone is visiting a friend.

b. Someone is going out into the cold.

c. Someone is crossing a street.

d. Someone is taking an exam.

e. Someone is driving a car.

f. Someone is giving directions.

g. Someone is exercising.

h. Someone is tasting some food.

i. Something is hot.

2 | HEALTHY SMOOTHIE

Grammar Notes 1a, 3

Look at the pictures showing how to make a banana-strawberry smoothie. Match a verb from column A with the appropriate words from column B to give instructions for making the smoothie. Then put the sentences in the correct order.

Column A	**Column B**
____ Add	the ingredients until smooth.
__1__ Slice	six strawberries.
____ Cut	a banana.
____ Wash	orange juice into the blender.
____ Blend	the strawberries in half.
____ Pour	the fruit to the orange juice.

Write each sentence under the appropriate picture.

1.  _Slice a banana._

2. _____

3. _____

4. _____

5. _____

6. _____

3 | MARTIAL ARTS

Complete the advertisement for a martial arts school. Use the affirmative or negative imperative form of the verbs in the box.

become	choose	decrease	increase	learn
miss	register	take	~~think~~	wait

MARTIAL ARTS ACADEMY

_____*Don't think*_____ that martial arts is only about physical training. A good
    1.
martial arts program offers many other benefits as well.

_____ self-defense and more at the Martial Arts Academy:
    2.

◆ _____ stress. Martial arts training helps you relax.
        3.

◆ _____ concentration. Martial arts students learn to
        4.
focus their attention.

◆ _____ fit. Strength and flexibility improve as you learn.
        5.
We are offering an introductory trial membership. _____ this
                                                            6.
special opportunity. _____ classes with Master Lorenzo
                            7.
Gibbons, a ninth-degree Black Belt Master.

_____ classes from our convenient
    8.
schedule. _____!
                9.
_____ now for a two-week trial.
    10.
Only $30. ◆ **Uniform included.**

4 | EDITING

Read this student's journal entry. There are five mistakes in the use of the imperative. The first mistake is already corrected. Find and correct four more.

For the Black Belt essay, Master Gibbons gave us this assignment:

Write

~~You write~~ about something important to you. My topic was "The Right

Way," the rules of life for the martial arts.

Three of these rules are very important to me:

- First, respects other people—treat them the way you want them to

  treat you.

- Second, helped people in need. In other words, use your strength for

  others, not use it just for your own good.

- Third, no lie or steal. You can't defend others when you feel guilty.

There are many other rules, but these are the three most important

ones to me.

Communication Practice

5 | LISTENING

🎧 *Listen to a TV chef describing how to make pancakes. Then listen again and number the instructions in the correct order.*

_____ Heat a frying pan and melt a small piece of butter in it.

_1_ Beat two egg whites in a large bowl.

_____ Add one and a quarter cups of whole wheat flour to the egg whites.

_____ Flip the pancakes over.

_____ Blend in some fruit.

_____ Mix thoroughly.

_____ Top them with fruit or yogurt.

_____ Pour some of the pancake mixture into the frying pan.

_____ Add a cup of low-fat milk.

6 | INFORMATION GAP: FIND THE WAY

Work in pairs (A and B). You are both going to give driving directions to places on the map.
Student A, follow the instructions on this page. Student B, turn to page 21.

1. Ask your partner for directions to the Martial Arts Academy. Draw the route.

    Example: **A:** I want to go to the Martial Arts Academy. Can you give me directions?
    B: Sure. Start at the corner of Carter and Adams.

2. Draw the route from Carter and Adams to the Sunrise Gym.
    (Be careful! One-way streets are marked →. Don't go the wrong way on a one-way street!)
    Give your partner directions.

    Example: **B:** I want to go to the Sunrise Gym. Can you give me directions?
    A: Sure. Start at the corner of Carter and Adams.

When giving directions, use sentences like these:

Start at the corner of Carter and Adams.	Go straight.	Continue on 9th Street.
(Don't) turn right.	Make a left turn.	Stay on Founders.

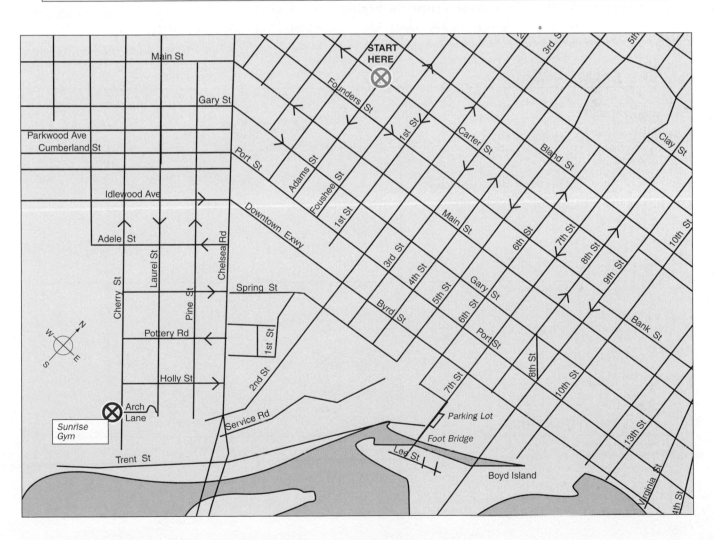

When you are finished, compare routes with your partner. Are they the same?

7 | RECIPE EXCHANGE

Work in small groups. Write down one of your favorite recipes. List the ingredients and write the instructions.

Example:

QUICK AND EASY BEAN TACOS
Ingredients: 1 can of beans (black, kidney, or pinto), 4 hard corn taco shells, 1 tomato, 1 onion, lettuce, salsa, spices (cumin, chili powder)
Instructions: Rinse and drain the beans. Add the spices. Simmer for 10 minutes. Chop the tomato and onion. Shred the lettuce. Fill the taco shells with the beans, tomato, and onion. Top with the lettuce and salsa.

Read your recipe to your group. Answer your classmates' questions.

Example: **A:** How long do you rinse the beans?
B: Until the water looks clear. Use cold water. Don't use hot water.

8 | CALM DOWN!

Work in small groups. Imagine you have been in a traffic jam for an hour. A friend is waiting to meet you on a street corner. What can you say to yourself to calm yourself down? Share your list with the other groups.

Example: **A:** Take a deep breath.
B: Don't think about the traffic.
C: . . .

9 | WRITING

Write directions from your school to another location. It can be your home, a store, the train station, or any place you choose.

Example: To get to my apartment from school, walk two blocks on Oak Street. Turn left on Tenth Avenue. Then take the bus to Main and . . .

10 | ON THE INTERNET

*As a class, choose a place that you would like to go to in your area. Then work in small groups. Do a search on **maps and directions** and look up directions to that place. Compare the directions. Are they the same? If not, how are they different? Which directions are the best? Why?*

INFORMATION GAP FOR STUDENT B

1. Draw the route from Carter and Adams to the Martial Arts Academy.
   (Be careful! One-way streets are marked →. Don't go the wrong way on a one-way street!)
   Give your partner directions.

   Example: **A:** I want to go to the Martial Arts Academy. Can you give me directions?
   B: Sure. Start at the corner of Carter and Adams.

2. Ask your partner for directions to the Sunrise Gym. Draw the route.

   Example: **B:** I want to go to the Sunrise Gym. Can you give me directions?
   A: Sure. Start at the corner of Carter and Adams.

When giving directions, use sentences like these:

Start at the corner of Carter and Adams.	Go straight.	Continue on 9th Street.
(Don't) turn right.	Make a left turn.	Stay on Founders.

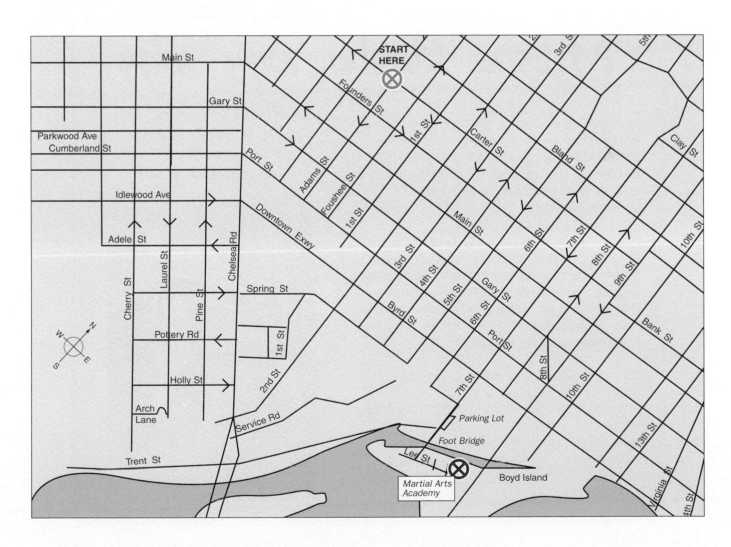

When you are finished, compare routes with your partner. Are they the same?

Grammar in Context

BEFORE YOU READ

🎧 *Look at the picture and the text above it. What did Matsuo Basho do? How long did he live? Read this short biography of Basho.*

Matsuo Basho, 1644–1694

Matsuo Basho **wrote** more than 1,000 *haiku* (three-line poems). He **chose** topics from nature, daily life, and human emotions. He **became** one of Japan's most famous poets, and his work **established** haiku as an important art form.

Basho **was** born Matsuo Munefusa near Kyoto in 1644. ("Basho" is the name he later **used** as a poet.) He **did not want** to become a samurai (warrior) like his father. Instead, he **moved** to Edo (present-day Tokyo) and **studied** poetry. Then he **became** a teacher, and by 1681 he **had** many students and admirers.

Basho, however, **was** restless. Starting in 1684, he **traveled** on foot and on horseback all over Japan. Sometimes his friends **joined** him and they **wrote** poetry together. Travel **was** difficult in the 17th century, and Basho often **got** sick. He **died** in 1694, during a journey to Osaka. At that time he **had** 2,000 students.

As for that flower
By the road —
My horse ate it!
— Matsuo Basho

AFTER YOU READ

Read the statements. Check **True** *or* **False**.

	True	False
1. Basho was born and studied in Japan.	☐	☐
2. Basho only traveled on foot.	☐	☐
3. He wrote poetry with his students.	☐	☐
4. He died at age 50.	☐	☐

Grammar Presentation

SIMPLE PAST: *BE*

Affirmative Statements

Subject	*Be*	
I	**was**	
You	**were**	
He She It	**was**	famous.
We You They	**were**	

Negative Statements

Subject	*Be + Not*	
I	**wasn't**	
You	**weren't**	
He She It	**wasn't**	famous.
We You They	**weren't**	

Yes / No Questions

Be	Subject	
Was	I	
Were	you	
Was	he she it	famous?
Were	we you they	

Short Answers

Affirmative				Negative		
Yes,	you	**were.**	**No,**	you	**weren't.**
	I	**was.**		I	**wasn't.**
	he she it	**was.**		he she it	**wasn't.**
	you we they	**were.**		you we they	**weren't.**

(continued)

Wh- Questions			
Wh- Word	*Be*	Subject	
Where When Why	**was**	I	famous?
	were	you	
	was	he she it	
	were	we you they	

SIMPLE PAST: REGULAR AND IRREGULAR VERBS

Affirmative Statements		
Subject	Verb	
I You He She It We You They	**moved traveled**	to Japan.
	came* **left***	in 1684.

Negative Statements			
Subject	*Did not*	Base Form of Verb	
I You He She It We You They	**didn't**	**move travel**	to Japan.
		come leave	in 1684.

**Come (came)* and *leave (left)* are irregular verbs. See Appendix 1 on page A-1 for a list of irregular verbs.

Yes / No Questions			
Did	Subject	Base Form of Verb	
Did	I you he she it we you they	**move travel**	to Japan?
		come leave	in 1684?

Short Answers					
Affirmative			Negative		
Yes,	you I he she it you we they	**did.**	**No,**	you I he she it you we they	**didn't.**

Wh- Questions				
Wh- Word	**Did**	Subject	Base Form of Verb	
When Why	**did**	I you he she it we you they	**move** **travel**	to Japan?
			come? **leave**?	

GRAMMAR NOTES

EXAMPLES

1. Use the **simple past** to talk about actions, states, or situations that are <u>finished</u>.

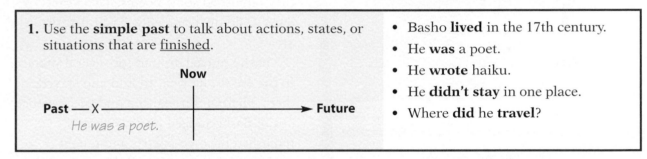

- Basho **lived** in the 17th century.
- He **was** a poet.
- He **wrote** haiku.
- He **didn't stay** in one place.
- Where **did** he **travel**?

2. You can use the simple past with **time expressions** that refer to the past. Some examples of past time expressions are *by 1681, in the 17th century, 300 years ago, last week*.

- *By 1681* he **had** many students.
- He **lived** *in the 17th century*.
- He **died** more than *300 years ago*.

3. The simple past of **regular** verbs is formed by adding *-d* or *-ed* to the base form of the verb.

▶ **BE CAREFUL!** There are often **spelling changes** when you add *-ed* to the verb.

BASE FORM		SIMPLE PAST
live	→	live**d**
join	→	join**ed**
study	→	stud**ied**
hop	→	hop**ped**
prefer	→	prefer**red**

4. Many common verbs are **irregular**. Their simple past is not formed by adding *-d* or *-ed*.

BASE FORM		SIMPLE PAST
be	→	**was / were**
get	→	**got**
go	→	**went**
have	→	**had**

Reference Notes

For **spelling rules** for the **simple past of regular verbs**, see Appendix 22 on page A-10.
For **pronunciation rules** for the **simple past of regular verbs**, see Appendix 30 on page A-15.
For a list of **irregular verbs**, see Appendix 1 on page A-1.

Focused Practice

1 | DISCOVER THE GRAMMAR

Read more about Basho. Underline all the verbs in the simple past. Then complete the time line on the left.

1644	Basho was born.
1656	Basho's father died.
1664	_____
1666	_____
	_____
_____	Students built the Basho Hut.
1683	_____
1684	_____
_____	Basho traveled to northern Honshu.
_____	Basho locked his gate to visitors.
1694	_____
	_____

As the son of a samurai, Basho grew up in the household of Todo Yoshitada, a young lord. After his father's death in 1656, Basho stayed in the Yoshitada household. He and Todo wrote poetry together, and in 1664 they published some poems. Two years later, Todo died suddenly. Basho left the area.

Basho moved around for several years. In the 1670s, he went to Edo and stayed there. He found friendship and success once again. Basho judged poetry contests, published his own poetry, and taught students. His students built him a home outside the city in 1681. They planted a banana tree (*basho* in Japanese) in front and called his home "Basho Hut." That is how the poet got his name: Basho.

In spite of this success, Basho became unhappy. He often wrote about loneliness. His mother died in 1683, and he began his travels a year later. His trip to the northern part of Honshu in 1689 was difficult, but his travel diary about this journey, *Narrow Road to the Deep North*, became one of Japan's greatest works of literature.

As a famous poet, Basho had many visitors—too many, in fact. In 1693 he locked his gate for a month, stayed alone, and wrote. The following year he took his final journey, to Osaka. He died there among his friends.

2 | EMILY DICKINSON

Complete this biography of American poet Emily Dickinson. Use the simple past form of the verbs in parentheses. Go to Appendix 1 on page A-1 for help with the irregular verbs.

Emily Dickinson, one of the most popular American poets, _____*lived*_____
1. (live)

from 1830 to 1886. She _____ about love, nature, and time.
2. (write)

These _____ her favorite themes.
3. (be)

Dickinson _____ an unusual life. After just one year
4. (lead)

of college, she _____ a recluse—she almost never
5. (become)

_____ her house in Amherst, Massachusetts. At home,
6. (leave)

she _____ visitors, and she only _____
7. (not have)   8. (wear)

white.

3 | MORE ABOUT EMILY DICKINSON

Complete this list of facts about Emily Dickinson. Use the simple past form of the verbs in parentheses. Go to Appendix 1 on page A-1 for help with the irregular verbs.

1. Dickinson _____*liked*_____ science.
   (like)

2. She _____ it in school.
   (study)

3. She _____ very interested in chemistry.
   (become)

4. Later she _____ about Arctic exploration.
   (read)

5. She _____ ideas from science in many of her poems.
   (use)

6. Emily Dickinson _____ only poems.
   (not write)

7. She also _____ letters.
   (write)

8. But she _____ the envelopes.
   (not address)

9. Other people always _____ that for her.
   (do)

10. During her lifetime, only 7 of her 1,700 poems _____ in print.
    (appear)

11. This _____ without her knowledge or permission.
    (be)

4 | A POEM BY EMILY DICKINSON
Grammar Notes 1–4

Now complete these lines from a poem by Emily Dickinson. Use the simple past form of the verbs in the box. Go to Appendix 1 on page A-1 for help with the irregular verbs.

bite	~~come~~	drink	eat	hop	see

A bird ___came___ down the walk:
1.

He did not know I _____;
2.

He _____ an angle-worm in halves
3.

And _____ the fellow raw.
4.

And then he _____ a dew
5.

From a convenient grass,

And then _____ sidewise to the wall
6.

To let a beetle pass.

5 | BASHO AND DICKINSON
Grammar Notes 1–4

Read these statements about Basho. Then write questions about Emily Dickinson. Write a yes/no question if a verb is underlined , or a wh- question if other words are underlined. Then answer your questions using the information from Exercises 2 and 3.

1. Basho <u>was</u> a poet.

   Q: *Was Dickinson a poet?*

   A: *Yes, she was.*

2. He was born <u>in 1644</u>.

   Q: *When was Dickinson born?*

   A: *She was born in 1830.*

3. He <u>became</u> famous during his lifetime.

   Q: _____

   A: _____

4. Basho <u>received</u> many visitors.

   Q: _____

   A: _____

5. He <u>traveled</u> a lot.

   Q: _____

   A: _____

6. Basho wrote <u>more than 1,000 poems</u>.

   Q: _____

   A: _____

7. He wrote <u>about nature</u>.

   Q: _____

   A: _____

8. He died <u>in 1694</u>.

   Q: _____

   A: _____

6 | **ANA CASTILLO**   *Grammar Notes 1–4*

Read this article about a modern writer. Then answer the questions on the next page.

ANA CASTILLO is a modern poet, novelist, short story writer, and teacher. She was born in Chicago in 1953, and she lived there for 32 years. *Otro Canto*, her first book of poetry, appeared in 1977.

In her work, Castillo uses humor and a lively mixture of Spanish and English (Spanglish). She got her special writer's "voice" by living in a neighborhood with many different ethnic groups. She also thanks her father for her writing style. "He had an outgoing and easy personality, and this . . . sense of humor. I got a lot from him . . ."

Castillo attended high school, college, and graduate school in Chicago. In the 1970s, she taught English and Mexican history. She received a Ph.D. in American Studies from Bremen University in Germany in 1992.

(continued)

*Read the statements. Write **That's right** or **That's wrong** and correct the incorrect statements.*

1. Ana Castillo was born in Mexico City.

  That's wrong. She wasn't born in Mexico City. She was born in Chicago.

2. She lived in Chicago until 1977.

_____

3. Her father was very shy.

_____

4. She grew up among people of different cultures.

_____

5. Castillo got most of her education in Chicago.

_____

6. She taught Spanish in the 1970s.

_____

7. She went to France for her Ph.D.

_____

7 | EDITING

Read this student's journal. There are ten mistakes in the use of the simple past. The first mistake is already corrected. Find and correct nine more.

> Today in class we read a poem by American poet Robert Frost. I
> really ~~enjoy~~ *enjoyed* it. It was about a person who choosed between two roads
> in a forest. Many people believed the person were Frost. He thinked
> about his choice for a long time. The two roads didn't looked very
> different. Finally, he didn't took the road most people take. He took
> the one less traveled on. At that time, he didn't thought it was an
> important decision, but his choice change his life.
>
> Sometimes I feel a little like Frost. Two years ago I decide to
> move to a new country. Did I made the right decision?

Communication Practice

8 | LISTENING

🎧 *Listen to part of an interview with a poet. Then listen again, and write the years on the time line.*

was born	parents left Turkey	moved to the U.S.	began to write poetry	graduated from college	won a poetry award	became a teacher

1970

9 | INFORMATION GAP: COMPLETE THE BIOGRAPHY

Work in pairs (A and B). Student A, follow the instructions on this page. Student B, turn to page 33.

1. Read the short biography below. Ask your partner questions to complete the missing information.

    Example: **A:** Where was Vladimir born?

    B: He was born in Kiev.

2. Answer your partner's questions.

    Example: **B:** When was he born?

    A: He was born on May 6, 1981.

Vladimir Liapunov was born on May 6, 1981, in _____ *Kiev* _____. His mother

was a _____, and his father made shoes.

At home they spoke _____. In 1999

Vlad and his family moved to _____. At

first Vlad felt _____. Then he got a

part-time job as a _____. He worked in

a Russian restaurant. He met _____ at

work, and they got married in 2001. They had a baby in 2002.

_____ ago, Vlad enrolled at the local

community college. His goal is to own his own restaurant someday.

When you are finished, compare the biographies. Are they the same?

10 | DIFFERENT LIVES

Work in pairs. Reread the information about Matsuo Basho (see pages 22 and 26) and Emily Dickinson (see page 27). In what ways were the two poets similar? How were they different? With your partner, write as many ideas as you can. Compare your ideas with those of your classmates.

> **Example:** A: Both Basho and Dickinson were poets.
> B: Basho lived in the 17th century. Dickinson lived in the 19th century.

11 | RHYMING WORDS

In poetry, the last word of a line sometimes rhymes with the last word of another line. For example, look at these first two lines of a famous poem by Joyce Kilmer. In these lines, **see** *rhymes with* **tree.**

> I think that I shall never **see**
> A poem lovely as a **tree.**

Work with a partner. Write down as many simple past verbs as you can that rhyme with the verbs in the box.

> | bought | drew | kept | sent | spoke |

> **Example:** **Sent** rhymes with **bent, lent, meant, spent,** and **went.**

Compare your lists with those of other students. Who has the most rhyming words?

12 | WRITING

Write a short autobiography. Do not put your name on it. Your teacher will collect all the papers, mix them up, and redistribute them to the class. Read the autobiography your teacher gives you. Then ask your classmates questions to try to find its writer.

> **Example:** Did you come here in 1990? OR When did you come here?

13 | ON THE INTERNET

Look up a poetry website. Find a poem that you like and tell someone about the poem.

> **Example:** I read a / an _____ poem yesterday. It was about . . .
> I really liked / didn't like it because . . .
> When I read the poem, I thought about . . .

INFORMATION GAP FOR STUDENT B

1. Read the short biography below. Answer your partner's questions.

    Example: **A:** Where was Vladimir born?

                  B: He was born in Kiev.

2. Ask your partner questions to complete the missing information.

    Example: **B:** When was he born?

                  A: He was born on May 6, 1981.

Vladimir Liapunov was born on _____ *May 6, 1981* _____, in Kiev. His mother was a dressmaker, and his father made _____.

At home they spoke Russian. In _____ Vlad and his family moved to Boston. At first Vlad felt lonely.

Then he got a part-time job as a cook. He worked in a _____. He met Elena at work, and they got married in _____. They had a baby in _____. A month ago, Vlad enrolled at the local _____. His goal is to own his own restaurant someday.

When you are finished, compare the biographies. Are they the same?

Past Progressive and Simple Past

Grammar in Context

BEFORE YOU READ

🎧 *Look at the picture. What do you think happened at Ligo Diamonds last Friday night? What was the weather like that night? Read this transcript of a radio play.*

THE ALIBI

[Ding-dong!]

SANDERS: Coming!… Coming!… Oh! Hi, Officer. Sorry I took so long. I **was exercising** in the basement when you **rang**.

OFFICER: Officer Barker, City Police. Are you Sal Sanders?

SANDERS: Yes, I am.

OFFICER: Is your wife home? I'd like to ask her a few questions.

SANDERS: No, Eve is at work. She's a manager at Ligo Diamonds. You know, she **was** very upset when she **heard** about the burglary.

OFFICER: **Was** your wife **working** the night of the burglary?

SANDERS: No, she **wasn't**. We **were staying** at Cypress Ski Lodge when it **happened**. Don't tell me we're suspects!

OFFICER: Just for the record, what **were** you and Mrs. Sanders **doing** between 6:00 P.M. and 9:00 P.M. last Friday?

SANDERS: We **were having** dinner in our room.

OFFICER: **Were** you still **eating** at 7:00?

SANDERS: No. Eve **was making** a call.

OFFICER: What **were** you **doing** while your wife **was talking**?

SANDERS: I **was watching** *Wall Street Watch*.

OFFICER: Hmmm . . . But the electricity **was** out because of the blizzard . . .

AFTER YOU READ

What did Sal Sanders tell the officer? Check the sentences.

☐   **1.** He started to exercise before the doorbell rang.

☐   **2.** He and his wife were home when the burglary happened.

☐   **3.** They were eating dinner at 7:00 P.M. on the night of the burglary.

☐   **4.** He was watching TV at 7:00 P.M. that night.

Grammar Presentation

PAST PROGRESSIVE

Statements				
Subject	*Was / Were*	*(Not)*	**Base Form of Verb + *-ing***	
I	**was**			
You	**were**			
He She It	**was**	**(not)**	**eating working sleeping**	yesterday at 7:00 P.M. when Eve **called**. while Sal **was talking**.
We You They	**were**			

Yes / No Questions				
Was / Were	**Subject**	**Base Form of Verb + *-ing***		
Was	I			
Were	you			
Was	he she it	**eating working sleeping**	yesterday at 7:00 P.M.? when Eve **called**? while Sal **was talking**?	
Were	we you they			

Short Answers						
Affirmative			**Negative**			
	you	**were.**			you	**weren't.**
	I	**was.**			I	**wasn't.**
Yes,	he she it	**was.**	**No,**		he she it	**wasn't.**
	you we they	**were.**			you we they	**weren't.**

(continued)

Wh- Questions				
Wh- Word	**Was / Were**	**Subject**	**Base Form of Verb + *ing***	
Why	**was**	I	**eating** **working** **sleeping**	yesterday at 7:00 P.M.? when Eve **called**? while Sal **was talking**?
	were	you		
	was	he she it		
	were	we you they		

GRAMMAR NOTES

EXAMPLES

1. Use the **past progressive** to describe an action that was <u>in progress</u> at a specific time in the past. The action began before the specific time and may or may not continue after the specific time.

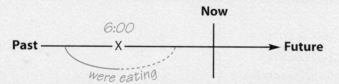

▶ **BE CAREFUL!** **Non-action verbs** are not usually used in the progressive.

- My wife and I **were eating** at 6:00.
- What **were** you **doing** at 7:00?
- They **weren't working** that night.

- She **heard** about the burglary. NOT She ~~was hearing~~ about the burglary.

2. Use the **past progressive** with the **simple past** to talk about an action that was <u>interrupted</u> by another action. Use the simple past for the interrupting action.

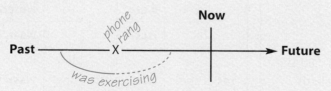

- Use *when* to introduce the **simple past** action.
- Use *while* to introduce the **past progressive** action.

- I **was exercising** when he **called**. (*I was exercising. The phone rang and interrupted my exercising.*)

- He was skiing *when* he **fell**.
- *While* he **was skiing**, he fell.

3. Use the **past progressive** with *while* to talk about two actions in progress <u>at the same time</u> in the past. Use the past progressive in both clauses.

- *While* I **was watching** TV, my wife **was talking** on the phone.

  OR

- My wife **was talking** on the phone *while* I **was watching** TV.

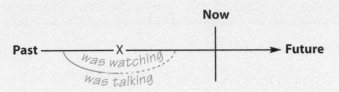

4. Notice that the **time clause** (the part of the sentence with *when* or *while*) can come at the beginning or the end of the sentence.

Use a **comma** after the time clause when it comes at the beginning. Do not use a comma when it comes at the end.

- *When* **you called,** I was eating.

  OR

- I was eating *when* **you called**.

  NOT I was eating~~,~~when you called.

5. BE CAREFUL! A sentence with both clauses in the simple past has a very <u>different meaning</u> from a sentence with one clause in the simple past and one clause in the past progressive.

   a. Both clauses in the **simple past**:

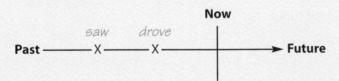

   b. One clause in the **simple past**, the other in the **past progressive**:

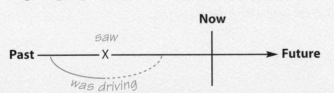

- When she **saw** the storm clouds, she **drove** home.
  (First she saw the storm clouds; then she drove home.)

- When she **saw** the storm clouds, she **was driving** home.
  (First she was driving home; then she saw the storm clouds.)

6. Use the **past progressive** to focus on the <u>duration</u> of an action, not its completion.

Use the **simple past** to focus on the <u>completion</u> of an action.

- Paul **was reading** a book last night.
  (We don't know if he finished it.)

- Paul **read** a book last night.
  (He finished it.)

Reference Note
For a list of **non-action verbs**, see Appendix 2 on page A-2.

Focused Practice

1 | DISCOVER THE GRAMMAR

Read the question. Then circle the letter of the correct sentence.

1. In which sentence do we know that the diamond necklace is gone?
   a. He was stealing a diamond necklace.
   b. He stole a diamond necklace.

2. Which sentence tells us that the people arrived at the mountains?
   a. They were driving to the mountains.
   b. They drove to the mountains.

3. In which sentence was the action interrupted?
   a. When the phone rang, he answered it.
   b. When the phone rang, he was looking for his bag.

4. Which sentence talks about two actions that were in progress at the same time?
   a. While the officer was questioning Sal, Eve was leaving town.
   b. When the officer questioned Sal, Eve left town.

5. In which sentence did the friends arrive before lunch began?
   a. When our friends arrived, we were eating lunch.
   b. When our friends arrived, we ate lunch.

2 | A TRAFFIC ACCIDENT   *Grammar Notes 1–6*

∩ *Complete the conversation with the past progressive or the simple past form of the verbs in parentheses. Use Appendix 1 on page 000 for help with irregular verbs.*

REPORTER: What was the cause of the accident, Officer?

OFFICER: Well, it looks like there were many causes. First of all, when the accident

_____happened_____, the driver _____was driving_____ much too fast. The driver
    1. (happen)   2. (drive)

is a suspect in a burglary, and she _____ town. While she
                                        3. (leave)

_____, she _____ to someone on her cell phone.
    4. (drive)   5. (speak)

When she _____ the pedestrian, she immediately _____
              6. (see)   7. (step)

on the brakes, but it was too late. The victim wasn't paying attention, either. He

_____ the street against a red light when the car _____
    8. (cross)   9. (hit)

him. He _____ the approaching car because he _____ to
          10. (not see)   11. (talk)

his friend. The friend _____ attention, either. He _____ to
                        12. (not pay)   **13. (listen)**

music with his headphones. When he _____ the car, he _____
                                    14. (notice)   **15. (try)**

to push his friend out of the way, but it was too late.

REPORTER: How is the victim doing?

OFFICER: Well, when the ambulance _____, he _____ from a head
                                  16. (arrive)   **17. (bleed)**

wound, but the doctors _____ the bleeding and they think he'll be OK.
                        18. (stop)

3 | **ANSWER CAREFULLY**   *Grammar Notes 1–6*

*The police are questioning another suspect in last Friday's burglary. Read this suspect's
answers. Use the words in parentheses and the past progressive or simple past to write the
police officer's questions.*

1. OFFICER: *What were you doing Friday night?* _____
                                      (What / you / do / Friday night)

   SUSPECT: I was visiting a friend.

2. OFFICER: _____
                        (Who exactly / you / visit)

   SUSPECT: My girlfriend. I got to her house at 5:30, and then I drove her to work.

3. OFFICER: _____
                        (she / work / at 7:00)

   SUSPECT: Yes, she was working the late shift.

4. OFFICER: _____
                        (anyone else / work / with her)

   SUSPECT: No, she was working alone.

5. OFFICER: _____
                        (What / you / do / while she / work)

   SUSPECT: I was reading the paper in her office.

6. OFFICER: But there was a terrible blizzard Friday night. The lights went out.

   _____
                        (What / you / do / when the lights / go out)

   SUSPECT: I took out my flashlight and looked for my girlfriend.

7. OFFICER: _____
                        (What / she / do / when you / find her)

   SUSPECT: She was looking for *me*.

8. OFFICER: Then _____
                        (What / you / do)

   SUSPECT: We quickly left the building.

9. OFFICER: _____
                        (Why / run / when the police / see you)

   SUSPECT: We were running because we wanted to get out of the storm.

4 | BLIZZARD

Grammar Notes 1–6

Combine the pairs of sentences. Use the past progressive or the simple past form of the verb. Remember to use commas when necessary.

1. The blizzard started. Mr. Ligo attended a party.

   When *the blizzard started, Mr. Ligo was attending a party.*

2. The wind began to blow. The electricity went out.

   When _____

3. He drove home. He listened to his car radio.

   While _____

4. He pulled over to the side of the road. He couldn't see anything.

   _____ when _____

5. He listened to the news. He heard about the burglary.

   While _____

6. It stopped snowing. Mr. Ligo went to the police station.

   When _____

5 | EDITING

Read this personal journal entry. There are seven mistakes in the use of the past progressive and the simple past. The first mistake is already corrected. Find and correct six more. Remember to look at punctuation!

> happened
> What ~~was happening~~ to me this morning was so unbelievable! I walked down the street while a woman stopped in front of me and asked me for directions to the nearest bank. At that moment, I was seeing my friend Bill across the street. I called out to him and asked him to wait for me. Luckily for me, he did. Bill saw everything: While I talking to the woman, a pickpocket was put his hand into my backpack. Bill started to walk away. I thought he didn't want to wait for me, but I was wrong. When Bill saw the pickpocket he went to call the police. They were arriving immediately. The police arrested the woman and the pickpocket. What an experience!

Communication Practice

6 | LISTENING

🎧 *Listen to a witness describe a traffic incident. Then listen again. According to the witness, which set of pictures is the most accurate? Circle the number.*

1.

2.

3.

7 | ROLE PLAY: THE REAL STORY

Work in groups of four. Follow these steps:

1. Three students are witnesses; the fourth is a police officer. Look at the pictures in Exercise 6.

2. The police officer asks the witnesses questions about the accident.

3. Each of the witnesses chooses one set of pictures to describe.

Example: A: Can you describe the accident?

B: Yes, two men were crossing the street.

8 | ARE YOU A GOOD WITNESS?

Look at this picture for ten seconds. Then close your book and write down what was happening. See how many details you can remember. What were the people doing? What were they wearing? Was anything unusual going on?

Example: A man and a woman were standing by the fireplace. The woman was wearing . . .

Compare your list with those of your classmates. Who remembered the most?

9 | WRITING

Write a description of an event that you witnessed: an accident, a crime, a reunion, a wedding, or another event. Use the past progressive and the simple past to describe what was happening and what happened during the event.

Example: While I was going to lunch today, I saw a wedding party. People were waiting for the bride and groom outside a temple. When they saw the couple, they . . .

10 | ON THE INTERNET

Do a search for your date of birth. Find out what was happening in the world at that time. Tell your classmates.

Example: I was born on March 1, 1965. At that time, the Beatles were touring the United States. . . .

Used to

Grammar in Context

BEFORE YOU READ

🎧 *What is a blog or weblog? Look at the pictures. What do you think this blog is about? What toys, TV shows, clothes, and hairstyles do you remember from your childhood? Read Sandra's weblog about the 1980s.*

 # The Awesome Eighties

Today's blog is a walk down memory lane. Were you a kid in the 1980s? What toys **did** you **use to play** with? What **did** you **use to watch** on TV?

Did you **use to watch** cartoons Saturday mornings? I **used to love** *She-Ra, Princess of Power*. I collected the toys and acted out the stories with my friends. It's hard to believe, but we **didn't use to play** video games then!

A puzzle called the Rubik's cube **used to be** very popular in the 1980s. My older sister Linda carried one in her backpack all the time. She and her friends **used to have** contests. She didn't win very often, but she loved it anyway.

This is my mother, dressed for work. She **used to love** suits with big shoulders. She said they made her feel strong, like She-Ra, Princess of Power. She **used to call** this one her "power suit."

My brother Gary and his friends had a rock band. They **used to practice** in the garage. They **never used to study**. Gary **used to get** some strange haircuts. He's a lawyer now, and he's lost his hair!

AFTER YOU READ

Read the statements. Check **True** *or* **False**.

		True	False
1. Sandra didn't watch TV on Saturdays.		☐	☐
2. She played video games a lot.		☐	☐
3. Her sister Linda played with a Rubik's cube.		☐	☐
4. Her mother wore a suit to work.		☐	☐
5. Her brother's band practiced in the garage.		☐	☐
6. Her brother and his friends studied all the time.		☐	☐
7. Her brother likes strange haircuts now.		☐	☐

Grammar Presentation

USED TO

Statements			
Subject	*Used to*	**Base Form of Verb**	
I You He She It We You They	**used to** **didn't use to**	**be**	popular.

Yes / No Questions				
Did	**Subject**	*Use to*	**Base Form of Verb**	
Did	I you he she it we you they	**use to**	**be**	popular?

Short Answers					
Affirmative			Negative		
Yes,	you I he she it you we they	**did.**	**No,**	you I he she it you we they	**didn't.**

Wh- Questions					
Wh- Word	Did	Subject	Use to	Base Form of Verb	
When	**did**	I you he she it we you they	**use to**	**be**	popular?

GRAMMAR NOTES

EXAMPLES

1. Use *used to* + **base form** of the verb to talk about <u>past habits</u> or <u>past situations</u> that no longer exist in the present.

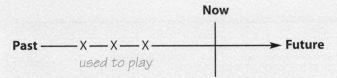

▶ **BE CAREFUL!** *Used to* always refers to the past. There is no present form.

- He **used to play** in a band.
  (*He played in a band in the past, but he doesn't play in a band now.*)

- She **used to love** cartoons.
  NOT She ~~uses~~ to love cartoons.

2. Use *used to* in sentences that <u>contrast the past and the present</u>. We often use time expressions such as *now*, *no longer*, and *not anymore* with the present to emphasize the contrast.

- I **used to have** very long hair, but *now* my hair is very short.
- We **used to play** with Rubik's cubes, but we do**n't** like them **anymore**.

3. Form the **negative** with:
didn't + *use to*

USAGE NOTE: In negative statements, ***never* + *used to*** is more common than *didn't use to*.

- He *didn't* **use to study**.
  NOT He didn't ~~used~~ to study.

- He *never* **used to study**.

4. Form **questions** with:
did + *use to*

USAGE NOTE: In questions, the simple past is more common than *did* + *use to*.

- **Did** you **use to have** long hair?
  NOT Did you ~~used~~ to have long hair?

- **Did** you **have** long hair when you were younger?

Pronunciation Note
Used to and *use to* are pronounced the same: /ˈyustə/.

(continued)

5. BE CAREFUL! Do not confuse *used to* + **base form** of the verb with the following expressions:

- *be used to* + **base form** + *-ing* (*be accustomed to*)

- *get used to* + **base form** + *-ing* (*get accustomed to*)

- She **used to work**.
  (*She doesn't work now.*)

- She **is used to working**.
  (*She is accustomed to working.*)

- She'll **get used to working**.
  (*She'll get accustomed to working.*)

Focused Practice

1 | DISCOVER THE GRAMMAR

Read these responses to "The Awesome Eighties" blog. Underline the verb forms that refer to past habits.

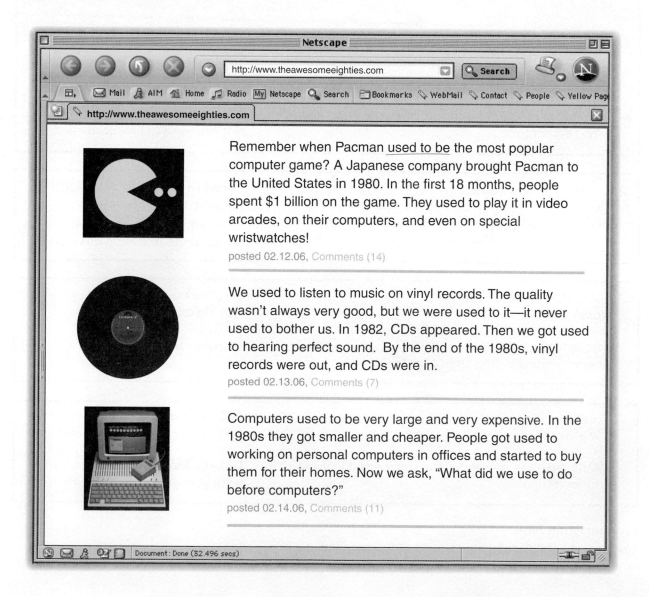

Remember when Pacman <u>used to be</u> the most popular computer game? A Japanese company brought Pacman to the United States in 1980. In the first 18 months, people spent $1 billion on the game. They used to play it in video arcades, on their computers, and even on special wristwatches!

posted 02.12.06, Comments (14)

We used to listen to music on vinyl records. The quality wasn't always very good, but we were used to it—it never used to bother us. In 1982, CDs appeared. Then we got used to hearing perfect sound. By the end of the 1980s, vinyl records were out, and CDs were in.

posted 02.13.06, Comments (7)

Computers used to be very large and very expensive. In the 1980s they got smaller and cheaper. People got used to working on personal computers in offices and started to buy them for their homes. Now we ask, "What did we use to do before computers?"

posted 02.14.06, Comments (11)

2 | SCHOOL REUNION

Sandra is at her class reunion. Complete the conversations with the correct form of **used to** *and the words in parentheses.*

1. SANDRA: You look familiar. ____*Did*____ you _____*use to be*_____ in the drama club?

   a. (be)

   ROSA: Sandra! It's me—Rosa! I _____ long hair. Remember?

   b. (have)

2. ROSA: There's Glen—all alone. Was he always that shy?

   SANDRA: Glen? He never _____ talking. Let's go say hi to him.

   a. (stop)

3. ROSA: _____ you _____ with Gary's band, the Backyard Boys?

   a. (play)

   GLEN: Sometimes. We _____ in Gary's garage after school.

   b. (practice)

   SANDRA: Tell the truth, Glen. You really _____ to see my sister Linda!

   c. (come)

4. GLEN: There's Jim and Laura. I think they got married a couple of years ago.

   SANDRA: Really? In high school, they _____ each other at all.

   a. (not like)

5. LAURA: I see Sandra! We _____ next to each other in math class.

   a. (sit)

   JIM: She looks so different now. She _____ glasses.

   b. (not wear)

   LAURA: We all look different now. We _____ a lot younger back then.

   c. (be)

3 | LOOKING BACK

Sandra is showing her daughter Megan an old photo album. Complete their conversation. Use **used to** *and the correct verb from the box.*

be	drive	~~have~~	love	play	visit	wear

MEGAN: Wow! Uncle Gary ____*used to have*____ a lot of hair!

1.

SANDRA: Not for long. Right after this photo, he shaved his head.

MEGAN: In this picture, were you going to the gym?

SANDRA: No. We _____ exercise clothes everywhere.

2.

MEGAN: You looked cute!

SANDRA: This was your Aunt Linda's car. She _____ her friends to school every

3.

day.

MEGAN: That's not Uncle Fred with her.

SANDRA: No, that's Glen. He _____ her boyfriend before she met Fred.

4.

(continued)

MEGAN: Oh! You had a Barbie doll!

SANDRA: Of course. I _____ with it every day.
5.

MEGAN: And that's me with Grandma and Grandpa!

SANDRA: Right. You _____ them at the beach every summer.
6.

You _____ the water.
7.

4 | EDITING

Read this journal entry about a high school reunion in Timmins, Ontario, a small town 500 miles north of Toronto. There are seven mistakes in the use of **used to.** *The first mistake is already corrected. Find and correct six more.*

Shania Twain

The high school reunion was great! I talked to Eileen Edwards. Well, she's the famous Shania Twain now. In high school, she ~~was~~ used to be just one of us, and tonight we all called her Eileen. She graduated in 1983, a year before me. Today she lives in a chateau in Switzerland and models for Revlon, but her life didn't used to be like that at all! She uses to be very poor, and her grandma used to made all her clothes because her family couldn't afford to buy them. She was always a good musician, though. In fact, she used to earn money for her family that way. She performed with a local rock band, and my friends and I use to go hear her. She could really sing! Her new name, Shania, means "on my way" in Ojibwa (her stepfather's Native American language). After she left Timmins, I got used to think that Timmins wasn't important to her anymore—but I was wrong. She is always doing good things for our community. And tonight she was just the way she used be in high school—simple and friendly!

Communication Practice

5 | LISTENING

🎧 *Two friends are talking about their past. Listen to their conversation. Then listen again. Check the things they used to do in the* **past** *and the things they do* **now**.

	Past	Now
1. get up very early without an alarm clock	☑	☐
2. use an alarm clock	☐	☐
3. have a big breakfast	☐	☐
4. have a cup of coffee	☐	☐
5. look at the newspaper	☐	☐
6. have endless energy	☐	☐
7. do aerobics	☐	☐
8. meet at class reunions	☐	☐
9. take car trips on weekends	☐	☐

6 | PEOPLE CHANGE

Work with a partner. Look at the pairs of pictures and talk about how the people have changed. Then write sentences that describe the changes. Compare your sentences with those of your classmates.

THEN NOW

1. Sharifa *used to be very busy, but now she is more relaxed.*

   She used to wear glasses, but now she doesn't.

_____

(continued)

THEN

NOW

2. Jean-Marc _____

_____

_____

THEN

NOW

3. Lyric _____

_____

_____

THEN

NOW

4. Mike _____

_____

_____

7 | THE WAY I USED TO BE

Work in small groups. Bring in a picture of yourself when you were much younger. Talk about the differences in how you used to be and how you are now. What did you use to do? How did you use to dress?

Example: I used to have very long hair. Now I wear my hair short.

8 | WRITING

Write a two-paragraph essay. Contrast your life in the past and your life now. In the first paragraph, describe how your life used to be at some time in the past. In the second paragraph, describe your life today.

Example: I used to live in Russia. I attended St. Petersburg University.
In those days I used to . . .
Today I am living in Florida and attending Miami University . . .

9 | ON THE INTERNET

Work in small groups. Each group picks a recent decade (ten-year period): 1950s, 1960s, 1970s, 1980s, or 1990s. Each member of the group does a web search on that decade.

1. Look for the fashions, styles, music, or movies of that time.

2. Share the information you find with your group.

3. As a group, share your information with the rest of the class. You can also bring in pictures you find.

Example: Here are some examples of the clothes people used to wear in the 1960s.
Young girls really used to wear their skirts short . . .
And here are some examples of the way people used to wear their hair.
Boys used to let their hair grow very long . . .

Grammar in Context

BEFORE YOU READ

🎧 *Think about the year 2050 and try to predict which business will create the most jobs. Computers? Robots? Space travel? Read this article about jobs of the future.*

Where to Look for Jobs in the Future

Computers

Robots

Space Travel

Which business **will create** the most jobs?

Did you guess space travel? If so, Professor Patrick Collins, a professor of economics in Japan, agrees with you. At a recent lecture he said, "It **won't be** long before people **will call** their travel agents and **book** their flights to the Moon. Imagine! Yes, there is room on tomorrow's flight to the Moon. It **leaves** at 9:00 A.M. It's **going to be** full so please arrive early for check-in."

Of course, many people disagree with Collins. They think space travel **will cost** too much and not many people **will travel**. They also think that people **won't feel** safe enough to travel into space. But Collins's research shows that the majority of people think it **will be** worth saving their money to travel into space. He claims that while it **will** probably **start out** as an activity for a few rich individuals, it **will grow** very quickly—just like the aviation (airplane) industry grew in the last 100 years. After all, Collins reminds us, the Wright brothers flew their first plane in 1903.

Where to Look for Jobs in the Future

If Collins is right that people **will travel** to space as tourists, then, like all tourists, they **are going to stay** in hotels. They **are going to want** tours and they **will** certainly **expect** some entertainment. All of this **will require** many people, and that **will mean** many new jobs.

Some of these space jobs **will be** similar to Earth jobs, but they **will have** some unique challenges. For instance, how **will** a space waiter **serve** food in a gravity-free restaurant? And what about fitness trainers? Teaching an aerobics class in space **will require** some new moves in addition to a lot more flexibility—in all directions! But not all space jobs **will be** more difficult. Some **will be** easier, the job of a porter for instance. No more carrying heavy luggage; it **will** just **float** along. Well, one thing is certain about these space jobs—they **won't be** boring!

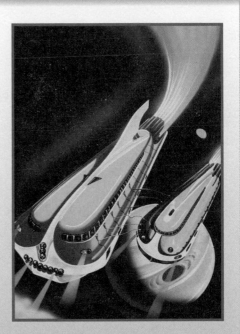

PLEASE NOTE: If you missed this great lecture, Professor Collins **is speaking** again at the space conference tomorrow night at 7:00 P.M.

AFTER YOU READ

What's Professor Collins's opinion? Read each statement and write **T (True)** *or* **F (False)** *under* **Collins**. *Write your own opinion under* **You**.

	Collins	You
1. Space travel will create more jobs in the future.	_____	_____
2. People won't feel safe enough to travel in space.	_____	_____
3. The space travel business won't grow very quickly.	_____	_____
4. At first, only rich people are going to travel as space tourists.	_____	_____
5. People will save money to travel into space.	_____	_____
6. There will be hotels in space.	_____	_____
7. Space jobs will be completely different from Earth jobs.	_____	_____
8. Space jobs will have some interesting new problems.	_____	_____

Grammar Presentation

BE GOING TO FOR THE FUTURE

Statements				
Subject	*Be*	(*Not*) *Going to*	Base Form of Verb	
I	**am***			
You	**are**			
He She It	**is**	(**not**) **going to**	**leave**	soon.
We You They	**are**			

* For contractions of *I am*, *you are*, etc., see Appendix 26 on page A-12.

Yes / No Questions				
Be	Subject	*Going to*	Base Form of Verb	
Am	I			
Are	you			
Is	he she it	**going to**	**leave**	soon?
Are	we you they			

Short Answers						
Affirmative				Negative		
Yes,	you	**are**.	**No**,	you**'re**		**not**.
	I	**am**.		I**'m**		
	he she it	**is**.		he**'s** she**'s** it**'s**		
	you we they	**are**.		you**'re** we**'re** they**'re**		

Wh- Questions				
Wh- Word	*Be*	Subject	*Going to*	Base Form of Verb
When Why	**are**	you	**going to**	**leave**?

WILL FOR THE FUTURE

Statements			
Subject	*Will* (*not*)	**Base Form of Verb**	
I You He She It We You They	**will** (**not**)*	**leave**	soon.

* For contractions of *I will*, *you will*, etc., see Appendix 26, page A-12.

Yes / No Questions			
Will	**Subject**	**Base Form of Verb**	
Will	I you he she it we you they	**leave**	soon?

Short Answers						
Affirmative			**Negative**			
Yes,	you I he she it you we they	**will**.	**No,**	you I he she it you we they	**won't**.

Wh- Questions			
Wh- Word	*Will*	**Subject**	**Base Form of Verb**
When	**will**	you	**leave**?

PRESENT PROGRESSIVE* FOR THE FUTURE

Statements		
Subject + *Be*	(*Not*) + Base Form + *-ing*	
We**'re**	(**not**) **leaving**	soon.
It**'s**		

SIMPLE PRESENT* FOR THE FUTURE

Statements		
Subject	**Verb**	
We	**leave**	Monday at 6:45 A.M.
It	**leaves**	

*For a complete presentation of present progressive and simple present forms, see Unit 1, page 3.

GRAMMAR NOTES	**EXAMPLES**

1. There are several ways to talk about the **future**. You can use:

- *be going to*
- *will*
- **present progressive**
- **simple present**

USAGE NOTE: Sometimes only one form of the future is appropriate, but in many cases more than one form is possible.

- They**'re going to have** a meeting.
- I think I**'ll go**.
- It**'s taking** place next week.
- It **starts** at 9:00 A.M. on Monday.

---

2. To make **predictions** or **guesses** about the future, use:

- *be going to*

    OR

- *will*

▶ **BE CAREFUL!** Use *be going to* instead of *will* when something in the present helps you make the prediction about the future.

- People **are going to travel** to space.

    OR

- People **will travel** to space.

- Look at those dark clouds! It**'s going to** rain. Not It'll rain.

---

3. To talk about future **intentions** or **plans**, use:

- *be going to*

    OR

- *will*

    OR

- **present progressive**

We often use *will* when we decide something at the moment of speaking.

We often use the **present progressive** when we talk about future plans that are already arranged.

- I**'m going to fly** to Mars next week.

    OR

- I**'ll fly** to Mars next week.

    OR

- I**'m flying** to Mars next week.

A: The show is opening next week.
B: Sounds interesting. I think I**'ll go**.

- I**'m flying** to Chicago next month. I already have a ticket.

Pronunciation Note
In informal speech, *going to* is often pronounced "gonna" /gənə/.

> **4.** To talk about **scheduled future events** (timetables, programs, schedules), use the **simple present**. Verbs such as *start*, *leave*, *end*, and *begin* are often used this way.
>
> - The shuttle **leaves** at 9:00 A.M.
> - The conference **starts** tomorrow morning.

Reference Note
Will can also be used for **making a request**; see Unit 13 on page 146.

Focused Practice

1 | DISCOVER THE GRAMMAR

Read this transcript of a radio program. The host, Dr. David Livingston, is interviewing Professor Patrick Collins. There are eighteen verb forms that refer to the future. Find and underline them. The first one is already underlined. Find and underline seventeen more.

THE SPACE SHOW

LIVINGSTON: Good evening, everybody, and welcome to my new program, *The Space Show*. I am your host, Dr. David Livingston, and my show <u>will bring</u> you information on anything and everything related to the exploration of space. And today's guest, Professor Patrick Collins, is going to talk about space travel. Professor Collins is speaking to us from Azabu University in Japan. He is an expert on space travel, and he believes that space travel is coming to us sooner than we think. Welcome to the show, Professor. Tell us: Why do you think space travel is going to be so popular and why so soon?

COLLINS: It's simple. Ask most people and they'll tell you they are very curious about outer space. There's already a lot of excitement about space travel.

LIVINGSTON: But how will the average person be able to afford it? It will be very expensive, no?

COLLINS: I know that some people say it'll cost too much. But space travel is also going to create jobs. And with those new jobs, the world's economy will improve. This means that people will have more money to spend, and more people will want to try space travel. And I'd like to add that travel to the Moon is only a start. We won't stop there. Putting people on Mars won't take much longer. We all know this beautiful planet Earth has limited resources. Soon we will have no choice but to look elsewhere, and that means to look into space.

LIVINGSTON: Very interesting. It's time for a short break, but first I want to remind everyone that Professor Collins is speaking at the Annual Space Transportation Conference in Virginia next week. Also, don't forget that *The Space Show* is moving to a new time. Next week's show begins at 8:00 P.M. Pacific Standard Time.

2 | IT'S GOING TO HAPPEN

Grammar Note 2

Look at the pictures. They show events from a day in the life of Professor Starr. Write predictions or guesses. Use the words in the box and a form of **be going to** *or* **not be going to**.

answer the phone	drive	get out of bed	~~get very wet~~	give a speech
go to sleep	have dinner	rain	~~take a trip~~	watch TV

1. _____ *He's going to take a trip.* _____

2. _____

3. _____

4. _____

5. _____

6. _____

7. _____

8. _____

9. _____   10. _____

3 | PROFESSOR STARR'S SCHEDULE

Grammar Note 3

Write about Professor Starr's plans for next week. Use the information from his calendar and the present progressive.

	Monday	Tuesday	Wednesday	Thursday	Friday	Saturday
A.M.	Teach my economics class	Take the train to Tokyo	Do the interview for <u>The Space Show</u>	Work on the Space Future website	Go to an exercise class	Answer e-mails from the Space Future website
P.M.		Meet friends from England for dinner	Answer questions from the online chat	↓	Fly to New York for the Space Transportation Conference	Write a speech for the next space travel conference

1. On Monday morning *he's teaching his economics class.* _____

2. On Tuesday morning _____

3. On Tuesday evening _____

4. On Wednesday morning _____

5. On Wednesday afternoon _____

6. All day Thursday _____

7. On Friday morning _____

8. On Friday evening _____

9. On Saturday morning _____

10. On Saturday afternoon _____

4 | SPACE FUTURE Q & A

It is the year 2020 and an international group of space tourists are getting ready for their space flight. Part of the preparation includes a Question and Answer (Q & A) session with astronaut William R. Pogue. Complete the questions and answers. Use the verbs in parentheses with **will** *or* **won't**.

You'll get used to it!

Q: _____Will_____ it _____take_____ a long time to get used to zero gravity?
1. (take)

A: No, _____it won't_____. Every day you _____ more comfortable, and after
2.   3. (feel)

three days you _____ used to being in space.
4. (become)

★ ★ ★

Q: _____ I _____ sick?
5. (feel)

A: Yes, you might feel sick for a little while. But it _____ long.
6. (last)

★ ★ ★

Q: I love to read. How _____ I _____ to keep a book open to the right page?
7. (be able)

A: Actually, reading a book in space can be quite a problem. You _____ strong
8. (need)

clips to hold the book open. It can be a little frustrating at first, but after a while you

_____ used to it.
9. (get)

★ ★ ★

Q: _____ I _____ the same?
10. (look)

A: Actually, you _____ the same at all. Your face and eyes _____
11. (look)   12. (get)

puffy. The first time you look in a mirror, you probably _____ yourself.
13. (recognize)

★ ★ ★

Q: _____ I _____ in my sleep?
14. (float)

A: Yes, if you are not tied down. And then you should be careful because you _____
15. (bump)

into things all night long. Trust me. You can get hurt!

★ ★ ★

Q: I like salt and pepper on my food. _____ I _____ to use salt and pepper on
16. (be able)

my food?

A: Yes, you _____ salt and pepper, but not like you do on Earth—the grains just
17. (have)

float away in zero gravity. You _____ small, squeezable bottles with salt water
18. (use)

and pepper water. You just squeeze it on your food. It tastes great!

5 | MOON SHUTTLE

It is June 2050. You and a friend are planning a trip to the Moon. Your friend just got the schedule, and you are deciding which shuttle to take. Use the words in parentheses to ask questions, and look at the schedule to write the answers. Use the simple present.

2050 SHUTTLE SERVICE TO THE MOON
September–November 2050

All times given in Earth's Eastern Standard Time

SEPTEMBER		OCTOBER		NOVEMBER	
Leave Earth	Arrive Moon	Leave Earth	Arrive Moon	Leave Earth	Arrive Moon
9/4 7:00 A.M.	9/7 6:00 P.M.	10/15 4:00 A.M.	10/18 3:00 P.M.	11/4 1:00 P.M.	11/8 12:00 A.M.
9/20 10:00 A.M.	9/23 9:00 P.M.	10/27 11:00 A.M.	10/30 10:00 P.M.	11/19 6:00 P.M.	11/23 5:00 A.M.

1. (During which months / the shuttle / fly to the Moon this year)

   A: *During which months does the shuttle fly to the Moon this year?*

   B: *It flies to the Moon in September, October, and November.*

2. (How many / shuttle flights / leave this year)

   A: _____

   B: _____

3. (How often / shuttle / depart for the Moon each month)

   A: _____

   B: _____

4. (When / the earliest morning flight / leave Earth)

   A: _____

   B: _____

5. (At what time / the latest shuttle / leave Earth)

   A: _____

   B: _____

6 | CHOOSE THE FUTURE

⌒ *Two people are traveling to a conference. Read their conversation and circle the most appropriate future forms.*

JASON: I just heard the weather report. It's raining / (It's going to rain) tomorrow.
        1.

ARIEL: Oh no. I hate driving in the rain. And it's a long drive to the conference.

JASON: Wait! I have an idea. We'll take / We're going to take the train instead!
        2.

ARIEL: Good idea! Do you have a train schedule?

JASON: Yes. Here's one. There's a train that will leave / leaves at 7:00 A.M.
        3.

ARIEL: What about lunch? Oh, I know. I'll make / I'm making some sandwiches for us.
        4.

JASON: OK. You know, it's a long trip. What are we doing / are we going to do all those hours?
        5.

ARIEL: Don't worry. We'll think / We're thinking of something.
        6.

JASON: You know, we have to get up really early. I think I'm going / I'll go home now.
        7.

ARIEL: OK. I'm seeing you / I'll see you tomorrow. Good night.
   8.

7 | EDITING

Read this student's report on space travel. There are eleven mistakes in the use of the future. The first mistake is already corrected. Find and correct ten more.

>   *travel*
>   Both astronauts and space tourists will ~~traveling~~ in space, but tourists going to have a much different experience. Space tourists is going to travel for fun, not for work. So, they willn't have to worry about many of the technical problems that astronauts worry about. For example, space tourists will need not to figure out how to use a screwdriver without gravity. And they isn't going to try new experiments outside the space shuttle. For the most part, space tourists will just going to see the sights and have a good time.
>
>   Still, there will be similarities. Regular activities be the same for astronauts and space tourists. For example, eating, washing, and sleeping will turned into exciting challenges for everyone in space. Everyone is going to doing exercises to stay fit in zero gravity. And both astronauts and space tourists will going to have many new adventures!

Communication Practice

8 | LISTENING

🎧 *Listen to the short conversations. Decide if the people are talking about something happening* **Now** *or in the* **Future**. *Then listen again and check the correct column.*

	Now	Future
1.	☐	☑
2.	☐	☐
3.	☐	☐
4.	☐	☐
5.	☐	☐
6.	☐	☐

9 | WHEN ARE YOU FREE?

Complete your weekend schedule. If you have no plans, write **free.**

	Friday	Saturday	Sunday
12:00 P.M.			
1:00 P.M.			
2:00 P.M.			
3:00 P.M.			
4:00 P.M.			
5:00 P.M.			
6:00 P.M.			
7:00 P.M.			
8:00 P.M.			
9:00 P.M.			

Now work with a partner. Ask questions to decide on a time when you are both free to do something together.

Example: A: What are you doing Friday afternoon? Do you want to go to the movies?

B: I'm studying at the library. How about Friday night? Are you doing anything?

10 | CHOOSE A TIME

There is a space conference in town this weekend. Work with your partner from Exercise 9. Look at the schedule of events below. Then look at your schedules from Exercise 9. Decide which events to attend and when.

SPACE TOURISM

Friday

8:00 A.M.–4:00 P.M.	Training for Space Travel
10:00 A.M.–12:00 P.M.	Eating in Space
7:00 P.M.	Advertising and Videos of Moon Resorts
8:00 P.M.	Meet Yang Liwei, China's First Astronaut

Saturday

2:00 P.M.–3:00 P.M.	Writing a Résumé for Space Employment
2:00 P.M.–4:00 P.M.	Personal Care in Space, or "How Do I Wash My Hair?"
6:00 P.M.	Advertising and Videos of Moon Resorts
8:00 P.M.	Space Sports

Sunday

8:00 A.M.–4:00 P.M.	Training for Space Travel
12:00 P.M.–2:00 P.M.	Live Taping of *The Space Show*
6:00 P.M.	Lecture: Who Should Invest in Space Tourism?

Example: A: What are you doing Friday? Do you want to go to "Training for Space Travel"?
B: Not really. That will take up the whole day. What else is there on Friday?

11 | WRITING

Imagine you are a travel agent advertising a dream vacation in space. Use your imagination to write about what your clients will do, what they will see, and how they will feel. What will hotel accommodations look like? What kinds of activities are there going to be? What types of food will people eat? Be creative!

Example: This is an experience you will never forget! Come with us to the Moon. We'll show you the sights and what Earth looks like from space . . .

12 | ON THE INTERNET

🔍 *Do a search on* **space sports**. *Read about the possibilities of new games and sports in zero gravity. Describe a game you read about or design your own game. Some websites allow you to submit your new ideas. Try it! Maybe yours will appear on the website too!*

Example: This game is called space water soccer. You will play it in a zero-gravity water room. Large blobs of water will float through the air, and each team will have to move the water blobs to one side of the room . . .

Future Time Clauses

Grammar in Context

BEFORE YOU READ

Look at the picture. What is the girl thinking? Read this article about setting goals.

GO FOR IT! What are your dreams for the future?

Are you going to get your degree **by the time you're 22**? Will you start your own business **before you turn 40**? We all have dreams, but they'll remain just dreams **until we change them to goals**. Here's how.

■ **PUT YOUR DREAMS ON PAPER. After you write a dream down,** it will start to become a goal. Your path will be a lot clearer. For example, Latoya Jones wrote:

> **Before I turn 30,** I'm going to be a successful businessperson.

Now her dream is starting to become her goal.

■ **LIST YOUR REASONS. When things get difficult,** you can read this list to yourself and it will help you to go on. This is what Latoya put at the top of her list:

> My parents will be proud of me **when I'm a successful businessperson**.

■ **WRITE DOWN AN ACTION PLAN.** What are you planning to do to achieve your goal? This is Latoya's action plan:

> I'm going to go to business school **as soon as I save enough money**.
>
> **When I have my degree,** I'll get a job with a big company.

■ **TAKE YOUR FIRST STEPS TODAY.** Here are the first steps Latoya is going to take:

> **Before I apply to schools,** I'm going to order some school catalogs.
>
> I won't decide on a school **until I visit several of them**.

You can do exactly what Latoya did to achieve your own goals. Keep this article in a safe place. **When you decide to start,** you'll know what to do. Remember, the longest journey starts with the first step!

AFTER YOU READ

For each pair of sentences (a or b), check the action that comes first.

Latoya's action plan:

1. _____ **a.** She will order school catalogs.   _____ **b.** She will apply to schools.

2. _____ **a.** She will save money.   _____ **b.** She will go to business school.

3. _____ **a.** She will get a job with a big company.   _____ **b.** She will get her degree.

Grammar Presentation

FUTURE TIME CLAUSES

Statements			
Main Clause		**Time Clause**	
I **will** I **am going to**			I **graduate**.
She **will** She **is going to**	**get** a job	**when**	she **graduates**.
They **will** They **are going to**			they **graduate**.

Yes / No Questions			
Main Clause		**Time Clause**	
Will I **Am** I **going to**			I **graduate**?
Will she **Is** she **going to**	**get** a job	**when**	she **graduates**?
Will they **Are** they **going to**			they **graduate**?

Short Answers					
Affirmative			**Negative**		
Yes,	you	**will.** **are.**	**No,**	you	**won't.** **aren't.**
	she	**will.** **is.**		she	**won't.** **isn't.**
	they	**will.** **are.**		they	**won't.** **aren't.**

Wh- Questions				
Main Clause			**Time Clause**	
Where	**will** I **am** I **going to**			I **graduate**?
	will she **is** she **going to**	**get** a job	**when**	she **graduates**?
	will they **are** they **going to**			they **graduate**?

GRAMMAR NOTES

EXAMPLES

1. When a **sentence about future time** has two clauses, the verb in the main clause is often in the future (*will* or *be going to*). But the verb in the **time clause** is often in the **simple present**.

> ▶ **BE CAREFUL!** Do not use *will* or *be going to* in a future time clause.

The **time clause** can come at the beginning or at the end of the sentence. The meaning is the same.

Use a **comma** after the time clause when it comes at the beginning. Do not use a comma when it comes at the end.

main clause   time clause
- She**'ll look** for a job *when* she **graduates.**

main clause   time clause
- He**'s going to work** *after* he **graduates.**

NOT when she ~~will graduate~~.

NOT after he ~~is going to graduate~~.

- *Before* she applies, she'll visit schools.

OR

- She'll visit schools *before* she applies.
  NOT She'll visit school‚ before she applies.

---

2. Here are some common **time expressions** you can use to begin future time clauses.

a. *When*, *after*, *not until*, and *as soon as* often introduce the event that happens <u>first</u>.

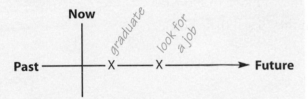

- *When* **I graduate**, I'll look for a job.
- I'll look for a job *after* **I graduate**.
- I wo**n't** look for a job *until* **I graduate**.
- *As soon as* **I graduate**, I'll look for a job.
  (*First I'll graduate. Then I'll look for a job.*)

b. *Before*, *until*, and *by the time* often introduce the event that happens <u>second</u>.

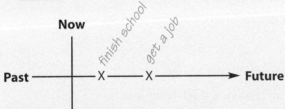

- *Before* **I get a job**, I'll finish school.
- I'll stay in school *until* **I get a job**.
- *By the time* **I get a job**, I'll be out of school.
  (*First I'll finish school. Then I'll get a job.*)

c. *While* introduces an event that will happen <u>at the same time</u> as another event.

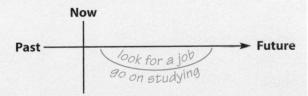

- *While* **I look for a job**, I'll go on studying.
  (*I will look for a job and study at the same time.*)

Focused Practice

1 | DISCOVER THE GRAMMAR

Read the numbered sentence. Then circle the letter of the two sentences that have a similar meaning.

1. Amber will open her own business when she finishes school.
   a. Amber will open her own business. Then she'll finish school.
   b. Amber will finish school. Then she'll open her own business.

2. Denzell won't quit until he finds another job.
   a. Denzell will find another job. Then he'll quit.
   b. Denzell will quit. Then he'll find another job.

3. Jake will retire as soon as he turns 60.
   a. Jake will retire. Then he'll turn 60.
   b. Jake will turn 60. Then he'll retire.

4. After the Morrisons sell their house, they'll move to Florida.
   a. The Morrisons will sell their house. Then they'll move to Florida.
   b. The Morrisons will move to Florida. Then they'll sell their house.

5. Marisa will call you when she gets home.
   a. Marisa will call you. Then she'll get home.
   b. Marisa will get home. Then she'll call you.

6. Dimitri is going to live with his parents until he gets married.
   a. Dimitri is going to get married. Then he'll live with his parents.
   b. Dimitri will live with his parents. Then he'll get married.

7. While Li-jing is in school, she'll work part-time.
   a. Li-jing will finish school. Then she'll get a part-time job.
   b. Li-jing will go to school. At the same time she'll have a part-time job.

8. By the time Marta gets her diploma, she'll be 21.
   a. Marta will get her diploma. Then she'll turn 21.
   b. Marta will turn 21. Then she'll get her diploma.

9. Adel and Farah won't buy a house until their son is two years old.
   a. They'll buy a house. Then their son will turn two.
   b. Their son will turn two. Then they'll buy a house.

10. Ina will live in Paris while she studies French cooking.
    a. First she'll study French cooking. Then she will move to Paris.
    b. She'll study French cooking. At the same time, she'll live in Paris.

2 | **LOOKING AHEAD**

Complete this student's worksheet. Use the correct form of the verbs in parentheses.

GOAL PLANNING WORKSHEET

A. What is your most important goal?

- I _____*'ll get*_____ a job after I _____.
     1. (get)   2. (graduate)

B. List the reasons you want to achieve this goal.

- When I _____ a job, I _____ more money.
         3. (get)   4. (have)
- When I _____ enough money, I _____ a used car.
         5. (save)   6. (buy)
- I _____ happier when I _____ employed.
     7. (feel)   8. (be)
- I _____ new skills while I _____.
     9. (learn)   10. (work)

C. What is your action plan?

- Every morning when I _____, I _____ the newspaper
                         11. (get up)   12. (buy)
   to look at the employment ads.

- When I _____ to my friends, I _____ them if they know
           13. (talk)   14. (ask)
   of any jobs.

- I _____ at the job notices board when I _____ to the
       15. (look)   16. (go)
   supermarket.

- Before I _____ on an interview, I _____ my computer
           17. (go)   18. (improve)
   skills. I want to learn Excel and PowerPoint.

D. What are the steps you will take right away?

- Before I _____ anything else, I _____ a list of people to
           19. (do)   20. (write)
   contact for help.

- As soon as I _____ all the people on my list, I _____ on
               21. (contact)   22. (work)
   fixing up my résumé.

3 | WHAT'S NEXT?

Combine these pairs of sentences. Use the future or the simple present form of the verb.
Remember to use commas when necessary.

1. Sandy and Jeff will get married. Then Sandy will graduate.

   _____*Sandy and Jeff will get married*_____ before _____*Sandy graduates.*_____

2. Jeff is going to get a raise. Then they are going to move to a larger apartment.

   _____ as soon as _____

3. They're going to move to a larger apartment. Then they're going to have a baby.

   After _____

4. They'll have their first child. Then Sandy will get a part-time job.

   _____ after _____

5. Their child will be two. Then Sandy will go back to work full-time.

   When _____

6. Sandy will work full-time, and Jeff will go to school.

   _____ while _____

7. Jeff will graduate. Then he'll find another job.

   _____ when _____

4 | EDITING

Read this journal entry. There are ten mistakes in the use of future time clauses. The first
mistake is already corrected. Find and correct nine more. Remember to look at punctuation!

Graduation is next month! I need to make some plans now because when exams ~~will start~~ *start*,
I don't have any free time. What am I going to do when I will finish school? My roommate
is going to take a vacation before she will look for a job. I can't do that because I need
to earn some money soon. I think that after I will graduate I am going to take a word
processing class. As soon as I learn word processing I look for a job as a bilingual office
assistant. It's hard to find full-time jobs, though. Part-time jobs are easier to find. Maybe
I'll take a part-time job after I find a good full-time one. Or maybe I'll take a workshop in
making decisions, before I do anything!

Communication Practice

5 | LISTENING

🎧 *Listen to a woman calling Jobs Are Us Employment Agency. Read the sentences that follow. Then listen again and number the events in order.*

The woman is going to:

_____ **a.** speak to a job counselor

_____ **b.** have an interview at the agency

__1__ **c.** send a résumé

_____ **d.** receive more job training

_____ **e.** go to companies

_____ **f.** take a skills test

6 | UNTIL WHEN?

Complete these sentences. Then compare your answers with those of your classmates. How many different answers are there? Remember that all sentences refer to future time.

1. I'm going to continue studying English until_____

2. While I'm in this class, _____

3. When I finish this class, _____

4. I'll stay in this country until_____

   Example: I'm going to continue studying English until I pass the TOEFL exam.

7 | INTERVIEW

Work with a partner. Interview him or her about some future plans. Ask questions such as:

- What will you do when _____?
- Where will you go after _____?
- Will you _____ while you _____?
- Before you _____, will you _____?

Take notes and then write a short paragraph about your classmate's plans.

   Example: Soo Mi is going to get married next year. Before she gets married, she's going to return home to visit her family. While she's away, she'll miss her boyfriend, but she'll e-mail him every day.

8 | WRITING

Complete this worksheet for yourself. Use future time clauses.

GOAL PLANNING WORKSHEET

A. What is your most important goal?

1. _____

B. List the reasons you want to achieve this goal.

1. _____

2. _____

3. _____

4. _____

C. What is your action plan?

1. _____

2. _____

3. _____

4. _____

D. What are the steps you will take right away?

1. _____

2. _____

3. _____

---

9 | ON THE INTERNET

Choose one personal dream. Write it down to make it a goal. What are the first steps you will take? Do a search to find the information you need. Report to the class on the information you find. Use future time clauses.

Example: GOAL: When I finish this English course, I will go to college.
SEARCH: Look up **colleges**.
REPORT: My goal is that when I finish this English course, I'll go to college. I looked up information about colleges. As soon as I am ready, I will apply to City College.

Wh- Questions: Subject and Object

Grammar in Context

BEFORE YOU READ

🎧 *Look at the drawing by a courtroom artist. A lawyer is questioning a crime witness. What kind of questions do you think the lawyer is asking? Read this excerpt from a court transcript.*

STATE OF ILLINOIS V. HARRY M. ADAMS   MARCH 31, 2006

LAWYER: **What happened on the night of May 12?** Please tell the court.

WITNESS: I went to Al's Grill.

LAWYER: **Who did you see there?**

WITNESS: I saw one of the defendants.

LAWYER: **Which one did you see?**

WITNESS: It was that man.

LAWYER: Let the record show that the witness is pointing to the defendant, Harry Adams. OK, you saw Mr. Adams. Did he see you?

WITNESS: No, he didn't see me.

LAWYER: But somebody saw you. **Who saw you?**

WITNESS: A woman. He was talking to a woman. She saw me.

LAWYER: OK. **What happened next?**

WITNESS: The woman gave him a box.

LAWYER: A box! **What did it look like?**

WITNESS: It was about this long . . .

LAWYER: So, about a foot and a half. **What did Mr. Adams do then?**

WITNESS: He took the box. He looked frightened.

LAWYER: **Why did he look frightened? What was in the box?**

WITNESS: I don't know. He didn't open it. He just took it and left in a hurry.

LAWYER: **Where did he go?**

WITNESS: Toward the parking lot.

LAWYER: **When did the woman leave?**

WITNESS: She was still there when we heard his car speed away.

AFTER YOU READ

Read the statements. Check **True** *or* **False**.

	True	False
1. The witness saw Harry Adams.	☐	☐
2. Harry Adams saw the witness.	☐	☐
3. The witness saw a woman.	☐	☐
4. The woman saw the witness.	☐	☐

Grammar Presentation

WH- QUESTIONS: SUBJECT AND OBJECT

Questions About the Subject		
Wh- Word Subject	Verb	Object
Who	saw	Harry?
		the box?

Answers		
Subject	Verb	Object
Marta	saw	him.
		it.

Questions About the Object			
*Wh-*Word Object	Auxiliary Verb	Subject	Main Verb
Who(m)	did	Marta	see?
What			

Answers		
Subject	Verb	Object
She	saw	Harry.
		the box.

GRAMMAR NOTES

EXAMPLES

1. Use **wh- questions** (also called *information questions*) to ask for specific information.

   Wh- questions begin with **wh- words** such as *who, what, where, when, why, which, whose, how, how many, how much,* and *how long*.

A: **Who** did you see at Al's Grill?
B: Harry Adams.

A: **When** did you go there?
B: On May 12.

A: **How many** people saw you?
B: Two.

2. When you are asking about the **subject**, use:

- a *wh-* word in place of the subject, and statement word order: **subject + verb**

For questions beginning with **which**, **whose**, **how much**, and **how many**, we often use **wh- word + noun** in place of the subject.

subject   subject
<u>Someone</u> saw you. <u>Something</u> happened.
↓   ↓
Who saw you?   **What** happened?

- **Which witness** told the truth?
- **How many people** saw the trial?

3. When the verb is a form of **be** *(am, is, are, was, were)* use:

- *wh-* **word +** *be*

<u>Harry Adams</u> is the defendant.
↓
- **Who is** the defendant?

Harry Adams is <u>the defendant</u>.
↓
- **Who is** Harry Adams?

4. When you are asking about the **object**, use:

- a *wh-* word, and the following word order: **auxiliary verb + subject + main verb**

For questions beginning with **which**, **whose**, **how much**, and **how many**, we often use **wh- word + noun** in place of the object.

REMEMBER: An **auxiliary** verb is a verb such as **do** *(does, did)*, **have** *(has, had)*, **can**, or **will**. **Be** can be an auxiliary too.

object   object
You saw <u>someone</u>. He said <u>something</u>.
↓   ↓
Who did you see? **What** did he say?

- **Which witness** did you believe?
- **How much time** did the jury need?

- **Who does** she defend?
- **Who is** she helping?

5. **USAGE NOTE:** In **very formal** English when asking about people as object, **whom** is sometimes used instead of *who*.

▶ **BE CAREFUL!** If the main verb is a form of **be**, you cannot use *whom*.

VERY FORMAL
- **Whom** did you see?

MORE COMMON
- **Who** did you see?

- **Who is** the next witness?
  NOT ~~Whom~~ is the next witness?

6. *Wh-* questions with **why**, **when**, or **where** have the following word order:

- **auxiliary verb + subject + main verb**

This is the same word order as in *wh-* questions about the object.

- **Why does** she want to defend him?
- **When did** she arrive?
- **Where will** she go?

Focused Practice

1 | DISCOVER THE GRAMMAR

Match the questions and answers.

__f__ 1. Who did you see?

_____ 2. Who saw you?

_____ 3. What hit her?

_____ 4. What did she hit?

_____ 5. Which man did you give the money to?

_____ 6. Which man gave you the money?

a. His wife saw me.

b. She hit a car.

c. Harry gave me the money.

d. A car hit her.

e. I gave the money to Harry.

f. I saw the defendant.

2 | CROSS-EXAMINATION

Grammar Notes 1–6

Complete the cross-examination. Write the lawyer's questions.

1. LAWYER: _What time did you return home?_
      (What time / you / return home)
   WITNESS: I returned home just before midnight.

2. LAWYER: _____
      (How / you / get home)
   WITNESS: Someone gave me a ride.

3. LAWYER: _____
      (Who / give / you / a ride)
   WITNESS: A friend from work.

4. LAWYER: _____
      (What / happen / next)
   WITNESS: I opened my door and saw someone on my living room floor.

5. LAWYER: _____
      (Who / you / see)
   WITNESS: Deborah Collins.

6. LAWYER: _____
      (Who / be / Deborah Collins)
   WITNESS: She's my wife's boss. I mean, she *was* my wife's boss. She's dead now.

7. LAWYER: _____
      (What / you / do)
   WITNESS: I called the police.

8. LAWYER: _____
      (When / the police / arrive)
   WITNESS: In about 10 minutes.

9. LAWYER: _____

(What / they / ask you)

WITNESS: They asked me to describe the crime scene.

10. LAWYER: _____

(How many police officers / come)

WITNESS: I don't remember. Why?

LAWYER: I'm asking the questions here. Please just answer.

3 | Q & A   *Grammar Notes 1–6*

Read the answers. Then ask questions about the underlined words.

1. Court begins <u>at 9:00 A.M.</u>

   When does court begin?

2. <u>Something horrible</u> happened.

   _____

3. <u>Five</u> witnesses testified.

   _____

4. The witness recognized <u>Harry Adams</u>.

   _____

5. <u>The witness</u> recognized Harry Adams.

   _____

6. The district attorney questioned <u>the restaurant manager</u>.

   _____

7. <u>The judge</u> spoke to the jury.

   _____

8. The verdict was <u>"guilty."</u>

   _____

9. The jury found Adams guilty <u>because he didn't have an alibi</u>.

   _____

10. The trial lasted <u>two weeks</u>.

   _____

11. Adams paid his lawyer <u>$2,000</u>.

   _____

4 | EDITING

Read a reporter's notes. There are eight mistakes in the use of wh- questions. The first mistake is already corrected. Find and correct seven more.

Questions

Where ~~Jones went~~ on January 15? *(did Jones go)*

Who went with him?

What time he return home?

Who he called?

How much money he had with him?

Whom saw him at the station the next day?

How did he look?

How many suitcases did he have?

When the witness call the police?

What did happen next?

What his alibi was?

Communication Practice

5 | LISTENING

🎧 You are on the phone with a friend. There is a bad connection. Listen to the following sentences. Then listen again. Circle the letter of the question you need to ask in order to get the correct information.

1. **a.** Who did you see at the restaurant?
   b. Who saw you at the restaurant?

2. **a.** Which car did the truck hit?
   b. Which car hit the truck?

3. **a.** When did it happen?
   b. Why did it happen?

4. **a.** Whose mother did you call?
   b. Whose mother called you?

5. **a.** Who did you report it to?
   b. Who reported it?

6. **a.** How many people heard the shouts?
   b. How many shouts did you hear?

7. **a.** Who saw the man?
   b. Who did the man see?

8. **a.** Why do you have to hang up?
   b. When do you have to hang up?

6 | WHAT HAPPENED NEXT?

Work with a partner. Look at the court transcript on page 73 again. Read it aloud. Then continue the lawyer's questioning of the witness. Ask at least six more questions.

Example: LAWYER: When did the woman leave?
WITNESS: She was still there when we heard his car speed away.
LAWYER: What happened next?

7 | INFORMATION GAP: POLICE CRIME INVESTIGATION

Two detectives (Maigret and Poirot) are investigating a case. All the suspects work at the same office. The detectives interviewed Mary Rogers, the office manager. Each detective took notes, but their notes are incomplete. You have to complete them. Work in pairs (A and B). Student A, follow the instructions on this page. Student B, turn to page 81.

1. Read Maigret's notes below.

2. Ask your partner for the information you need to complete Maigret's notes.

Example: **A:** Who did Mary Rogers see at 8:00 P.M.?
B: Rick Simon.

3. Maigret's notes have the information your partner needs to complete Poirot's notes. Answer your partner's questions.

Example: **B:** Where did Mary Rogers see Rick Simon?
A: She saw him at Al's Grill.

INTERVIEW WITH: Mary Rogers		DETECTIVE: Maigret	
SUSPECT (Who?)	**TIME** (When?)	**LOCATION** (Where?)	**OTHER WITNESSES** (Who else?)
Rick Simon	8:00 P.M.	Al's Grill	
Alice May		Fifth Avenue	Bob May
Jake Bordon	6:30 P.M.		the janitor
	7:15 P.M.		some children
John Daniels	7:00 P.M.		

When you are finished, compare Maigret's and Poirot's completed notes. Are they the same?

8 | STAR REPORTERS

Work in small groups. You are going to interview a ten-year-old child genius who is attending law school. You have five minutes to think of as many wh- *questions as you can. One student should write down all the questions.*

Examples: When did you decide to become a lawyer?
Who influenced you to become a lawyer?

You will be allowed to ask only six questions. Choose the six best questions. Now work in pairs. Role-play the interview. Use the six questions your group chose. Then write up the interview for a magazine article.

9 | WRITING

Work with a partner. Think of something exciting or interesting that you once saw. Tell your partner. Then write a list of questions and interview your partner to get more information. Take notes and write up the interview.

Example: A: I once saw a bad car accident.
B: Where did it happen?
A: On the highway.
B: How many cars were in the accident?
A: There was one car and a truck.
B: What did you do?
A: I . . .

10 | ON THE INTERNET

First do an online search for the definitions of these words. Write the definitions.

defense attorney	judge	jury	prosecutor	verdict	victim

The trial in this unit took place in the state of Illinois. Do a search on **criminal trial process in the United States**. *Do a web search or look at an online encyclopedia. Answer these questions:*

- Who does the defense attorney work for?
- Who represents the victim?
- Who chooses the jury?
- How many people sit on the jury?
- What does the judge do?
- Who gives the verdict?

When you are done, compare your answers with those of your classmates.

INFORMATION GAP FOR STUDENT B

1. Read Poirot's notes below.

2. Poirot's notes have the information your partner needs to complete Maigret's notes. Answer your partner's questions.

   Example: **A:** Who did Mary Rogers see at 8:00 P.M.?
   B: Rick Simon.

3. Ask your partner for the information you need to complete Poirot's notes.

   Example: **B:** Where did Mary Rogers see Rick Simon?
   A: She saw him at Al's Grill.

INTERVIEW WITH: Mary Rogers		**DETECTIVE:** Poirot	
SUSPECT (Who?)	**TIME** (When?)	**LOCATION** (Where?)	**OTHER WITNESSES** (Who else?)
Rick Simon	8:00 P.M.	Al's Grill	the waiter
Alice May	7:30 P.M.		
Jake Bordon	6:30 P.M.	the office	
Lilly Green	7:15 P.M.	in the park	
		Tony's Pizza	two customers

When you are finished, compare Maigret's and Poirot's completed notes. Are they the same?

From **Grammar** to **Writing**
Combining Sentences with Time Words

You can often improve your writing by combining two short sentences into one longer sentence that connects the two ideas. The two sentences can be combined by using time words such as *while, when, as soon as, before, after,* or *until*. The resulting longer sentence is made up of a main clause and a time clause.

Example: I was shopping. I saw the perfect dress for her. ⟶

     time clause   main clause

     While I was shopping, I saw the perfect dress for her.

     main clause   time clause

     I saw the perfect dress for her **while** I was shopping.

Notice that the time clause can come first or second. When it comes first, a comma separates the two clauses.

1 Read this paragraph. Underline all the sentences that are combined with a time word. Circle the time words.

> I always exchange holiday presents with my girlfriend, Shao Fen. Last year, (while) I was shopping for her, I saw an umbrella in her favorite color. As soon as I saw it, I thought of her. I bought the umbrella and a scarf in the same color. When Shao Fen opened the present, she looked really upset. She didn't say anything, and she didn't look at me. I felt hurt and confused by her reaction. Later she explained that in Chinese the word for "umbrella" sounds like the word for "separation." When she saw the umbrella, she misunderstood. She thought I wanted to end the relationship. After I heard that, I was very upset! I decided that next year, before I buy something, I'm going to check with her sister!

2 | *Look at this student's paragraph. Combine the pairs of underlined sentences with time words such as* **when, while, as soon as, before,** *and* **after**. *Use your own paper.*

I usually keep my wallet in my back pocket when I go out. <u>Two weeks ago, I was walking on a crowded street. I felt something.</u> I didn't pay any attention to it at the time. <u>I got home. I noticed that my wallet was missing.</u> I was very upset. It didn't have much money in it, but my credit card and my driver's license were there. <u>I was thinking about the situation. My brother came home.</u> He told me to report it to the police. <u>I called the police. They weren't very encouraging.</u> They said that wallets often get "picked" from back pockets. They didn't think I would get it back. <u>Tomorrow, I'm going to the movies. I'll keep my new wallet in my front pocket.</u>

Example: Two weeks ago, **while** I was walking on a crowded street, I felt something.

3 | *Before you write . . .*

1. We often say, "Learn from your mistakes." Think about a misunderstanding or a mistake that you experienced or observed. How did your behavior or thinking change because of your experience?

2. Describe the experience to a partner. Listen to your partner's experience.

3. Ask and answer questions about your experiences, for example: *When did it happen? Why did you . . . ? Where were you when . . . ? What will you do . . . ?*

4 | *Write a draft of your story. Follow the model below. Remember to use some of these time words and include information that your partner asked about.*

as soon as	before	until	when	while

I (OR My friend) always / often / usually / never _____

_____

_____

Last week / Yesterday / In 2003, _____

_____

_____

_____

_____

In the future / Next time, _____

_____

5 | *Exchange stories with a different partner. Complete the chart.*

1. The writer used time words to connect ideas. **Yes** _____ **No** _____

2. What I liked in the story:

_____

_____

_____

3. Questions I'd like the writer to answer about the story:

Who _____?

What _____?

When _____?

Where _____?

How _____?

(Other) _____?

6 | *Work with your partner. Discuss each other's chart from Exercise 5. Then rewrite your own paragraph and make any necessary changes.*

Review Test

I Complete each sentence with the simple present or present progressive form of the verb in parentheses.

1. You _____ *'re breathing* _____ hard. Sit down and rest for a while.
   (breathe / are breathing)

2. Dolphins are mammals. They have lungs and they _____ air.
   (breathe / are breathing)

3. Fred just left. He _____ to his biology class right now.
   (goes / is going)

4. He _____ to biology class twice a week.
   (goes / is going)

5. In our area, it _____ a lot in March.
   (rains / is raining)

6. It _____ right now, and I don't have my umbrella.
   (rains / is raining)

7. We _____. Is the music too loud for you?
   (dance / are dancing)

8. We _____ every day. It's good exercise.
   (dance / are dancing)

II Complete the conversations with the simple present or present progressive of the verbs in parentheses. Write short answers when necessary.

1. **A:** _____ *Are* _____ you _____ *getting* _____ ready for school? It's 7:45.
              a. (get)

   B: Yes, I _____ *am* _____. I _____ my teeth right now.
                    b.   c. (brush)

   A: How about Sue? _____ she _____ dressed?
                                              d. (get)

   B: I _____ so. She _____ for her shoes.
              e. (think)   f. (look)

2. **A:** Something _____ good. What _____ you _____?
                      a. (smell)   b. (cook)

   B: Pancakes. Hey, _____ you _____ your book bag?
                                              c. (have)

   A: No, I _____. _____ you _____ where it is?
                   d.   e. (know)

   B: You _____ it in your room these days, right?
                 f. (keep)

   A: I _____ in my room right now, but I _____ it.
                g. (stand)   h. (not see)

(continued)

3. **A:** Yuck. This milk _____ awful. I'm going to have juice instead.

a. (taste)

   B: Look, I _____ one sandwich for lunch. _____ that enough?

b. (pack)   c. (be)

   A: I _____ any lunch. I _____ hungry today.

d. (not want)   e. (not be)

   B: You _____ pale. _____ you _____ OK?

f. (look)   g. (feel)

   A: Yes, I _____. I'm just a little nervous about my spelling test.

h.

   B: Oh no! Look at the time. I think I _____ the school bus.

i. (hear)

   A: Don't worry. We _____ right now. Bye!

j. (leave)

III   *Complete each sentence with an affirmative or negative imperative. Use the verbs in the box. Use some verbs more than once.*

call	enjoy	forget	have	lock	put	walk

1. Please _____*walk*_____ the dog in the morning and afternoon.

2. But _____ her near the Wongs' house. She chases their cat.

3. Please _____ the back door before you go out. The key is in the door.

4. Also, _____ to turn out the lights. We have high electric bills.

5. _____ the newspapers in the garbage. They go in a separate recycling bin.

6. _____ the garbage cans on the sidewalk on Tuesday morning.

7. _____ me if you have any problems.

8. But _____ after 11:00. We go to bed early when we're on vacation.

9. _____ fun, and _____ the house.

IV   *Complete the conversation with the simple past form of the verbs in parentheses. Write short answers when necessary.*

A: Are you from Baltimore?

B: No, I'm not. I _____*was born*_____ in China, but I _____ here 10 years ago.

1. (be born)   2. (move)

A: Where _____ you _____ in China?

3. (live)

B: In Shanghai.

A: Oh really? I _____ in Shanghai last year. I _____ English there
4. (be)   5. (teach)

for three years.

B: That's interesting. _____ you _____ it?
6. (like)

A: Yes, I _____. Very much.
7.

B: _____ the United States _____ strange to you after China?
8. (appear)

A: Yes, it _____. I _____ comfortable in Baltimore for months.
9.   10. (not be)

For one thing, my students here_____ very polite.
11. (not seem)

B: I think it's called "reverse culture shock". I _____ uncomfortable when
12. (be)

I _____ back to China a few years ago.
13. (go)

A: _____ you uncomfortable for a long time?
14. (be)

B: No, I _____. Things _____ to feel normal again after a
15.   16. (begin)

few weeks.

A: _____ you _____ to feel culture shock in your own culture?
17. (expect)

B: No, I _____! But I'll be prepared the next time I visit!
18.

V | *Circle the correct verbs to complete the conversation.*

A: When you were young, did you use to ate / (eat) in restaurants a lot?
1.

B: No, not that often. We used to cooking / cook dinner at home.
2.

A: How about prices? Were / Did they lower when you were a kid?
3.

B: They sure were. Here's an example. A movie got used to / used to cost a dollar.
4.

A: Wow! Did you go / went to the movies a lot?
5.

B: Yes. We were going / went every Saturday afternoon. Hey, how about eating that
6.

hamburger?

A: OK—but one last question. Did / Are you like everything better in those days?
7.

B: Nope. In those days, I wasn't having / didn't have you to talk to. I like things much
8.

better now.

VI *Complete the telephone conversation with the simple past or past progressive form of the verbs in parentheses.*

A: Hi, I'm glad you're home! No one _____*answered*_____ a few minutes ago.
   1. (answer)

B: I _____ the lawn when the phone _____. What's up?
   2. (mow)   **3. (ring)**

A: I _____ a little accident with the car. Nothing serious—no injuries.
   4. (have)

B: Oh, that's good. How about the car?

A: It's OK. There _____ much damage. I _____ fast when
   5. (not be)   **6. (not drive)**

   I _____ the bus.
   7. (hit)

B: The bus! How _____ you _____ that?
                                8. (do)

A: I _____ to find a special radio station, so I _____ attention.
   9. (try)   **10. (not pay)**

B: _____ you _____ the police?
                        11. (call)

A: No. It _____ in front of a police station. An officer _____
      12. (happen)   **13. (appear)**

   before I even _____ out of the car. After the officer _____,
              14. (get)   **15. (leave)**

   I _____ the insurance company.
   16. (call)

B: Well, I'm just glad you're OK.

VII *Circle the correct verb to complete each conversation.*

1. A: Do you and Nora have plans for the weekend?
   B: Yes, we ('re going) / 'll go to a concert on Saturday. I just bought the tickets.

2. A: I can't believe I got into medical school.
   B: You are / 'll be a doctor in just a few years!

3. A: Oh no! I forgot to deposit my paycheck yesterday.
   B: I 'll / 'm going to deposit it for you. It's on my way.

4. A: I'm taking the train to Boston tomorrow.
   B: Oh. What time does / did it leave?

5. **A:** Take your umbrella. It<u>'s going to / 'll</u> rain.

   B: Thanks. I didn't listen to the weather report this morning.

6. **A:** My son is really interested in science fiction.

   B: Maybe he <u>has / 'll have</u> a career in space exploration when he grows up.

7. **A:** Look at Rachel's face. I think she<u>'s going to / 'll</u> cry.

   B: Poor kid. She really wants to come with us today.

8. **A:** It's almost June. What <u>are we going to / do we</u> do for the summer?

   B: How about summer school?

9. **A:** <u>Will / Does</u> Mahmoud call back this afternoon?

   B: He promised to call, but he's usually in class all afternoon.

10. **A:** Should I make a reservation at Dino's for tonight?

    B: It's already arranged. We <u>are / were</u> meeting there at 6:00.

VIII *Complete the sentences with the correct forms of the verbs in parentheses. Use **will** in one clause of each sentence.*

1. Laila _____*will need*_____ some new furniture when she _____*moves*_____ .
   a. (need)   b. (move)

2. As soon as you _____ to Oak Street, you _____ the library.
   a. (get)   b. (see)

3. We _____ here tonight until we _____ the report.
   a. (stay)   b. (finish)

4. After Sid _____ next June, he _____ in the city.
   a. (graduate)   b. (live)

5. I _____ the newspaper while I _____ breakfast.
   a. (read)   b. (eat)

6. They _____ a car when they _____ enough money.
   a. (buy)   b. (save)

7. Carmen _____ me before she _____ .
   a. (call)   b. (leave)

8. By the time you _____ 30, there _____ a shuttle
   a. (turn)   b. (be)

   to the moon.

IX *Complete the conversations with **wh-** questions.*

1. **A:** <u>Where did you go</u> last night?
   _{a.}

   B: I went to the movies.

   A: Really? _____ with you?
   _{b.}

   B: Mona did. She goes every weekend.

   A: _____?
   _{c.}

   B: We saw *Earthquake*.

2. **A:** You look upset. _____?
   _{a.}

   B: Nothing happened. I'm just tired.

   A: _____ on the math test?
   _{b.}

   B: I got an A.

   A: Wow! Big improvement. _____ with?
   _{c.}

   B: I studied with Ana. It really helped.

X *Circle the letter of the correct answer to complete each sentence.*

1. What _____? You look fascinated.   (A) B C D
   (**A**) are you reading   (**C**) will you read
   (**B**) do you read   (**D**) did you read

2. I'm reading about the Internet. Did you know it _____   A B C D
   in the 1960s?
   (**A**) begins   (**C**) began
   (**B**) 's going to begin   (**D**) is beginning

3. Jill, please _____ me your e-mail address again. I lost it.   A B C D
   (**A**) gives   (**C**) give
   (**B**) is giving   (**D**) gave

4. My e-mail address is jillski4@data.com. _____ it again!   A B C D
   (**A**) Not lose   (**C**) Aren't losing
   (**B**) Won't lose   (**D**) Don't lose

5. How are you, Naruyo? You _____ a little tired these days.   **A   B   C   D**
   - (**A**) 'll seem
   - (**B**) seem
   - (**C**) were seeming
   - (**D**) seemed

6. I _____ some evening classes this semester, and I have a lot of homework.   **A   B   C   D**
   - (**A**) 'm taking
   - (**B**) take
   - (**C**) 'm going to take
   - (**D**) was taking

7. I remember you. You _____ to go to school here.   **A   B   C   D**
   - (**A**) used
   - (**B**) were used
   - (**C**) using
   - (**D**) use

8. You have a good memory. I _____ here for only a month.   **A   B   C   D**
   - (**A**) go
   - (**B**) went
   - (**C**) was going to go
   - (**D**) 'm going

9. Will you buy an electric car when they _____ cheaper?   **A   B   C   D**
   - (**A**) will become
   - (**B**) are becoming
   - (**C**) became
   - (**D**) become

10. I think I _____ until electric cars are really cheap.   **A   B   C   D**
    - (**A**) waited
    - (**B**) 'll wait
    - (**C**) wait
    - (**D**) was waiting

11. _____ when it started to rain?   **A   B   C   D**
    - (**A**) Were you driving
    - (**B**) Are you driving
    - (**C**) Do you drive
    - (**D**) Will you drive

12. We were having dinner while it _____.   **A   B   C   D**
    - (**A**) rains
    - (**B**) 's going to rain
    - (**C**) raining
    - (**D**) was raining

13. He _____ a good job when he graduates next year.   **A   B   C   D**
    - (**A**) finds
    - (**B**) 'll find
    - (**C**) 's finding
    - (**D**) found

14. What classes _____ taking now?   **A   B   C   D**
    - (**A**) do you
    - (**B**) were you
    - (**C**) are you
    - (**D**) you are

XI *Each sentence has four underlined words or phrases. The four underlined parts of the sentence are marked A, B, C, or D. Circle the letter of the <u>one</u> underlined word or phrase that is NOT CORRECT.*

1. <u>Before</u> I <u>moved</u> to Chicago, I <u>use to</u> <u>live</u> in the country.
   A   B   C   D   A B Ⓒ D

2. We <u>are going to</u> <u>study</u> tonight <u>until</u> we <u>finished</u> the chapter.
   A   B   C   D   A B C D

3. It<u>'s</u> a one-way street, <u>so</u> <u>no</u> <u>turn</u> left here.
   A   B C D   A B C D

4. <u>When</u> Sid <u>will graduate</u> next June<u>,</u> he <u>will live</u> in the city.
   A   B   C   D   A B C D

5. <u>Where</u> <u>you went</u> <u>after</u> you <u>left</u> last night?
   A   B   C   D   A B C D

6. Who <u>did</u> <u>saw</u> you <u>while</u> you <u>were leaving</u> the bank?
   A B   C   D   A B C D

7. It <u>usually</u> <u>is raining</u> a lot here every winter, <u>but</u> last year it <u>didn't</u>.
   A   B   C   D   A B C D

8. <u>Were</u> you <u>watching</u> TV <u>when</u> I <u>call</u> you last night?
   A   B   C D   A B C D

9. You<u>'ll see</u> the bank<u>,</u> <u>when</u> you <u>get</u> to Main Street.
   A   B C   D   A B C D

10. We <u>didn't hear</u> the doorbell <u>when</u> he <u>arrived</u> because we <u>ate</u>.
    A   B   C   D   A B C D

11. Years <u>ago</u>, I didn't <u>used to</u> like rock music, <u>but</u> now I <u>love</u> it.
    A   B   C   D   A B C D

12. The movie <u>starts</u> <u>at</u> 7:30, so I <u>think</u> I <u>go</u>.
    A B   C D   A B C D

13. <u>Are you wanting</u> to <u>go</u> with me, or <u>are you</u> <u>studying</u> tonight?
    A   B   C   D   A B C D

▶ *To check your answers, go to the Answer Key on page RT-1.*

QUIZ RESULTS FOR UNIT 1, EXERCISE 6

If you checked . . .   *you are in the . . .*

1 and 2	Honeymoon Stage
3 and 4 and 5	Rejection Stage
6 and 7	Adjustment Stage
8	Adaptation Stage

PART II

Pronouns and Phrasal Verbs

Reflexive and Reciprocal Pronouns

BEFORE YOU READ

🎧 *What do you think* self-talk *is? Look at the examples of self-talk in the photos. Which are positive? Which are negative? Read this article from a psychology magazine.*

SELF-TALK

> It was all my fault.

> I'll never find another job.

> I'm the best worker they had.

> I'll find a better job soon.

Self-talk is the way we explain a problem to **ourselves**. It can affect how we feel and how we act. Take the case of Tom and Sara. They both got laid off from their jobs at the same company, but their reactions were totally different. Sara frequently talked on the phone with her friends, continued her free-time activities, and kept **herself** fit. Tom, on the other hand, spent all of his time **by himself**, didn't allow **himself** to have a good time, and gained 10 pounds.

Why were their reactions so very different from **one another**? They both lost their jobs, so the situation **itself** can't explain Tom's problems. The main difference was the way Tom and Sara explained the problem to **themselves**. Sara told **herself** that the problem was temporary and that she **herself** could change it. Tom saw **himself** as helpless and likely to be unemployed forever.

Tom and Sara both got their jobs back. Their reactions when they talked to **each other** were, again, very different. For his part, Tom grumbled, "Oh, I guess they were really desperate." Sara, on the other hand, smiled and said, "Well! They finally realized that they need me!"

AFTER YOU READ

Who did the following things? Check the correct answers.

	Tom	Sara	Tom and Sara
1. Stayed in good physical condition	☐	☐	☐
2. Spent a lot of time alone	☐	☐	☐
3. Thought the problem was temporary	☐	☐	☐
4. Felt helpless	☐	☐	☐
5. Had a conversation back at work	☐	☐	☐

Grammar Presentation

REFLEXIVE AND RECIPROCAL PRONOUNS

Reflexive Pronouns			
Subject Pronoun		**Reflexive Pronoun**	
I		**myself**	
You		**yourself**	
He		**himself**	
She		**herself**	
It	looked at	**itself**	in the mirror.
We		**ourselves**	
You		**yourselves**	
They		**themselves**	

Reciprocal Pronouns		
Subject Pronoun		**Reciprocal Pronoun**
We You They	looked at	**each other**. **one another**.

GRAMMAR NOTES

EXAMPLES

1. Use a **reflexive pronoun** when the subject and object of a sentence refer to the same people or things.

subject   =   object
- **Sara** looked at **herself** in the mirror.
  (Sara looked at her own face.)

subject   =   object
- **They** felt proud of **themselves**.
  (They were proud of their own actions.)

subject   =   object
- My **office light** turns **itself** off.
  (It turns off automatically.)

(continued)

2. In **imperative sentences** with reflexive pronouns, use:

- *yourself* when the subject is <u>singular</u>

- *yourselves* when the subject is <u>plural</u>

REMEMBER: In imperative sentences, the subject is *you*, and *you* can be either singular or plural.

- "Don't push **yourself** so hard, **Tom**," Sara said. (*talking to one friend*)

- "Don't push **yourselves** so hard, **guys**," Sara said. (*talking to several friends*)

---

3. Use a reflexive pronoun to **emphasize a noun**. In this case, the reflexive pronoun usually follows the noun directly.

- Tom was upset when he lost his job. The **job itself** wasn't important to him, but he needed the money.

---

4. *By* **+ a reflexive pronoun** means *alone* or *without any help*.

Be **+ a reflexive pronoun** means *act in the usual way*.

- Sara lives **by herself**. (*Sara lives alone.*)

- We finished the job **by ourselves**. (*No one helped us.*)

- Just **be yourself** at your interview.

---

5. Use a **reciprocal pronoun** when the subject and object of a sentence refer to the same people, and these people have a two-way relationship.

- Use *each other* for <u>two</u> people.

- Use *one another* for <u>more than two</u> people.

USAGE NOTE: Many people use *each other* and *one another* in the same way.

▶ **BE CAREFUL!** Reciprocal pronouns and plural reflexive pronouns have **different meanings**.

       subject   =   object
- **Tom and Sara** met **each other** at work. (*Tom met Sara, and Sara met Tom.*)

       subject   =   object
- **We all** told **one another** about our jobs. (*Each person exchanged news with every other person.*)

- **Sara and Tom** talked to **each other**. OR
- **Sara and Tom** talked to **one another**.

- Fred and Jane blamed **each other**. (*Fred blamed Jane, and Jane blamed Fred.*)

- Fred and Jane blamed **themselves**. (*Fred blamed himself, and Jane blamed herself.*)

---

6. Reciprocal pronouns have **possessive forms**: *each other's, one another's*.

- Tom and Sara took **each other's** number. (*Tom took Sara's number, and Sara took Tom's.*)

Reference Note
For a list of **verbs and expressions that often take reflexive pronouns**, see Appendix 3 on page A-2.

Focused Practice

1 | DISCOVER THE GRAMMAR

Read the rest of the article about self-talk. Underline the reflexive pronouns once and the reciprocal pronouns twice. Draw an arrow to the words that these pronouns refer to.

SELF-TALK *(continued)*

Positive self-talk can make the difference between winning and losing. Top athletes not only compete against one another, they also compete against themselves when they try to improve their performances. Many athletes use self-talk to help themselves reach new goals. For example, golf pro Jack Nicklaus used to imagine himself making a winning shot just before he played. Olympic swimmer Summer Sanders prepares herself for a race by smiling.

One sports psychologist believes that Olympic athletes are not very different from one another—they are all the best in their sports. When two top athletes compete against each other, the winner is the one with the most powerful positive "mental movies."

Psychologists say that ordinary people themselves can use these techniques as well. We can create "mental movies" to help ourselves succeed in difficult situations.

2 | THE OFFICE PARTY

Grammar Notes 1–2, 4–5

🎧 *Tom and Sara's company had an office party. Choose the correct reflexive or reciprocal pronouns to complete the conversations.*

1. **A:** Listen, guys! The food and drinks are over here. Please come and help ____yourselves____.
   (yourselves / themselves)

   B: Thanks. We will.

2. **A:** Isn't that the new head of the accounting department over there?

   B: I think so. Let's go over and introduce _____.
   (himself / ourselves)

3. **A:** I'm really nervous about my date with Nicole after the party. I cut _____
   (herself / myself)

   twice while shaving, and then I lost my car keys.

   B: Come on. This is a party. Just relax and be _____. You'll do fine.
   (yourself / yourselves)

4. **A:** What are you giving your boss for the holidays this year?

   B: We always give _____ the same holiday gifts.
   (ourselves / each other)

   Every year I give him a book, and he gives me a box of candy.

(continued)

5. **A:** What do you think of the new computer program?

   B: I'm not sure. In our department, we're still teaching _____ how to use it.
   (ourselves / themselves)

6. **A:** Jessica looks upset. Didn't she get a promotion?

   B: No, and she keeps blaming _____. I'll lend her that article about self-talk.
   (herself / himself)

7. **A:** The Aguayos are going to Japan on vacation this year.

   B: Are they going by _____ or with a tour group?
   (each other / themselves)

8. **A:** This was a great party.

   B: Yeah. We really enjoyed _____.
   (ourselves / myself)

3 | WE LEARN FROM ONE ANOTHER   *Grammar Notes 1–6*

Read this interview with George Prudeau, a high school French teacher. Complete the interview with the correct reflexive or reciprocal pronouns.

INTERVIEWER: How did you become a teacher?

GEORGE: When I got laid off from my 9:00–5:00 job, I told _____*myself*_____ "Here's my
                                                              1.
chance to do what I really want." One of the great things about teaching is the

freedom I have. I run the class by _____—just the way I want to.
                                      2.
I also like the way my students and I learn from _____. My students
                                                    3.
teach me a lot.

INTERVIEWER: What about discipline? Is that a problem?

GEORGE: We have just a few rules. I tell my students, "Keep _____ busy.
                                                                4.
Discuss the lessons, but don't interfere with _____'s work."
                                                5.

INTERVIEWER: What do you like to teach best?

GEORGE: I love French, but the subject _____ really isn't all that important. A
                                            6.
good teacher helps students learn by _____ and encourages them not
                                       7.
to give up when they have problems. For instance, John, one of my students, just

taught _____ how to bake French bread. The first few loaves were
        8.
failures. I encouraged him to use positive self-talk, and in the end he succeeded.

INTERVIEWER: What teaching materials do you use?

GEORGE: Very simple ones. I pride _____ on the fact that I can teach anywhere,
9.

even on a street corner.

INTERVIEWER: What do you like least about your job?

GEORGE: The salary. I teach French culture, but I can't afford to travel to France.

I have to satisfy _____ with trips to French restaurants!
10.

4 | GOING TO THE PARTY
Grammar Notes 1, 4–5

*Sara and Tom went to an office party. Look at each picture and write a sentence describing
what happened. Use a verb from the box with a reflexive or reciprocal pronoun. You will
use one verb more than once.*

| buy | cut | drive | greet | introduce to | smile at | talk to |

1. *Sara bought herself a new dress.*   2. _____

3. _____   4. _____

(continued)

5. _____

6. _____

7. _____

8. _____

5 | EDITING

Read this woman's diary. There are seven mistakes in the use of reflexive and reciprocal pronouns. The first mistake is already corrected. Find and correct six more.

> Jan's birthday was Wednesday, and I forgot to call him. I reminded ~~me~~ myself all day, and then I forgot anyway! I felt terrible. My sister Anna said, "Don't be so hard on yourselves," but I didn't believe her. She prides herself on remembering everything. Then I remembered the article on self-talk. It said that people can change the way they explain problems to theirselves. Well, I listened to the way I talked to me, and it sounded really insulting — like the way our high school math teacher used to talk to us. I thought, Jan and I are good friends, and we treat each others well. In fact, he forgave myself for my mistake right away. And I forgave him for forgetting our dinner date two weeks ago. Friends can forgive themselves, so I guess I can forgive myself.

Communication Practice

6 | LISTENING

🎧 *Listen to the conversations at an office party. Then listen again and circle the pronouns that you hear.*

1. **A:** The guys in Mark's department did a great job this year.

   B: I know. They should be really proud of <u>themselves</u> / (<u>each other</u>).

2. **A:** What's wrong? You look upset.

   B: I just heard Ed and Jeff talking. You know Ed blames <u>him</u> / <u>himself</u> for everything.

3. **A:** I hear you're going to Japan on vacation this year. Are you going by <u>yourself</u> / <u>yourselves</u>

   or with a tour?

   B: Oh, with a tour.

4. **A:** Jennifer looks happy tonight. Did Megan give her the promotion?

   B: No, not yet. Megan keeps asking <u>herself</u> / <u>her</u> if she can do the job.

5. **A:** How do you like the new computer system?

   B: I'm not sure. In our department, we're still teaching <u>each other</u> / <u>ourselves</u> how to use it.

6. **A:** So long, now. Thanks for coming. It was good to see you.

   B: Oh, it was a great party.

   A: I'm glad you enjoyed <u>yourself</u> / <u>yourselves</u>.

7 | CHEER YOURSELF UP!

What do you tell yourself in a difficult situation? Work with a partner and discuss each other's self-talk in the situations below. Then report to the class.

- You're going to take a big test.
- You're stuck in traffic.
- You have a roommate you don't like.
- You're going to compete in a sports event.
- You're having an argument with a friend or relative.
- You forgot something important.

Example: **A:** What do you tell yourself when you're going to take a big test?
B: I tell myself that I prepared myself well and that I'll do fine.

8 | THE OPTIMIST TEST

Test yourself by completing this questionnaire.

Are you an optimist or a pessimist?

What do you tell yourself when things go wrong? Check your most likely self-talk for each situation below. Then find out if you're an optimist or a pessimist.

1. Your boss doesn't say good morning to you.
- ☐ **a.** She isn't herself today.
- ☐ **b.** She doesn't like me.

2. Your family forgets your birthday.
- ☐ **a.** Next year we should keep in touch with one another more.
- ☐ **b.** They only think about themselves.

3. You gain 10 pounds.
- ☐ **a.** I promise myself to eat properly from now on.
- ☐ **b.** Diets never work for me.

4. Your boyfriend or girlfriend decides to go out with other people.
- ☐ **a.** We didn't spend enough time with each other.
- ☐ **b.** We're wrong for each other.

5. You're feeling tired lately.
- ☐ **a.** I pushed myself too hard this week.
- ☐ **b.** I never take care of myself.

6. Your friend forgets an appointment with you.
- ☐ **a.** He sometimes forgets to read his appointment book.
- ☐ **b.** He never reminds himself about important things.

Score your questionnaire
Optimists see bad situations as temporary or limited. Pessimists see them as permanent. All the **a** answers are optimistic, and all the **b** answers are pessimistic. Give yourself **0** for every **a** answer and **1** for every **b** answer.

If You Scored	You Are
0–2	very optimistic
3–4	somewhat optimistic
5–6	pessimistic

Now interview five classmates and find out how they answered the questions. Report the results to another group.

Example: For question 1, three people checked: "She isn't herself today."
Two people checked: "She doesn't like me."

9 | THE MEMORY GAME

Work with a partner. First look at the picture carefully for 30 seconds. Then shut your books and do the following.

1. Write down as many things as you can remember about what the people in the picture are doing.

2. Then compare your notes. Use reciprocal and reflexive pronouns in your description.

   Example: A: Two men are waving at each other.

   B: No, I think the people waving at each other are women.

When you are finished, open your books and check your answers. Who remembered the most? What did you leave out?

10 | WHAT ARE THEY THINKING?

With your partner, imagine the self-talk of some of the people at the party.

Examples: The man at the mirror: "I'll never give myself a haircut again."

The woman on the couch: "I don't know many people here. Should I introduce myself?"

11 | WRITING

Imagine you receive an e-mail from a friend who attends school in another city. Your friend is not doing well at school and is having problems with a boyfriend or girlfriend. Write your friend an e-mail. Explain the kind of self-talk you use when things are not going well.

Example: Annette, I'm sorry you are having problems in school. Here's what I tell myself when I have problems . . .

12 | ON THE INTERNET

Do a search on **self-help**. *Find different websites that show people how to help themselves. Choose one that you find interesting and bring information about it to class.*

Example: I found a website on teaching yourself how to meditate. They suggest working with a partner so that you can help each other . . .

Phrasal Verbs

Grammar in Context

BEFORE YOU READ

🎧 *Look at the photograph. What kind of work do you think the man does? Read this article about Dr. Eloy Rodriguez.*

Planting Ideas

A s a child, Eloy Rodriguez picked cotton to help support his family. He also **picked up** an interest in plants. Dr. Rodriguez is now a famous scientist, but he is still interested in plants. Every summer he **takes off** his lab coat, **puts on** his mosquito repellent, and travels to the Amazon region of Venezuela with his students. There, they search for medicinal plants.

Dr. Rodriguez **grew up** in Texas. The adults in his very large family (67 cousins lived nearby) **brought** their children **up** to be honest, fair, and *vivo*, or quick-thinking. Rodriguez did well in high school, especially in chemistry, and he **went on** to college. He took a job there cleaning a laboratory. He became a science major and then **went on** to graduate school. Soon he was managing the lab.

Eloy Rodriguez and anthropologist Richard Wrangham once noticed that sick animals often **pick out** certain plants to eat. They **turned** their observations **into** a new area of science—zoopharmacognosy (the study of how animals use plants as medicine). Today Rodriguez is one of the most brilliant scientists in the United States. Rodriguez thanks his family. He **points out** that 64 of his cousins graduated from college, 11 with advanced degrees. "Although poverty was there, family was what helped us **get by** in life."

AFTER YOU READ

Find a phrasal verb from the article that means . . .

1. became an adult _____

2. continued _____

3. survive _____

4. raised _____

5. select _____

6. removes _____

7. developed _____

8. covers himself with _____

Grammar Presentation

PHRASAL VERBS

Transitive Phrasal Verbs			
Subject	**Verb**	**Particle**	**Object (Noun)**
He	**put**	**on**	his lab coat.
	helped	**out**	his students.

		Object (Noun / Pronoun)	Particle
Subject	**Verb**		
He	**put**	his lab coat	**on.**
		it	
	helped	his students	**out.**
		them	

Intransitive Phrasal Verbs			
Subject	**Verb**	**Particle**	
She	**started**	**over.**	
He	**grew**	**up**	in Texas.
They	**got**	**back**	early.

GRAMMAR NOTES	EXAMPLES
1. Phrasal verbs (also called *two-word verbs*) are made up of a **verb + particle**.	verb + particle • He **put on** his lab coat.
On, off, up, down, in, and *out* are common particles.	verb + particle • She **pointed out** a problem.
Particles and prepositions look the same. However, particles are part of the verb phrase, and they often <u>change the meaning</u> of the verb.	verb + preposition • She's **looking up** at the sky. *(She's looking in the direction of the sky.)* verb + particle • She's **looking up** the word. *(She's searching for the word in the dictionary.)*

	PHRASAL VERB (LESS FORMAL)	**ONE-WORD VERB** (MORE FORMAL)
2. USAGE NOTE: Many **phrasal verbs** and one-word verbs have similar meanings. Phrasal verbs are often <u>less formal</u>, and they are more common in everyday speech.	**bring up**	raise
	figure out	solve
	go on	continue
	pick out	select
	take off	remove
	wake up	awaken

3. Phrasal verbs can be transitive or intransitive. **Transitive phrasal verbs** have <u>objects</u>.	phrasal verb + object • He **set up** *an experiment*. phrasal verb + object • They **figured out** *the problems*.
Most transitive phrasal verbs are **separable**. This means that the object can come: • <u>after</u> the verb + particle OR • <u>between</u> the verb and its particle	verb + particle + object • We **dropped off** *the students*. OR verb + object + particle • We **dropped** *the students* **off**. object • We **dropped** *them* **off**. NOT We dropped off them.
▶ **BE CAREFUL!** When the object is a **pronoun**, it must come <u>between</u> the verb and the particle.	

4. Some phrasal verbs are intransitive. **Intransitive phrasal verbs** do not have objects.	• Dr. Rodriguez **grew up** in Texas. • He **got back** late.

Reference Notes
For a list of **transitive phrasal verbs** and their meanings, see Appendix 4 on page A-3.
For a list of **intransitive phrasal verbs** and their meanings, see Appendix 5 on page A-4.

Focused Practice

1 | DISCOVER THE GRAMMAR

Read the article. Underline the phrasal verbs. Circle the objects of the transitive phrasal verbs.

In Eloy Rodriguez's elementary school in Edinburg, Texas, teachers passed Chicano* students over for special honors classes. They also punished them for speaking Spanish. When Rodriguez became the first U.S.-born Chicano biology instructor at his university, he worked 18 hours a day and slept in his lab. "I was very aware that I was the first this, and the first that, and I knew that some people were waiting for me to slip up." Rodriguez didn't slip up. However, he knows that when students feel teachers don't treat them fairly, it turns them off education. Many of them just give up.

Today, Dr. Rodriguez is passing his own success on. When he became a professor at Cornell University, he set out to find Latino** graduate students. He takes these students with him on many of his trips and works hard to turn them into top scientists. In 1990 he set up KIDS (Kids Investigating and Discovering Science)—a science program for minority elementary school children. They put on white lab coats and investigate science with university teachers who treat them like research scientists. They observe nature and figure out problems. In interviews, Rodriguez always brings up role models. "I saw my first snowflake before I saw my first Chicano scientist," he says. Because of Rodriguez's efforts, many students will not face the same problem.

* Chicano—Mexican-American
** Latino—from a Spanish-speaking country in Central or South America

*Read these sentences and decide if they are **True (T)** or **False (F)**.*

__F__ 1. In Rodriguez's elementary school, teachers chose Chicano students for honors classes.

_____ 2. When Rodriguez became a biology instructor, some people expected him to fail.

_____ 3. Unfair treatment makes students less interested in education.

_____ 4. Today, Rodriguez wants to forget his own success.

_____ 5. He searches for Latino graduate students for his program at Cornell.

_____ 6. In 1990 Rodriguez visited a program called KIDS.

_____ 7. Children in KIDS wear the same lab clothes as the scientists.

_____ 8. Rodriguez rarely mentions role models.

2 | COME ALONG!

Complete this advertisement for a field trip to the Amazon. Choose the phrasal verb from the box that is closest in meaning to the verb in parentheses. Use the correct form of the phrasal verb. Use Appendices 4 and 5 on pages A-3 and A-4 for help.

fill out	find out	~~get up~~	hand in	keep on	pass up
pick up	set up	~~sign up~~	talk over	try out	work out

Two Weeks in the Amazon! _____Sign up_____ *Now!*
1. (register)

The Biology Department is now _____ its summer field trip to the
2. (preparing)

Amazonian rain forest in Venezuela. _____ your application from the
3. (get)

Department Office (Room 215), and _____ it _____ right
4. (complete)

away. _____ it _____ by May 1.
5. (submit)

Last summer we collected

plants and identified them. This

summer we plan to talk to local

people and _____
6. (discover)

how they use plants in traditional

medicine. This trip is challenging.

We travel to our camp by canoe.

When there are problems, we

_____ them _____ by ourselves. We _____
7. (solve)   **8. (arise)**

very early, and we _____ working until dark. There is also some danger, so
9. (continue)

_____ the trip _____ with your families before you
10. (discuss)

decide. This is a chance to _____ your research skills and make a real
11. (use)

contribution. We hope you won't _____ this opportunity to do important
12. (reject)

"hands-on" science.

3 | FOOD FOR THOUGHT   *Grammar Notes 1–2*

Circle the correct particle to complete each phrasal verb. Use Appendices 4 and 5 on pages A-3 and A-4 for help.

EAT SOME LEAVES AND CALL ME IN THE MORNING

In 1972, Richard Wrangham of Harvard University set (out) / up to study chimpanzees in Tanzania. He
1.
observed that these chimps get <u>by / up</u> at dawn
2.
to eat the leaves of *Aspilia*. They clearly hate the
taste. This brought <u>back / up</u> a question: Why do
3.
chimpanzees pick <u>out / over</u> this plant but pass
4.
<u>out / up</u> delicious fruit nearby? Wrangham thought
5.
this question <u>over / up</u> for several years. He then asked Eloy Rodriguez to help him
6.
<u>in / out</u> with the analysis. Together, they worked <u>over / out</u> the puzzle: *Aspilia*
7.   **8.**
contains an antibiotic. Zoopharmacognosy—the study of how animals "doctor"
themselves with plants—was born.

---

4 | IN THE FIELD   *Grammar Note 3*

Complete the conversations. Use phrasal verbs and pronouns.

1. A: Don't forget to put on your mosquito repellent!

  B: Don't worry! I _____*put it on*_____ as soon as we got here.

2. A: Can we take off our hats? It's really hot.

  B: Don't _____. They protect you from the sun.

3. A: How do you turn on the generator?

  B: It's easy. You _____ with this switch.

4. A: Did you cover up the leftover food? We don't want the ants to get at it.

  B: Don't worry. We'll _____.

5. A: Is Dr. Rodriguez going to call off the field trip tomorrow?

  B: He'll only _____ if someone gets sick.

6. A: Good night. Oh, can someone wake Mike up tomorrow morning?

  B: No problem. I'll _____.

5 | IN THE LAB

Unscramble the words to make sentences. If more than one answer is possible, give both answers.

1. on / Put / your lab coats   Put your lab coats on.   OR   Put on your lab coats.

2. the experiment / Set / up   _____

3. out / it / Carry   _____

4. down / Sit / when you're done   _____

5. to page 26 / on / Go   _____

6. up / your reports / Write   _____

7. in / them / Hand   _____

8. off / Take / your lab coats   _____

9. them / Put / away   _____

10. the lab / Clean / up   _____

6 | EDITING

Read this student's journal notes. There are nine mistakes in the use of phrasal verbs. The first mistake is already corrected. Find and correct eight more.

I just got from Venezuela back! [*back* inserted] I spent two weeks in the Amazon rain forest with Dr. Rodriguez's research group. We carried out research there on plants that the Piaroa people use as medicine. We made down a list of these plants, and we're going to analyze them when we get back to school next week.

We set down camp near the Orinoco River, hundreds of miles from any major city. Life there is hard. You get very early up every morning. You must always watch up and never touch a new insect or plant. If you pick up it, you can get a bad skin rash. But plants can also cure. One day, I felt sick. One of the Piaroa gave me the stem of a certain plant to chew. It worked! Later I found at that the same plant helps cure insect bites. And believe me, insects are a big problem in the rain forest. I used up many bottles of repellent. But even when I put on it, it didn't totally keep the insects away.

This trip changed my life! I'm now thinking about switching my major to pharmacology. I want to find over more about how people can use the same plants that animals use as medicine.

Communication Practice

7 | LISTENING

🎧 *Some college students are taking a science class. Listen to these conversations. Circle the phrasal verbs that you hear. Then listen again and check your answers.*

1. **A:** What's Terry doing?

   B: She's <u>handing in</u> / <u>handing out</u> some lab reports.

2. **A:** Are you done with your report, Rea?

   B: Almost. I just have to <u>look up</u> / <u>look over</u> some information.

3. **A:** Hey, guys. That music is disturbing us.

   B: Sorry. We'll <u>turn it down</u> / <u>turn it off</u>.

4. **A:** Jason is discouraged.

   B: I know. He says he can't <u>keep on</u> / <u>keep up</u> with the class.

5. **A:** Did you hear about Lila?

   B: Yes, we were all surprised when she <u>dropped in</u> / <u>dropped out</u> yesterday.

6. **A:** OK, class. It's time to <u>take back</u> / <u>take off</u> your lab coats.

   B: Oh, could we have a few more minutes? We're almost done.

7. **A:** Hi. Can I help you?

   B: Yes, thanks. I need to <u>pick up</u> / <u>pick out</u> a book for my biology report.

8. **A:** Did you see Professor Diaz in lab today?

   B: Yes. He <u>brought up</u> / <u>brought back</u> those plants from the field trip. Very interesting.

Now look at your completed sentences. Decide if the statements below are **True (T)** *or* **False (F)**.

___F___ 9. Terry is giving some reports to the teacher.

_____ 10. Rea is going to look for some information in a reference book.

_____ 11. They're going to make the music lower.

_____ 12. Jason feels that the class is going too fast for him.

_____ 13. Lila visited the class yesterday.

_____ 14. It's time to return the lab coats.

_____ 15. She needs to choose a book for her report.

_____ 16. Professor Diaz returned the plants.

8 | LET'S TALK IT OVER

Work in groups. Imagine that you are going to take a class field trip. Decide where to go—for example, the zoo, a museum, a park. Then assign tasks and make a list. Try to include some of the phrasal verbs from the box. You can also use Appendices 4 and 5 on pages A-3 and A-4 for help.

call up	clean up	figure out	hand out	look over	look up
make up	pass out	pick out	pick up	talk over	write down

Example: A: I'll write down the To Do list.
B: Good idea. I'll call up to find out the hours.
C: I can pick up a bus schedule.

9 | A NEW LEAF

Discuss the pictures with a partner. Who are the people, and what are they doing in each picture? Make up a story about the pictures, and write a number under each picture to show the sequence. Then write your story. Compare your story to those of your classmates. Talk over any differences. There is more than one way to tell a story!

Example: In this picture, one of the men is looking up information about a plant . . .

a. _____

b. _____

c. _____

d. _____

e. _____

f. _____

10 | WRITING

Dr. Eloy Rodriguez is a role model to his students. Who was your most important role model when you were growing up? Why did you pick this person? What problems did your role model help you out with? What ideas and actions did you pick up from this person? Write a paragraph. Use phrasal verbs.

Example: When I was growing up, my role model was my high school chemistry teacher. I picked Ms. Suarez because she was a good teacher. She helped me out when I didn't understand the lesson, and she . . .

11 | ON THE INTERNET

Do a search on **science lab safety rules**. *Find rules that use phrasal verbs. Write them down. Share the rules with the rest of your class. Create one list to put up on the board.*

Example: Always clean up spills immediately.

From **Grammar** to **Writing**
Using Pronouns for Coherence

When you write a paragraph, it is usually better to use pronouns than to repeat the same noun. Pronouns can make your writing smoother and more connected.

Example: **My apartment** is pretty cozy. I hope you enjoy staying in **my apartment**. ⟶
My apartment is pretty cozy. I hope you enjoy staying in **it**.

1 | *Read this note from Ted, thanking Felicia in advance for house-sitting. Circle all the pronouns. Above each pronoun, write the noun that it refers to.*

Dear Felicia,

Thanks for staying in my apartment next weekend and taking care of the

dog. Help (yourself) to the food in the fridge —you can use it all up if you want.
Felicia

I rented some videos for you. They're on top of the TV. I picked out some action

movies. I hope you like them. The VCR is easy to use, but remember to turn it

down at 11:00 P.M. My upstairs neighbor is very touchy about noise. There are

just a few other things to remember. Red's friendly, but please keep her away

from my neighbor's poodle. They don't like each other. Her bowl is on the kitchen

counter. Fill it up once a day with dry food. Please walk her twice a day. When

you go out, remember to turn on the answering machine. It's in the living room.

The Sunday newspaper arrives at about 8:00 A.M. Pick it up early —sometimes

it disappears! When you leave for work Monday, just leave the keys with

Mrs. Delgado next door. I'll get them from her when I get back.

Thanks again!

Ted

2 | *Read this note. Change the nouns to pronouns when you can. With phrasal verbs, remember to put the pronoun between the main verb and the particle.*

Dear Dara,

Welcome! I hope you enjoy staying here this week. Here are a few things to keep in mind:

• The mail is delivered every day around noon. You'll find ~~the mail~~ *it* in the mailbox in front of the building. Please pick up the mail and put the mail on the dining room table.

• Feel free to use the air conditioner, but please turn off the air conditioner when you leave the house.

• There's plenty of food in the refrigerator! Please feel free to use up the food.

• I'm expecting a few phone calls. If you're home, could you please take a message? Just write down the message on the yellow pad in the top left desk drawer.

I think you'll find that the apartment is pretty comfortable. I hope you enjoy staying in the apartment. Make yourself at home!

See you in a week.

Rachel

---

3 | Before you write . . .

1. Imagine that a friend is going to take care of your home while you are away. What will your friend's responsibilities be? What special things do you need to tell him or her about your home or neighborhood? Make a list.

2. Exchange lists with a partner. Ask questions about your partner's list. Answer your partner's questions.

Example: **A:** How often should I take out the garbage?
B: Oh, you can take it out every other day.
Where do you keep the dog food?
A: It's in the cupboard under the kitchen sink.

4 │ *Write a note to your friend. Use your own paper. Give instructions about taking care of your home. Include answers to your partner's questions in Exercise 3. Use pronouns and phrasal verbs.*

5 │ *Exchange notes with a different partner. Complete the chart.*

---

1. Did the writer use pronouns where necessary?   **Yes** _____   **No** _____

2. Put a question mark (?) over each pronoun you think is in the wrong place.

3. Complete this chart of daily tasks with information from your partner's note. If you have a question, ask your partner, and write the answer on the chart.

   Examples: Sunday: water the plants, feed the pets, pick up the newspaper
                  Monday: feed the pets, pick up the mail and put it on the hall table

Day	Tasks
_____	_____
_____	_____
_____	_____
_____	_____
_____	_____
_____	_____
_____	_____

---

6 │ *Work with your partner. Discuss each other's editing questions from Exercise 5. Then rewrite your note. Make any necessary changes in your use of pronouns. Add information that your partner requested.*

II

Review Test

I *Circle the correct pronouns to complete the article.*

When Marta's company laid (her) / herself off, she told her / herself it was time to start her own
____1.____ ____2.____
business. Like Marta, a lot of people dream about starting their / one another's own businesses
____3.____
and working for them / themselves. Unfortunately, very few succeed. Are you a self-starter? Read
____4.____
about the qualities of successful business owners and decide for you / yourself.
____5.____

• Do you have a lot of energy? Self-starters have lots of energy. They push itself / themselves
____6.____

 very hard, and their families often have to force them / itself to take a break.
____7.____

• Can you lead others? Good team members work well with one another / themselves, but
____8.____

 self-starters must lead them / themselves.
____9.____

• Do you like to challenge you / yourself? Self-starters get bored when things are too easy.
____10.____

• Are you self-confident? Self-starters have lots of self-confidence. You need to believe in

 herself / yourself even when nobody else believes in you / yourself.
____11.____ ____12.____

• Do you have social support? Self-starters need good friends and family, so don't forget

 themselves / them when you get busy. Even independent people listen to each other's / his
____13.____ ____14.____
 problems.

II *Complete the article. Choose the phrasal verb from the box that is closest in
meaning to the words in parentheses. Use the correct form of the phrasal verb.*

find out	get back	get by	go on	~~grow up~~	hand over
help out	look up	pass over	pick out	set up	turn into

When you were _____*growing up*_____, did you think that tomatoes grew in
 1.(becoming an adult)
supermarkets? Did you realize that cotton was a plant before it _____
 2.(became)

your new gym socks? New Yorker Wendy Dubit _____ that a lot of city
3. (learned)

kids don't know anything about farms. She used her own money to _____
4. (establish)

Farm Hands/City Hands. This organization buses city people to small farms. Children and adults

from all social classes _____ on family farms and receive room and food
5. (assist)

in exchange. They also learn things you can't _____. One lawyer noted,
6. (try to find in a book)

"I worked with the tomatoes for weeks. Now I can _____ the perfectly
7. (choose)

ripe ones and _____ the ones that need a few more days on the vine."
8. (decide not to use)

Many people start small gardens of their own when they _____ to the city.
9. (return)

After the success of Farm Hands/City Hands, Dubit _____ to invent
10. (continued)

Project Ongoing to train homeless people in farm work and food services. The project has been so

successful that participants _____ on the food that they grow. They sell
11. (survive)

any extra. They _____ the profits _____ to the
12. (give)

program.

III   *Complete each conversation with a phrasal verb and a pronoun.*

1. **A:** This field trip will be difficult. Please think over your decision carefully.

   B: OK. I'll _____ *think it over* _____ this weekend and let you know on Monday.

2. **A:** Did you write down the flight number for our trip?

   B: Yes, I _____ on an envelope. Now where did I put the envelope?

3. **A:** Are we going to pick up Pam on the way to the airport?

   B: No. We don't have to _____. She has a ride.

4. **A:** Don't forget to put on your hat. That sun is hot.

   B: I'll _____ before I leave.

5. **A:** Someone please help out Ramón. That pack's too heavy for one person.

   B: OK. I'll _____. We can carry it together.

6. **A:** Why did you pick out cat's claw to study? It's such a common plant.

   B: I _____ because people use it for a lot of different things.

7. **A:** When are you going to write up your notes?

   B: I'll _____ as soon as we get back.

IV *Circle the letter of the correct answer to complete each sentence.*

1. Maria often goes to the movies by _____.　　　　A　B　C　Ⓓ
   (**A**) themselves　　　　(**C**) alone
   (**B**) her　　　　(**D**) herself

2. Paul set _____ his own business in 1999.　　　　A　B　C　D
   (**A**) out　　　　(**C**) down
   (**B**) up　　　　(**D**) at

3. That frog is poisonous. Don't _____!　　　　A　B　C　D
   (**A**) pick it up　　　　(**C**) pick up
   (**B**) pick up it　　　　(**D**) pick it

4. Sharon didn't want to study, but she talked _____ into it.　　　　A　B　C　D
   (**A**) each other　　　　(**C**) them
   (**B**) himself　　　　(**D**) herself

5. We're going your way. Do you want us to _____ at home?　　　　A　B　C　D
   (**A**) drop you off　　　　(**C**) drop you down
   (**B**) dropping you off　　　　(**D**) drop off you

6. When Brad and I study together, we help _____ a lot.　　　　A　B　C　D
   (**A**) us　　　　(**C**) each other
   (**B**) them　　　　(**D**) her

7. After I graduated from high school, I went _____ to college.　　　　A　B　C　D
   (**A**) over　　　　(**C**) on
   (**B**) herself　　　　(**D**) himself

8. He borrowed two books from me; he hasn't given _____ yet.　　　　A　B　C　D
   (**A**) them back　　　　(**C**) back them
   (**B**) it back　　　　(**D**) back it

9. Could you turn _____ the music so we can sleep?　　　　A　B　C　D
   (**A**) down　　　　(**C**) over
   (**B**) away　　　　(**D**) up

10. We'll turn _____ and go to sleep too.　　　　A　B　C　D
    (**A**) it off　　　　(**C**) it away
    (**B**) off it　　　　(**D**) away it

V   *Read this student's essay. There are eight mistakes in the use of phrasal verbs and pronouns. The first mistake is already corrected. Find and correct seven more.*

> I have three older brothers, but my role model is my next oldest
>
> brother, Orlando. Orlando was always there for ~~myself~~ [*me*] when we were
>
> growing up. I was very small, and he always kept the bullies away.
>
> When I couldn't figure up homework problems by myself, he helped out
>
> me. Orlando never gave up when he had problems. Once in high school,
>
> my baseball team passed myself up for pitcher. I wanted to quit the
>
> team, but he talked me over playing. In fact, he woke early every
>
> morning up to practice with me. When they chose me for pitcher the
>
> following year, we were really proud of ourselves— he was proud of me for
>
> succeeding, and I was proud of himself for being such a great coach.

▶ *To check your answers, go to the Answer Key on page RT-2.*

PART III

Modals and Similar Expressions

11 Ability: *Can, Could, Be able to*

BEFORE YOU READ

🎧 *What are the people in the photo doing? Look at the title of the article. Guess the main point. Read the article.*

Born to Dance

by V. Gupta

"**W**ho made up the rule that you **can** only **dance** on your two feet?" asks Mary Verdi-Fletcher, president and founding director of Dancing Wheels. She is also one of its main dancers. Verdi-Fletcher was born with a medical condition that affects the nervous system. By the age of 12, she **wasn't able to stand** or **walk**. But that didn't stop her from dancing. People said, "You **can't walk**; how **can** you **be** a dancer?" Verdi-Fletcher, however, *knew* it was possible to dance in a wheelchair because, as she says, "Dance is an emotion that comes from within."

When she entered her first dance competition, the audience was confused. "She's in a wheelchair. How **can** she **dance**?" But at the end of the performance, they stood and applauded. Not only **could** she **dance**, but she **could hypnotize** an audience with her talent. When the artistic director of the Cleveland Ballet first saw her, he thought, "*That* is a dancer. . . . You **can't take** your eyes off her."

Dancing Wheels has both "sitdown dancers" and "standup dancers." The group offers a new definition of dance. It also changes the perception of what people **can** or **cannot do**. "Through our dance," says Verdi-Fletcher, "we want to show that anything is possible and achievable. . . . People need to see they **can achieve** their dreams and aspirations—but not without a lot of hard work and dedication."

AFTER YOU READ

Read the statements. Check **True**, **False**, *or* **Don't Know**.

	True	False	Don't Know
1. Verdi-Fletcher is a professional dancer.	☐	☐	☐
2. She's also a singer.	☐	☐	☐
3. The audience loves her performance.	☐	☐	☐
4. The director of the Cleveland Ballet didn't like her work.	☐	☐	☐
5. Verdi-Fletcher has changed ideas about people's abilities.	☐	☐	☐

Grammar Presentation

ABILITY: *CAN* AND *COULD*

Statements			
Subject	*Can / Could* (*not*)	Base Form of Verb	
I You He She We You They	**can** (**not**)	**dance**	now.
	could (**not**)		last year.

Contractions		
cannot can not	=	**can't**
could not	=	**couldn't**

Yes / No Questions		
Can / Could	Subject	Base Form of Verb
Can	I you he she we you they	**dance**?
Could		

Short Answers					
Affirmative			Negative		
Yes,	you I he she you we they	**can.** **could.**	**No,**	you I he she you we they	**can't.** **couldn't.**

Wh- Questions			
Wh- Word	*Can / Could*	Subject	Base Form of Verb
How well	**can** **could**	she you	**dance**?

(continued)

ABILITY: *BE ABLE TO*

Statements			
Subject	*Be*	*(Not) Able to*	Base Form of Verb
I	**am**	**(not) able to**	**practice.**
You	**are**		
He She	**is**		
We You They	**are**		

Yes / No Questions			
Be	Subject	*Able to*	Base Form of Verb
Is	she	**able to**	**practice?**
Are	you		

Short Answers						
Affirmative			Negative			
Yes,	she	**is.**	No,	she	**isn't.**
	I	**am.**		I'm	**not.**

Wh- Questions				
Wh- Word	*Be*	Subject	*Able to*	Base Form of Verb
When	**is**	she	**able to**	**practice?**
How often	**are**	you		

GRAMMAR NOTES

1. *Can* and *could* are **modals**. Like all modals:

- They are followed by the base form of a verb.

- They have the same form for all subjects. (They do not use *-s* for the third-person singular.)

- They form the negative with *not*. (They do not use *do*.)

- They go before the subject in questions. (They do not use *do*.)

The expression **be able to** has the same meaning of ability as *can* and *could*. This meaning makes it similar to a modal. Notice that unlike real modals, it has different forms (*am, is, are; was, were; will be*).

EXAMPLES

- Mary **can dance**.

- I **can** dance, and she **can** dance too. NOT She ~~cans~~ dance.

- She **can't** sing. NOT She ~~doesn't~~ can sing.

- **Can** Antonio dance too? NOT ~~Does~~ can Antonio dance too?

- **Are** they **able to** dance? *(Can they dance?)*

- She **wasn't able to** dance then. *(She couldn't dance then.)*

2. Use *can*, *can't*, *could*, *couldn't*, or a form of *be able to* to express **ability**.	• She **can dance**, but she **can't sing**. • We **could ride** bikes then, but we **couldn't drive** cars. • Next year you**'ll be able to write** to me in English.

3. Use *can* or *can't* for **present ability**.	• She **can speak** English, but she **can't speak** French.

4. Use *can* for **future ability** when you are talking about <u>plans or arrangements</u>. ▶ **BE CAREFUL!** Don't use *can* for future ability when you are talking about <u>things you learn</u>. Use ***will be able to***.	• I **can buy** tickets on the way home *tomorrow*. • When I finish this course, **I'll be able to speak** French well. NOT When I finish this course, I ~~can~~ speak French well.

5. Use *could* or *couldn't* for **past ability**. ▶ **BE CAREFUL!** Don't use *could* in affirmative statements for a <u>single event</u> in the past. Use ***was / were able to***.	A: **Could** he **dance** as a child? B: No, he **couldn't dance** then. • In 2002 they **were able to win** first prize in the dance competition. NOT In 2002 they ~~could~~ win . . .

6. You can use a form of *be able to* for **present**, **future**, or **past ability**.	**PRESENT:**	**Are** you **able to drive** this car?
	FUTURE:	We**'ll be able to do** that dance soon.
	PAST:	Li **wasn't able to win** first prize last year.
Be able to can also be a **gerund** or **infinitive**.	**GERUND:**	**Being able to dance** is important to him.
	INFINITIVE:	I want **to be able to drive** by June.
USAGE NOTE: *Can* is much more common than *be able to* in everyday speech about the present.	**MORE COMMON:**	**Can** you dance?
	LESS COMMON:	**Are** you **able to** dance?

Reference Notes

Can and *could* are also used to ask and give **permission** (see Unit 12) and make **requests** (see Unit 13).
Can't and *could* are also used to draw **conclusions** (see Unit 37).
Could is also used to make **suggestions** (see Unit 15) and express **future possibility** (see Unit 36).
For a list of **modals and their functions,** see Appendix 19 on page A-8.

Focused Practice

1 | DISCOVER THE GRAMMAR

Look at this information about Mary Verdi-Fletcher. Then decide whether the statements below are True (T) or False (F). Put a question mark (?) if there isn't enough information.

Mary Verdi-Fletcher

1955	born in Ohio
1975	graduated from high school got job as keypunch operator
1978	learned to drive
1979	entered Dance Fever Competition
1980	began Dancing Wheels enrolled in Lakeland Community College, Ohio took course in public speaking
1980–1988	worked for Independent Living Center
1984	married Robert Fletcher
1989–1990	tour director for Cleveland Ballet
1990–present	founding director and dancer, Dancing Wheels teaches dance to people with and without disabilities
Awards	Outstanding Young Clevelander Award (1990) Oracle Merit Award (1991) Invacare Award of Excellence in the Arts (1994) Governor's Award for Outreach (1998)
Other Interests	watching football and soccer games

___T___ 1. Verdi-Fletcher was able to get a job after high school.

_____ 2. She can't drive a car.

_____ 3. She couldn't participate in dance competitions.

_____ 4. She can speak foreign languages.

_____ 5. She was able to start a dance company.

_____ 6. She couldn't finish college.

_____ 7. She can probably speak well in front of large groups of people.

_____ 8. She'll be able to help people with disabilities learn to dance.

_____ 9. She can play the piano.

_____10. She's so busy she can't have other interests.

2 | NOW I CAN

Complete the paragraphs with **can, can't, could,** *or* **couldn't.**

1. For a long time, Jim and Marie _____couldn't_____ agree on a family sport. Jim loves tennis,

   and Marie takes lessons, but she still _____ play. Marie _____

   swim, but Jim hates the water. They recently took up dancing. Now, they _____

   do the swing *and* spend time together.

2. Stefan has made a lot of progress in English. Last semester he _____ order a

   meal in a restaurant or talk on the telephone. His friends helped him do everything. Now he

   _____ speak English in a lot of situations.

3. Bill almost _____ make his class presentation last semester because he was so

   nervous. He _____ communicate well in small groups, but not in big ones. He

   plans to take a course in public speaking. He _____ register online next week.

4. Last year I _____ dance at all, but when I met Stan, I signed up for a class right

   away. He _____ really dance, and I wanted to dance with him. Now I

   _____ do the basic steps. I _____ do the waltz yet, but we're

   planning to waltz at our wedding next month.

3 | AT THE DANCE STUDIO

Complete each conversation with the correct form of **be able to** *and the verb in parentheses. Choose between affirmative and negative.*

1. **A:** I heard your sister wanted to take lessons. __Was__ she __able to start__?
   a. (start)

   B: Yes, she was. She started last month. She can do the fox-trot now, but she still

   _____ the waltz.
   b. (do)

2. **A:** Why are you taking dance lessons?

   B: I want to _____ at my wedding!
   a. (dance)

3. **A:** _____ you _____ Mrs. Suraikin at the studio yesterday?
   a. (find)

   B: Yes. She told me I _____ in the tango contest next month!
   b. (compete)

   A: Great! I know that's really important to you.

   B: Yes. _____ the tango in a contest means a lot to me.
   c. (do)

(continued)

4. A: _____ you _____ Russian as a child, Mrs. Suraikin?
   a. (speak)

   B: Yes, I was. We spoke it at home, so I _____ it fluently.
   b. (speak)

   A: _____ your children _____ Russian too?
   c. (speak)

   B: No, unfortunately my children never learned Russian. They only speak English.

5. A: I _____ the waltz last weekend because I hurt my ankle.
   a. (practice)

   B: That's too bad. _____ you _____ next week?
   b. (practice)

4 | AT THE THEATER

Two friends are at a dance performance. Complete their conversations with **can**, **could**, *or* **be able to** *and the correct verb from the box. You will use some of these verbs more than once. Use* **can** *or* **could** *when possible. Choose between affirmative and negative.*

| dance | do | get | lend | pay | pronounce | see |

1. NINA: _____Can_____ you _____see_____ the stage OK?
   a.

   LEÓN: Yes, I _____ it fine. What about you?
   b.

   NINA: No. I _____ it very well at all. The man in front of me is too tall.
   c.

   LEÓN: Change seats with me. You _____ it better then.
   d.

2. LEÓN: Wow! This performance is great. This group _____ really beautifully!
   a.

   NINA: I know. I'm glad I _____ tickets. Last year I _____ any.
   b.   c.

   They were sold out.

   LEÓN: What's their name?

   NINA: I'll spell it for you. It's P-i-l-o-b-o-l-u-s. I'm not sure I _____ it correctly!
   d.

3. LEÓN: It's intermission. Would you like to get something to eat?

   NINA: Oh, I'm afraid I _____ anything. I left my wallet at home by mistake.
   a.

   LEÓN: No problem. I _____ you some money.
   b.

   NINA: Thanks. I _____ you back tomorrow.
   c.

4. NINA: _____ you _____ the tango?
   a.

   LEÓN: Not yet! But I'm taking dance lessons, so I _____ it soon!
   b.

5 | EDITING

Read this review of a dance performance. There are ten mistakes in the use of **can**, **could**, *and* **be able to**. *The first mistake is already corrected. Find and correct nine more.*

The Dance Desk

How ~~They Can~~ Do That?

Can They

By Jennifer Andrews

Pilobolus Dance Theatre, photo by John Kane

Last night was the first time I saw the group Pilobolus perform. And what a performance it was! I would like to can tell you that I fully understood the performance, but I can't. I *can* to say, however, that the experience was completely wonderful.

Pilobolus is a very unusual group. The performers have no background in dance. When they began, they thought, "Maybe we can't dancing, so why try?" So they just made interesting shapes with their bodies. Well, this group certainly cans dance, and they are able to do much more. The six dancers in the group are athletic, artistic, and very talented. They are able do amazing things with their bodies. In many dances, they move together as a single unit.

My theater companion and I had great seats. We could saw the entire stage (not always true in some theaters). The sound system, though, had a few problems, and we didn't able to hear the music clearly all the time.

Some people in the audience asked: "Is it dance or is it gymnastics?" You can decide for yourself. Many people weren't able to got tickets for the first two performances of this series, but you can still buy tickets for next week. This is the type of dance performance everyone can enjoys.

Highly recommended.

Communication Practice

6 | LISTENING

🎧 *Karl is interviewing for the job of office manager at Carmen's Dance Studio. Listen to the conversation. Then listen again and check all the things that Karl can do now.*

☑ **1.** answer the phones   ☐ **5.** design a monthly newsletter

☐ **2.** speak another language   ☐ **6.** schedule appointments

☐ **3.** use a computer   ☐ **7.** drive

☐ **4.** type 50 words per minute   ☐ **8.** dance

7 | INFORMATION GAP: CAN THEY DO THE TANGO?

Students at Carmen's Dance Studio are preparing for a dance recital in June. It is now the end of April. Can students do all the dances featured in the recital at this time? Work in pairs (A and B). Student A, follow the instructions on this page. Student B, turn to page 134 and follow the instructions there.

1. Ask your partner for the information you need to complete the schedule below.

> **Example:** **A:** Can the students do the Argentine tango?
> **B:** No, they can't. But they'll be able to do it by the end of May.

2. Your schedule has the information your partner needs to complete his or her schedule. Answer your partner's questions.

> **Example:** **B:** Can they do the cha-cha?
> **A:** Yes, they can. They could do it in March.

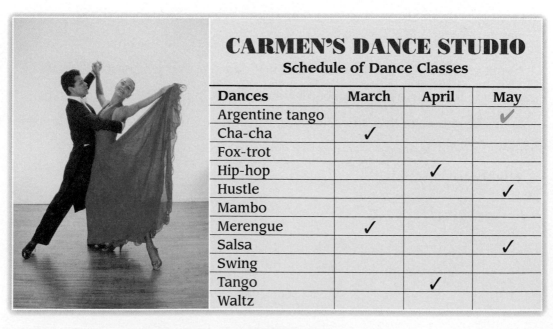

CARMEN'S DANCE STUDIO
Schedule of Dance Classes

Dances	March	April	May
Argentine tango			✔
Cha-cha	✓		
Fox-trot			
Hip-hop		✓	
Hustle			✓
Mambo			
Merengue	✓		
Salsa			✓
Swing			
Tango		✓	
Waltz			

When you are finished, compare schedules. Are they the same?

8 | CLASS PRESENTATION

Work in small groups. Imagine you are planning a class presentation. Look at the list of skills and tell each other what you **can** *and* **can't** *do. Add to the list.*

- do research online
- create a website
- make charts and graphs
- do a spreadsheet
- photocopy handouts
- take photographs
- videotape the presentation
- interview people
- give a PowerPoint presentation
- _____
- _____

Example: A: Can you do research online?
              B: Sure. But I can't create a website yet.

9 | ON THE INTERNET

Many people have disabilities. Research one of the famous people listed below. Tell the class about that person. Who is / was the person? What is / was the person's disability? What are / were some of the person's accomplishments?

Ludwig van Beethoven

Andrea Bocelli

Stephen Hawking

Frida Kahlo

Marlee Matlin

Christopher Reeve

Auguste Renoir

Marla Runyan

Example: Ludwig van Beethoven was one of the most famous composers in the world. As the result of an illness toward the end of his life, he lost the ability to hear. Even though he couldn't hear at all, he was able to continue to compose beautiful music that people still listen to today.

10 | WRITING

Write one or two paragraphs about a person who has succeeded in spite of some kind of disability or problem. Use one of the people from Exercise 9, or choose another person.

Example: My aunt had a difficult childhood. She grew up in a poor family. When she was 16, she quit school because she had to stay home and help her mother take care of her younger brothers and sisters. She made all the meals, and by the time she was 18, she could cook and bake very well. She was even able to win a local baking contest. People began ordering cakes from her, and before long she was able to save enough money to start her own small business . . .

INFORMATION GAP FOR STUDENT B

1. The schedule below has the information your partner needs to complete his or her schedule. Answer your partner's questions.

    Example: A: Can the students do the Argentine tango?
    B: No, they can't. But they'll be able to do it by the end of May.

2. Ask your partner for the information you need to complete your schedule.

    Example: B: Can they do the cha-cha?
    A: Yes, they can. They could do it in March.

CARMEN'S DANCE STUDIO
Schedule of Dance Classes

Dances	March	April	May
Argentine tango			✓
Cha-cha	✓		
Fox-trot		✓	
Hip-hop			
Hustle			
Mambo		✓	
Merengue			
Salsa			
Swing	✓		
Tango			
Waltz	✓		

When you are finished, compare schedules. Are they the same?

Permission: *Can, Could, May, Do you mind if*

Grammar in Context

BEFORE YOU READ

🎧 *Look at the cartoons. Where are these people? What is their relationship? What do two of the people want? How do the others feel about it? Read the article.*

Oh, you're awake! **Can** I **wear** your new jacket today?

Could my friend **stay** here for a few weeks?

Always Ask First

Heather immediately liked Tara, her neat, non-smoking roommate. Their first week together was great. The second week, the cookies from Heather's mom disappeared. Tara didn't ask Heather, "**Could** I **have** one?" Tara's friends always shared food without asking permission. The third week, Tara looked annoyed whenever Heather's friends stopped by to visit. Heather never asked Tara, "Hey, **do you mind if** they **hang out** here for a while?" At home, Heather's friends were always welcome. By October, Heather and Tara weren't speaking to each other.

Luckily, their dorm counselor was able to help them fix their relationship with three simple rules.

1. Always ask permission before you touch your roommate's stuff. Say: "My computer isn't working. **May** I **use** yours for a few hours?"
2. Set times when it's OK to have visitors. If it's not "visiting hours," ask your roommate's permission: "**Can** Luis and Ming-Hwa **work** here tonight? We're doing a presentation in class tomorrow."
3. Try to solve problems. Say: "Your music is too loud, but you **can borrow** my headphones."

Follow these guidelines, and who knows? You may gain a happier roommate *and* a good friend.

AFTER YOU READ

Read the statements. Check **True** *or* **False**.

	True	False
1. Some roommates don't know when to ask permission.	☐	☐
2. Tara gave Heather permission to eat her cookies.	☐	☐
3. Heather didn't ask for permission to have visitors.	☐	☐
4. It's very important to ask for permission to borrow things.	☐	☐

Grammar Presentation

PERMISSION: *CAN, COULD, MAY, DO YOU MIND IF*

Questions: *Can / Could / May*			
Can / Could / May*	Subject	Base Form of Verb	
Can **Could** **May**	I he she we they	**stay**	here?

*Can, *could*, and *may* are modals. Modals have only one form. They do not have *-s* in the third-person singular.

Short Answers					
Affirmative			Negative		
Yes,	you he she you they	**can.** **may.**	**No,**	you he she you they	**can't.** **may not.**

NOTE: *May not* is not contracted.

Statements: *Can / May*			
Subject	*Can / May (not)*	Base Form of Verb	
You He They	**can** (**not**) **may** (**not**)	**stay**	here.

Questions: *Do you mind if*			
Do you mind if	Subject	Verb	
Do you mind if	I we they	**stay**	here?
	he she it	**stays**	

Short Answers	
Affirmative	Negative
Not at all. **No,** I **don't.** Go right ahead.	**Yes,** I **do.**

NOTE: See Grammar Note 4 for a full explanation.

GRAMMAR NOTES	**EXAMPLES**

1. Use the modals *can*, *could*, and *may* to **ask permission**.

Notice that when you use *could* for permission, it is not the past.

USAGE NOTE: *May* is more formal than *can* and *could*.

less formal

- **Can** I **borrow** your book?
- **Could** he **come** tomorrow?
- **May** I **leave** now, Dr. Lee?

more formal

2. We often say *please* when we ask permission. Note the word order.

- **May** I **ask** a question, *please*?
  OR
- **May** I *please* **ask** a question?

3. Use *can* or *may* in **answers**. Don't use *could*.

▶ BE CAREFUL! Do not contract *may not*.

USAGE NOTES: In conversation, we usually use <u>informal expressions</u> instead of modals in answers.

When people **refuse permission**, they usually apologize and give an explanation.

A: **Could** I borrow this pencil?
B: **Yes**, of course you **can**.
   NOT Yes, you ~~could~~.
C: **No**, you **may not**.
   NOT No, you ~~mayn't~~.

A: **Could** I close the window?
B: *Sure.* OR *Certainly.* OR *Go ahead.*
C: *No, please don't.* It's hot in here.

A: **Can** I please use your computer?
B: *I'm sorry, but I need it today.*

4. Use *Do you mind if* to ask permission when your action may <u>annoy or inconvenience</u> someone.

▶ BE CAREFUL! When we answer with *Not at all* or *No, I don't*, we're really saying: *It's OK.* We're giving permission.

And when we answer with *Yes, I do*, we're really saying: *It's NOT OK.* We're refusing permission.

A: **Do you mind if I clean up** later?
B: Yes, actually, I do. I hate to see a mess in the kitchen.

A: **Do you mind if I eat** these tacos?
B: *Not at all.* OR *No, I don't.*
   (It's OK for you to eat these tacos.)
C: *Yes, I do.* I bought them for Kyle.
   (It's NOT OK for you to eat the tacos.)

Reference Notes
For general information on **modals**, see Unit 11, Grammar Note 1, on page 126.
Can and *could* are also used to talk about **ability** (see Unit 11) and make **requests** (see Unit 13).
Could and *may* are also used to express **future possibility** (see Unit 36) and to draw **conclusions** (see Unit 37).
For a list of **modals and their functions**, see Appendix 19 on page A-8.

Focused Practice

1 | DISCOVER THE GRAMMAR

Read this quiz. Underline all the modals and expressions for permission. Then if you'd like to, you can take the quiz. The answers are below.

Are You a Good Roommate?

Take this short quiz and find out.

1. You want to use your roommate's computer.
   You say:
   ○ **a.** I may use your computer tonight.
   ○ **b.** <u>May I use</u> your computer tonight?
   ○ **c.** I'm using your computer tonight.

2. You don't have any food in the house.
   You say:
   ○ **a.** Can you make dinner for me?
   ○ **b.** I don't mind eating some of your food.
   ○ **c.** Do you mind if I have some of your food?

3. You may not have time to wash the dishes tonight.
   You say:
   ○ **a.** Could you wash the dishes?
   ○ **b.** I can't wash the dishes.
   ○ **c.** Can I wash the dishes tomorrow?

4. Your roommate asks you: "Could my best friend stay overnight?"
   You answer:
   ○ **a.** Can she stay in a hotel instead?
   ○ **b.** Sure.
   ○ **c.** I'm sure she could, but I don't want her to!

5. You can find nothing to wear to the party next Friday.
   You say:
   ○ **a.** May I please borrow your new sweater?
   ○ **b.** I may borrow your new sweater.
   ○ **c.** You could lend me your new sweater.

6. You and your roommate need the dorm counselor's permission to have a party in your room.
   You say:
   ○ **a.** Could we have a party in our room on Saturday?
   ○ **b.** Maybe we could have a party in our room on Saturday.
   ○ **c.** Could you have a party in your room on Saturday?

ANSWERS: 1. b, 2. c, 3. c, 4. b, 5. a, 6. a

2 | RULES AND REGULATIONS

Look at the signs. Complete each conversation with the words in parentheses and the correct pronouns. Write appropriate short answers.

1. (do you mind if)

JEAN-PIERRE: _____*Do you mind if*_____ I _____*eat*_____
                                                 a. (eat)

                my lunch here while I get on the Internet?

LAB ASSISTANT: _____*Sorry, but I do*_____. Look at the sign.
                                 b.

Computer Lab

2. (can)

EMIL: Wow! Those guys next door sure are making a lot of noise!

TORY: Well, they _____ music now. It's
                      a. (play)

       8:00 A.M.

EMIL: I know. _____ I _____
                                 b. (borrow)

       your earplugs? I have to study for my English test.

Quiet Hours
11:00 p.m. - 7:00 a.m.
Sunday - Saturday

3. (may)

CARMEN: _____ we _____ our
                                 a. (ride)

       bikes here?

GUARD: _____.
                   b.

4. (could)

DONOVAN: _____ I _____ my
                               a. (bring)

       dog next semester? My roommate doesn't mind.

COUNSELOR: _____. But some of the other
                             b.

       dorms allow pets.

Kent Hall

5. (may)

GABRIELLE: _____ I _____ my cell
                               a. (use)

       phone in here?

LIBRARIAN: _____.
                   b.

3 | PARTY TIME

Heather and her roommate Tara are planning a party in Kent Hall. Use the words in parentheses to ask for permission. Answer the questions.

1. Tara's friend Troy is in town. She wants him to come to the party.

   TARA: *Do you mind if Troy comes to the party?* _____
   (Do you mind if)

   HEATHER: *Not at all.* _____ I'd love to meet him.

2. Heather wants to borrow her roommate's black sweater.

   HEATHER: I have nothing to wear. _____
   (Can)

   TARA: _____ I'm planning to wear it myself!

3. Tara's sister is coming from out of town. Tara wants her to stay in their room.

   TARA: _____
   (Do you mind if)

   HEATHER: _____ She can sleep on the couch.

4. Heather and Tara would like to have the party in the dormitory lounge. Heather asks her

   dormitory counselor for permission.

   HEATHER: _____
   (May / please)

   COUNSELOR: _____ It's available next Friday.

5. Heather and Tara would like to hang decorations from the ceiling of the lounge.

   HEATHER: _____
   (May / please)

   COUNSELOR: _____ Fire regulations won't allow it.

6. Heather and Tara want to party until midnight.

   HEATHER: _____
   (Could / please)

   COUNSELOR: _____ Quiet hours start at 11:00 on Friday.

7. Tara wants to play some of her friend Erica's CDs at the party.

   TARA: _____
   (Could)

   ERICA: _____ Which ones should I bring?

8. It's Friday night. A student wants to study in the lounge.

   STUDENT: _____
   (Can)

   HEATHER: _____ We're having a party. Want to join us?

4 | EDITING

Read Emil's English test. There are seven mistakes in the use of **can**, **could**, **may**, *and* **do you mind if**. *The first mistake is already corrected. Find and correct six more.*

Class: _English 102_ **Name:** _Emil Kuhn_

Directions: These conversations take place on a train. Find and correct the mistakes.

1. **A:** May we board the train yet?
           can't OR may not
   B: No, you ~~mayn't~~ board until 12:30.

2. **A:** Can he comes on the train with me?

   B: Sorry. Only passengers can board.

3. **A:** Do you mind if I'm sitting here?

   B: No, I don't. My friend is sitting here.

4. **A:** Could I looked at your newspaper?

   B: Yes, of course you could.

5. **A:** Do you mind if my son play his

       computer game?

   B: No, not at all. It won't disturb me.

   A: Thanks.

Communication Practice

5 | LISTENING

🎧 *Listen and write the number of each conversation. Then listen again and decide if permission was given or refused. Check the appropriate column.*

	Permission Given	Permission Refused
_____ **a.** roommate / roommate	☐	☐
_____ **b.** child / parent	☐	☐
_____ **c.** travel agent / customer	☐	☐
_1_ **d.** police officer / driver	☑	☐
_____ **e.** boyfriend / girlfriend's mother	☐	☐
_____ **f.** employee / employer	☐	☐
_____ **g.** student / teacher	☐	☐

6 | ASKING PERMISSION

Work in small groups. Read the following situations and decide what to say. Think of as many things to say as possible.

1. You have a small apartment. Two of your friends are coming to visit your town for a week, and they want to stay with you. What can you say to your roommate?

   Examples: Do you mind if Larry and Zoë stay here for a week?
   Could Larry practice his guitar in the evening?
   Can Zoë keep her bike in the hall?

2. You're visiting some good friends. The weather is very cold, but they don't seem to mind. Their windows are open, and the heat is off. You're freezing.

3. You're at a concert with some friends. You like the performer very much. You have your camcorder and your camera with you. Sometimes this performer talks to fans and signs programs after the concert.

4. You have formed a study group with some classmates. You want to use a classroom on Thursday evenings to study. You would like to use one of your school's video cams for speaking practice. Some of your classmates come directly from work. They would like permission to eat their dinner in the classroom. What can you say to your teacher?

7 | ROLE PLAY

Work in pairs. Read the following situations. Take turns being Student A and Student B.

Student A

1. You were absent from class yesterday. Student B, your classmate, always takes good notes.

   Example: A: May I copy your notes from class yesterday?
   B: Sure. Here they are.
   A: Could I call you tonight if I have questions?
   B: Of course.

2. You're at work. You have a terrible headache. Student B is your boss.

3. You're a teenager. You and your friend want to travel to another city to see a concert. You want to borrow your mother's (Student B's) car. Your friend has a license and wants to drive.

4. Student B has invited you to a small party. At the last minute, your two cousins show up. They have nothing to do the night of the party.

Student B

1. Student A is in your class. You are always willing to help your classmates.

2. Student A is your employee. You have a lot of work for Student A to do today.

3. Student A is your son / daughter. You like this friend, and you have no objection to lending him or her the car. However, you want the friend to be careful.

4. Your party is a small party for a few of your close friends. It's also at a restaurant, and you have already arranged for a certain number of people to attend.

8 | WRITING

Write two short notes asking permission. Choose situations from Exercise 7 or use situations of your own. Then exchange notes with two classmates. Write responses to your classmates' notes.

Examples:

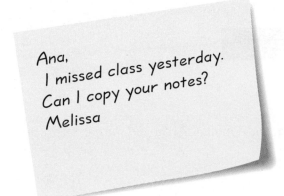

Ana,
I missed class yesterday.
Can I copy your notes?
Melissa

Sorry, Melissa, but
I missed class too!
Ana

9 | ON THE INTERNET

Do a search on **dormitory rules***. Choose a school that interests you and print out or write down some of their rules. Then work with a partner. Role-play a conversation between a student and a dorm counselor.*

1. Ask for information about the rules for the dorm your partner researched. You can ask about:

    - visitors
    - decorating your room
    - study areas
    - quiet hours

2. Answer your partner's questions about the dorm you researched.

    Example: A: Can my sister stay overnight with me?
    B: Yes, she can. But only for two days.

13 Requests: *Can, Could, Will, Would, Would you mind*

Grammar in Context

BEFORE YOU READ

🎧 *What is Marcia's e-mail address? Who did Marcia send e-mails to? Who did she get e-mails from? Read her e-mail messages.*

Mail's Here!

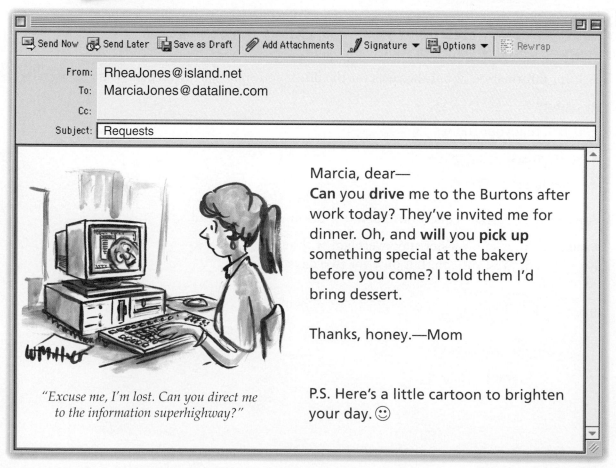

Send Now | Send Later | Save as Draft | Add Attachments | Signature ▾ | Options ▾ | Rewrap

From: RheaJones@island.net
To: MarciaJones@dataline.com
Cc:
Subject: Requests

Marcia, dear—
Can you **drive** me to the Burtons after work today? They've invited me for dinner. Oh, and **will** you **pick up** something special at the bakery before you come? I told them I'd bring dessert.

Thanks, honey.—Mom

P.S. Here's a little cartoon to brighten your day. ☺

"Excuse me, I'm lost. Can you direct me to the information superhighway?"

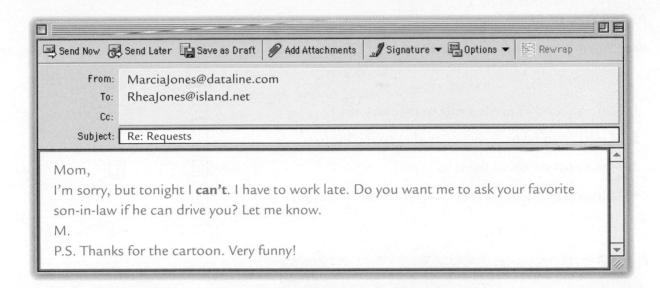

Mom,

I'm sorry, but tonight I **can't**. I have to work late. Do you want me to ask your favorite son-in-law if he can drive you? Let me know.

M.

P.S. Thanks for the cartoon. Very funny!

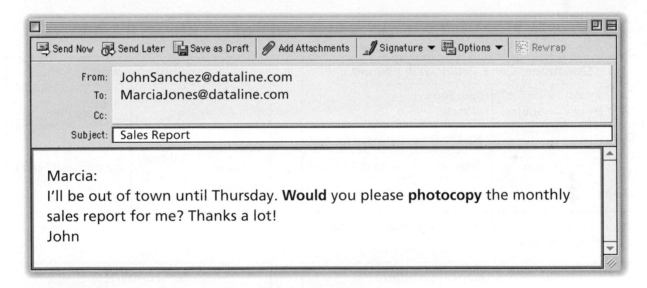

Marcia:

I'll be out of town until Thursday. **Would** you please **photocopy** the monthly sales report for me? Thanks a lot!

John

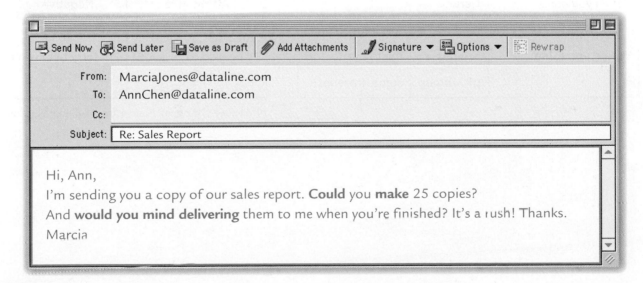

Hi, Ann,

I'm sending you a copy of our sales report. **Could** you **make** 25 copies?

And **would you mind delivering** them to me when you're finished? It's a rush! Thanks.

Marcia

AFTER YOU READ

Read the statements. Check **True** *or* **False**.

	True	False
1. Marcia's mother needs a ride to the Burtons.	☐	☐
2. Marcia is going to drive her mother to the Burtons.	☐	☐
3. John needs copies of the sales report.	☐	☐
4. Marcia is going to make the copies herself.	☐	☐

Grammar Presentation

REQUESTS: *CAN, COULD, WILL, WOULD, WOULD YOU MIND*

Questions: *Can / Could / Will / Would*			
*Can / Could Will / Would**	Subject	Base Form of Verb	
Can **Could** **Will** **Would**	you	**mail**	this letter for me?
		drive	me to the doctor?
		pick up	some groceries?

*Can, could, will, and *would* are modals. Modals do not have *-s* in the third-person singular.

Short Answers		
Affirmative		Negative
Sure Certainly Of course	(I **can**). (I **will**).	I'm sorry, but I **can't**.

Questions: *Would you mind*		
Would you mind	Gerund	
Would you mind	**mailing**	this letter for me?
	driving	me to the doctor?
	picking up	some groceries?

Short Answers	
Affirmative	Negative
Not at all. I'd be glad to. No problem.	I'm sorry, but I **can't**.

NOTE: See Grammar Note 4 for a full explanation.

GRAMMAR NOTES	**EXAMPLES**
1. Use the modals *can*, *could*, *will*, and *would* to make a **request** (ask someone to do something). **USAGE NOTE:** We use *could* and *would* to <u>soften requests</u> and make them more polite.	 • **Can** you **turn on** the TV? • **Will** you **bring** dessert? • **Could** you **call** me later? • **Would** you **close** the door?
2. You can also use *please* to make the request <u>more polite</u>. Note the word order.	• **Would** you **close** the door, *please*? OR • **Would** you *please* **close** the door?
3. In **affirmative answers** to requests, we usually use expressions such as *sure*, *certainly*, *of course*, and *no problem*. In **negative answers**, we usually apologize and give an explanation. ▶ **BE CAREFUL!** Do not use *could* or *would* in response to polite requests.	A: **Would** you **shut** the window, please? B: *Sure.* OR *Sure I will.* OR *Certainly.* A: **Could** you **take** this to Ron's office, please? B: *I'm sorry, I can't. I'm expecting a call.* NOT I'm sorry, I ~~couldn't~~. NOT Sure I ~~would~~.
4. We also use ***Would you mind* + gerund** (verb + *-ing*) to make <u>polite requests</u>. ▶ **BE CAREFUL!** When we <u>answer</u> this type of request with ***Not at all***, it means that we will do what the person requests.	A: **Would you mind waiting** a minute? Mr. Caras is still in a meeting. B: *Not at all.* *(OK. I'll do it.)*

Reference Notes
For general information on **modals**, see Unit 11, Grammar Note 1, page 126.
Can and *could* are also used to talk about **ability** (see Unit 11) and ask **permission** (see Unit 12).
Can't and *could* are also used to draw **conclusions** (see Unit 37).
Could is also used to express **future possibility** (see Unit 36).
Will is also used to talk about the **future** (see Units 6 and 7).
For a list of **modals and their functions**, see Appendix 19 on page A-8.

Focused Practice

1 | DISCOVER THE GRAMMAR

◯ *Marcia has a new co-worker. Read their conversations. Underline all the requests.*

1. MARCIA: Hi. You must be the new assistant. I'm Marcia. Let me know if you need anything.

   LORNA: Thanks, Marcia. <u>Could you show</u> me the coat closet?

   MARCIA: Certainly. It's right over here.

2. LORNA: Marcia, would you help me with the photocopier? I'm having trouble with it.

   MARCIA: Sure. Just put your original in, like this, and press this button.

3. MARCIA: I'm leaving for lunch. Would you like to come?

   LORNA: Thanks, but I can't right now. I'm really busy.

   MARCIA: Do you want a sandwich from the coffee shop?

   LORNA: That would be great. Can you get me a tuna sandwich and a soda?

   MARCIA: Sure. Will you answer my phone until I get back?

   LORNA: No problem.

4. MARCIA: Lorna, would you mind making a pot of coffee? Some clients are coming in a few
            minutes, and I have to set up the PowerPoint presentation.

   LORNA: I'm sorry, but I can't do it now. I've got to finish this letter before 2:00.

   MARCIA: That's OK. Thanks anyway.

5. CLIENT: I'm Michael Rodrigues. Could you tell Marcia that I'm here for our meeting?

   LORNA: Certainly. I'll call her right now.

6. LORNA: Hi, Marcia. Mr. Rodrigues is here for your meeting.

   MARCIA: Thanks. Could you take him to the conference room? I'll be there in a few minutes.

   LORNA: No problem.

   MARCIA: And would you mind offering him a cup of coffee while he waits?

7. MARCIA: I'm going home now. Don't forget to turn off the printer before you leave.

   LORNA: I won't.

   MARCIA: By the way, could you give this report to John Sanchez for me?

   LORNA: Sure.

2 | ASKING FOR FAVORS

Mike's roommate, Jeff, is having problems today. Read Jeff's requests. Then circle the letter of the appropriate response to each request.

1. Mike, would you please drive me to class today? My car won't start.
   a. Yes, I would.   **b.** I'd be glad to.

2. Would you mind lending me $5? I'm getting paid tomorrow.
   a. Not at all.   **b.** Yes.

3. Mike, can you take these books back to the library for me? I'm running late this morning.
   a. Sorry. I'm late for class too.   **b.** No, I can't.

4. Could you lock the door on your way out? My hands are full.
   a. Yes, I could.   **b.** Sure.

5. Can you turn the radio down? I need to study for my math quiz this morning.
   a. Certainly.   **b.** Not at all.

6. Will you pick up some milk on the way home this afternoon?
   a. No, I won't.   **b.** I'm sorry, I can't. I'll be at work until 8:00.

3 | WOULD YOU MIND?

Look at the pictures on this and the next page. What is each person thinking? Write the letter of the correct sentence from the box.

a. Repair the photocopier.	**d.** ~~File these reports.~~	**g.** Buy some cereal.
b. Call back later.	**e.** Shut the door.	**h.** Wait for a few minutes.
c. Get that book.	**f.** Close the window.	**i.** Wash your cups and dishes.

1. ___*d*___   2. _____   3. _____

(continued)

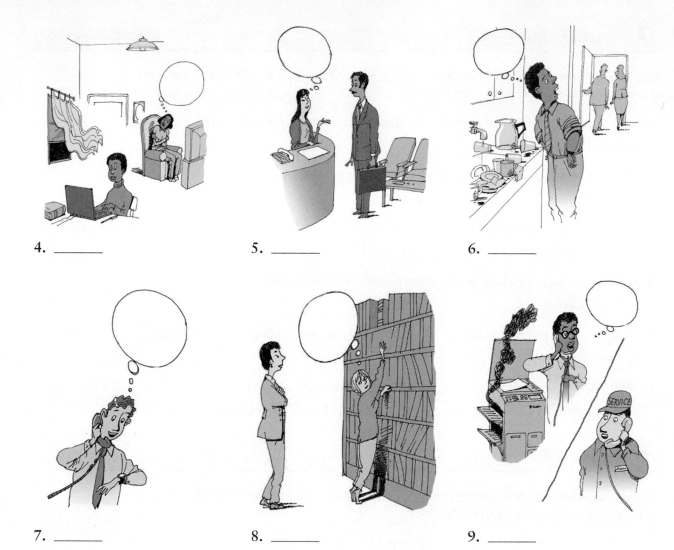

4. _____   5. _____   6. _____

7. _____   8. _____   9. _____

What are these people going to say? Complete their requests. Use the words in parentheses and the information from the pictures.

1. ___*Could you file these reports, please?*___ I've finished reading them.
   (Could)

2. _____ I can't think with all that noise in the hall.
   (Would)

3. _____ on the way home? We don't have any left.
   (Will)

4. _____ It's freezing in here.
   (Can)

5. _____ Mr. Rivera is still in a meeting.
   (Would you mind)

6. _____ It's getting messy in here.
   (Would you mind)

7. _____ I have to leave for a meeting now.
   (Could)

8. _____ I can't reach it.
   (Can)

9. _____ I need to make copies right away.
   (Could)

4 | EDITING

*Read Marcia Jones's response to an e-mail message from her boss. (Her answers are in **red** print.) There are seven mistakes in making and responding to requests. The first mistake is already corrected. Find and correct six more.*

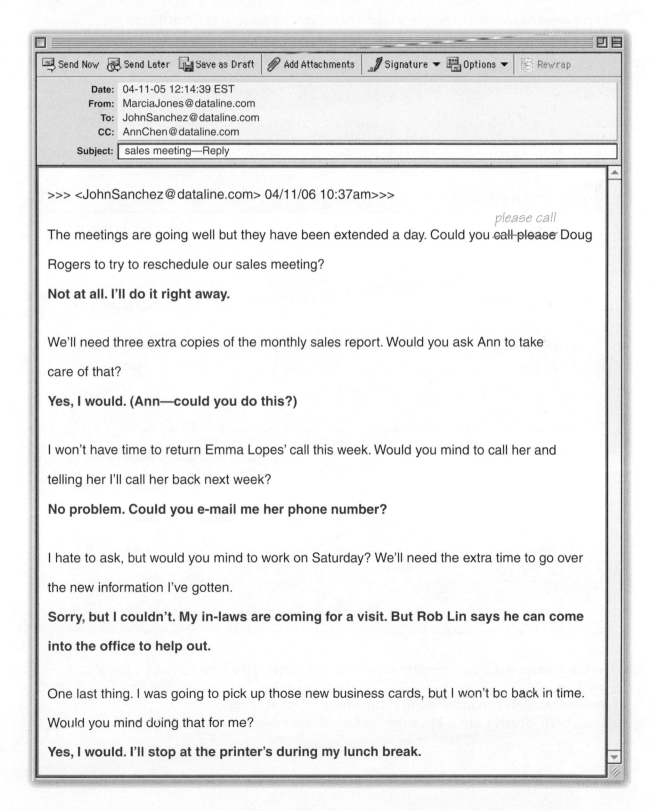

| Send Now | Send Later | Save as Draft | Add Attachments | Signature ▼ | Options ▼ | Rewrap |

Date: 04-11-05 12:14:39 EST
From: MarciaJones@dataline.com
To: JohnSanchez@dataline.com
CC: AnnChen@dataline.com

Subject: sales meeting—Reply

>>> <JohnSanchez@dataline.com> 04/11/06 10:37am>>>

The meetings are going well but they have been extended a day. Could you ~~call please~~ *please call* Doug Rogers to try to reschedule our sales meeting?

Not at all. I'll do it right away.

We'll need three extra copies of the monthly sales report. Would you ask Ann to take care of that?

Yes, I would. (Ann—could you do this?)

I won't have time to return Emma Lopes' call this week. Would you mind to call her and telling her I'll call her back next week?

No problem. Could you e-mail me her phone number?

I hate to ask, but would you mind to work on Saturday? We'll need the extra time to go over the new information I've gotten.

Sorry, but I couldn't. My in-laws are coming for a visit. But Rob Lin says he can come into the office to help out.

One last thing. I was going to pick up those new business cards, but I won't be back in time. Would you mind doing that for me?

Yes, I would. I'll stop at the printer's during my lunch break.

Communication Practice

5 | LISTENING

🎧 *Marcia Jones has planned a busy weekend. Listen to the conversations. Then listen again and check the things that belong on her schedule.*

☑ 1. take Ethan to the dentist   ☐ 5. go to the movies

☐ 2. take kids to the library   ☐ 6. walk Mom's dog

☐ 3. babysit for Kelly's daughter   ☐ 7. pick up the car at the garage

☐ 4. go to Kelly's party   ☐ 8. go to the gym with Jade

6 | I'D BE GLAD TO

Fill out your schedule for the weekend.

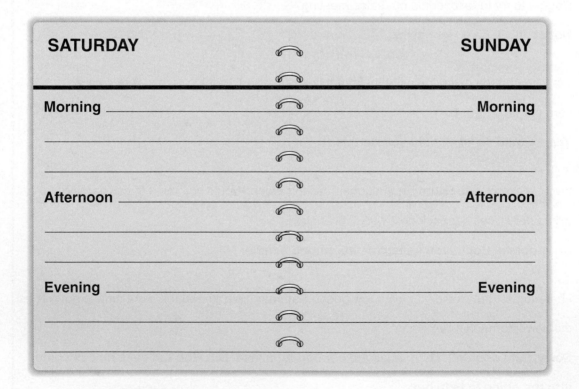

SATURDAY		SUNDAY
Morning _____		**Morning**
_____		
_____		
Afternoon _____		**Afternoon**
_____		
_____		
Evening _____		**Evening**
_____		
_____		

Now work in a group. Ask group members to help you with some of the things on your schedule.

Example: A: Can you drive me to the mall Saturday morning?
B: Sorry, I can't. I'm working Saturday morning. OR Sure, I'd be glad to.

7 | WRITING

Read the following situations. For each one, write a note making one or more requests.

1. Your roommate is going away for the weekend. Your sister from out of town will be visiting you. Write a note to your roommate.

Example:

> Hi Viktor,
>
> My sister is visiting this weekend. Would you mind lending her your bike? I'd like to take her for a ride in the park.
>
> Thanks,
> Kunio

2. You work at a restaurant on Mondays, Wednesdays, and Fridays. You have to go to the dentist, but he or she can only see you on Wednesday. Write a note to a co-worker.

3. You're in school. You have to leave class early in order to help your parents. Write a note to a classmate.

4. You're going to have a party at your home. You've invited 20 people. Write a note to your neighbor.

8 | ON THE INTERNET

Send e-mail messages to several classmates. Make a request in each one. Answer messages you receive from your classmates.

Example: Hi Carlos,
I have to miss class tomorrow. Could you make a copy of your notes for me? Also, would you mind . . .

14 Advice: *Should, Ought to, Had better*

Grammar in Context

BEFORE YOU READ

🎧 *Do you talk to people on the Internet? What are some advantages of Internet communication? What are some problems? Read the article about being polite on the Internet. If you don't understand a cyber word, look up its meaning on the next page.*

Netiquette 101

by Emilia Poster

E-mail, bulletin boards, and chat rooms open up a new world of communication—and, sometimes, misunderstanding. To avoid problems, you **should know** these simple rules of netiquette:

😉 When **should** you **post** to a bulletin board or chat room? Newbies **shouldn't jump in** right away—they **ought to lurk** a little first. Look through old messages for answers to common questions. Many sites also have FAQs for basic information. After that, post when you have something new to say. You **should keep** your post short and simple.

😉 **Should** you **use** capital letters to make a strong statement? NO! A MESSAGE ALL IN CAPITAL LETTERS SEEMS LIKE SHOUTING. You **should follow** the normal rules for capital (big) and lowercase (small) letters.

😉 Did someone make you angry? You**'d better not reply** right away. Count to 10 first. Don't flame another board or chat room member. You **should** never **forget** that people on the Internet are real people with real feelings.

😉 Emoticons help avoid misunderstandings. You **should learn** how to use them to show your feelings.

😉 Internet safety is part of netiquette. When you post to a bulletin board or a chat room, you **should** always **use** a screen name. Never give your real name or other personal information.

Practice these five rules of netiquette, and most of your emoticons will be smilies! ☺

Cyber Words

bulletin board an Internet site where members can post ideas about a special interest

chat room a site for online conversations in "real" time

emoticon a picture of a feeling, for example:

FAQ Frequently Asked Questions

flame send insulting messages to someone

lurk read messages on a bulletin board but not post any messages

netiquette Internet etiquette (rules for polite behavior)

newbie (or newb) someone new to an Internet site

post send messages to a bulletin board or chat room

"Got your e-mail, thanks."

AFTER YOU READ

Read the statements. Check **OK** *or* **Not OK**.

	OK	Not OK
1. Read some messages before you post.	☐	☐
2. Reply immediately when you're angry.	☐	☐
3. Use all capital letters in your posts.	☐	☐
4. Use emoticons to show feelings.	☐	☐
5. Use your real name in chat rooms.	☐	☐
6. Learn the rules of netiquette.	☐	☐
7. Always flame people when you don't like their messages.	☐	☐
8. Write long, complicated messages.	☐	☐
9. Think about people's feelings when you post a message.	☐	☐

Grammar Presentation

ADVICE: *SHOULD, OUGHT TO, HAD BETTER*

Statements		
Subject	*Should / Ought to / Had Better**	Base Form of Verb
I You He She We You They	**should** (**not**) **ought to** **had better** (**not**)	**reply**.

Contractions		
should not	=	**shouldn't**
had better	=	**'d better**

*Should and *ought to* are modals. *Had better* is similar to a modal. These forms do not have *-s* in the third-person singular.

Yes / No Questions		
Should	Subject	Base Form of Verb
Should	I he she we they	**reply**?

Short Answers					
Affirmative			Negative		
Yes,	you he she you they	**should**.	**No**,	you he she you they	**shouldn't**.

Wh- Questions				
Wh- Word	*Should*	Subject	Base Form of Verb	
How When Where	**should**	I he she we they	**send**	it?

GRAMMAR NOTES	EXAMPLES
1. Use the modals *should* and *ought to* to say that something is **advisable** (a good idea). **USAGE NOTES:** We do not usually use the <u>negative</u> of *ought to* in American English. We use *shouldn't* instead. We often <u>soften advice</u> with *maybe, perhaps,* or *I think.*	• Derek **should answer** that e-mail. • You **ought to read** the FAQ. • We **shouldn't post** long messages. NOT COMMON We ~~ought not to~~ post long messages. • Ryan, *maybe* you **shouldn't spend** so much time on the Internet.

Pronunciation Note
Ought to is often pronounced "oughta" in informal speech.

2. Use *had better* for **strong advice**—when you believe that something bad will happen if the person does not follow the advice. **USAGE NOTE:** The full form *had better* is very formal. We usually use the **contraction.** The <u>negative</u> of *had better* is **had better not.** ▶ **BE CAREFUL!** *Had better* always refers to the **present** or the **future,** never to the past (even though it uses the word *had*).	• Kids, you**'d better get** off-line now or you won't have time for your homework. • You**'d better choose** a screen name. NOT COMMON You ~~had better~~ choose a screen name. • You**'d better not use** your real name. NOT You ~~had not better~~ use your real name. • You**'d better not call** them *now.* They're probably sleeping. • You**'d better post** that *tomorrow* or it'll be late.

3. Use *should* for **questions.** We do not usually use *ought to* or *had better* for questions.	• **Should** I **join** this chat room? • When **should** I **sign on**?

Reference Notes
For general information on **modals,** see Unit 11, Grammar Note 1 on page 126.
Sometimes we use *must* or *have to* to give **very strong advice.** This kind of advice is similar to talking about **necessity** or **obligation** (see Unit 34).
For a list of **modals and their functions,** see Appendix 19 on page A-8.

Focused Practice

1 | DISCOVER THE GRAMMAR

Read these posts to an online bulletin board for high school students. Underline the words that give or ask for advice.

Subject: HELP!
From: Hothead

MY BRAIN IS EXPLODING!!! SAVE ME!! What <u>should</u> I <u>do</u>? I'm taking all honors courses this year, and I'm on the debate team, in the school congress, and on the soccer team. OH! I'd better not forget piano lessons! I'm so busy I shouldn't even be online now. 🙁

From: Tweety

First of all, you should stop shouting. You'll feel better. Then you really ought to ask yourself, "Why am I doing all this?" Is it for you or are you trying to please somebody else?

From: Loki

Tweety's right, Hothead. Do you really want to do all that stuff? No? You'd better not do it then. You'll burn out before you graduate. 🐣

From: gud4me

You're such a loser. You should get a life. I mean a REAL life. Do you have any friends? Do you ever just sit around and do nothing?

From: Tweety

Hey, gud4me, no flaming allowed! We shouldn't fight. Try to help or keep quiet. 🙂

2 | FRIENDLY ADVICE

Grammar Notes 1–2

Read these posts to a chat room about learning English. Complete them with the correct form (affirmative or negative) of the words in parentheses. Use contractions when possible.

curly: I think I _____*should watch*_____ more movies to improve my English. Any ideas?
                              1. (should / watch)

usedit: I loved *Sixth Sense*. But you _____ it if you don't like scary films.
                                              2. (had better / rent)

agurl: That's right. You _____ the remote in your hand. That way you
                                        3. (had better / keep)
can fast-forward through the scary parts.

592XY: I think you _____ *Groundhog Day*. The same thing happens
                                  4. (ought to / see)
again and again. It's great listening practice—and it's funny!

pati: Do you have a DVD player? If not, maybe you _____ one.
5. (should / get)

DVDs have English subtitles.

usedit: But you _____ the subtitles right away. First you
6. (should / use)

_____ a few times. That's what rewind buttons are for!
7. (should / listen)

592XY: Good advice. And you really _____ a plot summary before you
8. (ought to / read)

watch. You can find one online. It's so much easier when you know the story.

agurl: Curly, you're a math major, right? You _____ *A Beautiful Mind.*
9. (ought to / watch)

It's about a math genius.

curly: Thanks, guys. Those are great ideas. But you _____ me any
10. (had better / give)

more advice, or I'll never work on my other courses!

---

3 | COMPUTER TIPS   *Grammar Note 3*

Complete these posts to an online bulletin board. Choose the correct words from the box to complete the questions. Give short answers.

ask them to stop	buy one online	check the spelling
forward the e-mail	~~post right away~~	try to repair it

1. Q: I want to join a new online discussion group. *Should I post right away* _____?

   A: *No, you shouldn't* _____. It's always a good idea to "lurk" before you post.

2. Q: My friends e-mail me a lot of jokes. A few of them are funny, but I really don't like

     receiving them. _____?

   A: _____. These jokes can waste a lot of time!

3. Q: My computer is seven years old and has problems. _____?

   A: _____. That's very old for a computer! Buy a new one!

4. Q: I just received a warning about a computer virus. The e-mail says to tell everyone I know

     about it. _____?

   A: _____. These warnings are almost always false.

5. Q: I hate to go shopping, but I really need a jacket. _____?

   A: _____. It's safe. Just buy from a company you know.

6. Q: I type fast and make spelling mistakes. Is that bad? _____?

   A: _____. Use a spell checker! Mistakes are bad netiquette!

4 | SAFETY RULES!

Rewrite these Internet safety tips. Use **should**, **ought to**, *or* **had better**. *Choose between affirmative and negative.*

> ### The Internet is a wonderful place to visit and hang out. Here are some tips to make your trip there a safe one!

1. I often use my real name online. Is that a problem?

Yes! *You should always use a screen name.*
(Always use a screen name.)

Protect your identity!

2. Someone in my chat group just asked for my address.

_____
(Don't give out any personal information.)

People can use it to steal your identity and your money.

3. My brother wants my password to check out a group before joining.

_____
(Don't give it to anyone.)

Not even your brother! He might share it, and then people can steal your information.

4. I sent a file to someone, and she told me it had a virus.

_____
(Get virus protection and use it.)

A virus can hurt your computer and destroy important files (and other people's too).

5. I update my virus protection every month. Is that really necessary?

Yes!_____
(Keep your virus protection up-to-date.)

Remember: *Old* virus protection is *no* virus protection!

6. I got an e-mail about a home-based business. I could make $15,000 a month.

_____
(Don't believe any "get rich quick" offers.)

They sound good, but people almost always lose money.

7. I got an interesting e-mail. I don't know who sent it, but it's got a file attached.

_____
(Don't open any e-mail attachments from strangers.)

They could contain dangerous viruses.

8. The Internet sounds too dangerous for me!

Not really. _____ ,
(Be careful!)

but enjoy yourself—it's an exciting world out there!

5 | EDITING

Read these posts to a bulletin board for international students in the United States. There are twelve mistakes in the use of **should,** **ought to,** *and* **had better.** *The first mistake is already corrected. Find and correct eleven more.*

Justme: My friend asked me to dinner and she told me I should ~~to~~ bring some food! What kind of an invitation is that? What I should bring to this strange dinner party?

Sasha: LOL!* Your friend is having a potluck—a dinner party where everybody brings something. It's really a lot of fun. You ought bring a dish from your country. People will enjoy that.

Toby: HELP! My first day of class, and I lost my wallet! What ought I do first? My student ID, credit card, and cash are all gone.

R2D2: First of all, you'd not better panic because you need to be calm so you can speak clearly. You should to call your credit card company right away. Did you lose your wallet at school? Then you ought to going to the Lost and Found Department at your school.

Smiley: What should an international student does to make friends? At my college people always smile and say, "Hi, how are you?" but they don't wait for an answer!

4gud: New students should joining some clubs and international student organizations. They also ought to find a student in each class to study with and ask about homework assignments.

Newguy: Hi. I'm new to this board. I'm from Vietnam, and I'm going to school in Canada next year. How should I will get ready?

Smiley: Welcome Newguy! I'm at school in Montreal, and my best advice is—you're better bring a lot of warm clothes. You won't believe how cold it gets here.

Sasha: You ought check the school's website. They might have a Vietnam Students' Association. If they do, you should e-mail the Association with your questions. Good luck!

*LOL = Laughing out Loud

Communication Practice

6 | LISTENING

🎧 *A radio show host is giving advice to callers about buying a new computer. Listen to the show. Then listen again and check the sentences that agree with his advice.*

☐ 1. Repair a seven-year-old computer.

☑ 2. Read online computer reviews.

☐ 3. Throw away your old computer.

☐ 4. Always buy the cheapest computer.

☐ 5. Order a computer from a big online company.

☐ 6. Shop at a local computer store.

☐ 7. Consider a service contract.

☐ 8. Get the most memory you can afford.

7 | NEW COUNTRY, NEW CUSTOMS

Work with a partner. Imagine that your partner has been offered a job in a country that you know very well. Give some advice about customs there. Then switch roles. Use the topics below and some of your own.

- calling your boss by his or her first name
- shaking hands when you first meet someone
- calling a co-worker by a nickname
- asking for a second helping of food when you are a guest
- crossing the street before the light turns green

Add your own topics.

- _____
- _____

Examples: You'd better not call your boss by her first name.
You should shake hands when you first meet someone.

8 | PROBLEM SOLVING

Work in small groups. Take turns telling each other about problems you are having. They can be real problems or invented problems, or you can choose from the problems below. Your classmates will give you advice.

- having trouble making friends

- not earning enough money

- not having enough free time

Example: A: I'm having trouble making friends.
B: Maybe you should come to the student lounge.
C: I think you ought to spend more time with the rest of us.

9 | THIS PLACE NEEDS WORK!

Work in pairs. Look at a classroom at the EFL Computer Training Institute. Give advice for ways to improve the institute. Then compare your ideas with the ideas of another pair.

Example: A: They should empty the trash.
B: Yes, and they ought to . . .

10 | WRITING

Look at the picture in Exercise 9. Imagine you are a student at the EFL Computer Training Institute. Write a letter of complaint to Mr. Thompson, the owner of the school. Give advice on improvements the institute should make.

Example: Dear Mr. Thompson:

I am a student at the EFL Computer Training Institute. My classes are very good, but the Institute had better make some improvements or many students are going to leave. First, I think you should . . .

11 | ON THE INTERNET

ⓒ *Do a search on* **advice on learning English**. *Then discuss your search results with your classmates.*

Example: A: You should always speak English with your classmates.

B: You shouldn't worry about speaking fast. It's not important.

C: I think . . .

Do you agree with the advice?

Suggestions: *Let's, Could, Why don't, Why not, How about*

Grammar in Context

BEFORE YOU READ

🎧 *What do you know about youth hostels? Would you like to stay in one of the hostels in the photos below? Read the information from a youth hostel website.*

Let's Travel!

A LOT OF STUDENTS WANT TO TRAVEL—but they don't have much money or don't want to travel alone. Sound familiar? If so, **why don't** you **travel** and **stay** at youth hostels? They are cheap, and you'll meet friendly people from all over the world.

There are more than 4,000 hostels in over 60 different countries. They vary from simple buildings to magnificent old castles. Interested in a more active vacation? **How about checking into** a lodge near a volcano in Costa Rica? Hike through the rain forest during the day. In the evening, you **could watch** red-hot lava coming out of the volcano.

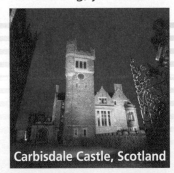

Carbisdale Castle, Scotland

Arenal Observatory Lodge, Costa Rica

Do you prefer cities? **Why not stay** at the Jockey Club Mt. Davis Youth Hostel in Hong Kong? It overlooks the harbor and isn't far from the excitement of downtown.

Tired of being on land? **How about a room** on the *af Chapman* in Stockholm, Sweden? Built in 1888, this sailing ship has been rocking tired tourists to sleep for more than 50 years.

Wherever you go, you'll meet talkative travelers, share stories with them, and gain a greater understanding of the world and its people. So what are you waiting for?

(select a country) ▼ and **let's go**!

AFTER YOU READ

Check the correct answers.

The website suggests _____.

☐ **1.** spending your vacation in the dorm

☐ **2.** staying at expensive hotels

☐ **3.** checking into a lodge

☐ **4.** avoiding the Jockey Club Mt. Davis Youth Hostel

☐ **5.** sleeping on the *af Chapman*

☐ **6.** talking to other travelers

Grammar Presentation

SUGGESTIONS: *LET'S, COULD, WHY DON'T, WHY NOT, HOW ABOUT*

Let's		
Let's (not)	**Base Form of Verb**	
Let's (not)	**take**	the ferry.
	stay	in a castle.

Could			
Subject	**Could***	**Base Form of Verb**	
I You He She We They	**could**	**take**	the ferry.
		stay	in a castle.

*Could is a modal. Modals have only one form. They do not have *-s* in the third-person singular.

Why don't				
Why	**Don't**	**Subject**	**Base Form of Verb**	
Why	**don't**	I we you they	**take**	the ferry?
	doesn't	he she	**stay**	in a castle?

Why not		
Why not	**Base Form of Verb**	
Why not	**take**	the ferry?
	stay	in a castle?

How about		
How about	Gerund / Noun	
How about	**staying**	in a castle?
	a castle?	

GRAMMAR NOTES

EXAMPLES

1. Use *let's*, *could*, *why don't*, *why not*, and *how about* to make **suggestions**.

A: Let's take a trip this summer.

B: We **could go** to Costa Rica.

A: Why don't we **ask** Luke to go too?

B: OK. **Why doesn't** Tom **call** him tonight?

A: Why not call him right now?

B: How about staying at youth hostels?

A: How about a lodge in the rain forest?

USAGE NOTE: We often use *maybe* in suggestions with *could*.

• *Maybe* we **could stay** near the volcano.

2. *Let's* always includes the speaker. It means "Here's a suggestion for you and me."

• **Let's go** to Miami. We need a vacation.
  (I suggest that we go to Miami.)

• **Let's not stay** at a hostel.
  (I suggest that we don't stay at a hostel.)

3. Note the **different forms** to use with these expressions.

BASE FORM OF THE VERB

• **Let's** *take* the ferry.

• We **could** *take* the ferry.

• **Why don't** we *take* the ferry?

• **Why not** *take* the ferry?

GERUND OR NOUN

• **How about** *taking* the ferry?

• **How about** *the ferry*?

4. Notice the **punctuation** at the end of each kind of suggestion.

STATEMENTS

• **Let's** go to a concert**.**

• **Maybe** we **could** go to a concert**.**

QUESTIONS

• **Why don't** we go to a concert**?**

• **Why not** go to a concert**?**

• **How about** going to a concert**?**

(continued)

<table>
<tr>
<td>5. To agree with a suggestion, we usually answer with an <u>informal expression</u>.</td>
<td>A: Let's take a walk.
B: Good idea.
Great.
I'd like that.
OK.
Sure.</td>
</tr>
<tr>
<td>To disagree, we often give an explanation and make another suggestion.</td>
<td>A: Why don't we go to the park?
B: We go there a lot. How about the river?</td>
</tr>
</table>

Reference Note
Making suggestions is sometimes similar to **giving advice** (see Unit 14).

Focused Practice

1 | DISCOVER THE GRAMMAR

🎧 *Emily and Megan are visiting Hong Kong. Read their conversation. Underline all the suggestions.*

EMILY: <u>Why don't we go to the races?</u> I hear they're really exciting.

MEGAN: I'd like to, but I need to go shopping.

EMILY: Then let's go to the Temple Street Market tonight. We might even see some Chinese opera in the street while we're there.

MEGAN: That sounds like fun. But if we do that, why not go to the races this afternoon?

EMILY: OK, but let's get something to eat first in one of those floating restaurants.

MEGAN: I don't think we'll have time. Maybe we could do that tomorrow. Right now, how about getting *dim sum* at the Kau Kee Restaurant next door? Then we could take the Star Ferry to Hong Kong Island and the racecourse.

EMILY: Sounds good. Here's an idea for tomorrow. Why not take one of those small boats—*kaido*—to Lantau Island? When we come back, we could have dinner at the Jumbo Palace.

MEGAN: Let's do that. It's a little expensive, but it sounds like fun.

Now look at this page from a Hong Kong guidebook and check the places Emily and Megan will visit and the transportation they will take.

HONG KONG
Highlights

- **Hong Kong Space Museum.** One of the world's most advanced. See the Sky Show and a movie on the Omnimax movie screen.

✓ **Temple Street Night Market.** Find great bargains, visit a fortune-teller, and, with luck, hear Chinese opera performed in the street.

- **Harbour City.** Shop for clothing, electronics, and antiques in this huge, modern mall. Beautiful harbour views from the open rooftop.

- **Happy Valley Racecourse.** Watch Hong Kong's favorite sport. Feel the excitement as millions of Hong Kong dollars ride on every horse race.

TRANSPORTATION

- **Railway lines** make local stops in both Kowloon and on Hong Kong Island. Use the Kwung Tong Line in Kowloon and the Island Line on Hong Kong Island.

- **The Star Ferry** is the queen of Hong Kong water transportation, and it's a bargain, too. There are several routes connecting Kowloon and Hong Kong Island.

- *Kaido* are small wooden ferries that carry 20–40 passengers.

- **Citybus** passengers ride the double-decker buses in air-conditioned comfort all over Hong Kong, Kowloon, and nearby islands. Tourists like the view from the top deck.

PLACES TO EAT

- **Jumbo Palace ($$$)** A traditional-style floating restaurant specializing in seafood.

- **Yunk Kee Restaurant ($)** Award-winning Cantonese food—famous for its roast duck.

- **Kau Kee Restaurant ($)** A favorite place for *dim sum*—a great way to try a variety of dishes.

- **Bo Kong Vegetarian Restaurant ($$)** Simple but tasty dishes. This attractive restaurant is popular with local celebrities.

- **Peak Lookout ($$$)** The food is not exciting, but you won't notice because the view of the harbour and the islands is so spectacular.

2 | MAKING PLANS

Complete the conversations with the appropriate expression in parentheses.

1. **A:** I feel like having seafood for dinner, but we went to Jumbo Palace last night.

   B: _____*Why not*_____ go again? The food's great, and so is the view.
   (Why not / Let's not)

2. **A:** I'm really tired. _____ resting before we go out?
   (Let's / How about)

   B: That's a good idea. I'm tired too.

3. **A:** I want to explore downtown Hong Kong.

   B: _____ take a double-decker Citybus? We'll see a lot more that way.
   (Let's not / Why don't we)

4. **A:** A group of foreign students just checked into the hostel.

   B: _____ ask them to join us for dinner.
   (How about / Maybe we could)

5. **A:** I don't want to go home tomorrow. I'm having a really good time here.

   B: So am I. _____ leave tomorrow.
   (Let's / Let's not)

3 | LET'S . . .

Complete the suggestions with phrases from the box. Add pronouns and change the verbs as necessary. Punctuate correctly.

buy another one	~~buy tickets~~	come with us
go to the beach	take a trip together	try that new seafood place

1. **A:** There's an Oasis concert at the Hong Kong Convention Centre next weekend.

   B: We're near there now. Why don't _we buy tickets?_____

2. **A:** It's going to be hot tomorrow.

   B: I know. How about_____

3. **A:** Sweaters are on sale. Maybe we could buy one for Brian's birthday.

   B: We got him a sweater last year. Let's not_____

4. **A:** I don't know what to do on spring vacation. I'm sick of staying in the dorm.

   B: Me too. Maybe _____

5. **A:** Emily doesn't have any plans either.

   B: Why doesn't_____

6. **A:** I'm hungry.

   B: Let's _____

4 | EDITING

Read these comments from a suggestions book at a hostel. There are nine mistakes in the use of expressions of suggestion. The first mistake is already corrected. Find and correct eight more. Remember to check the punctuation.

SUGGESTIONS

have
The rooms here are very nice, but why don't you ~~having~~ better lamps so we can read at night?
Petra De Graff, Netherlands

How about have a list of inexpensive restaurants in the area?
Jessica Edwards, Canada

The breakfast is delicious, but why not has music in the breakfast room? Everyone likes music.
Liv Lindberg, Sweden

The countryside around here is very beautiful. Maybe you could having some bikes for us to use so we could explore a little?
Yan Ying Tan, Taiwan

I like staying in old, historic hostels, but I miss some of the modern conveniences. How about having Internet access. It would be nice to send and get e-mail! And why not accepting credit cards?
Carlos Ezcurra, Argentina

You provide sheets, so why you don't provide towels too? They're just as important as sheets!
Ian Harlow, Scotland

Here's a suggestion for all of us hostel guests. Let's don't be so messy! It will be more pleasant for everyone if we clean up our own stuff.
Anonymous

Communication Practice

5 | LISTENING

🎧 *Emily and Megan have just arrived on Lantau Island in Hong Kong. Look at the map. Then listen to the conversation. Listen again. On the map, check the things they decide to do and the places they decide to see.*

Tian Tan Buddha and Po Lin Monastery

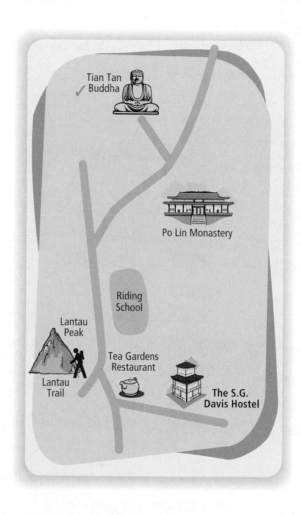

6 | HOW ABOUT . . . ?

Work with a partner. Imagine you are both visiting Hong Kong. Look at the guidebook on page 169 and talk about what you would like to do. Make suggestions about activities.

Example: A: I want to buy some souvenirs.
B: Let's go to the Temple Street Night Market.

7 | THINGS TO DO

Work with a group to plan a trip to an interesting place in your area. Discuss the following:

- where to go
- when to go
- how to get there
- what to do there
- who will call or write for more information

Example: A: How about visiting San Diego?
B: Maybe we could go next weekend.
C: How about going to the zoo?
A: Why not take the bus?
B: Why don't the two of you call for information?

8 | WRITING

Write a letter to someone who is going to visit you. Make suggestions about the things you can do together.

Example: Dear Kim,
I am so excited about your visit! Let's make some plans right now. You arrive on Friday, the 10th. Why don't we spend the next day at the museum? There's a great exhibit on . . .

9 | ON THE INTERNET

Ⓒ *Work with a partner. First choose a country and city you are both interested in visiting. Then research the hostels there. (You could check out* **Hostelling International***). Discuss the hostel possibilities and agree on one to stay at.*

Example: A: Let's go to England.
B: I've been there. How about Scotland? It's a beautiful country, and we could still practice our English . . .
A: Maybe we could stay at Carbisdale Castle. It looks great in the photo.
B: That's true. But why don't we stay in Edinburgh? There are several hostels in the old section of the city . . .

From **Grammar** to **Writing**
Using Appropriate Modals

When you write a note, you do more than give information. You perform social functions such as asking for permission and making requests. Modals help you perform these functions politely.

Example: I want you to call me in the morning. ⟶
Could you **please** call me in the morning?

1 *Read this note from Ed to his co-worker, Chen. Work with a partner and decide which sentences should have modals. Underline the sentences.*

> *From the Desk of Ed Hansen . . .*
>
> Chen,—Here is our project summary. <u>Read it.</u> I really think it's much too long.
>
> What do you think? Tell me whether to shorten it. We will meet tomorrow to
>
> discuss it. My advice is that we finish the draft by Friday. By the way, Nadia
>
> is in town. I want to invite her to our meeting. —Ed

2 *Complete a second draft of the note. Use modals to express the functions in parentheses.*

> *From the Desk of Ed Hansen . . .*
>
> Chen,—Here is our project summary. _____Would you mind_____ reading it? I really think
>   **(make a request)**
>
> it's much too long. What do you think? _____ I shorten it?
>   **(ask advice)**
>
> _____ meet tomorrow to discuss it. We _____ finish
>   **(make a suggestion)**   **(give advice)**
>
> the final draft by Friday. By the way, Nadia is in town. _____ I
>   **(ask permission)**
>
> invite her to our meeting? —Ed

3 Complete Chen's note to Ed. Use modals to express the following ideas:

- Shorten the summary. *(advice)*
- I want to meet tomorrow morning instead. *(suggestion)*
- Reserve the conference room for the meeting. *(request)*
- Of course Nadia will come to the meeting. *(permission)*
- We're going to have lunch together after the meeting. *(suggestion)*

❦ *From the Desk of Chen Wu . . .*

Ed—Sorry, I was very busy this morning, so I wasn't able to
finish reading the summary until now. *I think you should shorten it.*

_____

_____

_____

_____

See you tomorrow morning. —Chen

---

4 Before you write . . .

1. Work with a partner. Choose one of the situations below. Role-play the situation.
   Use modals to express the ideas.

   SITUATION 1: **A salesperson and his or her boss**
   You work in a sales office. Recently a customer complained to your boss because he
   had to wait for service. You want to meet with your boss to explain what happened.
   You'd like to bring a co-worker who saw the incident. You think the company needs
   another receptionist for busy times.

   SITUATION 2: **A student and his or her English teacher**
   You would like your English teacher to write a letter of recommendation for you.
   You want him or her to mention that you have good computer skills and are an
   A student in the class. You're not sure how many hours to work a week, so you ask
   your teacher. You want to miss class so that you can go to your job interview.

2. Work with another pair. Watch their role play. Make a list of functions they expressed
   (for example, advice, suggestion, ability) and the modals they used to express those
   functions. Discuss your list with them—did they express what they wanted to?

3. Perform your role play and discuss it with the other pair.

5 Write a note as one of the characters in the role play. Use modals and information
from the feedback you received on your role play.

Review Test

I   *Circle the letter of the appropriate response to each question.*

1. Could you speak English when you were a child?
    a. I'd be glad to.
    (b.) Yes, I could.

2. Can you swim?
    a. Yes, I can. I'd be glad to.
    b. Yes, I can. I really enjoy it.

3. Would you turn off the lights before you leave?
    a. Of course.
    b. Yes, I would.

4. May I ask a question?
    a. Yes, you may. What is it?
    b. You may. I'm not sure.

5. Would you mind lending me some money? I left my wallet at home.
    a. Yes, I would. Here's $10.
    b. Not at all. Here's $10.

6. Why don't we go to the beach today?
    a. Good idea.
    b. Because the car broke down.

7. Could you explain this word to me?
    a. Sorry, but I don't understand it either.
    b. No, I couldn't. I never heard it before!

8. Maybe I'll wear a suit. What do you think?
    a. Maybe you shouldn't.
    b. Maybe you won't.

9. Were you able to get tickets for the concert last week?
    a. No, I wasn't.
    b. Why not?

II *Read each sentence. Write its function. Use the words in the box.*

ability	advice	permission	request	suggestion

1. Passengers may not use cell phones on the airplane. _____*permission*_____

2. Could you please turn the light out before you leave? _____

3. Why not take the train? _____

4. Of course you can use my pen. _____

5. When Eva was little, she couldn't reach the elevator button. _____

6. Do you mind if my sister comes with us? _____

7. Let's take a taxi. _____

8. If you don't know who sent that e-mail, you'd better not open it. _____

9. Would you mind calling back in about half an hour? _____

10. Will you please explain that to me again? _____

11. I can't lift that box by myself. _____

12. Maybe we could go to a later movie. _____

13. You shouldn't use your real name in an Internet chat room. _____

14. Ty didn't study hard, but he was able to pass the final exam. _____

III *Circle the correct words to complete the conversations.*

1. **A:** This dorm room is depressing me.

   B: <u>May we /</u> (<u>Why not</u>) redecorate? We have some free time.

　　　　　a.

   A: OK. Where <u>should we / were we able to</u> start?

　　　　　　　　　b.

   B: Maybe we <u>could / couldn't</u> put up new curtains.

　　　　　　　c.

   A: Great. <u>Let's / Why not</u> go to the store right now?

　　　　　d.

   B: We <u>can't / 'd better</u> measure the windows first.

　　　　e.

   A: These curtains are pretty. <u>Why not / How about</u> putting them up right away?

　　　　　　　　　　　　f.

   B: We <u>may / should</u> wash the windows first. They're really dirty.

　　　　g.

   A: OK. The windows are clean. <u>Let's / May we</u> put up the curtains now.

　　　　　　　　　　　h.

   B: The room looks great. <u>Why don't we / We should</u> buy some new posters next.

　　　　　　　　　i.

(continued)

2. A: Dancing Wheels is performing next weekend. <u>Let's / Would you mind</u> get tickets.
a.

B: Good idea. <u>Could / Should</u> you pick them up? I'm really busy this week.
b.

A: No problem. I'll <u>can / be able to</u> get them after class today. <u>Do you mind if / Why not</u>
c.d.

I get a ticket for Carlos too?

B: <u>Yes, I do. / Not at all.</u> I haven't seen him in ages. Maybe we <u>could / will</u> all go out to
e.f.

dinner before the theater. I hear that new Indian restaurant is very good.

A: OK, but we <u>could / 'd better</u> make a reservation. It's also very popular.
g.

3. A: I'm buying a new computer this year. Any suggestions?

B: <u>How about / Why don't</u> you ask Anatol? He knows a lot about computers.
a.

A: Good idea. <u>Could / Should</u> you give me his e-mail address?
b.

B: I don't have it, but you <u>'d better / could</u> ask Karin. She'll have it.
c.

A: <u>Do you mind if / Would you mind</u> asking her for me? You know her better.
d.

B: Sure.

IV *Each sentence has four underlined words or phrases. The four underlined parts of the sentences are marked A, B, C, or D. Circle the letter of the <u>one</u> underlined word or phrase that is NOT CORRECT.*

1. <u>When</u> I was 10, I <u>could</u> hit a ball far, but I <u>wasn't</u> able <u>run</u> fast.   **A B C Ⓓ**
ABCD

2. Why <u>don't</u> we <u>have</u> dinner and then <u>go</u> see *Possible Dreams.*   **A B C D**
ABCD

3. You <u>drove</u> all day today, so <u>maybe</u> you'd <u>not better</u> <u>drive</u> tonight.   **A B C D**
ABCD

4. <u>Will</u> you mind <u>bringing</u> your camera to the party <u>tomorrow</u> <u>?</u>   **A B C D**
ABCD

5. Dad, <u>may</u> I <u>borrow</u> the car tomorrow or <u>does</u> Mom <u>has</u> to use it?   **A B C D**
ABCD

6. I <u>can't</u> <u>help</u> you with this, so <u>maybe</u> you should <u>to talk</u> to Mr. Ho.   **A B C D**
ABCD

7. <u>Should</u> I <u>give</u> my host flowers, or <u>should</u> I <u>bringing</u> candy?   **A B C D**
ABCD

8. <u>May be</u> you <u>ought</u> <u>to</u> just <u>bring</u> flowers.   **A   B   C   D**
   A   B C   D

9. Silva <u>wasn't</u> a strong child, but she <u>could</u> win first prize in   **A   B   C   D**
         A   B

    gymnastics <u>when</u> she <u>was</u> ten.
                C   D

10. I think I <u>was</u> able <u>to</u> <u>finish</u> my <u>homework</u> early tomorrow.   **A   B   C   D**
            A   B C   D

11. <u>It's</u> really late, so <u>let's</u> <u>us</u> <u>go</u> out to dinner tonight, OK?   **A   B   C   D**
    A   B C D

V   *Find and correct the mistake in each conversation.*

1. **A:** Can Elena ~~dances~~? *dance*

    B: Yes, she's great. She's able to do all kinds of difficult steps.

2. **A:** When you were a child, were you able to skate?

    B: Yes. In fact, I once could win a competition in my school.

3. **A:** Could please you help me?

    B: Sure. What seems to be the problem?

4. **A:** Would you mind giving me a ride home?

    B: Yes, I would. When would you like to leave?

5. **A:** You really ought update your virus protection.

    B: OK. I'll do it today.

6. **A:** We would better hurry, or we'll be late.

    B: Don't worry. We can still get there on time.

7. **A:** Could I borrow the car tonight?

    B: Sorry, but you couldn't. I need it myself.

8. **A:** Do you mind if my friend coming to the party with me?

    B: Not at all. There's always room for one more!

▶ *To check your answers, go to the Answer Key on page RT-2.*

PART
IV

Present Perfect

16 Present Perfect: *Since* and *For*

Grammar in Context

BEFORE YOU READ

🎧 *Where can you find an article like this? Look at the information below the photo. How long has Bob Burnquist been a professional? Read the article about this champion skateboarder.*

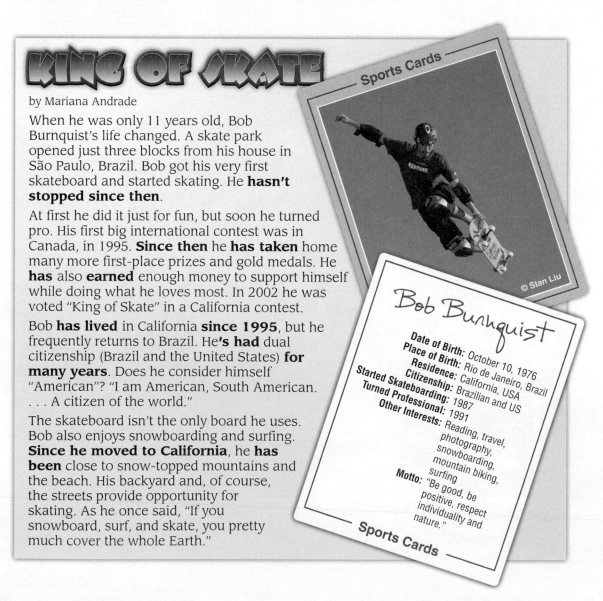

KING OF SKATE

by Mariana Andrade

When he was only 11 years old, Bob Burnquist's life changed. A skate park opened just three blocks from his house in São Paulo, Brazil. Bob got his very first skateboard and started skating. He **hasn't stopped since then**.

At first he did it just for fun, but soon he turned pro. His first big international contest was in Canada, in 1995. **Since then** he **has taken** home many more first-place prizes and gold medals. He **has** also **earned** enough money to support himself while doing what he loves most. In 2002 he was voted "King of Skate" in a California contest.

Bob **has lived** in California **since 1995**, but he frequently returns to Brazil. He**'s had** dual citizenship (Brazil and the United States) **for many years**. Does he consider himself "American"? "I am American, South American. . . . A citizen of the world."

The skateboard isn't the only board he uses. Bob also enjoys snowboarding and surfing. **Since he moved to California**, he **has been** close to snow-topped mountains and the beach. His backyard and, of course, the streets provide opportunity for skating. As he once said, "If you snowboard, surf, and skate, you pretty much cover the whole Earth."

Sports Cards

© Stan Liu

Bob Burnquist

Date of Birth: October 10, 1976
Place of Birth: Rio de Janeiro, Brazil
Residence: California, USA
Citizenship: Brazilian and US
Started Skateboarding: 1987
Turned Professional: 1991
Other Interests: Reading, travel, photography, snowboarding, mountain biking, surfing
Motto: "Be good, be positive, respect individuality and nature."

Sports Cards

AFTER YOU READ

Read the statements. Check **True** *or* **False**.

	True	False
1. Bob Burnquist still skates.	☐	☐
2. His only first-place prize was in 1995.	☐	☐
3. He lives in Brazil.	☐	☐
4. He lives close to the beach.	☐	☐

Grammar Presentation

PRESENT PERFECT: *SINCE* AND *FOR*

Statements				
Subject	*Have (not)*	**Past Participle**		*Since / For*
I You* We They	**have** (not)	**been**†	here	**since** 1995. **for** a long time.
He She It	**has** (not)	**lived**		

* *You* is both singular and plural.
† *Been* is an irregular past participle. See Grammar Notes on page 185 and Appendix 1 on page A-1 for a list of irregular verbs.

Yes / No Questions				
Have	**Subject**	**Past Participle**		*Since / For*
Have	I you we they	**been**	here	**since** 1995? **for** a long time?
Has	he she it	**lived**		

Short Answers					
Affirmative			**Negative**		
Yes,	you I / we you they	**have.**	**No,**	you I / we you they	**haven't.**
	he she it	**has.**		he she it	**hasn't.**

(continued)

Wh- Questions				
Wh- Word	*Have*	Subject	Past Participle	
How long	**have**	I you we they	**been**	here?
	has	he she it	**lived**	

Short Answers
Since 1995. **For** many years.

Contractions	
Affirmative	**Negative**
I have = **I've** he has = **he's** you have = **you've** she has = **she's** we have = **we've** it has = **it's** they have = **they've**	have not = **haven't** has not = **hasn't**

GRAMMAR NOTES

EXAMPLES

---

1. Use the **present perfect** with *since* or *for* to talk about something that <u>began</u> in the past and <u>continues</u> into the present (and may continue into the future).

- Bob **has been** a skater *since* 1987. *(He became a skater in 1987, and he is still a skater.)*
- He **has been** a skater *for* many years. *(He became a skater many years ago, and he is still a skater.)*

---

2. Use *since* **+ point in time** *(since yesterday, since 5:00, since Monday, since 1995)* to show <u>when</u> something started.

    Since can also introduce a time clause.

- He **has won** many contests *since 1995*.
- He **has become** famous *since then*.

- He **has loved** sports *since he was a child*.

---

3. Use *for* **+ length of time** *(for 10 minutes, for two weeks, for years, for a long time)* to show <u>how long</u> something has lasted.

- Bob **has owned** a restaurant *for years*.

4. Form the present perfect with:
have **+ past participle**

- He **has lived** there for years.
- They **have been** skating partners since 1998.

Past participles can be regular or irregular.

a. The **regular** form of the past participle is **base form of verb + -*d*** or **-*ed***.

This form is the same as the regular simple past form of the verb.

- He has **loved** sports since he was a kid.
- He has **wanted** to skate for a long time.

▶ **BE CAREFUL!** There are often **spelling changes** when you add **-*ed*** to the verb.

- He hasn't **stopped** since then.

b. There are many **irregular** past participles. A few common ones are listed below. Notice that irregular verbs with similar base forms often have similar past participles.

- He has **bought** two new skateboards since March.
- They haven't **won** a contest for several years.

Base Form of the Verb	Past Participle	Base Form of the Verb	Past Participle
be	**been**	pay	**paid**
see	**seen**	say	**said**
meet	**met**	do	**done**
sleep	**slept**	go	**gone**
sell	**sold**	drive	**driven**
tell	**told**	give	**given**
buy	**bought**	know	**known**
think	**thought**	grow	**grown**
begin	**begun**	eat	**eaten**
sing	**sung**	fall	**fallen**
have	**had**	speak	**spoken**
make	**made**	break	**broken**
put	**put**	get	**gotten**
read	**read**	write	**written**

Reference Note
For a more complete list of **irregular past participles**,
   see Appendix 1 on page A-1.

Focused Practice

1 | DISCOVER THE GRAMMAR

*Read the information about Caterina and Roque. Then circle the letter of the sentence (**a** or **b**) that best describes the situation.*

1. Caterina has been a skater since 1998.
   a. She is still a skater.
   b. She is not a skater anymore.

2. She has had long hair since she was a little girl.
   a. She has short hair now.
   b. She has long hair now.

3. She has lived in the same apartment for ten years.
   a. She lived in a different apartment eleven years ago.
   b. She moved a few years ago.

4. Caterina and Roque have been married for five years.
   a. They are not married now.
   b. They got married five years ago.

5. They haven't been on a vacation since 2001.
   a. They are on a vacation now.
   b. They were on a vacation in 2001.

6. Caterina hasn't won a contest for two years.
   a. She won a championship two years ago.
   b. She didn't win a championship two years ago.

2 | FOR LOVE OF THE SPORT

Grammar Notes 1–3

*Complete these sentences about Brazilian sportswriter Mariana Andrade. Use **since** or **for**.*

1. Mariana Andrade has lived in São Paulo ___since___ 1995.

2. She has been a sportswriter _____ four years.

3. _____ June she has written several articles about skateboarding.

4. This sport has been very popular in Brazil _____ many years.

5. Mariana has met Burnquist twice _____ she started her job.

6. She loves to skate, but she hasn't skated _____ a long time.

7. She has been married to Alvaro, another skater, _____ 2003.

8. They've had their own house _____ two years, and they've been parents _____ July.

3 | SKATING SUCCESS

Grammar Note 4

Complete this article about Roque Guterres with the correct form of the verbs in parentheses. Use Appendix 1 on page A-1 for help with irregular verbs.

Roque Guterres _____ *has loved* _____ skating since he was a little boy. He began
                                 1. (love)

skating when he was 10, and he _____ since that time. Roque
                                              2. (not stop)

_____ a professional skater now for several years. He and Caterina
          3. (be)

_____ in Rio since they got married. They _____
          4. (live)   **5. (have)**

the same one-bedroom apartment for five years. They _____ a vacation
                                                                   6. (not take)

for many years, but they _____ to several skating contests since Roque
                                    7. (go)

turned pro. Roque _____ in four international contests since last year.
                            8. (skate)

He _____ two second-place prizes since then. Since he was a child, he
              9. (win)

_____ to be a pro. His dream _____ true
          10. (want)   **11. (come)**

since then.

4 | SKATEBOARDING FACTS

Grammar Notes 1–4

*Complete these sentences with the present perfect form of the verbs in parentheses and
with **since** or **for**. Use Appendix 1 on page A-1 for help with irregular verbs.*

Skateboarding _____ *has been* _____ popular ___ *for* ___ more than 50 years.
                                 1. (be)   **2.**

Skateboards _____ around _____ the 1930s. The first ones
                         3. (be)   **4.**

were simple wooden boxes on metal wheels. They _____ a lot
                                                              5. (change)

_____ then!
    6.

The first skateboarding contest took place in California in 1963. _____ then,
                                                                                    7.

thousands of contests _____ place all over the world.
                                 8. (take)

In 1976, the first outdoor skate park opened in Florida. _____ then, hundreds of
                                                                            9.

parks _____ in countries around the world.
            10. (open)

Skateboarding can be dangerous. _____ last year, more than 15,600 people in the
                                               11.

United States alone _____ to hospital emergency rooms because
                              12. (go)

of injuries.

(continued)

✍ When he was seven years old, Jon Comer lost his right foot as a result of a car accident.

But that didn't stop him. _____ then, he _____ one of the
         13.   14. (become)

best-known professional skateboarders in the world.

✍ Tony Hawk _____ professionally _____ many years, but he
            15. (not compete)   16.

is still the most famous and successful skateboarder in the world.

5 | A RÉSUMÉ   *Grammar Notes 1–4*

*Ingrid Schwab is applying for a job as a college sports instructor. Look at her résumé and
the interviewer's notes. Complete the interview. Use the words in parentheses to write
questions. Then answer the questions. Use contractions when possible.
Note:* **The year is 2006.**

Ingrid Schwab
2136 East Travis Street
San Antonio, Texas 78284

INTERVIEWED
09/18/06

Education:
1998   Certificate (American College of Sports Medicine)
1995   M.A. Physical Education (University of Texas)   moved to
                                                       San Antonio
                                                       in 1991

Employment:
1997–present   part-time physical education teacher (high school)
1995–present   sports trainer (private)
                                   teaches tennis, swimming

Skills:
speak German, Portuguese, and Spanish
martial arts   got black belt
                                      in tae kwon do
                                      2 mos. ago

Other Interests:
travel, photography, skateboarding

Awards:
1998   Teacher of the Year Award
1995   silver medal in Texas Skateboarding Contest

Memberships:
1998–present   member of National Education Association (NEA)

1. (How long / live in San Antonio)

INTERVIEWER: *How long have you lived in San Antonio?*

INGRID: *I've lived in San Antonio for 15 years.*

OR

I've lived in San Antonio since 1991.

2. (How long / have your M.A. degree)

INTERVIEWER: _____

INGRID: _____

3. (have any more training since you got your M.A.)

INTERVIEWER: _____

INGRID: _____

4. (How long / be a physical education teacher)

INTERVIEWER: _____

INGRID: _____

5. (How long / work as a sports trainer)

INTERVIEWER: _____

INGRID: _____

6. (How long / have a black belt in tae kwon do)

INTERVIEWER: _____

INGRID: _____

7. (win any awards since then)

INTERVIEWER: I see you won a medal in skateboarding. _____

INGRID: _____. I won the Teacher of the Year Award in 1998.

8. (How long / be a member of the NEA)

INTERVIEWER: _____

INGRID: _____

6 | EDITING

*Read these posts to an online skateboard message board. There are ten mistakes in the use of the present perfect with **since** and **for**. The first mistake is already corrected. Find and correct nine more.*

The Skateboarding Board
Tell us your skating stories here!

I've had
~~I have~~ my skateboard for two years. For me, it's much more than just a sport. It's a form of transportation. It's much faster than walking!

Jennifer, USA

I've been a skater since five years. Since December I won two contests. I'd love to go pro one day.

Paulo, Brazil

Help! I've broken three boards for January!!! Is this normal? How long you have had your board?

Sang-Ook, Korea

Broken boards?! That's nothing! I've break my wrist twice since I started skating!

Marta, Mexico

Last year, my board hit a rock while I was skating in the street. I fell and hit my head and had to go to the emergency room. I always worn a helmet since then!

Megan, Australia

I live in California since 2001. My first love is surfing, but when there aren't any waves, I jump on my skateboard and take to the streets!

Ming, USA

Wow! Yesterday, my friend gave me a copy of the video "OP King of Skate." I've watch it three times since then. The Burnquist part is awesome!

Todd, Canada

At last! A skate park opened near my home last week. Since then I gone every day. It's a lot more fun than skating in the streets!

Sylvie, France

Communication Practice

7 | LISTENING

🎧 *Antonio Serrano is looking for a job as a radio sports announcer. Listen to this interview. Then listen again and complete the interviewer's notes. Use* **since** *and* **for**.

> ## *WSPR* Radio
>
> *Antonio Serrano*   *interviewed 9/8*
>
> *He's been a sports announcer* ___*for 20 years*___ .
>   **1.**
>
> *He's had two jobs* _____ .
>   **2.**
>
> *He's lived in Los Angeles* _____ .
>   **3.**
>
> *He hasn't worked* _____ .
>   **4.**
>
> *He's been a student at UCLA* _____ .
>   **5.**

8 | ROLE PLAY: A JOB INTERVIEW

Write a résumé. Use Ingrid's résumé on page 188 as a model. You can use real or imaginary information. Then role-play a job interview with a partner. Take turns being the interviewer and the candidate. Use the script below to help you complete the interview.

Example: **A:** How long have you been a lab technician?
                B: I've been a lab technician for five years.

INTERVIEWER: How long have you been a(n) _____?

CANDIDATE: I've _____.

INTERVIEWER: And how many jobs have you had since _____?

CANDIDATE: I've _____.

INTERVIEWER: I see from your résumé that you live in _____.
How long have you lived there?

CANDIDATE: _____.

INTERVIEWER: Your English is quite good. How long have you studied it?

CANDIDATE: _____.

INTERVIEWER: Well, thank you very much. We'll be in touch with you.

9 | **THE BEST PERSON FOR THE JOB**

A business college needs a new math teacher. Look at these two résumés. In small groups, decide who to hire and why. Use **since** *and* **for**.

Example: **A:** Wu Hao has had the same job since he got his Ph.D.
B: Erika Jones has a lot of experience. She's been a teacher since 1981.

Wu Hao

Education:
1995 Ph.D in Mathematics (UCLA)

Teaching Experience:
1995–present   Bryant University

Courses Taught:
Algebra
Trigonometry
Calculus
Business Mathematics

Publications:
"Introducing Computers into the College Math Class" (*The Journal of Mathematics*, 1997)

Awards:
Teacher of the Year, 1997
Distinguished Professor, 2004

Erika Jones

Education:
1981 Ph.D in Mathematics (UCLA)

Teaching Experience:
2001–present   NYC Technical College
1996–2000   UCLA
1987–1995   University of Wisconsin, Madison
1984–1986   Brown University
1981–1983   UCLA

Courses Taught:
Mathematical Analysis 1
Mathematical Analysis 2

Publications:
"Imaginary Numbers" (*MJS*, 1986)
"Number Theory" (*Mathematics*, 1986)
"How Real Are Real Numbers?" (*Math Education*, 1989)

---

10 | **WRITING**

Write a paragraph about someone's accomplishments. It can be someone famous or someone you know. Use the present perfect with **since** *or* **for**.

Example: Ingrid has been a high school physical education teacher and a private sports trainer for many years. She has received two awards since 1998, one for teaching and the other for skateboarding. She has been a member of the National Education Association since 1998. Ingrid speaks four languages. She has been a student of martial arts for a long time, and she has had her black belt in tae kwon do for two months.

11 | **ON THE INTERNET**

Ⓒ *Find information online about a current famous professional athlete. How long has that person been professional? How many events has he or she won since 2005? What else has he or she accomplished?*

Present Perfect: Already and Yet

Grammar in Context

BEFORE YOU READ

🎧 *How do you feel about parties? Which do you prefer: giving a party or going to one? Why? Read the magazine article.*

It's Party Time!

It's almost the end of the year, and you**'ve already been** to several parties, but you **haven't given** one **yet**. You're a little nervous, but you decide it's time to take the plunge.

First things first: **Have** you **chosen** the day **yet**? What about the time?

OK. You**'ve already chosen** the day and the time and **sent** the invitations. But you **haven't decided** on the menu **yet**, and now your party is just a week away! Don't panic!

We spoke to Patty Cake, a professional party planner. She says, "It *is* very important to be organized, but remember: You don't need a whole new set of skills. Think about your everyday life. You**'ve already done** many of the things you need to do for a party. You know how to shop for food, put it on plates, and introduce friends to one another. Now, you just need to bring all these skills together."

Still need help? Party planners, like Patty Cake, can offer specific advice. "We**'ve already helped** hundreds of people plan successful parties—big and small. If you **haven't tried** a party-planning service **yet**, you should give it a chance," says Cake. And you don't have to spend a lot of money. Free advice is available on the Internet. There, you will also find handy lists where you can check off things you**'ve already done** (and see the things you **haven't done yet**!). So, take a deep breath, relax, and enjoy the party!

AFTER YOU READ

Reread the first three paragraphs of the article. Check the correct answers.

The person _____.

☐ **1.** went to several parties

☐ **2.** gave a party

☐ **3.** chose a date for the party

☐ **4.** chose the time

☐ **5.** sent invitations

☐ **6.** decided on a menu

Grammar Presentation

PRESENT PERFECT: *ALREADY* AND *YET*

Affirmative Statements: *Already*				
Subject	*Have*	*Already*	Past Participle	
They	**have**	*already*	**mailed**	the invitations.
She	**has**		**gotten**	her invitation.

Negative Statements: *Yet*				
Subject	*Have not*	Past Participle		*Yet*
They	**haven't**	**mailed**	the invitations	*yet*.
She	**hasn't**	**gotten**	her invitation	

Yes / No Questions: *Yet*				
Have	Subject	Past Participle		*Yet*
Have	they	**mailed**	the invitations	*yet*?
Has	she	**gotten**	her invitation	

Short Answers				
Affirmative		Negative		
Yes,	they **have**.	No,	they **haven't**.	
	she **has**.		she **hasn't**.	

GRAMMAR NOTES

EXAMPLES

1. Use the **present perfect** with *already* in <u>affirmative statements</u> to talk about something that has happened before now.

▶ **BE CAREFUL!** We do not usually use past time expressions with the present perfect and *already*.

- I've *already* **mailed** the invitations.
- Jenna **has** *already* **met** Carlos.

NOT Jenna has already met Carlos ~~last month~~.

---

2. *Already* usually goes between *have* and the past participle.

Already can also go at the end of the clause.

- I've *already* **baked** the cake.

OR

- I've **baked** the cake *already*.

---

3. Use the **present perfect** with *yet* in <u>negative statements</u> to talk about something that has not happened before now.

It is possible that we expected something to have happened earlier, and it is still possible that it will happen in the future.

- I **haven't cleaned** *yet*.

A: Jenna **hasn't called** *yet*.
B: Oh, I'm sure we'll hear from her later.

---

4. *Yet* usually goes at the end of the clause.

Yet can also go between *have not* and the past participle.

- They **haven't arrived** *yet*.

OR

- They **haven't** *yet* **arrived**.

---

5. Use *yet* in <u>questions</u> to ask if something has happened before now.

USAGE NOTE: We sometimes use *already* in <u>questions</u> to express surprise that something happened sooner than expected.

- **Have** you **bought** the soda *yet*?

- **Has** Carlos **arrived** *already*?
  The party doesn't start until 8:00!

---

6. For **negative answers** to *yes / no* questions, you can use *haven't* or *not yet*.

A: Has the party started yet?
B: No, it **hasn't**.

OR

No, **not yet**.

OR

Not yet.

Reference Note
For a list of **irregular past participles,** see Appendix 1 on page A-1.

Focused Practice

1 | DISCOVER THE GRAMMAR

*Read the first sentence. Then decide if the second sentence is **True (T)** or **False (F)**.*

1. I've already given many parties.

___F___   This will be my first party.

2. I haven't baked the cake yet.

_____   I plan to bake a cake.

3. Have the guests arrived yet?

_____   I'm surprised that the guests are here.

4. Has Jenna left already?

_____   I'm surprised that Jenna left.

5. Have you had a cup of tea yet?

_____   I don't know if you had a cup of tea.

6. Carlos has already met my sister.

_____   I need to introduce Carlos to my sister.

2 | PARTY TALK

Grammar Notes 1–6

*Complete these conversations. Use the present perfect form of the verbs in parentheses with **already** or **yet** and short answers. Use contractions when possible. Go to Appendix 1 on page A-1 for help with irregular verbs.*

1. **A:** This is a great party. _____*Have*_____ you _____*tried*_____ the cake _____*yet*_____?
   (try)

   B: _____*No*_____, I _____*haven't*_____. But I'm going to have a piece now.

2. **A:** Jenna, I'd like you to meet my friend Carlos.

   B: We _____ _____ _____. Marta introduced us.
   (meet)

3. **A:** Would you like another cup of coffee?

   B: No, thanks. I _____ _____ _____ three cups!
   (have)

4. **A:** I don't see Jenna. _____ she _____ _____? It's still early!
   (leave)

   B: _____ , she _____. She's in the kitchen.

5. **A:** _____ you _____ Coppola's new movie _____?
   (see)

   B: _____ , I _____. It's great. What about you?

   A: I _____ _____ it _____, but I want to.
   (see)

6. **A:** This was a great party. I'm giving my own party next week.

   I _____ _____ _____ the whole thing, but I'm
   (plan)

   still a little nervous about it.

   B: Don't worry. If you do all the planning, the rest will take care of itself!

3 | FIRST THINGS FIRST   *Grammar Notes 1–4*

Read Fabrizio's party-planning checklist. Write statements about the things that he **has already done** *and the things that he* **hasn't done yet**. *Use contractions when possible. Go to Appendix 1 on page A-1 for help with irregular verbs.*

Things to Do

- ✓ pick a date
- ☐ choose a time
- ✓ find a location
- ✓ write a guest list
- ✓ buy invitations
- ☐ send invitations
- ☐ ask friends to help
- ☐ plan the menu
- ✓ pick out music
- ☐ shop for food
- ☐ clean the house
- ✓ borrow some chairs

1. *He's already picked a date.*

2. *He hasn't chosen a time yet.*

3. _____

4. _____

5. _____

6. _____

7. _____

8. _____

9. _____

10. _____

11. _____

12. _____

4 | EDITING

*Read this online bulletin board. There are nine mistakes in the use of the present perfect with **already** and **yet**. The first mistake is already corrected. Find and correct eight more.*

Ask the Party Planner!

Doug asked: Help! My party is next week and I haven't figured out the food ~~already~~ *yet*! I've yet wasted three days worrying, and I still don't have any ideas. What should I do?

The Party Planner's Advice is: Don't panic! Your guests have started arriving yet, so there's still time. Ask everyone to bring something! (You've already invite people, right?) Or order pizza. I haven't met anyone already who doesn't like pizza.

• •

Rosa asked: I'd like to find a "theme" for my next birthday party. I've already have a pasta party (10 kinds of pasta!), and I've already gave a movie party (everyone dressed up as a movie character). Any ideas?

The Party Planner's Advice is: Sure. Has you tried this one yet? No yet? Ask each guest to bring a baby photo of him- or herself. Collect the photos. People try to match the photos with the guests! Your guests will love it!

Communication Practice

5 | LISTENING

🎧 *Some friends are planning a party. Listen to their conversation. Listen again and check the things they've already done.*

✓ 1. find a place
2. invite people
3. borrow extra chairs
4. figure out food
5. buy soda
6. select music

6 | INFORMATION GAP: CHORES

Work in pairs (A and B). Student A, follow the instructions on this page. Student B, turn to page 201 and follow the instructions there.

1. Look at the picture of the Meiers' dining room and at Gisela's To Do list. Cross out the chores that Gisela has already done.

2. Answer your partner's questions about Gisela's chores.

   Example: **B:** Has Gisela vacuumed the carpet yet?
   A: No, she hasn't.   OR   No, not yet.

3. Look at Helmut's To Do list. Ask your partner questions to find out which chores Helmut has already done. Cross out those chores.

   Example: **A:** Has Helmut bought film yet?
   B: Yes, he has.   OR   Yes, he's already bought film.

To Do—Helmut
~~buy film~~
bake the cake
put the turkey in the oven
mop the floor
wash the dishes
cut up the vegetables

To Do—Gisela
vacuum the carpet
buy flowers
wash the windows
set the table
hang the balloons
wrap the gift

Now compare lists with your partner. Are they the same?

7 | WHAT ABOUT YOU?

Write a list of things that you planned or wanted to do by this time (for example, find a new job, paint the apartment). Include things that you have already done and things that you haven't done yet. Exchange lists with a classmate and ask and answer questions about the items on the lists.

Example: A: Have you found a new job yet?

B: No, not yet. I'm still looking. OR Yes, I have.

8 | WRITING

Imagine you and a friend are giving a party tonight. Leave a note for your friend to explain what you've already done and what you haven't done yet.

Example: I've already bought the soda, but I haven't gotten the potato chips yet . . .

9 | ON THE INTERNET

Think of an activity you are planning—a job search, travel, a car purchase, moving, a party. Look for an online To Do list. For example, type in **to do list + job search**. *What have you already done? What haven't you done yet? Discuss your list with a partner.*

Example: I'm looking for a job. I've already written a résumé, but I haven't gotten any references yet.

INFORMATION GAP FOR STUDENT B

1. Look at the picture of the Meiers' kitchen and at Helmut's To Do list. Cross out the chores that Helmut has already done.

2. Look at Gisela's To Do list. Ask your partner questions to find out which chores Gisela has already done. Cross out those chores.

   Example: **B:** Has Gisela vacuumed the carpet yet?
   A: No, she hasn't.   OR   No, not yet.

3. Answer your partner's questions about Helmut's chores.

   Example: **A:** Has Helmut bought film yet?
   B: Yes, he has.   OR   Yes, he's already bought film.

To Do—Helmut
~~buy film~~
bake the cake
put the turkey in the oven
mop the floor
wash the dishes
cut up the vegetables

To Do—Gisela
vacuum the carpet
buy flowers
wash the windows
set the table
hang the balloons
wrap the gift

Now compare lists with your partner. Are they the same?

18 Present Perfect: Indefinite Past

Grammar in Context

BEFORE YOU READ

🎧 *What do you think the article is about? Would you like to do the things in the photos? Why or why not? Read the article.*

Been There? Done That? Maybe it's time for something new… (or maybe not!)

by Rosa García

Today's world is getting smaller. People are traveling the globe in record numbers. They**'ve been** to Rome. They**'ve seen** the ancient pyramids of Egypt. They**'ve gone** skiing in the Swiss Alps. Now, they're looking for new places to see and new things to do. They want adventure. *Travel Today* **has just come out** with its annual survey. As part of the survey, the magazine asks its readers the following question: "What would you like to do that you**'ve never done** before?"

Here are some of their answers:

I**'ve made** several trips to Egypt, but I**'ve never ridden** a camel. I'd like to do that some day.

Hot-air ballooning! My boyfriend **has tried** this several times, but I**'ve never done** it.

I**'ve ice skated** and I**'ve climbed** mountains, but I**'ve never been** ice climbing. That's something I'd definitely like to try!

Moving along.
Camel safari in the desert

Up, up, and away!
Hot-air ballooning over Turkey

Work or play?
Ice climbing in the USA

These are just a few activities that travelers can choose from today. All you need is time, money (a lot of it!), and a sense of adventure. But you don't have to go to a faraway place in an unusual type of transportation to have a great vacation! **Have** you **ever spent** the day walking in the woods or **watched** the sun set over the ocean? These can be wonderful adventures too! And a lot more affordable!

AFTER YOU READ

Which activities have the readers of Travel Today *tried? Check them.*

☐ **1.** skiing in the Alps   ☐ **4.** ice skating

☐ **2.** riding a camel   ☐ **5.** mountain climbing

☐ **3.** hot-air ballooning   ☐ **6.** ice climbing

Grammar Presentation

PRESENT PERFECT: INDEFINITE PAST

Statements			
Subject	*Have (not)*	**Past Participle**	
They	**have (not)**	**visited**	Egypt.
She	**has (not)**	**been**	there.

See page 183 in Unit 16 for a complete presentation of present perfect forms.

Statements with Adverbs					
Subject	*Have (not)*	**Adverb**	**Past Participle**		**Adverb**
They	**have**	*never* *just* *recently*	**visited**	Egypt.	
She	**has**		**been**	there.	
They	**have (not)**		**visited**	Egypt	*twice.* *lately.* *recently.*
She	**has (not)**		**been**	there	

Yes / No Questions				
Have	**Subject**	*(Ever)*	**Past Participle**	
Have	they	*(ever)*	**visited**	Egypt?
Has	she		**been**	there?

Short Answers			
Affirmative		**Negative**	
Yes,	they **have.**	**No,**	they **haven't.**
	she **has.**		she **hasn't.**

Wh- Questions				
Wh- Word	*Have*	**Subject**	**Past Participle**	
How often	**have**	they	**visited**	Egypt?
	has	she	**been**	there?

GRAMMAR NOTES	EXAMPLES

1. Use the **present perfect** to talk about things that happened at an **indefinite time** in the past.

You can use the present perfect when you <u>don't know</u> when something happened or when the specific time is <u>not important</u>.

- They**'ve traveled** to Egypt.
  (You don't know exactly when.)

- We**'ve been** to Rome.
  (The specific time isn't important.)

2. Use the **present perfect** with **adverbs** like *twice* or *often* to talk about <u>repeated actions</u> at some indefinite time in the past.

Adverbs such as *twice* and expressions such as *many times* usually go at the <u>end of the sentence</u>.

Adverbs of frequency such as *always*, *often*, and *never* usually go <u>before the past participle</u>.

- They**'ve visited** Rome *twice*.
- We**'ve** *often* **stayed** at that hotel.

- I**'ve stayed** there *many times*.

- I**'ve** *always* **stayed** there.

3. You can use *ever* with the **present perfect** to ask <u>questions</u>. It means *at any time up until the present*.

Use *never* to <u>answer negatively</u>.

A: **Have** you *ever* **been** to Rome?

B: **No**, I**'ve** *never* **been** there.   OR
No, *never*.

4. Use the **present perfect** with *just*, *lately*, and *recently* to emphasize that something happened in the <u>very recent</u> (but still indefinite) <u>past</u>.

- *Just* goes <u>before</u> the past participle.
- *Lately* goes at the <u>end</u> of the sentence.
- *Recently* can go <u>before</u> the past participle or at the <u>end</u> of the sentence.

USAGE NOTE: In American English, people often use *just* and *recently* with the <u>simple past</u>.

- I**'ve** *just* **gotten** back from China.
- They **haven't been** there *lately*.
- He**'s** *recently* **flown** a lot.   OR
  He**'s flown** a lot *recently*.

- I *just* **got** back from China.

Reference Note
For a list of **irregular past participles**, see Appendix 1 on page A-1.

Focused Practice

1 | DISCOVER THE GRAMMAR

*Read the first sentence. Then decide if the second sentence is **True (T)** or **False (F)**.*

1. Adventure vacations have become very popular.

____T____ They are popular now.

2. I have never been to the Himalayas.

_____ I went to the Himalayas a long time ago.

3. I've just returned from China.

_____ I was in China a short time ago.

4. Greg asks you, "Have you ever been to Costa Rica?"

_____ Greg wants to know when you were in Costa Rica.

5. Marta asks you, "Have you read any good travel books lately?"

_____ Marta wants to know about a travel book you read last year.

6. We have visited Egypt several times.

_____ This is not our first visit to Egypt.

2 | INTERVIEW

Grammar Notes 1–4

🎧 *Complete this interview between* Travel Today **(TT)** *and travel writer Rosa García* **(RG).** *Use the present perfect form of the verbs in parentheses. Use contractions when possible.*

TT: As a travel writer, you _____'ve visited_____ many places. Any favorites?
　　　　　　　　　　　　　　　　1. (visit)

RG: Thailand. It's a beautiful, amazing country. I _____ there five times, and I can't
　　　　　　　　　　　　　　　　　　　　　　　　　2. (be)

wait to go back.

TT: What _____ your most unusual travel experience?
　　　　　　　　3. (be)

RG: My *most* unusual? I _____ so many! I _____ near sharks
　　　　　　　　　　　　　　4. (have)　　　　　　　　　5. (swim)

(in a cage, of course!), I _____ dinner next to an active volcano,
　　　　　　　　　　　　　　6. (eat)

I _____ in an ice hotel in Finland . . .
　　　7. (sleep)

TT: The world _____ a lot smaller. There are fewer and fewer "undiscovered"
　　　　　　　　　8. (become)

places. _____ you ever _____ a really great place and decided not to tell
　　　　　　　　　　　　　　9. (find)

your readers about it?

(continued)

RG: No. I _____ about doing that a few times, but I _____ never

     10. (think)

_____ a place secret. I _____ always _____ about it.

    11. (keep)   12. (write)

TT: Where _____ you just _____ back from?

                              13. (come)

RG: I _____ just _____ from a hot-air ballooning trip in Australia.

                  14. (return)

    It was really fantastic.

TT: Where are you going next?

RG: On an African safari! I _____ never _____ on one, and I'm really excited.

                                    15. (go)

TT: Good luck! I look forward to your African safari article.

3 | SURVEY

Grammar Note 1

*Look at the survey. Then write sentences about things Andy **has done** and things he **hasn't done**. Use contractions when possible.*

Travel Time Survey

Name: _____Andy Cheng_____

Have you ever done the following activities?
Check the ones you have done.

1. rent a car ☐
2. rent a motorcycle ☑
3. ride a camel ☐
4. jump out of an airplane with a parachute ☑
5. go up in a hot-air balloon ☑
6. spend time on a desert island ☐
7. eat some really unusual food ☑
8. take photos of wild animals up close ☐
9. cross the Andes on horseback ☐
10. sail a boat on the Nile River ☑
11. swim with dolphins in the ocean ☑
12. be on a safari ☐
13. fly around the world ☐
14. go on an organized trip ☐

1. *He hasn't rented a car.* OR *He's never rented a car.*

2. *He's rented a motorcycle.*

3. _____

4. _____

5. _____

6. _____

7. _____

8. _____

9. _____

10. _____

11. _____

12. _____

13. _____

14. _____

4 | FIRST TIME UP

Grammar Notes 1–4

🎧 *Complete this conversation with the words in parentheses and the present perfect form of the verbs. Include short answers. Use contractions when possible.*

EVAN: Hot-air ballooning! What's it like? *I've never done this before* _____!
        1. (I / never / do / this / before)

ANDY: You'll love it. _____ a few times,
                              2. (I / go up)

      but _____.
                  3. (I / not do / it / lately)

EVAN: _____?
            4. (you / travel / a lot)

ANDY: Yes, _____. I'm a travel writer, so it's part of my job.
              5.

EVAN: That's great! _____ on a safari?
                          6. (you / ever / be)

ANDY: No, _____, but _____.
            7.   8. (I / always / want / to go)

EVAN: Me too. _____.
                  9. (I / be / to Africa / several times)

      In fact, _____ back from a trip there.
                    10. (I / just / get)

      But _____ on a safari.
                11. (I / never / be)

ANDY: Look. _____ getting the balloon ready.
                  12. (They / just / finish)

      It's time to go up!

5 | SOUVENIRS

Look at some of Rosa's things. Write sentences using the present perfect form of the verbs in the box.

be	ride	see	stay	travel	write

1. _____ *She's been to Egypt twice.* _____

2. _____

3. _____

4. _____

5. _____

6. _____

6 | EDITING

Read these comments found on a hot-air ballooning website. There are twelve mistakes in the use of the present perfect and adverbs. The first mistake is already corrected. Find and correct eleven more.

---

upandaway.com

We ~~has~~ *have* received many comments from our clients. We'd like to share some with you.

Comments

I have always be afraid of heights. But after I saw the beautiful photos on your website, I knew I had to go hot-air ballooning! This have been one of the best experiences of my life. Thank you!

Britta Kessler, Germany

We've returned just from the best vacation we've ever have. I've told all my friends about your company.

James Hudson, Canada

I've always wanted to go up in a hot-air balloon. I was not disappointed!

Antonio Vega, Mexico

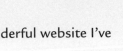

I just gotten my photos back! Fantastic!

Bill Hampton, USA

I've never went hot-air ballooning, but after visiting your wonderful website I've decided to sign up!

Amalia Lopes, Brazil

We gave our parents a balloon trip as an anniversary gift. They've just wrote to say it was fantastic. They've ever been very adventurous, but now they want to go rafting!

Pat Calahan, Ireland

You have ever seen the face of a kid on a hot-air balloon ride? The cost of the ride: a lot. That look on her face: priceless!

Lydia Hassan, New Zealand

I broke my leg last month, so I haven't lately been able to do sports—boring! Your mountain balloon trip has just gave me a lift—in more than one way!

May Roa, Philippines

Communication Practice

7 | LISTENING

🎧 *Olivia is talking to a travel agent about different vacation possibilities. Look at the choices below. Listen to the conversation. Then listen again and check the activities she's done before. Then circle the number of the best vacation choice for her.*

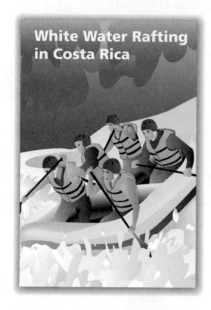

White Water Rafting in Costa Rica

1. ☑

Shark Diving in South Africa

2. ☐

Snow Mobiling in Canada

3. ☐

Relaxing on a Desert Island

4. ☐

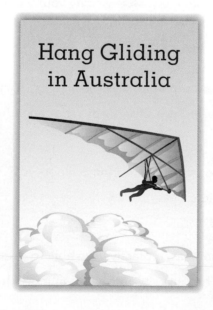

Hang Gliding in Australia

5. ☐

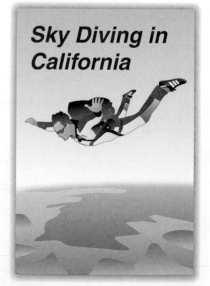

Sky Diving in California

6. ☐

8 | HAVE YOU EVER?

Ask your classmates questions. Find out how many people have ever done any of the following things. Add four more activities. When someone answers yes, *ask more questions. Get the stories behind the answers. Share your answers and stories with the class.*

- ride a horse
- take a long trip by car
- climb a mountain
- swim in a river
- sail a boat
- go camping
- _____
- _____
- _____
- _____

Example: A: Have you ever ridden a horse?
   B: Yes, I have. I was visiting a friend . . .

9 | WRITING

Read this quote. Then write a paragraph that answers the questions below.

"My favorite thing is to go where I've never been."
   Diane Arbus (1923–1971, photographer, USA)

What does Arbus mean? Do you feel the same way? Where have you been? Where have you never been that you would like to go?

Example: I've read the quote by Diane Arbus. I think it means . . .

10 | ON THE INTERNET

Do a search on **adventure vacation**. *Describe some of the activities you find. Have you ever done any of them? Would you like to try one? Why or why not?*

Example: I've never been on an African safari, but I'd like to go on one. I love animals . . .

Grammar in Context

BEFORE YOU READ

🎧 *What do you think a "commuter marriage" is? What is happening in the cartoon? How do you think the people feel? Read the excerpt from an article in* Modern Day *magazine.*

LIFESTYLES

Commuter Marriages

Many modern marriages are finding interesting solutions to difficult problems. Take Joe and Maria Tresante, for example. Joe and Maria **married** in June 2000. They **lived** in Detroit for three years. Then in 2003 Joe, a college professor, **got** a great job offer in Los Angeles. At the same time, Maria's company **moved** to Boston. They are still married, but they **have lived** apart ever since. They **have decided** to travel back and forth between Boston and Los Angeles until one of them finds a different job. Sociologists call this kind of marriage a "commuter marriage." "It **hasn't been** easy," says Maria. "Last month I **saw** Joe three times, but this month I**'ve** only **seen** him once."

It also **hasn't been** inexpensive. In addition to the cost of frequent air flights, their phone bills **have gone up**. Last month, they **started** to communicate more by e-mail with the hope of lowering their expenses.

Is all this trouble and expense worth it? "Yes," says the couple. "It **was** a difficult decision, but so far it **has worked out** for us. It's better for us both to have jobs that we like." The Tresantes **have had to** work hard to make their marriage succeed, but the effort **has paid off**. The couple notes, "We**'ve been** geographically separated, but we**'ve grown** closer emotionally."

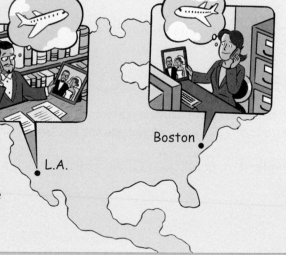

Boston

L.A.

AFTER YOU READ

Read the statements. Check **True** *or* **False**.

	True	False
1. Joe and Maria used to live in Detroit.	☐	☐
2. They are now living together in Los Angeles.	☐	☐
3. They are happy with their marriage.	☐	☐
4. It costs a lot to live apart.	☐	☐
5. Joe and Maria communicate by e-mail.	☐	☐

Grammar Presentation

PRESENT PERFECT AND SIMPLE PAST

Present Perfect
She **has been** here since 2003.
They**'ve lived** here for 20 years.
We**'ve spoken** once today.
He **hasn't flown** this month.
Has she **called** him today?

Simple Past
She **was** in Detroit in 2000.
They **lived** there for 10 years.
We **spoke** twice yesterday.
She **didn't fly** last month.
Did she **call** him yesterday?

GRAMMAR NOTES

EXAMPLES

1. Use the **present perfect** to talk about things that started in the past, <u>continue up to the present</u>, and may continue into the future.

Use the **simple past** to talk about things that happened in the past and have <u>no connection to the present</u>.

* They **have lived** apart for the past three years.
(They started living apart three years ago and are still living apart.)

* They **lived** together in Detroit for three years.
(They lived in Detroit until 2003. They no longer live in Detroit.)

(continued)

2. Use the **present perfect** to talk about things that happened at an <u>indefinite time</u> in the past.

Use the **simple past** to talk about things that happened at a <u>specific time</u> in the past. The exact time is known and sometimes stated.

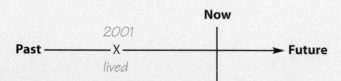

▶ **BE CAREFUL!** Do not use the present perfect with a specific point in time. The only exception is with *since*.

- They **have decided** to travel back and forth.
  (We don't know exactly when the decision was made, or the time of the decision is not important.)

- They **lived** in Detroit *in 2001*.

- I **lived** in Detroit *in 2002*.
  NOT <s>I've lived</s> in Detroit in 2002.
- **I've lived** in Detroit *since 2002*.

---

3. Use the **present perfect** to talk about things that have happened in a time period that is <u>not finished</u>, such as *today, this morning, this month, this year*.

Use the **simple past** to talk about things that happened in a time period that is <u>finished</u>, such as *yesterday, last month, last year*.

▶ **BE CAREFUL!** Some time expressions such as *this morning*, *this month*, or *this year* can refer to an <u>unfinished or finished</u> time period. Use the present perfect if the time period is unfinished. Use the simple past if the time period is finished.

- He **'s called** three times *today*.
  (Today isn't finished, and it's possible that he'll call again.)

- He **called** three times *yesterday*.
  (Yesterday is finished.)

- It's 10:00 A.M. She **'s had** three cups of coffee *this morning*.
  (The morning isn't finished.)
- It's 1:00 P.M. She **had** three cups of coffee *this morning*.
  (The morning is finished.)

Reference Notes
For the **simple past**, see Unit 3.
For the **present perfect** with *since* and *for*, see Unit 16.
For the **present perfect** for **indefinite past**, see Unit 18.
For a list of **irregular verbs**, see Appendix 1 on page A-1.

Focused Practice

1 | DISCOVER THE GRAMMAR

*Read the information about Joe and Maria. Then circle the letter of the sentence (**a** or **b**) that best describes the situation.*

1. It's 2005. Joe's family moved to Houston in 1995. They still live there.
   a. Joe's family lived in Houston for 10 years.
   b. Joe's family has lived in Houston for 10 years.

2. Last year Joe and Maria enjoyed their vacation in Canada.
   a. They had a good time.
   b. They've had a good time.

3. Joe is telling his friend about his present job. His friend asks,
   a. "How long were you there?"
   b. "How long have you been there?"

4. Joe is telling Maria that the weather in Los Angeles has been too hot for the past five days.
   a. The weather is uncomfortable now.
   b. The weather is comfortable now.

5. Joe studied the piano for 10 years, but he doesn't play anymore.
   a. Joe has played the piano for 10 years.
   b. Joe played the piano for 10 years.

6. Maria wants to move to Los Angeles from Boston, but she must find a job first.
   She is interviewing for a job in Los Angeles. She says,
   a. "I lived in Boston for two years."
   b. "I've lived in Boston for two years."

7. This month Maria and Joe have met once in Boston and once in Los Angeles.
   They will meet once more in New York.
   a. They've seen each other twice this month.
   b. They saw each other twice this month.

8. Maria's mother visited Maria in Boston. When she got home, she wrote,
   a. "It was a great visit."
   b. "It has been a great visit."

9. Maria and Joe haven't e-mailed each other this week.
   a. Joe's computer was broken.
   b. Joe's computer has been broken.

2 | IT HASN'T BEEN EASY

Complete this entry in Maria's journal. Circle the correct verb forms.

Thursday, September 28

It's 8:00 P.M. It (**'s been**)/ was a hard day, and it's not over yet! I still have to work on that
1.

report. I **'ve begun / began** it last night, but so far I **'ve written / wrote** only two pages. And it's due
2.   3.

tomorrow! Work **has been / was** so difficult lately. I **'ve worked / worked** late every night this
4.   5.

week. I feel exhausted and I **haven't gotten / didn't get** much sleep last night. And, of course, I
6.

miss Joe. Even though I **'ve seen / saw** him last week, it seems like a long time ago. This commuter
7.

relationship is beginning to get me down. We **'ve lived / lived** apart for too long. Oh, there's the
8.

phone. I hope it's Joe.

3 | PHONE CONVERSATION

⌒ *Complete the phone conversation between Maria and Joe. Use the present perfect or
the simple past form of the verbs in parentheses.*

JOE: Hi, hon! How _____*was*_____ your day? I bet you're glad it's over.
                              1. (be)

MARIA: I'm OK—a little tired. I only _____ a few hours last night. I'm
                                            2. (sleep)

   writing this big report, and I _____ worrying about it all week.
                                        3. (not stop)

JOE: You _____ tired for weeks. You need to relax a little. Listen—
          4. (be)

   why don't I come see you this weekend? We _____ each other
                                                    5. (see)

   only twice this month.

MARIA: Sounds great, but remember the last time you _____?
                                                          6. (come)

   I _____ any work, and I still _____.
        7. (not do)   8. (not catch up)

JOE: I understand. Now, why don't you have a cup of coffee and relax?

MARIA: Coffee! You're kidding! I _____ five cups today. And yesterday
                                      9. (already have)

   I _____ at least six. I can't drink another drop.
        10. (drink)

JOE: You _____ a rough week. Try to get some sleep.
          11. (have)

MARIA: I can't go to sleep yet. I _____ my report, and it's due tomorrow.
                                        12. (not finish)

JOE: Well, I hope it goes fast. Good night, hon. I'll call you tomorrow.

MARIA: Bye honey. Speak to you tomorrow.

4 | CHANGES

Grammar Notes 1–2

Joe and Maria met in the 1990s. Since then Joe has changed. Use the words below and write down how Joe has changed.

In the 1990s	**Since then**
1. have / long hair	wear his hair / very short
2. be / clean shaven	grow / a beard
3. be / heavy	lose / weight
4. be / a student	become / a professor
5. live / in a dormitory	buy / a house
6. be / single	get / married

1. *In the 1990s Joe had long hair.*

   Since then, he has worn his hair very short.

2. _____

   _____

3. _____

   _____

4. _____

   _____

5. _____

   _____

6. _____

   _____

5 | AN INTERVIEW

Grammar Notes 1–3

Read the magazine article on page 212 again. Imagine that you wrote the article. You asked Joe and Maria questions to get your information. What were they? Use the words in parentheses and write the questions.

1. (How long / be married)

   How long have you been married?

2. (How long / live in Detroit)

   _____

(continued)

3. (When / get a job offer)

_____

4. (When / your company move)

_____

5. (How long / live apart)

_____

6. (How often / see each other last month)

_____

7. (How often / see each other this month)

_____

8. (When / start to communicate by e-mail)

_____

6 | EDITING

Read this entry from Maria's journal. There are eight mistakes in the use of the present perfect and the simple past. The first mistake is already corrected. Find and correct seven more.

    I've just finished reading a fascinating article about Felicia Mabuza-Suttle.
Actually, ~~I read~~ I've read several articles about her this year. She's a very famous
international businesswoman and talk-show host in South Africa. Guess what! We
have something in common! She and her husband had a "commuter marriage" for
more than 15 years, and they are still happily married! She lives in Johannesburg,
South Africa; he lives in Atlanta, Georgia. That's a whole ocean apart! They have
met in the 1970s. In the first 10 years of their marriage they have lived in more
than 10 cities. Then, in the early 1990s she has returned to South Africa to help
her country. It wasn't an easy life, but they both feel it's been very worthwhile.

    Their situation makes our problems seem not that bad. Joe and I are only
3,000 miles apart, and we have managed to see each other a lot since we left
Detroit. But, to be honest, I have been happier when we have lived together in
Detroit. I hope we can live together again someday soon.

Communication Practice

7 | LISTENING

🎧 *A school newspaper is interviewing two college professors. Listen to the interview. Then listen again and check the items that are now true.*

The professors _____.

☑ **1.** are married

☐ **2.** live in different cities

☐ **3.** are at the same university

☐ **4.** live in Boston

☐ **5.** are in Austin

☐ **6.** have a house

8 | SOME NUMBERS

Look at the chart. Work in pairs and discuss the information. Use the words in the box.

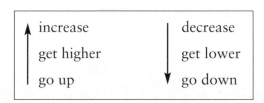

increase	decrease
get higher	get lower
go up	go down

Marriage Statistics for the United States				
	1980	**1990**	**1995**	**2000**
Number of marriages	2,406,700	2,448,000	2,336,000	2,329,000
Number of divorces	1,182,000	1,175,000	1,169,000	1,155,000
Percentage of men (20–24) never married	68.8%	79.7%	80.7%	83.7%
Percentage of women (20–24) never married	50.2%	64.1%	66.7%	72.8%
Average age of first marriage: men women	24.7 22.0	26.1 23.9	26.9 24.5	26.8 25.1

Example: **A:** The number of marriages has decreased since 1980.
B: That's right. In 1980 there were 2,406,700 marriages. And in 2000 there were 2,329,000.

9 | A COUNTRY YOU KNOW WELL

Work in small groups. Tell your classmates about some changes in a country you know well.

Example: In 2004, a new president took office. Since then, the economy has improved.

10 | LOOKING BACK

Work in pairs. Look at Maria's records from last year and this year. It's now the end of August. Compare what Maria did last year with what she's done this year.

LAST YEAR					
January	**February**	**March**	**April**	**May**	**June**
• business trip to N.Y. • L.A. – 2X	• L.A. – 2X • 1 seminar	• business trip to N.Y. • L.A. – 1X	• L.A. – 3X • 1 lecture	• 10 vacation days • Jay's wedding	• 2 seminars • L.A. – 2X
July	**August**	**September**	**October**	**November**	**December**
• L.A. – 1X • Sue's wedding	• L.A. – 1X	• L.A. – 2X • 1 lecture	• business trip to Little Rock	• 1 seminar	• 10 vacation days

THIS YEAR					
January	**February**	**March**	**April**	**May**	**June**
• L.A. – 1X	• business trip to N.Y. • 1 lecture	• L.A. – 1X • Nan's wedding	• L.A. – 1X	• business trip to Miami • L.A. – 1X	• 5 vacation days • 1 seminar
July	**August**	**September**	**October**	**November**	**December**
• Barry's wedding	• L.A. – 1X • 1 lecture				

Example: A: Last year she went on three business trips.
B: So far this year she's only gone on two.

11 | WRITING

How has your family changed in the last five years? Write a paragraph about some of the changes. Use the present perfect and the simple past.

> **Example:** Five years ago, all my brothers and sisters lived at home. Since then, we have all moved away . . .

12 | ON THE INTERNET

*Do a search on **Felicia Mabuza-Suttle**. What has she accomplished? What degrees has she gotten? What awards has she received? When did she receive them? Write about her. Use the present perfect and the simple past.*

> **Example:** Felicia Mabuza-Suttle has been a talk-show host in South Africa for many years . . .

Grammar in Context

BEFORE YOU READ

🎧 *Look at the key facts about African elephants. Why do you think the elephant population has changed so much? Look at the map of Africa. What parts of Africa have elephants? Professor Jane Owen has been studying elephants for several decades. Read the excerpt from her latest article in* Science Today.

AFRICAN ELEPHANTS

AFRICA

Jane Owen, Ph.D.

HABITAT

Elephants and their ancestors **have been living** on this planet for 5 million years. Scientists **have found** their bones in many places, including Europe and the Americas. Present-day African elephants **have** also **survived** in different kinds of environments, including very dry areas in Niger, grasslands in East Africa, and forests in West Africa.

KEY FACTS

Largest Size

Height: 13 feet	**Trunk:** 40 pounds
Length: 25 feet	**Tusks:** 11 feet
Weight: 8 tons	**Tail:** 4 feet

Life Span
60–65 years

Estimated Population

1979: 1,300,000	**1997:** 650,000
1989: 600,000	**2003:** 435,000

ELEPHANTS AND HUMANS

Because of their great size and strength, elephants **have** always **fascinated** humans. Our fascination **has caused** African elephants to become almost extinct. Poachers (illegal hunters) **have killed** hundreds of thousands of elephants for the ivory of their tusks. After 1989 it became illegal to sell ivory. The elephant population grew after that, but recently it **has been dropping** again. According to recent reports, many governments **have lost** control of poachers. At present, there may be only 400,000 African elephants left.

AFTER YOU READ

Read the statements. Check **True** *or* **False**.

	True	False
1. There were elephants on Earth 5 million years ago.	☐	☐
2. All elephants live in grasslands.	☐	☐
3. Poachers killed hundreds of thousands of elephants before 1989.	☐	☐
4. The number of elephants is increasing.	☐	☐

Grammar Presentation

PRESENT PERFECT PROGRESSIVE AND PRESENT PERFECT

PRESENT PERFECT PROGRESSIVE

Statements				
Subject	*Have* (*not*)	*Been*	Base Form of Verb + *-ing*	(*Since / For*)
I You* We They	**have** (**not**)	**been**	**writing**	(**since** 2004). (**for** years).
He She It	**has** (**not**)			

*You is both singular and plural.

Yes / No Questions				
Have	Subject	*Been*	Base Form of Verb + *-ing*	(*Since / For*)
Have	you	**been**	**writing**	(**since** 2004)? (**for** years)?
Has	he			

Short Answers						
Affirmative			Negative			
Yes,	I / we	**have.**	**No,**	I / we	**haven't.**	
	he	**has.**		he	**hasn't.**	

Wh- Questions				
Wh- Word	*Have*	Subject	*Been*	Base Form of Verb + *-ing*
How long	**have**	you	**been**	**writing**?
	has	he		

(continued)

PRESENT PERFECT PROGRESSIVE AND PRESENT PERFECT

Present Perfect Progressive
They **have been living** here for 5 million years.
I**'ve been reading** this book since Monday.
Dr. Owen **has been writing** articles since 1990.
She**'s been working** in Niger for a year.

Present Perfect
They **have lived** here for 5 million years.
I**'ve read** two books about elephants.
Dr. Owen **has written** many articles.
She**'s worked** in many countries.

GRAMMAR NOTES

EXAMPLES

1. The **present perfect progressive** often shows that something is <u>unfinished</u>. It started in the past and is still continuing. The emphasis is on the <u>continuation</u> of the action.

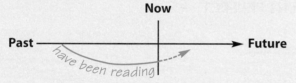

- I**'ve been reading** a book about elephants. *(I'm still reading it.)*
- She**'s been writing** an article. *(She's still writing it.)*

The **present perfect** often shows that something is <u>finished</u>. The emphasis is on the <u>result</u> of the action.

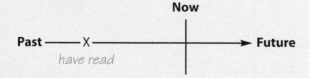

- I**'ve read** a book about elephants. *(I finished the book.)*
- She**'s written** an article. *(She finished the article.)*

▶ BE CAREFUL! **Non-action verbs** are not usually used in the progressive.

- I**'ve had** a headache all day. NOT I've been having a headache all day.

2. We often use the **present perfect progressive** to talk about <u>how long</u> something has been happening.

- I**'ve been reading** books about elephants *for two months*.

We often use the **present perfect** to talk about:

- <u>how much</u> someone has done
- <u>how many things</u> someone has done
- <u>how many times</u> someone has done something

- I**'ve read** *a lot* about it.
- She**'s written** *three* articles.
- I**'ve read** that book *twice*.

3. Sometimes you can use either the **present perfect progressive** or the **present perfect**. The meaning is basically the same. This is especially true with verbs such as *live*, *study*, *teach*, and *work* with *for* or *since*.	• She**'s been studying** African elephants *for* three years. OR • She**'s studied** African elephants *for* three years. *(In both cases, she is still studying them.)*
USAGE NOTES We often use the **present perfect progressive** to show that something is <u>temporary</u>. We use the **present perfect** to show that something is <u>permanent</u>.	• They**'ve been living** here *since* 1995, but they are moving next month. • They**'ve lived** here *since* they were children. They've always lived here.

Reference Notes

For a list of **non-action verbs**, see Appendix 2 on page A-2.
For use of the **present perfect** with *since* and *for*, see Unit 16 on page 184.

Focused Practice

1 | DISCOVER THE GRAMMAR

Read the first sentence. Then decide if the second sentence is **True (T)** *or* **False (F)**.

1. Professor Owen has been reading a book about African wildlife.

  _F_   She finished the book.

2. She's read a book about African wildlife.

  _____   She finished the book.

3. She's written a magazine article about the rain forest.

  _____   She finished the article.

4. She's been waiting for some supplies.

  _____   She received the supplies.

5. They've lived in Uganda since 1992.

  _____   They are still in Uganda.

6. They've been living in Uganda since 1992.

  _____   They are still in Uganda.

7. We've been discussing environmental problems with the leaders of many countries.

  _____   The discussions are probably over.

8. We've discussed these problems with many leaders.

  _____   The discussions are probably over.

2 | PROFESSOR OWEN'S WORK
Grammar Notes 1–3

Complete these statements. Circle the correct form of the verbs. In some cases, both forms are correct.

1. Professor Owen is working on two articles for the next issue of *National Wildlife* magazine. She has written / has been writing these articles since Monday.

2. *National Wildlife* magazine has published / has been publishing its annual report on the environment. It is an excellent report.

3. More than 500 African elephants have already died / have been dying this year.

4. Professor Owen has given / has been giving many talks about elephants in past lecture series.

5. She has spoken / has been speaking at our school many times.

6. Congress has created / has been creating a new study group to discuss the problem of endangered animals. The group has already met twice.

7. The new group has a lot of work to do. Lately, the members have studied / have been studying the problem of the spotted owl.

8. Professor Owen was late for a meeting with the members of Congress. When she arrived the chairperson said, "At last, you're here. We have waited / have been waiting for you."

9. Professor Owen has lived / has been living in Kenya for the last two years, but she will return to the United States in January.

10. She has worked / has been working with environmentalists in Kenya and Tanzania.

3 | WHAT'S BEEN HAPPENING?
Grammar Note 1

Compare these two pictures of Professor Jane Owen.

Complete the sentences describing what is going on in the pictures. Use the present perfect progressive form of the verbs in parentheses. Choose between affirmative and negative forms.

1. She _____*'s been working*_____ in her office.
   (work)

2. She _____ an elephant in the field.
   (follow)

3. She _____ an article.
   (write)

4. She _____ the newspaper.
   (read)

5. She _____ coffee.
   (drink)

6. She _____ tea.
   (drink)

7. She _____ her sandwich.
   (eat)

8. She _____ TV.
   (watch)

9. She _____ hard.
   (work)

10. It _____ all day.
   (rain)

4 | GRANDDAD

Grammar Notes 1–3

Complete this entry from Professor Owen's field journal. Use the present perfect progressive or the present perfect form of the verbs in parentheses.

We _____*'ve been hearing*_____ about Granddad since we arrived here in Amboseli Park.
1. (hear)

He is one of the last "tuskers." Two days ago, we finally saw him. His tusks are more than seven

feet long. I _____ never _____ anything like them.
2. (see)

Granddad _____ here for more than 60 years. He
3. (live)

_____ everything, and he _____ countless threats from
4. (experience)   5. (survive)

human beings. Young men _____ their courage against him, and poachers
6. (test)

_____ him for his ivory. His experience and courage
7. (hunt)

_____ him so far.
8. (save)

For the last two days, Granddad _____ slowly through the tall grass.
9. (move)

He _____ and _____. Luckily, it _____
10. (eat)   11. (rest)   12. (rain)

a lot this year, and even the biggest elephants _____ enough food and water.
13. (find)

Watching this elephant _____ an incredible experience. I hope he is still
14. (be)

here when we come back next year!

5 | HOW LONG AND HOW MUCH?

Grammar Note 2

Professor Owen is doing fieldwork in Africa. Imagine you are about to interview her. Use the words below to ask her questions. Use her notes to complete her answers. Choose between the present perfect progressive and the present perfect.

FIELD NOTES
3/23/05

GRANDDAD
　　Order: *Proboscidea*
　　Family: *Elephantidae*
　　Genus and Species: *Loxodonta africana*

• eats about 500 pounds of vegetation/day
• drinks about 40 gallons of water at a time
• walks 5 miles/hour (50 miles/day)

1. (How long / you / observe / Granddad)

   YOU: *How long have you been observing Granddad?* _____

   OWEN: *I've been observing him for* _____ two days.

2. (How much vegetation / he / eat)

   YOU: _____

   OWEN: _____

3. (How often / he / stop for water)

   YOU: _____

   OWEN: _____ four times.

4. (How much water / he / drink)

   YOU: _____

   OWEN: _____

5. (How long / he / walk today)

   YOU: _____

   OWEN: _____ nine hours.

6. (How far / he / travel today)

   YOU: _____

   OWEN: _____

6 | EDITING

Read this student's journal entry. There are eight mistakes in the use of the present perfect progressive and the present perfect. The first mistake is already corrected. Find and correct seven more.

> studying
> This year in class we've been ~~studied~~ endangered species.
> We've already been studying the panda and the tiger. Now
> we're learning about the African elephant. Elephants has been
> roaming the Earth for millions of years! I have to write a
> research paper on the topic. I've researched it on the Web
> since Monday. It's now Friday, and I haven't finished yet.
> There's so much information! I've already been reading more
> than ten articles, and I've even been ordered a book about
> endangered species. I really find this topic interesting, and I've
> been learning a lot! The paper has to be ten pages long. So far,
> I've been writing about five pages. I've been thinking about a
> title for my paper, but I haven't been deciding on one yet.

Communication Practice

7 | LISTENING

🎧 *Listen to the conversations. Then listen again and circle the letter of the pictures that illustrate the situations.*

1.

a.

b.

(continued)

2.

a.

b.

3.

a.

b.

4.

a.

b.

5.

a.

b.

8 | THINGS CHANGE

Have a class discussion. Talk about things that have changed or have been changing in your city or town. Use the present perfect progressive and the present perfect.

Example: A: Traffic has been getting worse. I've been spending a lot more time driving to class.
B: Me too. I think more and more people have been driving to work.

9 | ON THE INTERNET

These two animals have been on the World Wildlife Fund's list of the ten most endangered species. Do a search on one of them.

Arabian oryx

Monarch butterfly

Find out about its . . .

- geographic location (habitat)
- size
- habits

Learn . . .

- why it has become endangered
- what governments or other groups have been doing to save it

Now get together in small groups and discuss your findings.

10 | WRITING

Write a paragraph about one of the animals discussed in this unit. Use the topics from Exercise 9 to guide your writing.

Example: The Arabian oryx is about three feet tall. Its horns are . . .
It has become endangered because . . .

From **Grammar** to **Writing**
The Topic Sentence and Paragraph Unity

A paragraph is a group of sentences about one main idea. Writers often state the main idea in one sentence, called the topic sentence. The topic sentence is often near the beginning of the paragraph.

1 | *Read this personal statement for a job application. First cross out any sentences that do not belong in the paragraph. (Later you will choose a topic sentence.)*

Please describe your work experience.

_____
(topic sentence)

While I was in high school, I worked as a server at Darby's during the summer and on weekends. ~~Summers here are very hot and humid.~~ I worked with many different kinds of customers, and I learned to be polite even with difficult people. They serve excellent food at Darby's. I received a promotion after one year. Since high school, I have been working for Steak Hut as the night manager. I have developed management skills because I supervise six employees. One of them is a good friend of mine. I have also learned to order supplies and to plan menus. Sometimes I am very tired after a night's work.

Now choose one of the sentences below as the topic sentence, and write it as the first sentence of the paragraph.

- I feel that a high school education is necessary for anyone looking for a job.
- My restaurant experience has prepared me for a position with your company.
- Eating at both Darby's and Steak Hut in Greenville is very enjoyable.
- I prefer planning menus to any other task in the restaurant business.

2 You can use a tree diagram to develop and organize your ideas. Complete the tree diagram for the paragraph in Exercise 1.

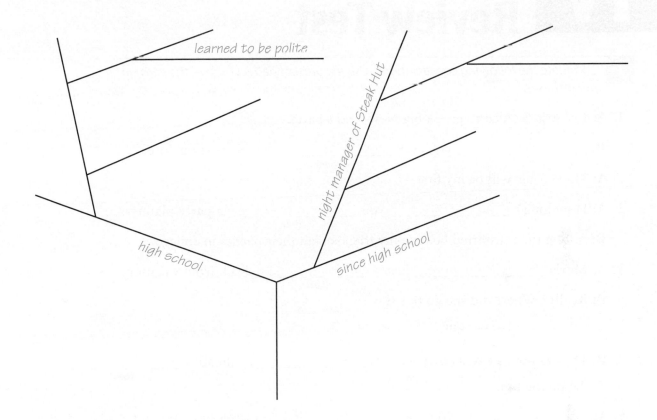

3 Before you write . . .

1. On a separate piece of paper, make a tree diagram for your accomplishments. Do not include a topic sentence.

2. Work with a small group. Look at each other's diagrams and develop a topic sentence for each one.

3. Ask and answer questions to develop more information about your accomplishments.

4 Write a personal statement about your accomplishments. Use your tree diagram as an outline.

Review Test

I *Complete the following conversations. Use the present perfect form of the verbs in parentheses.*

1. **A:** I've just decided to give a big New Year's party.

    B: _____*Have*_____ you ever _____*given*_____ a big party before?
    (give)

    A: Nope. This will be my first.

2. **A:** How long _____ you _____ a party planner?
    (be)

    B: A long time. I started helping my friends plan their parties in college.

3. **A:** Marla _____ just _____ back from vacation.
    (get)

    B: Really? Where did she go this time?

4. **A:** It's time to pay the bills.

    B: They're not as bad as they look. I _____ already _____
    (pay)
    the phone bill.

5. **A:** _____ you ever _____ a letter of complaint?
    (write)

    B: Yes, I have. I got great results.

6. **A:** Can I throw this magazine out?

    B: Not yet. Jennifer _____ it yet.
    (not read)

7. **A:** How many skating contests _____ you _____?
    (win)

    B: A lot. I've stopped counting.

8. **A:** What have you told the kids about our holiday plans?

    B: I _____ them anything yet. Let's wait until our plans are definite.
    (not tell)

9. **A:** _____ the letter carrier _____ yet?
    (come)

    B: Yes, he has. About an hour ago. You got two letters.

10. **A:** Would you like some coffee?

    B: No, thanks. I _____ three cups already.
    (have)

11. **A:** _____ you _____ a topic for your research paper?
    (choose)

    B: Yes. I'm going to write about Asian elephants.

II *Complete the conversations with **since** or **for**.*

1. **A:** What happened? I've been waiting for you ___since___ 7:00.

   B: My train broke down. I sat in the tunnel for an hour.

2. **A:** How long have you lived in San Francisco?

   B: _____ I was born. How about you?

   A: I've only been here _____ a few months.

3. **A:** When did you and Alan meet?

   B: I've known Alan _____ ages. We went to elementary school together.

4. **A:** Has Greg worked at Café Fidelio for a long time?

   B: Not too long. He's only been there _____ 2004.

5. **A:** Why didn't you answer the door? I've been standing here ringing the doorbell _____ five minutes.

   B: I didn't hear you. I was taking a shower.

6. **A:** How long have you had trouble sleeping, Mr. Yang?

   B: _____ March. It started when I moved.

7. **A:** Celia has been studying English _____ she was 10.

   B: That's why she speaks so well.

8. **A:** Did you know that Gary plans to change jobs?

   B: He's been saying that _____ the past two years. He never does anything about it.

III *Each sentence has four underlined words or phrases. The four underlined parts of the sentences are marked A, B, C, or D. Circle the letter of the one underlined word or phrase that is NOT CORRECT.*

1. I 've wanted to visit Bali since years, but I haven't been there yet.
      A   B   C   D
          A (B) C D

2. We went there last year after we have visited Japan.
      A   B   C D
          A B C D

3. Have you been living in California since a long time?
      A   B   C   D
          A B C D

4. I lived here since I got married in 1998.
     A   B   C   D
          A B C D

(continued)

5. We 've been <u>wait</u> for Chen <u>for</u> an hour, but he hasn't arrived <u>yet</u>.
    A   B   C   D

A B C D

6. Todd <u>is</u> excited right now <u>because</u> he's <u>lately</u> <u>won</u> an award.
      A   B   C D

A B C D

7. <u>It's</u> only 9:00, and <u>she already</u> <u>had</u> four cups of tea <u>this</u> morning.
    A   B   C   D

A B C D

8. I <u>'m watching</u> television <u>for</u> the last three <u>hours</u> and now I <u>feel</u>
       A   B   C   D
worried about that test tomorrow.

A B C D

9. Paz <u>been working</u> <u>for</u> Intellect <u>since</u> he <u>moved</u> to Silicon Valley.
         A   B   C   D

A B C D

10. <u>Has he moved</u> here a long time <u>ago</u>, or <u>has</u> he just <u>arrived</u>?
      A   B   C   D

A B C D

IV *Circle the letter of the correct answer to complete each sentence.*

1. _____ you ever appeared on a game show, Mr. Smith?
   - (**A**) Did
   - (**B**) Has
   - (**C**) Have
   - (**D**) Was

A B Ⓒ D

2. No, but I've _____ wanted to.
   - (**A**) ever
   - (**B**) yet
   - (**C**) don't
   - (**D**) always

A B C D

3. Why _____ you decide to try out for *Risk*?
   - (**A**) did
   - (**B**) were
   - (**C**) have
   - (**D**) are

A B C D

4. My wife _____ your show for years now.
   - (**A**) watches
   - (**B**) is watching
   - (**C**) was watching
   - (**D**) has been watching

A B C D

5. She has always _____ I should apply as a contestant.
   - (**A**) saying
   - (**B**) says
   - (**C**) said
   - (**D**) say

A B C D

6. You're a librarian. How long _____ that kind of work?
   - (**A**) did you do
   - (**B**) have you done
   - (**C**) do you do
   - (**D**) were you doing

A B C D

7. I've been a reference librarian since _____.   **A   B   C   D**

   (**A**) a long time   (**C**) 1998

   (**B**) three years   (**D**) I've graduated

8. Have you been interested in game shows since you _____ a librarian?   **A   B   C   D**

   (**A**) became   (**C**) become

   (**B**) have become   (**D**) have been becoming

9. I've only _____ them for about a year.   **A   B   C   D**

   (**A**) watching   (**C**) been watching

   (**B**) watch   (**D**) watches

10. Have you been studying the rules for the show _____ we called?   **A   B   C   D**

    (**A**) for   (**C**) since

    (**B**) when   (**D**) as soon as

11. I _____ them for weeks, but I still don't understand them.   **A   B   C   D**

    (**A**) read   (**C**) was reading

    (**B**) reading   (**D**) 've been reading

| **V** | *Complete each conversation with the correct form of the verb in parentheses. Choose between affirmative and negative forms.* |

1. (see)

   A: _____*Have*_____ you _____*seen*_____ *Day After Tomorrow* yet?

                                                     a.

   B: Yes, I have. I _____ it last night.

                          b.

2. (drink)

   A: Who _____ all the soda? We needed it for the party.

                          a.

   B: Not me. I _____ any soda at all since last week. I _____

                          b.   **c.**

   water all week. It's much healthier.

3. (write)

   A: Susan Jackson _____ a lot of travel books lately.

                                       a.

   B: _____ she _____ *Rafting in Costa Rica*?

                                         b.

   A: Yes, she did. She _____ that one about five years ago.

                             c.

(continued)

4. (cook)

A: You _____ for hours. When are we eating dinner?
   a.

B: I just finished. I _____ something special for you. It's called
   b.
   "ants on a tree."

A: Gross!

B: I _____ it for you many times before. It's just meatballs with rice.
   c.

5. (have)

A: I _____ a lot of trouble with my new car lately.
   a.

B: Really? You _____ it very long!
   b.

A: I know. I _____ it for only a year. I _____ my old car
   c.   d.
   for 10 years before I sold it. I _____ any trouble with it at all!
                                    e.

6. (look)

A: Linda _____ really discouraged yesterday afternoon.
   a.

B: I know. She _____ for an apartment and hasn't found anything yet.
   b.

A: There's an apartment available on the fourth floor in our building.

   _____ she _____ at it?
                       c.

B: She _____ at it last week, but she didn't rent it because it's too small.
   d.

VI *Find and correct the mistake in each sentence.*

      have
1. I ~~am~~ applied for the position of junior accountant in my department.

2. I have been working as a bookkeeper in this company since four years.

3. I have did a good job.

4. I have already been getting a promotion.

5. I has gained a lot of experience in retail sales.

6. In addition, I have took several accounting courses.

7. Since February my boss liked my work a lot.

8. She has gave me more and more responsibility.

9. I have already show my accounting skills.

10. This has been being a very good experience for me.

▶ *To check your answers, go to the Answer Key on page RT-3.*

PART V

Nouns and Articles: Review and Expansion

Grammar in Context

BEFORE YOU READ

🎧 *Look at the map and the photo. Where did each journey start and end? When do you think these journeys took place? Read the history text about a modern explorer's expeditions.*

WHO GOT THERE FIRST?

Was **Christopher Columbus** really the first **explorer** to discover the **Americas**? The great Norwegian **explorer Thor Heyerdahl** didn't think so. He believed that ancient **people** were able to build **boats** that could cross **oceans**.

To test his **ideas**, **Heyerdahl** decided to build a **copy** of the reed **boats** pictured in ancient Egyptian **paintings** and sail across the **Atlantic Ocean** from **North Africa** to **Barbados**. **Heyerdahl's team** also copied ancient Middle Eastern **pots** and filled them with *enough* **food** for their **journey**—dried **fish**, **honey**, **oil**, *some* **eggs** and **nuts**, and *a little* fresh **fruit**. Ra, the **expedition's boat**, carried an international **group** of **sailors** including a **Chadian**, an **Egyptian**, an **Iraqi**, a **Japanese**, a **Mexican**, and a **Norwegian**.

On **May** 25, 1969, **Ra** left **Safi** in **Morocco** and headed across the widest **part** of the **Atlantic**. The **boat** fell apart just before it reached **Barbados**, but all the **men** aboard survived and wanted to try again.

On **May** 17, 1970, **Ra II**, sailing under the **flag** of the **United Nations**, successfully crossed the **Atlantic** in 57 **days**. The **expedition** proved that ancient **civilizations** had *enough* **skill** to reach the **Americas** long before **Columbus** did.

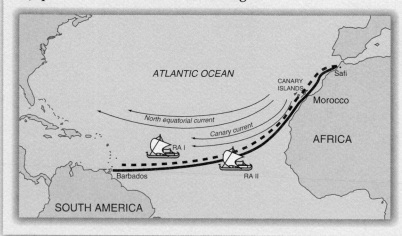

AFTER YOU READ

Read the statements. Check **True** *or* **False**.

	True	False
1. Heyerdahl believed that Columbus was the first explorer to discover the Americas.	☐	☐
2. Heyerdahl's team built a reed boat.	☐	☐
3. The team members were all from Egypt.	☐	☐
4. The first Ra expedition failed.	☐	☐
5. The second Ra expedition crossed the Pacific.	☐	☐

Grammar Presentation

NOUNS AND QUANTIFIERS

Count Nouns			
Article / Number	Noun	Verb	
A One	**sailor**	is	brave.
The Two	**sailors**	are	brave.

Non-count Nouns		
Noun	Verb	
Oil	is	necessary.
Sailing	is	dangerous.

Quantifiers and Count Nouns		
	Quantifier	Noun
I saw	*some* *enough* *a lot of*	sailors. islands. boats.
	a few *several* *many*	
I didn't see	*any* *enough* *a lot of* *many*	

Quantifiers and Non-count Nouns		
	Quantifier	Noun
I used	*some* *enough* *a lot of*	oil. salt. honey.
	a little *a great deal of* *much*	
I didn't use	*any* *enough* *a lot of* *much*	

GRAMMAR NOTES

EXAMPLES

---

1. **Proper nouns** are the <u>names</u> of particular people, places, or things. They are usually unique (there is only one).

People	Heyerdahl, Africans
Places	Egypt, the Atlantic
Months	September, October
Nationalities	Norwegian, Chinese
Seasons	spring, summer, fall, winter

<u>Capitalize</u> the first letter of proper nouns.

EXCEPTION: We often use *the* before seasons, and we usually don't capitalize the first letter.

• The second **Ra** expedition was successful.

• They arrived in **the spring**.

---

2. **Common nouns** refer to people, places, and things, but <u>not by their names</u>. For example, *explorer* is a common noun, but *Heyerdahl* is a proper noun.

People	explorer, sailor, builder
Places	continent, country, city
Things	pots, eggs, fish, honey

<u>Do not capitalize</u> the first letter of a common noun unless the noun is the first word in a sentence.

• Heyerdahl is an **explorer**.
  NOT Heyerdahl is an ~~Explorer~~.

---

3. Common nouns can be either count or non-count. **Count nouns** are people, places, or things that you can <u>count separately</u>: *one boat*, *two boats*, *three boats . . .*

• **a** sailor, **the** sailor, **two** sailors
• **an** island, **the** island, **three** islands
• **a** map, **the** map, **four** maps

• Count nouns can be <u>singular or plural</u>.
• They take <u>singular or plural verbs</u>.
• You can use *a / an* or *the* before them.

• He saw one **shark**. She saw two **sharks**.
• The **boat** *is* fine, but the **sailors** *are* sick.
• **A sailor** lives alone on **the island**.

---

4. **Non-count nouns** are things that you <u>cannot count separately</u>. For example, you can say *gold*, but you cannot say *one gold* or *two golds*.

Abstract words	courage, education, time
Activities	exploring, sailing, farming
Fields of study	geography, history
Foods	corn, chocolate, fish

Some common non-count nouns do not fit into categories.

equipment	homework	news
furniture	information	work

• Non-count nouns have <u>no plural</u> forms.
• They take <u>singular verbs and pronouns</u>.

• We usually do not use *a / an* with them.

• He had a lot of **courage**.
• **Anthropology** *is* an interesting subject.
  It *was* Heyerdahl's favorite subject.
  NOT ~~An anthropology~~ is an interesting subject.

5. Use the quantifiers *some*, *enough*, *a lot of*, and *any* with both **count nouns** and **non-count nouns**.

                     count   non-count
- We have *some* **eggs** and *some* **honey**.

                    count   non-count
- Are there *enough* **pots** and *enough* **oil**?

             count
- There were *a lot of* good **days**.

             non-count
- There was *a lot of* **danger** too.

Use *any* in <u>negative</u> sentences and <u>questions</u>.

             count
- We didn't see *any* **sharks**.

           non-count
- Is there *any* **tea** left?

---

6. Use *a few*, *several*, and *many* with **plural count nouns** in <u>affirmative</u> sentences.

- *A few* team **members** got sick.
- They experienced *several* large **storms**.
- *Many* **people** worried about them.

Use *a little*, *a great deal of*, and *much* with **non-count nouns** in <u>affirmative</u> sentences.

- They had *a little* **trouble** with the sail.
- They threw away *a great deal of* **food**.
- *Much* **planning** went into this.

USAGE NOTE: In <u>affirmative</u> sentences, *much* is very formal.

VERY FORMAL: We saw *much* **pollution**.

LESS FORMAL: We saw *a lot of* **pollution**.

▶ **BE CAREFUL!** Don't confuse *a few* and *a little* with *few* and *little*. *Few* and *little* usually mean "not enough."

- I received *a little* **news** during the voyage. (*not a lot, but enough*)
- I received *little* **news** during the voyage. (*not enough news*)

---

7. Use *many* with **count nouns** and *much* with **non-count nouns** in <u>questions</u> and <u>negative</u> sentences.

A: How *many* **ships** did they see?

B: They didn't see *many*.

USAGE NOTE: *Much* isn't formal in questions and negative sentences.

A: How *much* **water** did they carry?

B: They didn't carry *much*.

Reference Notes

For a list of **irregular plural nouns**, see Appendix 6 on page A-4.
For a list of **non-count nouns**, see Appendix 7 on page A-4.
For **categories of proper nouns**, see Appendix 8 on page A-5.
For **spelling rules** for **regular plural nouns**, see Appendix 25 on page A-11.
For **capitalization rules**, see Appendix 27 on page A-13.

Focused Practice

1 | DISCOVER THE GRAMMAR

🎧 *Uta Bremer* **(UB)** *sailed around the world alone on a small boat. Read her interview with* Adventure Travel **(AT)** *magazine. Underline the nouns.*

ADVENTURE TRAVEL

Around the World Alone

AT: It took a lot of <u>courage</u> to make this <u>journey</u>. When did you decide to sail around the world alone?

UB: When I got my boat, *Katya*, for my 19th birthday, I knew right away that I wanted to do this.

AT: When did you start?

UB: I left New York on May 15, two and a half years ago, and I headed for Panama.

AT: How far did you travel?

UB: Thirty thousand miles.

AT: How much equipment were you able to take with you?

UB: I didn't have much money, so I didn't bring many things. I used the stars to navigate by, not electronic technology.

AT: What did you eat?

UB: I bought food in different ports. I loved going to markets and learning about local cooking. And I collected water in a pot when it rained.

AT: How did you spend your time when you were sailing?

UB: At first I listened to the news a lot, but after a while I preferred music. And I did a lot of reading.

AT: What was difficult for you?

UB: The loneliness. I had my cat, Typhoon, but I missed my family.

AT: What did you like best about the trip?

UB: The sight of this harbor. I'm so glad to be back for Thanksgiving.

Write each noun in the correct column.

Proper Nouns	Common Nouns	
	Count Nouns	**Non-count Nouns**
Katya	*journey*	*courage*

2 | MAKING PLANS   *Grammar Notes 2–4*

🎧 *Megan and Jason are planning a hiking trip. Complete their conversation with the correct form of the words in parentheses. Use Appendix 7 on page A-4 for help with non-count nouns.*

JASON: There ___'s___ still a lot of ___work___ to do this evening. We have
     1. (be)   **2. (work)**

 to plan the food for the trip.

MEGAN: I've been reading this book about camping. There _____ some good
                3. (be)

 _____ about food in it.
 4. (advice)

JASON: What does it say?

MEGAN: We should bring a lot of _____ and _____.
          5. (bean)   **6. (rice)**

JASON: _____ _____ good on camping trips too.
   7. (potato)   **8. (be)**

MEGAN: Fresh _____ _____ too heavy to carry. Maybe we can get
     9. (vegetable)   **10. (be)**

 some when we pass through a town.

JASON: _____ the _____ ready? We should go over the checklist.
   11. (be)   **12. (equipment)**

MEGAN: I did that. We need some _____ for the radio.
         13. (battery)

JASON: Why do we need a radio? I thought we were running away from civilization.

MEGAN: But the _____ never _____. I still want to know what's
    14. (news)   **15. (stop)**

 happening.

JASON: That's OK with me. By the way, do we have enough warm _____? It gets
                16. (clothing)

 chilly in the mountains.

MEGAN: That's true. And the

 _____ really
 17. (cold)

 _____ me at night.
 18. (bother)

JASON: But we have warm sleeping

 _____.
 19. (bag)

3 | HAPPY CAMPERS

Complete these excerpts from a book about family camping. For each paragraph, use the quantifiers in parentheses. You will use some quantifiers more than once.

1. (a little / a few)

Try to get _____*a little*_____ exercise before a long camping trip. It will help you feel better
    a.

on the trip. _____ good stretching exercises every day will help.
    b.

_____ walking or swimming is also useful.
    c.

2. (many / a great deal of)

You will need _____ information for a long trip. Your public library has
    a.

_____ books about family camping. The National Park Service website can also
    b.

provide _____ advice.
    c.

3. (a / some) (much / many)

Making a fire is _____ skill, but it's easy to learn. You won't need
    a.

_____ practice before you can build a roaring campfire. Start with
    b.

_____ paper and leaves. Place the wood on top of these and leave spaces for air.
    c.

Don't use _____ big pieces of wood.
    d.

4. (any / enough) (How much / How many)

"There isn't _____ milk left! Who used it all?" _____ times have
    a.   b.

you heard this cry? To avoid this problem, plan your food in advance. _____
    c.

sandwiches are you going to make? _____ bread will you need? Make sure you
    d.

have _____ food and beverages before you leave.
    e.

5. (few / a few) (little / a little)

On our family's first camping trip, we had _____ equipment and almost no
    a.

experience, but we still had a lot of fun. It was a blast. We swam, we hiked, and we made new

friends. Of course, we had _____ problems, but not many. Anyway,
    b.

_____ inconvenience didn't interfere with our fun.
    c.

    Today millions of people enjoy camping. In fact, _____ campsites are
    d.

available in the summer without a reservation.

4 | EDITING

Read Uta's diary entries. There are seventeen mistakes in the use of nouns and in the use of verb and pronoun agreement. The first three mistakes are already corrected. Find and correct fourteen more.

                    Canary

October 27. I've been on the ~~canary~~ Islands for three days now. I'll start home when

          weather is

the ~~weathers are~~ better. I was so surprised when I picked up my mails today. My

family sent some birthday presents to me. My Birthday is the 31st.

october 29. I think the weather is getting worse. I heard thunders today, but there

wasn't many rain. Typhoon and I stayed in bed. I started reading <u>brave New World</u>.

October 30. I left the Canary Islands today—just like columbus. There's a strong wind

and plenty of sunshine now. I went 250 miles.

October 31. I'm 21 today. To celebrate, I drank little coffee for breakfast and I

opened my presents. I got some perfume and some pretty silver jewelries.

November 1. The electricities are low. I'd better save them until I get near land. I'll

need the radio then. It rained today, so I collected a few waters for cooking.

Communication Practice

5 | LISTENING

🎧 *Megan and Jason are planning to make cookies for their trip. Listen to them talk about the recipe. Then listen again and check the ingredients that they have enough of. Listen a third time and make a shopping list of ingredients that they need to buy.*

Ingredients

2 cups of butter	1 cup of cornflakes
✓ 3 cups of brown sugar	8 eggs
2 cups of oatmeal (uncooked)	1 cup of raisins
4 cups of flour	2 cups of chocolate chips

Shopping List

butter

_____

_____

_____

_____

6 | SHIPWRECKED!

Work with a group. Imagine that you are about to be shipwrecked near a deserted tropical island. You have room in your lifeboat for only five things. Look at the list. Decide what to take and give your reasons. Compare your choices with other groups' choices.

sugar	ax	fireworks
pasta	matches	telescope
beans	fishing equipment	compass
chocolate	radio	maps of the area
fresh water	portable TV set	a book, *Navigating by the Stars*
cooking pot	batteries	a book, *Tropical Plants You Can Eat*

Example: I think we should take a lot of beans. We might not find any food on the island.

7 | WRITING

Describe a trip that you have taken. Where did you go, and when? How long did you stay? Who went with you? What did you take along? What did you do there?

Example: Three years ago, I went to Amsterdam with my family. My father was on a short vacation, so we couldn't spend much time there . . .

8 | ON THE INTERNET

Work in groups and choose an explorer from the list below. Then individually do an Internet search for information to answer the questions. Share the information in your group.

Explorers

Ellen Ochoa   Ibn Battuta   Louise Arner Boyd   Jacques Cousteau   Zhang Qian

Questions

- Where was the explorer from?
- When did he or she live?
- What parts of the world did he or she explore?
- How did he or she travel?
- Why did he or she go?
- What were some of his or her achievements?

As a group, present your information to the class. Use maps and pictures from your research.

Example: Ellen Ochoa was the first Hispanic female astronaut.

Articles: Indefinite and Definite

Grammar in Context

BEFORE YOU READ

🎧 *Look at the pictures on this page and the next. Read the title of each story. What kind of a story do you think a fable is? Do you know a fable in your first language? Read the two fables.*

Two Fables

Aesop was **a famous storyteller** in Greece more than 2,000 years ago. **The fables** he told are still famous all over **the world**. Here are two of Aesop's fables.

The Ant and The Dove

An ant lived next to **a river**. One day, **the ant** went to **the river** to drink, and he fell into **the water**. **A dove** was sitting in **a tree** next to **the river**. **The dove** saw **the ant** struggling in **the water**. She picked **a leaf** from **the tree** and dropped it into **the river**. **The ant** climbed onto **the leaf** and floated safely to **the shore**.

An hour later, **a hunter** came to **the river** to catch **birds**. He was **the best hunter** in that part of **the country**, and all **the animals** feared him. When **the ant** saw **the hunter**, he wanted to save his friend, but he thought, "How can **a tiny ant** stop **a big man**?" Then he had **an idea**. He climbed on **the hunter's foot** and bit him hard. **The hunter** shouted in pain, and **the noise** made **the dove** fly away.

Help!

(continued)

The Town Mouse and The Country Mouse

A town mouse went to visit his cousin in **the country. The country cousin** was poor, but he gladly served his town cousin **the only food** he had—**some beans** and **some bread. The town mouse** ate **the bread** and laughed. He said, "What **poor food** you **country mice** eat! Come home with me. I will show you how to live." **The moon** was shining brightly that night, so **the mice** left immediately.

As soon as they arrived at **the town mouse's house**, they went into **the dining room**. There they found **the leftovers** of **a wonderful dinner**, and soon **the mice** were eating **jelly** and **cake** and many nice things. Suddenly, **the door** flew open, and **an enormous dog** ran in. **The mice** ran away quickly. "Good-bye, Cousin," said **the country mouse**. "Are you leaving so soon?" asked **the town mouse**. "Yes," his honest cousin replied. "This has been **a great adventure**, but I'd rather eat **bread** in peace than **cake** in fear."

AFTER YOU READ

Number these sentences from "The Ant and The Dove" in the correct order.

_____ An hour later, a hunter came to the river to catch birds.

_____ She picked a leaf from the tree and dropped it into the river.

_____ The dove saw the ant struggling in the water.

_____ A dove was sitting in a tree next to the river.

_____ The ant climbed onto the leaf and floated safely to the shore.

Now number these sentences from "The Town Mouse and The Country Mouse" in the correct order.

_____ The town mouse ate the bread and laughed.

_____ The mice ran away quickly.

_____ The country cousin was poor, but he gladly served his town cousin the only food he had.

_____ This has been a great adventure.

_____ A town mouse went to visit his cousin in the country.

Grammar Presentation

ARTICLES: INDEFINITE AND DEFINITE

INDEFINITE

Singular Count Nouns		
	A / An	(Adjective) Noun
Let's read	a	story.
This is	an	old story.

Plural Count Nouns / Non-count Nouns		
	(Some)	(Adjective) Noun
Let's listen to	(some)	stories on this CD.
This CD has		nice music too.

DEFINITE

Singular Count Nouns		
	The	(Adjective) Noun
Let's read	the	story by Aesop.
It's	the	oldest story.

Plural Count Nouns / Non-count Nouns		
	The	(Adjective) Noun
Let's listen to	the	stories by Aesop.
I like		old music on this CD.

GRAMMAR NOTES

EXAMPLES

1. We can use **nouns** in two ways:

a. A noun is **indefinite** when you and your listener <u>do not have a specific person, place, or thing in mind</u>.

b. A noun is **definite** when you and your listener both <u>know which person, place, or thing</u> you are talking about.

A: Let's buy **a book**.
B: Good idea. Which one should we buy?
(A and B are not talking about a specific book.)

A: I bought **the book** yesterday.
B: Good. You've wanted it for a while.
(A and B are talking about a specific book.)

2. Use the **indefinite article** *a / an* with <u>singular count nouns</u> that are **indefinite**.

- Use *a* before <u>consonant sounds</u>.
- Use *an* before <u>vowel sounds</u>.

► **BE CAREFUL!** It is the <u>sound</u>, not the letter, that determines whether you use *a* or *an*.

Use **no article** or *some* with <u>plural count nouns</u> and with <u>non-count nouns</u> that are **indefinite**. *Some* means an indefinite number.

A: I'm reading *a fable*.
B: Oh really? Which one?

- *a* river, *a* tiny ant
- *an* idea, *an* exciting story

- *a* European writer (a "Yuropean")
- *an* honest relative (an "ahnest")

plural count
- There are *(some)* **books** on the floor. Are they yours?

non-count
A: I had to buy *(some)* **food**.
B: Oh. What did you buy?

(continued)

3. Note these uses of *a / an*, **no article**, and *some*:

a. To **identify** (say what someone or something is), use:

• *a / an* with <u>singular count nouns</u>

A: What do you do?
singular count
B: I'm *a* **chef**.

• **no article** with <u>plural count nouns</u> and <u>non-count nouns</u>

A: What are these?
plural count
B: They're **beans**. I'm making soup.
A: And this?
non-count
B: It's **bread**. I just baked it.

b. To make **general statements**, use **no article** with <u>plural count nouns</u> and <u>non-count nouns</u>.

plural count   non-count
• Ava loves **stories** and **music**.
(stories and music in general)

c. *Some* in general statements means "some, but not all."

• I like *some* **stories**, but a lot of them are boring.

4. Use the **definite article** *the* with most <u>common nouns</u> (count and non-count, singular and plural) that are **definite**. Use *the* when:

a. a person, place, or thing is <u>unique</u>— there is only one

• Aesop is famous all over *the* **world**.
• *The* **moon** was shining brightly.

b. the <u>context</u> makes it clear which person, place, or thing you mean

A: Who is she?
B: She's *the* **teacher**.
(A and B are students in a classroom. A is a new student.)

A: *The* **food** was great.
B: I enjoyed it too.
(A and B are coming out of a restaurant.)

c. the noun is mentioned for the <u>second time</u> (it is often indefinite the first time it is mentioned)

• *An* **ant** lived next to *a* **river**. One day, *the* **ant** went to *the* **river** to drink.
• They ate **cake**. *The* **cake** was delicious.

d. a <u>phrase or adjective</u> such as *first, best, right, wrong,* or *only* identifies the noun

• He was *the best* **hunter** in the country.
• He served *the only* **food** he had.

5. Adjectives often go <u>directly before a noun</u>. When you use an article or *some*, the adjective goes between the article or *some* and the noun.

- *Old* **fables** are great.
- We read **the *first* story** in the book.
- He has **some *beautiful old* books**.

Reference Note
For a list of **non-count nouns**, see Appendix 7 on page A-4.

Focused Practice

1 | DISCOVER THE GRAMMAR

Read the conversations. Circle the letter of the statement that best describes each conversation.

1. CORA: Dad, could you read me a story?

    DAD: Sure, I'd love to.

    a. Dad knows which story Cora wants him to read.

    b. Cora isn't talking about a particular story.

2. FRED: Mom, where's the new book?

    MOM: Sorry, I haven't seen it.

    a. Mom knows that Fred bought a new book.

    b. Mom doesn't know that Fred bought a new book.

3. DAD: I'll bet it's in the hall. You always drop your things there.

    FRED: I'll go look.

    a. There are several halls in the house.

    b. There is only one hall in the house.

4. DAD: Was I right?

    FRED: You weren't even close. It was on a chair in the kitchen.

    a. There is only one chair in the kitchen.

    b. There are several chairs in the kitchen.

5. DAD: Wow! Look at that! The pictures are great.

    FRED: So are the stories.

    a. All books have good pictures and stories.

    b. The book Fred bought has good pictures and stories.

6. FRED: Oh, I forgot . . . I also got a computer game. Do you want to play?

    DAD: Sure. I love computer games.

    a. Dad is talking about computer games in general.

    b. Dad is talking about a particular computer game.

2 | THE LIFE OF AESOP

Grammar Notes 1–5

Circle the correct article to complete this paragraph. Circle Ø if you don't need an article.

People all over (the) / Ø world know a / the fables of Aesop,
                    1.   **2.**

but there is very little information about the / Ø life of this
                                             3.

famous Greek storyteller. Scholars agree that Aesop was born

around 620 B.C. In his early years, he was a / the slave, and he
                                               4.

lived on Samos, an / a island in an / the Aegean Sea. Even as
                5.   **6.**

a / the slave, Aesop had the / Ø wisdom and knowledge. His
7.   **8.**

master respected him so much that he freed him. When Aesop

became a / Ø free man, he traveled to many countries in order to
       9.

learn and to teach. In Lydia, the / Ø king invited him to stay in that country and gave Aesop some
                              10.

difficult jobs in a / the government. In his work, Aesop often used a / Ø fables to convince people
                  11.   **12.**

of his ideas. One time, a / the king sent Aesop to Delphi with a / Ø gold for a / the people of that
                        13.   **14.**   **15.**

city. Aesop became disgusted with the / Ø people's greed, so he sent the / Ø gold back to a / the
                                    16.   **17.**   **18.**

king. A / The people of Delphi were very angry at Aesop for this, and they killed him. After his
     19.

death, a / the famous sculptor made a / the statue of Aesop you see in a / the photo above.
      20.   **21.**   **22.**

3 | FUN AND GAMES

Grammar Notes 1–5

*Complete the conversations with **a**, **an**, or **the**.*

1. **AVA:** I'm sick of this computer game, and I've read all my books.

   DAD: Let's go to _____*the*_____ new bookstore on Main Street.

2. **AVA:** Can we buy _____ computer game too?

   DAD: OK. I'm sure they sell games there.

3. **DAD:** Maybe you should turn off _____ computer before we leave.

   AVA: I'll leave it on for Ethan. He likes this game.

4. **DAD:** Do you see the bookstore? I was sure it was on Main Street.

   AVA: I think it's on _____ side street, but I'm not sure which one.

   DAD: I'll try this one.

5. **DAD:** There it is.

   AVA: You can park right across _____ street.

6. **AVA:** There's _____ man with drums and a guitar at the back of the store.

   DAD: Maybe he's _____ storyteller. Let's go see.

7. **AVA:** That was _____ fastest hour I've ever spent.

   DAD: I know. It was _____ excellent performance.

8. **AVA:** I really enjoyed _____ story about the warrior princess.

   DAD: Me too. It's _____ really exciting story.

9. **AVA:** We were going to get _____ computer game too, remember?

   DAD: OK. I think the newest games are in _____ front of _____ store.

10. **AVA:** This is _____ awesome game. Can I get it?

    DAD: Sure. Let's bring everything to _____ cashier. She's right over there.

---

4 | FAST READERS   *Grammar Notes 1, 3–5*

Ben went to a bookstore to buy books for his young niece. Complete the sentences with **the** *where necessary. Leave a blank if you don't need an article.*

BEN: I'm looking for _____ books for my 14-year-old niece. What do you recommend?
                          1.

CLERK: Let's go to _____*the*_____ young adult section. Does she like _____ mysteries? Doris
                          2.   3.

   Duncan wrote some good ones for teenagers.

BEN: She's read all _____ mysteries by Duncan. She's _____ fastest reader in the family!
                        4.   5.

CLERK: It's hard to keep up with _____ fast readers. Here's a good one by Gillian Cross—
                                     6.

   Born of _____ *Sun.* It's about finding a lost Inca city.
             7.

BEN: She'll like that one. She loves _____ books about _____ history—and science too.
                                         8.   9.

CLERK: Then how about *A Short History of* _____ *Universe?* It's in _____ science section.
                                              10.   11.

BEN: This is great! She likes _____ books with beautiful pictures.
                                  12.

CLERK: Well, _____ pictures in this one are fantastic. *Nature Magazine* called this book
                 13.

   _____ best introduction to this subject.
   14.

BEN: OK, I'll take _____ mystery by Cross and _____ science book. Anything else?
                       15.   16.

CLERK: Well, _____ kids have fun with _____ trivia games. Here's a good one.
                 17.   18.

BEN: Great. I'll get _____ trivia game too. Thanks. You've been very helpful.
                         19.

5 | PERSON, PLACE, OR THING?

Grammar Notes 1–5

*This is a trivia game. Complete the clues for each item. Then, using the clues and the appropriate picture, write the answer. Use **a / an** or **the** where necessary. Leave a blank if you don't need an article. The answers to the trivia game are at the end of the exercise.*

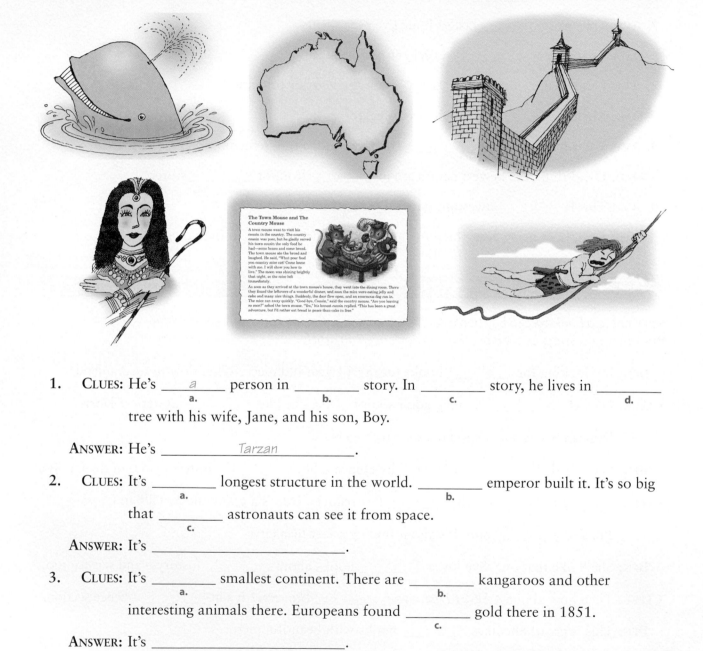

1. **CLUES:** He's ___*a*___ person in _____ story. In _____ story, he lives in _____
                  a.   **b.**   **c.**   **d.**

   tree with his wife, Jane, and his son, Boy.

   ANSWER: He's _____*Tarzan*_____.

2. **CLUES:** It's _____ longest structure in the world. _____ emperor built it. It's so big
                  a.   **b.**

   that _____ astronauts can see it from space.
            c.

   ANSWER: It's _____.

3. **CLUES:** It's _____ smallest continent. There are _____ kangaroos and other
                  a.   **b.**

   interesting animals there. Europeans found _____ gold there in 1851.
                                              c.

   ANSWER: It's _____.

4. **CLUES:** They are _____ very short stories. _____ stories are about _____
                  a.   **b.**   **c.**

   animals, but they teach _____ lessons about how people behave. Aesop wrote
                               d.

   _____ most famous ones.
      e.

   ANSWER: They're _____.

5. **CLUES:** She was _____ intelligent and beautiful woman. She was _____ most
   a.   b.

   famous queen of Egypt. She ruled _____ country with her brother.
   c.

   ANSWER: She was _____.

6. **CLUES:** They are _____ biggest animals that have ever lived. They have _____ fins,
   a.   b.

   but they aren't _____ fish.
   c.

   ANSWER: They're _____.

ANSWERS: 2. The Great Wall of China   3. Australia   4. fables   5. Cleopatra   6. whales

6 | EDITING

*Read the article about video games. There are thirteen mistakes in the use of **a**, **an**, and*
the. *The first mistake is already corrected. Find and correct twelve more.*

THE PLUMBER AND THE APE

Once there was a plumber named Mario.
The plumber
~~Plumber~~ had beautiful girlfriend. One day,

a ape fell in love with the girlfriend and

kidnapped her. The plumber chased ape to

rescue his girlfriend. This simple tale

became *Donkey Kong*, a first video game

with a story. It was invented by Shigeru

Miyamoto, an artist with Nintendo, Inc. Matsimoto loved the video games, but he

wanted to make them more interesting. He liked fairy tales, so he invented story

similar to a famous fairy tale. Story was an immediate success, and Nintendo

followed it with *The Mario Brothers* and then with *Super Mario*. The third game

became popular all over a world, and it is still most famous game in video history.

Nintendo has continued to add the new characters to the story, but success does not

change Mario. He is always brave little plumber in a red hat and work clothes.

Communication Practice

7 | LISTENING

🎧 *Listen to the conversations. Then listen again and circle the correct articles.*

1. **AMY:** What's that?

   BEN: Oh. It's a /(the) new video game. Do you want to try it?

2. **AMY:** I'm reading the story you recommended now. Who's Angelica? I can't figure it out.

   BEN: She's a / the princess with magic powers.

3. **AMY:** What about Aesop? Have you read a / the fable?

   BEN: No. I'm going to tonight.

4. **AMY:** You know, I'd like to buy a / the book of fables for Ava.

   BEN: Good idea. She loves fables.

5. **AMY:** Let's go to a / the bookstore this weekend.

   BEN: OK. We can go on Sunday after lunch.

6. **AMY:** Speaking of lunch, I'm hungry.

   BEN: Here. Why don't you have a / the sandwich?

Read your completed conversations. Circle the letter of the statement that best describes each conversation.

1. **a.** Ben and Amy have already spoken about this video game.
   b. Ben has never mentioned this video game before.

2. **a.** The story has several princesses. One of them has magic powers.
   b. The story has just one princess.

3. **a.** Ben and Amy have already spoken about this fable.
   b. Amy has never mentioned this fable before.

4. **a.** Amy has a specific book of fables in mind.
   b. Amy isn't thinking of a particular book of fables.

5. **a.** Amy has a specific bookstore in mind.
   b. Amy isn't thinking of a particular bookstore.

6. **a.** There is only one sandwich.
   b. There are several sandwiches.

8 | INFORMATION GAP: STORY TIME

Work in pairs (A and B). Student A, follow the instructions on this page. Student B, turn to page 261 and follow the instructions there.

1. Look at the picture below. Ask your partner for the information you need to finish labeling the picture.

   Example: **A:** Who's the man in the black cape?
   B: He's the magician.

2. Answer your partner's questions.

   Example: **B:** What's the magician holding?
   A: A magic wand.

When you are finished, compare pictures. Are the labels the same?

9 | QUIZ SHOW

Work with a group. Choose five interesting or famous things. Write three clues for each thing. Then join another group. Give your clues and ask the other group to guess what each thing is. Look at Exercise 5 for ideas.

Example: **A:** It's a planet. It's the closest one to the sun. There might be water there.
B: Does it have rings?

10 | THE MORAL OF THE STORY

Fables often have a moral—*a sentence at the end that explains the lesson of the story. Read the list of morals. What do you think they mean?*

- You can't please everyone.

- It's better to eat bread in peace than cake in fear.

- Sometimes a little friend turns out to be a great friend.

- Slow and steady wins the race.

- Look before you leap.

Example: "It's better to eat bread in peace than cake in fear."
I think this means it's better to have a good life situation with poorer things than a bad life situation with better things. You can't enjoy the better things if you are living in fear.

Which one could be the moral of "The Ant and The Dove" on page 249? Discuss your ideas with a group.

11 | WRITING

Choose one of the morals that you discussed in Exercise 10. Write a paragraph about an experience that you have had or know about that illustrates the meaning of the moral.

Example: "Slow and steady wins the race."
When I was in high school, I was a good student, but I always waited until the night before a test to study. I learned very fast, so I never had trouble. Then I took a class from Mr. Fox, the toughest teacher in the school . . .

12 | ON THE INTERNET

Do a search on **Aesop's fables.** *Choose a fable to read. Then work with a partner. Tell your partner the fable and listen to your partner's fable. Then discuss the answers to these questions about the two fables.*

- What is the title of the fable?

- Who are the characters in the fable?

- Where are they?

- What is the problem?

- How do they solve the problem?

- What is the moral of the fable?

INFORMATION GAP FOR STUDENT B

1. Look at the picture below. Answer your partner's questions.

    Example: **A:** Who's the man in the black cape?
    B: He's the magician.

2. Ask your partner for the information you need to finish labeling the picture.

    Example: **B:** What's the magician holding?
    A: A magic wand.

When you are finished, compare pictures. Are the labels the same?

From **Grammar** to **Writing**
Developing a Paragraph with Examples

One way to develop a paragraph is to add examples. Examples give your reader a clear idea of what you are writing about. They often give more information about the people, places, and things you are describing. They also make your writing more interesting.

> **Example:** We celebrate with **food.** ⟶
> We celebrate with **food. For example, we bake loaves of bread we call "souls."**

1 Read this paragraph about a holiday. Write the examples from the box in the correct place in the paragraph.

My family always hires a mariachi band.	For my sister, we offer toys.
~~we bake loaves of bread we call "souls."~~	We also decorate the altar with candy skulls.

In Mexico we celebrate *Los Días de los Muertos* ("The Days of the Dead") on November 1 and 2. On these days, we remember our relatives who have died. We celebrate with food, special gifts for the dead, and music. For example, _____*we bake loaves of bread we call "souls."*_____ They

1.

are shaped like people. _____

2.

In addition, we remember special things our relatives liked, and we buy them gifts. For example, for my grandfather, we always put out a new hat. _____ On the second day,

3.

everyone in my family meets at the cemetery. This sounds sad, but it is really a big party. _____,

4.

and we all sing. Some people think that *Los Días de los Muertos* is like Halloween, but they are wrong. At Halloween, people pretend to be afraid of evil spirits, but during *Los Días de los Muertos,* we invite the friendly spirits of our family to visit us.

2 | *Complete this outline of the paragraph in Exercise 1.*

1. The name of the holiday and when it is celebrated: _____.

2. The purpose of the holiday: _____.

3. How people celebrate the holiday:

   a. _____*food*_____

      Examples: ____*loaves of bread called "souls"*____ and _____

   b. _____

      Examples: ____*a new hat for my grandfather*____ and _____

   c. _____

      Examples: _____ and _____

3 | *Before you write . . .*

1. Develop an outline like the one in Exercise 2 for a paragraph about a holiday that is special to you.
2. Work with a partner. Exchange outlines. Ask questions about your partner's holiday. Answer your partner's questions.

4 | *Write a paragraph about a special holiday. Include information your partner asked you about.*

5 | *Exchange paragraphs with a different partner. Complete the chart with information from your partner's paragraph.*

	Yes	No
1. Does the paragraph include examples?	☐	☐
2. Do the examples give more information about people, places, and things?	☐	☐
3. Are there more examples that you would like to see?	☐	☐
4. If yes, what would you like an example of? _____		
5. What else would you like to know about this holiday?_____		

6 | *Work with your partner. Discuss each other's editing questions from Exercise 5. Then rewrite your own paragraph and make any necessary corrections.*

V

Review Test

I *Complete each conversation with the correct form of the words in parentheses.*

1. A: We got _____*a lot of mail*_____ today.
   _{a. (many / a lot of) (mail / mails)}

   B: How _____ came?
   _{b. (much / many) (letter / letters)}

2. A: Are you still majoring in mathematics?

   B: No, _____ interest me much anymore.
   _{a. (it / they) (doesn't / don't)}

3. A: There _____ some new furniture in the office.
   _{a. ('s / are)}

   B: I know. I saw _____ new _____ too.
   _{b. (several / a great deal of)}   _{c. (computer / computers)}

4. A: Do you enjoy reading?

   B: _____ OK, but I prefer listening to music.
   _{a. (It's / They're)}

5. A: I put _____ in the tomato sauce.
   _{a. (too much / too many) (salt / salts)}

   B: No, you didn't. _____ just fine to me.
   _{b. (It / They) (tastes / taste)}

6. A: Did you watch the six o'clock news?

   B: No. I missed _____ today.
   _{a. (it / them)}

7. A: I brought _____ luggage on this trip.
   _{a. (a lot of / a)}

   B: How _____ do you have?
   _{b. (much / many) (bag / bags)}

8. A: Did you find _____ information for your report on explorers?
   _{a. (much / many)}

   B: Yes, I did. I found _____ good articles online.
   _{b. (any / some)}

9. A: I love this music.

   B: I like _____ too.
   _{a. (it / them)}

II *Complete the conversation with the correct words or phrases in parentheses.*

A: Joe's birthday is tomorrow. Let's surprise him and give a party.

B: That's not _____*much*_____ time.
   _{1. (much / many)}

A: One day? That's _____. We still have candles and decorations left

2. (enough / too much)

from the last party.

B: Let's just make _____ hamburgers and fries. And I'll bake a cake.

3. (a lot of / a great deal of)

_____ chopped meat do we have?

4. (How much / How many)

A: Only _____. And we only have _____ rolls.

5. (a few / a little)   6. (a few / a little)

B: Put them on the list. I'll also need _____ eggs for the cake.

7. (some / any)

A: _____?

8. (How many / How much)

B: Two. Is there _____ flour and sugar?

9. (any / many)

A: Not _____. I'll get more.

10. (much / many)

B: I think that's it.

A: Not quite. Joe's got _____ friends. We'd better start calling them.

11. (a lot of / much)

B: Why don't you go shopping? I'll call _____ people while you're gone.

12. (a few / a little)

III   *Complete the conversations with* **a**, **an**, *or* **the**.

1. **A:** Did anyone feed ___the___ cat today?

   B: I did. Why?

   A: He's still hungry.

2. **A:** Look at this picture of Boots.

   B: It's really cute. What kind of cat is it?

   A: It's not _____ cat. It's _____ dog.

   B: You're kidding! What _____ unusual animal!

3. **A:** Please shut _____ door. It just blew open.

   B: OK.

4. **A:** It was cold last night.

   B: _____ ground is still frozen.

5. **A:** How's _____ weather in L.A.?

   B: Sunny. How's New York?

   A: You can't even see _____ sun.

6. **A:** Who's that woman in the uniform?

   B: She's _____ captain of this ship.

7. **A:** What does Martha do?

   B: She's _____ engineer. She works for World Cargo.

8. **A:** We need _____ new car.

   B: I know. But we'll have to wait.

9. **A:** I need _____ car today.

   B: OK. Can you drop me off at work?

   A: Sorry, I have _____ early meeting, so I can't help you.

IV *Complete the sentences with* **the** *where necessary. Capitalize the first letter when you don't use* **the**.

1. _____ F friendship is very important to most people.

2. ____The____ friendship of my classmates is very important to me.

3. Sue used _____ money in her bank account to pay her tuition.

4. _____ money isn't everything.

5. _____ travel can be educational. _____ staying at home can be educational too.

6. _____ vegetables in our garden aren't ripe yet.

7. _____ vegetables contain a lot of vitamins.

V *Complete the paragraphs with* **a, an, the**, *or* **some**.

1. Yesterday, I went to ____the____ biggest video store downtown to rent _____ movies.
                            a.   b.

   I found _____ comedy and _____ thriller. _____ comedy was very funny. I really
                   c.   d.   e.

   enjoyed it. _____ thriller wasn't that good.
                   f.

2. We need to buy _____ office supplies soon. We need _____ paper for _____
                           a.   b.   c.

   printer and _____ disks. _____ paper is more important than _____ disks.
                     d.   e.   f.

VI *Each sentence has four underlined words or phrases. The four underlined parts of the sentence are marked A, B, C, or D. Circle the letter of the* <u>one</u> *underlined word or phrase that is NOT CORRECT.*

1. <u>Many</u> popular <u>flavorings</u> <u>come</u> from <u>Native american</u> cultures.   **A   B   C   (D)**
   A   B   C   D

2. Chili <u>was</u> unknown in <u>an</u> <u>Asia or Europe</u> <u>a few</u> hundred years ago.   **A   B   C   D**
       A   B   C   D

3. Now <u>it's</u> <u>the</u> most popular spice in <u>a</u> <u>world</u>.   **A   B   C   D**
       A   B   C   D

4. It's hard to imagine <u>the</u> <u>Italian</u> or Szechuan <u>food</u> without <u>chili</u>.   **A   B   C   D**
                      A   B   C   D

5. Do you know that <u>a</u> <u>chocolate</u> also <u>comes</u> from <u>America</u>?   **A   B   C   D**
                    A   B   C   D

6. For <u>some</u> <u>American</u> cultures, it was <u>the</u> <u>medicine</u>.   **A   B   C   D**
       A   B   C   D

7. Now <u>People</u> all over <u>the world</u> <u>use</u> chocolate to flavor <u>food</u>.   **A   B   C   D**
       A   B   C   D

▶ *To check your answers, go to the Answer Key on page RT-3.*

PART VI

Adjectives and Adverbs

Grammar in Context

BEFORE YOU READ

🎧 *Look at the house. Is this a good place to live? Why or why not? What do you think is important when looking for a home? Read the ad for two apartments in this house.*

WAKEFIELD HOUSE

Are you looking for a **nice** neighborhood with **safe, quiet** streets? Do you love the **big sunny** rooms and **high** ceilings in **old** buildings—but want **modern** appliances too? Apartments in Wakefield House offer that and more. Here's your place to relax **completely** after a **long hard** day at school or work. We are located in a **peaceful residential** area near **famous** Lake Forest Park. And you'll still be a **convenient** drive or bus ride from downtown and the university. **Exciting** nightlife, shopping, and museums are just minutes away.

It sounds **very expensive**, right? But it's not! A **charming one-bedroom** apartment is **surprisingly affordable**. We have two **beautifully furnished** apartments **available** right now. But don't wait! Our apartments rent **very quickly**.
Call 555–1234 now for an appointment.

★ ★

Here's what some of our **satisfied** tenants are saying about life at Wakefield House:

"This neighborhood is like a **small** village. There are some **really friendly** people here."
—Maggie Chang

"This place is **absolutely perfect**. I'll **never** move again!"
—Luis Rivera

"We **often** spend the **whole** weekend here—walking through the **nearby** park or just sitting on the **front** porch."
—Alice Thompson

AFTER YOU READ

Read the statements. Check **True** *or* **False**.

	True	False
1. Wakefield House is in a dangerous neighborhood.	☐	☐
2. The apartments have a lot of light.	☐	☐
3. It's in an exciting area of the city.	☐	☐
4. You'll be surprised that the rent is so low.	☐	☐
5. There are two apartments for rent now.	☐	☐
6. One tenant likes to spend weekends at home.	☐	☐

Grammar Presentation

ADJECTIVES AND ADVERBS

Adjectives
They are **quiet** tenants.
It's a **fast** elevator.
The house looks **nice**.
It's absolutely **perfect**.

Adverbs
They talk **quietly**.
It moves **fast**.
She described it **nicely**.
It's **absolutely** perfect.

Participial Adjectives	
-ing Adjective	*-ed* Adjective
The apartment is **interesting**.	One couple is **interested** in the apartment.
It's an **interesting** one-bedroom apartment.	The **interested** couple called again.
My neighbor is **annoying**.	I'm **annoyed** by his loud music.
He's an **annoying** neighbor.	Another **annoyed** tenant complained.
This street map is **confusing**.	People were **confused** by the street map.
It's a **confusing** street map.	A **confused** driver asked for directions.

GRAMMAR NOTES	EXAMPLES

1. Use **adjectives** to describe or give more information about <u>nouns</u> (people, places, or things).

adjective   noun
- It's a **quiet building**.

noun   adjective
- The **building** is **quiet**.
  (Quiet *tells you more about the building.*)

An adjective usually goes right <u>before the noun</u> it describes.

adjective + noun
- This is a **small house**.

It can also go <u>after a non-action verb</u> such as *be, look, seem, appear, smell,* or *taste*.

verb + adjective
- This house **looks small**.

---

2. Use **adverbs** to describe or give more information about <u>verbs</u>, <u>adjectives</u>, or other <u>adverbs</u>.

An adverb usually goes right <u>after the verb</u> it describes.

verb + adverb
- The apartment **rented quickly**.

It usually goes right <u>before the adjective or adverb</u> it describes.

adverb + adjective
- It's an **extremely nice** house.

adverb + adverb
- They got it **very quickly**.

---

3. Use **adverbs of manner** to describe or give more information about <u>action verbs</u>. These adverbs often answer *"How?"* questions.

A: *How* did they decorate the apartment?
B: They decorated it **beautifully**!

▶ **BE CAREFUL!** Do not put an adverb of manner between the verb and the object.

verb   object   adverb
- She **decorated** the house **beautifully**.
  NOT She decorated ~~beautifully the house~~.

---

4. Adverbs of manner are often formed by adding **-ly** to adjectives:

adjective
- We need a **quick** decision.

adjective + -ly = adverb

adverb
- You should decide **quickly**.

▶ **BE CAREFUL!** Some adjectives also end in *-ly* —for example, *friendly, lonely, lovely,* and *silly*.

adjective
- It's a **lovely** apartment.

Some adverbs of manner have **two forms**: one with *-ly* and one without *-ly*. The form without *-ly* is the same as the adjective.

slowly	OR	**slow**
quickly	OR	**quick**
loudly	OR	**loud**
clearly	OR	**clear**

- Don't speak so **loudly**.
  OR
- Don't speak so **loud**.

USAGE NOTE: The form **without -ly** is common in <u>informal</u> speech.

5. Some **common adverbs of manner** are not formed by adding *-ly* to adjectives:

a. The adverb form of ***good*** is ***well***.

                 adjective   adverb
- He's a **good** driver. He drives **well**.

b. A few **adjectives** and **adverbs** have the <u>same form</u>—for example, *early, fast, hard, late,* and *wrong*.

                 adjective   adverb
- She is a **hard** worker. She works **hard**.

                 adjective   adverb
- The visitor was **late**. He woke up **late**.

▶ **BE CAREFUL!** ***Hardly*** is not the adverb form of *hard*. *Hardly* means "almost not."

- There's **hardly** enough room for a bed. *(There's almost not enough room for a bed.)*

Lately is not the adverb form of *late*. *Lately* means "recently."

- We haven't seen any nice houses **lately**. We're getting discouraged.

---

6. Use **adverbs of frequency** to say <u>how often</u> something happens.

- She *usually* **rents** to students.

Adverbs of frequency usually go <u>before</u> the main verb. They usually go <u>after</u> a form of ***be***.

- They *always* **share** a house with friends.
- My neighbors **are** *always* home on Sunday.

---

7. Participial adjectives are adjectives that end with ***-ing*** or ***-ed***. They come from <u>verbs</u>.

                           verb
- This story **amazes** me.

Participial adjectives often describe **feelings**.

             adjective   adjective
- It's an **amazing** story. I'm **amazed**.

- Use the ***-ing*** form for someone or something that <u>causes</u> a feeling.

- The fly is **disgusting**. *(The fly causes the feeling.)*

- Use the ***-ed*** form for the person who <u>has</u> the feeling.

- I'm **disgusted**. *(I have the feeling.)*

Reference Notes

For a list of **non-action verbs**, see Appendix 2 on page A-2.
For a discussion of **adverbs of frequency**, see Unit 1 on page 5.
For a list of **participial adjectives**, see Appendix 11 on page A-6.
For the **order of adjectives before a noun**, see Appendix 12 on page A-6.
For **spelling rules** for **base form of verb + -ing**, see Appendix 21 on page A-10.
For **spelling rules** for **base form of verb + -ed**, see Appendix 22 on page A-10.
For **spelling rules** for forming *-ly* adverbs, see Appendix 24 on page A-11.

Focused Practice

1 | DISCOVER THE GRAMMAR

Read this notice from a university bulletin board. Underline the adjectives and circle the adverbs. Then draw an arrow from the adjective or adverb to the word it is describing.

APT. FOR RENT
140 Grant Street, Apartment 4B

Are you looking for a place to live? This <u>lovely</u> apartment is in a new building and has two large bedrooms and a sunny kitchen. The building is (very) quiet—absolutely perfect for two serious students. You'll be close to campus. The bus stop is a short walk, and the express bus goes directly into town. You can run or ride your bike safely in nearby parks. The rent is very affordable. Small pets are welcome. Interested students should call Megan at 555-5050. Don't wait! This apartment will rent fast. Nonsmokers, please.

2 | WRITING HOME   *Grammar Notes 1–7*

Circle the correct words to complete Maggie's letter to her brother.

Dear Roger,

I wasn't sure I'd like living in a (large) / largely city, but I <u>real / really</u> love it! Maybe that's
        1.   2.

because my <u>new / newly</u> neighborhood is so <u>beautiful / beautifully</u>. Last Saturday I worked
          3.   4.

<u>hard / hardly</u> and unpacked all my stuff. Then I spent Sunday <u>happy / happily</u> exploring the
  5.   6.

neighborhood. I couldn't believe the <u>gorgeous / gorgeously</u> houses on these streets.
                         7.

My apartment is <u>great / greatly</u> and the other tenants are very <u>nice / nicely</u>. My next-door
         8.   9.

neighbor, Alice, seemed <u>shy / shyly</u> at first, but I think we're going to become <u>good / well</u>
                10.   11.

friends very <u>quick / quickly</u>. She's an art student, and she <u>usual / usually</u> visits museums on
        12.   13.

Saturdays. We're going together next week. Life in the city is <u>exciting / excitingly</u>, but I get
                                          14.

<u>terrible / terribly</u> homesick. So I hope you visit me soon!
  15.

                                              Love,
                                              Maggie

3 | DID YOU LIKE IT?

Grammar Notes 2, 4

Many different people went to see the apartment described in Exercise 1. Complete their comments about the apartment. Use the correct form of the words in parentheses. See Appendix 24 on page A-11 for help with spelling adverbs ending in **-ly**.

1. I am very interested. I think the apartment is _____*extremely nice*_____.

(extreme / nice)

2. I was expecting much bigger rooms. I was _____.

(terrible / disappointed)

3. I thought it would be hard to find, but it was _____.

(surprising / easy)

4. This neighborhood is _____.

(extreme / expensive)

5. This apartment is _____ for this neighborhood.

(amazing / cheap)

6. I think it's a great place. I'm sure it will rent _____.

(incredible / fast)

7. The notice said it was a quiet place, but I heard the neighbors _____.

(very / clear)

8. I heard them too. I thought their voices were _____.

(awful / loud)

9. The ad described the apartment _____.

(very / accurate)

10. I like the owner. She's _____.

(exceptional / friendly)

11. To be honest, this place is _____ for me!

(absolute / perfect)

12. I'm going to feel _____ if I don't get it.

(real / upset)

4 | IT'S HARD TO TELL WITH ALICE

Grammar Note 7

Maggie and Luis are talking about their neighbor. Read their conversation. Complete it with the correct participial adjective form (**-ing** *or* **-ed**) *of the verbs in parentheses.*

MAGGIE: What's the matter with Alice?

LUIS: Who knows? She's always _____*annoyed*_____ about something.

1. (annoy)

MAGGIE I know, but this time I'm really _____.

2. (confuse)

LUIS: Why? What's so _____ this time?

3. (confuse)

MAGGIE: Oh, I thought she was happy. She met an _____ man last week.

4. (interest)

LUIS: Great. Was she _____ in him?

5. (interest)

MAGGIE: I thought so. She said they saw a _____ movie together. So I thought . . .

6. (fascinate)

LUIS: Maybe she was _____ by the movie, but she was _____

7. (fascinate)   8. (disappoint)

with the guy.

MAGGIE: Maybe. It's hard to tell with Alice. Her moods are often very _____.

9. (surprise)

5 | EDITING

Read the evaluation Luis wrote about his teacher. There are twelve mistakes in the use of adjectives and adverbs. The first mistake is already corrected. Find and correct eleven more.

English 206   **EVALUATION**

exceptional
Mr. Delgado is an ~~exceptionally~~ teacher. He prepared careful for classes, and his lessons were almost always interested. He explained clearly the material, and he returned always our tests on time. This was not an easy class, but the time always passed fastly because the students were exciting by the material. I studied hardly for this class—more than two hours a night—because Mr. Delgado gave hard tests. His tests were very fairly though. We were never surprising by test questions because they were all from class work or the textbook. I did good in this class, and I'm sure other students will too. I recommend highly his class.

Communication Practice

6 | LISTENING

A couple is discussing newspaper apartment ads. Read the ads. Then listen to the conversation. Listen again, and number the ads from 1 to 4 to match the order in which the couple discusses them.

Section 6 Real Estate

CUMBERLAND **Wow! Cute/cozy 2 bed** in quiet area. No pets. $450/month. 555-2343 ext 27	**SMITHFIELD** ¹ **Large, lovely 2 bed** in new bldg, nr pub transport. $500/month. 555-3296
LINCOLN **Beautiful 2 bed** in completely renovated bldg. Mod. kitchen & ba. Available immediately $460/month. 555-7859	**FOSTER** **Light and bright 2 bed** on beautifully landscaped street. Newly painted, excel condition. Near shopping and schools. $600/month. 555-7749

7 | WHERE DO YOU LIVE?

Work in small groups. Describe where you live. Tell each other how you found the place.
Explain how you first felt about it (pleased, disappointed, etc.). Describe what it looks like.
Tell how you decorated it. What is special about your place?

Example: I found my apartment last summer when I was walking down the street. I saw an "Apartment for Rent" sign. I knocked on the door. At first, I was disappointed. It's a small apartment . . .

8 | HOME SWEET HOME

Work with a partner. There are many different types of housing. Describe the different
types listed below. How are they similar? How are they different? Use your dictionaries to
help you. Do these types of housing exist in other places you have lived?

- apartment
- boarding house
- dorm (dormitory)
- mansion
- mobile home
- private home
- rented room in someone's house
- studio apartment

Example: A mobile home can be very convenient. You can pull it behind your car.

9 | YOUR IDEAL NEIGHBOR

Work in small groups. Take turns describing your ideal neighbor. Describe the person and
his or her activities. Here are some words you can use.

Adjectives			Adverbs		
cheerful	considerate	gloomy	early	easily	happily
helpful	loud	messy	late	loudly	noisily
neat	reliable	serious	politely	quietly	seriously

Example: My ideal neighbor isn't loud and doesn't party too late. When we have a problem, we can talk about it politely.

10 | WRITING

Write an ad like the one for Wakefield House on page 268. Describe your ideal home.

Example: Do you want to live in an exciting neighborhood with great stores that stay open late? Do you want a large, modern apartment with a terrific view of all the action in the streets below? The apartments in the Atrium are . . .

11 | ON THE INTERNET

*Do a search on **real estate** or **off-campus housing** in your area or another location that interests you. Print out four ads and discuss them with a partner.*

Example: **A:** Here's an ad for a cozy one-bedroom apartment on a quiet street.
B: Cozy? That probably means small.

Adjectives: Comparisons with *As . . . as* and *Than*

Grammar in Context

BEFORE YOU READ

🎧 *How often do you eat out? What types of restaurant food do you enjoy? Would you like to order the pizza in the photo? Why or why not? Read the newspaper restaurant review.*

A New Place for Pizza
by Pete Tsa

AS FRESH AS IT GETS!

PIZZA PLACE, the chain of popular restaurants, has just opened a new one on Main Street, two blocks from the university. The day I ate there, the service was **not as good as** at the other Pizza Place restaurants in town. The young staff (mostly students) probably needs time to become **more professional**. But the pizza was incredible! It seemed **bigger** and **better than** at the other six locations. As with all food, **the fresher** the ingredients, **the better** the pizza. The ingredients at the new Pizza Place are **as fresh as** you can get (no mushrooms from a can here!), and the choices are much **more varied than** at their other restaurants. We ordered two different types. The one with mashed potatoes and garlic was a lot **more interesting than** the traditional pizza with cheese and tomato sauce, but both were delicious.

Each Pizza Place is different. The one on Main Street is a little **larger** (and **louder**) **than** the others. It's also **more crowded** because students love it. At lunchtime the lines outside this new eatery are getting **longer and longer**. Go early for a **quieter, more relaxed** meal.

AFTER YOU READ

Read the statements about Pizza Place. Check **True** *or* **False***.*

		True	False
1.	The service is great.	☐	☐
2.	The pizza is very good.	☐	☐
3.	The mushrooms are fresh.	☐	☐
4.	They have only two types of pizza.	☐	☐
5.	It's crowded because it's small.	☐	☐
6.	It's noisy at lunchtime.	☐	☐

Grammar Presentation

ADJECTIVES: COMPARISONS WITH *AS . . . AS* AND *THAN*

Comparisons with *As . . . as*				
	(Not) As	Adjective	*As*	
The new restaurant is	**(not) as**	**large** **busy** **good** **interesting** **expensive**	**as**	the other ones.

Comparisons with *Than*		
	Comparative Adjective Form	*Than*	
The new restaurant is	**larger** **busier** **better**	**than**	the other ones.
	more interesting **less expensive**		

GRAMMAR NOTES	EXAMPLES
1. Use *(not) as* + **adjective** + *as* to compare people, places, or things, and show how they are (or aren't) **similar**.	**A:** Pizza Place is **as good as** Joe's. **B:** But Joe's is**n't as expensive as** Pizza Place.
• Use *as* + **adjective** + *as* to show how they are <u>the same or equal</u>. Use *just* to make the comparison stronger.	• The new menu is *just* **as good as** the old. *(The new menu and the old menu are equally good.)*
• Use *not as* + **adjective** + *as* to show how they are <u>not the same or equal</u>.	• The new menu is**n't as varied as** the old. *(The old menu was more varied.)*
REMEMBER: It is not necessary to mention both parts of the comparison when the meaning is clear.	**A:** I liked the old menu. It had more choices. **B:** Too bad the new one is**n't as varied**. *(. . . as the old menu)*

2. Use **comparative adjectives** + *than* to show how people, places, or things are **different**.	• The new restaurant is **bigger than** the old restaurant. • The new waiters are **more professional than** the old waiters.

3. There are several ways of **forming comparative adjectives**.		
a. For **short adjectives** (one-syllable and two-syllable ending in *-y*), use **adjective + *-er***.	**ADJECTIVE** loud friendly	**COMPARATIVE** loud**er** friendl**ier**
There are often **spelling changes** when you add *-er*.	late big early	lat**er** big**ger** earl**ier**
Some adjectives have **irregular** comparative forms.	good bad	**better** **worse**
b. For **long adjectives** (two or more syllables), use *more / less* + **adjective**.	expensive	**more** expensive **less** expensive
c. For **some adjectives**, like *lively*, *lovely*, or *quiet*, you can use either *-er* or *more*.	• The Inn is **livelier** than Joe's. <div align="center">OR</div>• The Inn is **more lively** than Joe's.	

(continued)

4. Use *than* before the second part of the comparison.

REMEMBER: It's not necessary to mention both parts of the comparison when the meaning is clear.

- Our table is **smaller than** their table.

- The new tables are **smaller**.
  (. . . than the old tables)

5. Comparatives with *than* and comparisons with *as . . . as* often express the <u>same meaning</u> in different ways.

USAGE NOTE: With <u>one-syllable adjectives</u>, *not as . . . as* is more common than *less . . . than*.

- The Inn is **more expensive than** Joe's.
- Joe's is**n't as expensive as** the Inn.
- Joe's is **less expensive than** the Inn.
- Our server is**n't as fast as** theirs.
  NOT Our server is ~~less fast than~~ theirs.

6. Repeat the comparative adjective to show how something is <u>increasing or decreasing</u>:

comparative adjective + *and* + **comparative adjective**

With long adjectives, repeat only *more* or *less*.

- The lines are getting **longer and longer**.
  (Their length is increasing.)
- It's getting **more and more popular**.
  (Its popularity is increasing.)
- It's **less and less comfortable**.
  (The comfort is decreasing.)

7. Use **two comparative adjectives** to show <u>cause and effect</u>:

the + **comparative adjective** + *the* + **comparative adjective**

When both comparative adjectives describe the same person, place, or thing, we often <u>leave out the noun</u>.

- **The more crowded** the restaurant, **the slower** the service.
  (The service is slower because the restaurant is more crowded.)

A: The service is really fast here.
B: The faster, the better.
(The faster the service, the better the service.)

Reference Notes
For a list of **adjectives** that use **both forms of the comparative**, see Appendix 9 on page A-5.
For a list of **irregular comparative adjectives**, see Appendix 10 on page A-6.
For **spelling rules** for the **comparative form of adjectives**, see Appendix 23 on page A-11.

Focused Practice

1 | DISCOVER THE GRAMMAR

Read the information about two brands of frozen pizza. Then decide if each statement is
True (T) *or* **False (F).**

	Maria's Pizza	**John's Pizza**
Size	12 inches	12 inches
Weight	27 ounces	24 ounces
Price	$5.99	$6.99
Calories*	364	292
Salt content*	731 milligrams	600 milligrams
Baking time	20 minutes	16 minutes
Taste	★ ★ ★	★ ★ ★ ★

* for a five-ounce serving

___F___ **1.** Maria's pizza is bigger than John's.

_____ **2.** John's pizza is just as big as Maria's.

_____ **3.** John's isn't as heavy as Maria's.

_____ **4.** Maria's is just as expensive as John's.

_____ **5.** John's is more expensive than Maria's.

_____ **6.** Maria's is higher in calories than John's.

_____ **7.** Maria's is saltier than John's.

_____ **8.** The baking time for Maria's isn't as long as the baking time for John's.

_____ **9.** John's tastes better than Maria's.

2 | CHEESE CHECK

Grammar Note 1

Look at this consumer magazine chart comparing three brands of pizza cheese. Complete the
sentences. Use **as . . . as** *or* **not as . . . as** *and the correct form of the words in parentheses.*

PIZZA CHEESE	Better ●	◑	○ Worse
Brand	**Price (per serving)**	**Taste**	**Smell**
X	5¢	◑	●
Y	3¢	◑	◑
Z	3¢	○	◑

1. Brand Z ___is as expensive as___ Brand Y.
   (be / expensive)

2. Brand Y _____ Brand X.
   (be / expensive)

3. Brand X _____ Brand Y.
   (taste / good)

4. Brand Z _____ Brand Y.
   (taste / good)

5. Brand Y _____ Brand X.
   (smell / nice)

6. Brand Y _____ Brand Z.
   (smell / nice)

3 | **MENU**

Look at the menu. Then complete the sentences comparing items on the menu. Use the appropriate comparative form of the adjectives in parentheses and **than***.*

The Golden Palace

Take-out Menu
2465 Mineral Springs Rd.
Tel: (401) 555-4923

Open 7 days a week
Mon–Thurs: 11:00 A.M.–10:00 P.M.
Fri–Sat: 11:00 A.M.–11:00 P.M.
Sunday: 12:00 noon–10:00 P.M.

Place your order by phone and it will be ready when you arrive.

Broccoli with Garlic Sauce $6.25
Beef with Broccoli $7.75
Beef with Dried Red Pepper $7.25
Chicken with Broccoli $7.75
Chicken with Orange Sauce $7.25
Sweet-and-Sour Shrimp $8.25
Pork with Scallions $6.25
Steamed Mixed Vegetables $5.50
Steamed Scallops with Broccoli $7.75

Kid's Corner
Honey chicken wings $5.75
Pizza-style spring roll $4.50
Macaroni and cheese slices $4.00

Hot and Spicy   No sugar, salt, or oil

1. The sweet-and-sour shrimp is _____*more expensive than*_____ the steamed scallops.
                                            (expensive)

2. The beef with dried red pepper is _____ the beef with broccoli.
                                            (hot)

3. The pork with scallions is _____ the sweet-and-sour shrimp.
                                   (expensive)

4. The chicken with orange sauce is _____ the scallops with broccoli.
                                            (spicy)

5. The steamed mixed vegetables are _____ the pork with scallions.
                                            (salty)

6. The chicken with broccoli is _____ the chicken with orange sauce.
(mild)

7. The steamed vegetables are _____ the beef with dried red pepper.
(healthy)

8. The broccoli with garlic sauce is _____ the chicken with broccoli.
(cheap)

9. The pork with scallions is _____ the steamed mixed vegetables.
(oily)

10. The shrimp dish is _____ the scallop dish.
(sweet)

11. The restaurant's hours on Sunday are _____ they are on Saturday.
(short)

12. The children's menu is _____ the adult's menu.
(short)

13. The children's menu is _____ too.
(expensive)

14. The chicken wings are _____ the macaroni and cheese slices.
(sweet)

4 | THE MORE, THE MERRIER   Grammar Notes 6–7

Complete these conversations. Use the comparative form of the adjectives in parentheses to show an increase/decrease or a cause and effect.

1. **A:** Wow! The lines here are getting _longer and longer_.
(long)

   B: I know. And _the longer_ the wait, _the hungrier_ I get.
(long)   (hungry)

2. **A:** It's worth the wait. The food here is getting _____.
(good)

   B: But _____ the food, _____ the bill!
(good)   (high)

3. **A:** The lunch crowd is leaving. It's getting _____.
(crowded)

   B: Great. These books were starting to feel _____.
(heavy)

4. **A:** There's Professor Lee. You know, his course is getting _____.
(popular)

   B: It's amazing. _____ it is, _____ it gets.
(hard)   (popular)
   He's a great teacher.

5. **A:** Is it the hot sauce, or has your cough been getting _____?
(bad)

   B: It's the hot sauce, but I love it. For my taste, _____,
(spicy)
   _____.
(good)

6. **A:** The service used to be slow here, but it's getting _____.
(fast)

   B: Right. _____ the service, _____ the lines!
(fast)   (short)

5 | EDITING

Read this student's essay. There are nine mistakes in the use of **as . . . as** *and comparatives with* **than**. *The first mistake is already corrected. Find and correct eight more.*

When I was a teenager in the Philippines, I was an expert on snacks and

fast foods. I was growing fast, so the more I ate, the ~~hungry~~ *hungrier* I felt. The

street vendors in our town had the better snacks than anyone else. In the

morning, I used to buy rice muffins on the way to school. They are much

sweeter that American muffins. After school, I ate fish balls on a stick or

adidas (chicken feet). Snacks on a stick are small than American hot dogs

and burgers, but they are much varied. My friend thought *banana-cue*

(banana on a stick) was really great. However, they weren't as sweet from

kamote-cue (fried sweet potatoes and brown sugar), my favorite snack.

When I came to the United States, I didn't like American fast food at

first. To me, it was interesting than my native food and less tastier too.

Now I'm getting used to it, and it seems deliciouser and deliciouser.

Does anyone want to go out for a pizza?

Communication Practice

6 | LISTENING

🎧 *A couple is trying to choose between two brands of frozen pizza in the supermarket. Listen to their conversation. Then listen again and check the pizza that is better in each category.*

	Di Roma's	Angela's
1. cheap	☑	☐
2. big	☐	☐
3. healthy	☐	☐
4. tasty	☐	☐
5. fresh	☐	☐

7 | PIZZA AROUND THE WORLD

Look at some of these favorite international pizza toppings. Discuss them with a partner.
Make comparisons using some of the adjectives in the box.

| delicious | filling | healthy | interesting | spicy | tasty | traditional | unusual |

1. Australia

2. Mexico

3. Hong Kong

4. Greece

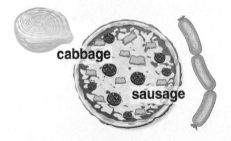

5. Poland

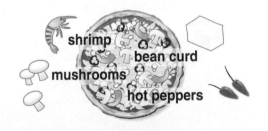

6. Indonesia

Example: **A:** The pizza from Poland seems more filling than the one from Greece.
B: Yes, and it's not as spicy.

8 | WHAT'S ON THE MENU?

Work in groups. Imagine that you have a restaurant. Give your restaurant a name and decide what to put on the menu. Discuss dishes and prices for each category. Use comparisons in your discussion.

Example: A: We need one more soup. How about chicken noodle?
B: Too boring! Gazpacho is more interesting.

_____

Soups and Appetizers

_____ . . . . $ _____
_____ . . . . $ _____
_____ . . . . $ _____
_____ . . . . $ _____

Entrées

_____ . . . . $ _____
_____ . . . . $ _____
_____ . . . . $ _____
_____ . . . . $ _____

Salads and Side Dishes

_____ . . . . $ _____
_____ . . . . $ _____
_____ . . . . $ _____
_____ . . . . $ _____

Desserts

_____ . . . . $ _____
_____ . . . . $ _____
_____ . . . . $ _____
_____ . . . . $ _____

Beverages

_____ . . . . $ _____
_____ . . . . $ _____
_____ . . . . $ _____

With your group, role-play ordering from your menu. One person is the server; the others are customers.

Example: CUSTOMER: Is the gazpacho as spicy as the hot-and-sour soup?
SERVER: No, the hot-and-sour soup is much spicier.

9 | INFORMATION GAP: THICK AND CHUNKY

Work in pairs (A and B). Student A, follow the instructions on this page. Student B, turn to page 288 and follow the instructions there.

1. Look at the charts below comparing two brands of spaghetti sauce.

2. Ask your partner questions to complete the charts.

> **Example:** A: Which brand is smoother?
> B: Frank's is smoother than Classic's.

3. Draw the following circles:
   - ● for the brand that has more of a certain quality
   - ◒ if the brands are equal
   - ○ for the brand that has less of a certain quality

4. Answer your partner's questions.

> **Example:** B: Which brand is thicker?
> A: Frank's is as thick as Classic's.

Spaghetti Sauce

● more   ◒ equal   ○ less

Quality	Frank's	Classic's
smooth	●	○
thick	◒	◒
chunky		
flavorful	○	●
sweet		
salty	●	○

Quality	Frank's	Classic's
spicy		
garlicky	●	○
fresh-tasting		
fattening	○	●
nutritious		
expensive	●	○

When you are finished, compare your charts. Are they the same? Choose a spaghetti sauce to buy. Explain your choice.

10 | WRITING

Write a paragraph comparing your country's food with the food of another country.

> **Example:** Food in Taiwan is fresher than food in the United States. Taiwan is a small island and there are a lot of farms . . .

11 | ON THE INTERNET

Work with a partner. Find two online menus for the same type of take-out restaurants in your city (for example, pizza places, hamburger places, Chinese restaurants). Print them out and compare them. Which restaurant would you prefer to eat at? Why?

> **Example:** **A:** The food at Mike's Place isn't as cheap as at the Plaza Grill.
> **B:** You're right. But it looks more varied and interesting.

INFORMATION GAP FOR STUDENT B

1. Look at the charts below comparing two brands of spaghetti sauce.

2. Answer your partner's questions.

> **Example:** **A:** Which brand is smoother?
> **B:** Frank's is smoother than Classic's.

3. Ask your partner questions to complete the charts.

> **Example:** **B:** Which brand is thicker.
> **A:** Frank's is as thick as Classic's.

4. Draw the following circles:

⬤ for the brand that has more of a certain quality

◒ if the brands are equal

◯ for the brand that has less of a certain quality

Spaghetti Sauce

⬤ more   ◒ equal   ◯ less

Quality	Frank's	Classic's
smooth	⬤	◯
thick	◒	◒
chunky	◯	⬤
flavorful		
sweet	⬤	◯
salty		

Quality	Frank's	Classic's
spicy	◯	⬤
garlicky		
fresh-tasting	◒	◒
fattening		
nutritious	◯	⬤
expensive		

When you are finished, compare your charts. Are they the same? Choose a spaghetti sauce to buy. Explain your choice.

Adjectives: Superlatives

BEFORE YOU READ

🎧 *Look at the photo. Do you recognize this city? Where do you think it is? What are some important features for a city to have? Read the travel brochure.*

The biggest!
The best!
The safest!
The most exciting!

The biggest!
The best!
The safest!
The most exciting!

A Superlative City

TORONTO. It's the capital of the province of Ontario. It's also . . .

🍁 **the largest** city in Canada

🍁 **the most important** economic and financial center of the country

🍁 one of **the most multi-cultural** cities on earth
(Over 100 languages are spoken!)

🍁 one of **the easiest** towns to get around
(It has **the** second **largest** public transportation system in North America.)

🍁 **the safest** city on the continent, and one of **the most peaceful** of all large, international cities

All of these features, and many more, make Toronto one of **the most exciting** cities in the world. Come visit and find out for yourself!

AFTER YOU READ

Read the statements. Check **True** *or* **False**.

	True	False
1. Some Canadian cities are larger than Toronto.	☐	☐
2. Some Canadian cities are more important economically than Toronto.	☐	☐
3. Many cities in the world aren't as diverse and multi-cultural as Toronto.	☐	☐
4. It's easy to get around Toronto.	☐	☐
5. No city in North America is safer than Toronto.	☐	☐

Toronto and the CN Tower seen from Lake Ontario

Grammar Presentation

ADJECTIVES: SUPERLATIVES

Superlatives			
	Superlative Adjective Form		
This is	**the largest** **the busiest** **the best**	city	in the world. of all. I've ever visited.
	the most interesting **the least expensive**		

GRAMMAR NOTES

EXAMPLES

1. Use **superlative adjectives** to compare <u>one</u> person, place, or thing with other people, places, or things in a <u>group</u>.

- The CN Tower is **the tallest** tower in the world.
- Toronto is **the most multi-cultural** city in Canada.

2. There are several ways of **forming superlative adjectives**.

ADJECTIVE	SUPERLATIVE
loud	**the** loud**est**
friendly	**the** friendli**est**

a. For **short adjectives** (one syllable and two syllables ending in -*y*), use: ***the* + adjective + -*est***.

There are often **spelling changes** when you add **-*est***.

late	**the** lat**est**
big	**the** big**gest**
early	**the** earl**iest**

Some adjectives have **irregular** superlative forms.

good	**the best**
bad	**the worst**

b. For **long adjectives** (two or more syllables), use ***the most / the least* + adjective**.

expensive	**the most** expensive
	the least expensive

c. For **some adjectives**, like *lively*, *lovely*, or *quiet*, you can use either ***the . . . -est*** or ***the most / the least***.

- Rio is **the liveliest** city in the world.

OR

- Rio is **the most lively** city in the world.

3. We often use the superlative with other **words and expressions**:

a. phrases with *in* and *of*

- This is **the least expensive** hotel *in town*.
- This was **the best** day *of our visit*.

b. *one of* or *some of*
Use a <u>plural noun</u> with these expressions.

- Toronto is *one of* **the most interesting** *cities* in the world.
NOT Toronto is one of the most interesting ~~city~~ in the world.

c. *second* (*third*, *fourth* . . .)

- It has **the** *second* **largest** transportation system.

d. *ever* + **present perfect**

- This is **the biggest** building *I've ever seen*.

Reference Notes
For a list of **adjectives** that use **both forms of the superlative**, see Appendix 9 on page A-5.
For a list of **irregular superlative adjectives**, see Appendix 10 on page A 6.
For **spelling rules** for the **superlative form of adjectives**, see Appendix 23 on page A-11.

Focused Practice

1 | DISCOVER THE GRAMMAR

Read more information about Toronto. Underline all the superlative adjectives.

What to Do and See in Toronto

🍁 **Go to the CN Tower**. It's <u>the tallest</u> free-standing structure in the world—even taller than the Petronas Towers in Malaysia. From there you can get the best view of the city and countryside.

🍁 **Drive along Yonge Street**. At 1,200 miles (1,800 km) it's the longest street in the world. For one weekend in July it's one of the liveliest too. Come and join 1 million others for the exciting Yonge Street Festival.

🍁 **Visit PATH**, the world's largest underground shopping complex.

🍁 **Explore the Old Town of York**. It has the most historic buildings in the whole city.

🍁 **Take the Yuk Yuk Comedy Tour** of the Entertainment District—you'll have a good time on the funniest bus ride in town.

🍁 **Visit the Toronto Zoo**. There's always something new and fascinating going on. Local people call it the best family outing in Toronto.

2 | CITY STATISTICS

Grammar Notes 1–2

Look at the chart and complete the sentences on the next page. Use the superlative form of the correct adjective.

		ATHENS	MEXICO CITY	SEOUL	TORONTO
👫	**Population**	748,110	8,591,309	9,853,972	2,571,400
📏	**Size**	428 square km/ 165 square miles	1,479 square km/ 571 square miles	627 square km/ 242 square miles	630 square km/ 243 square miles
🌡	**Average January Temperature**	10.2°C/ 50.4°F	13.3°C/ 55.9°F	−3.5°C/ 25.7°F	−6.4°C/ 20.5°F
🌡	**Average July Temperature**	27.9°C/ 82.2°F	16.7°C/ 62.1°F	24.4°C/ 75.9°F	20.7°C/ 69.3°F
☂	**Average Rainfall per Year**	394.8 mm/ 15.5 in.	634.3 mm/ 25 in.	1,364.8 mm/ 53.7 in.	877.7 mm/ 32.2 in.
☕	**Cost of a Cup of Coffee ($U.S.)**	$4.25	$1.20	$3.00	$3.35

1. Seoul has _____the largest_____ population of all four cities, but it isn't
   (large / small)
   _____ city in size.
   (big / small)

2. Mexico City is _____ city in area.
   (big / small)

3. Athens is _____ city in both population and size.
   (big / small)

4. In winter, _____ cities are Seoul and Toronto.
   (warm / cold)

5. Toronto also has some of _____ July temperatures, but Seoul doesn't.
   (hot / cool)

6. Of all the cities in the chart, Mexico City is _____ in July and
   (hot / cool)
   _____ in January. It has _____ climate of all.
   (warm / cold)   (comfortable / uncomfortable)

7. _____ city is Athens. It's also _____ in July.
   (dry / rainy)   (hot / cold)

8. Seoul is _____ city.
   (dry / rainy)

9. You'll find _____ cup of coffee in Mexico City.
   (cheap / expensive)

10. _____ cup of coffee is in Athens.
    (cheap / expensive)

3 | THE CN TOWER / *LA TOUR CN*   *Grammar Notes 1–3*

Read about the CN Tower. Complete the information. Use the superlative form of the correct adjective from the box.

clear	famous	fast	heavy	long	popular	~~tall~~

1. At 1,815 feet, 5 inches (553.33 m), the CN Tower is _____the tallest_____
   free-standing structure in the world.

2. Everyone recognizes the CN Tower. It is _____ building in Canada.

3. At 130,000 tons (117,910 metric tonnes), the CN Tower is one of _____
   buildings in the world.

4. With 2 million visitors every year, it is one of _____ tourist attractions in
   the country.

5. Because of its very high antenna, the tower provides the people of Toronto with some of
   _____ radio and TV reception in North America.

6. Moving at 15 miles (22 km) per hour, the six elevators are among _____
   in the world. The ride to the Look Out Level takes just 58 seconds.

7. If you don't want to take the elevator, you can try the stairs! The CN Tower has
   _____ metal staircase in the world.

4 | WHAT ABOUT YOU?

*Write superlative sentences about your own experiences. Use the words in parentheses with **the most** and **the least** + the present perfect. Write two sentences for each item. Go to Appendix 1, page A-1, for help with the irregular past participles.*

Example: Toronto is the most interesting city I've ever visited.
             Meadville is the least interesting place I've ever visited.

1. (interesting / city / visit)

_____

_____

2. (comfortable / place / stay)

_____

_____

3. (friendly / people / meet)

_____

_____

4. (expensive / trip / take)

_____

_____

5 | EDITING

Read this postcard. There are seven mistakes in the use of superlative adjectives. The first mistake is already corrected. Find and correct six more.

 most beautiful
Greetings from Toronto —the ~~beautifulest~~ city I've ever visited. Yesterday we went to the CN Tower —the more recognizable structure in all of Canada. From there you get the best view of the city. The restaurant was the most expensivest I've ever seen, so we just enjoyed the view and then went to Kensington Market to eat. This place has the baddest crowds but the cheapest and the goodest food we've had so far. We're staying in East Toronto. It's not the closer place to downtown, but it has some of most historic buildings. In fact, our bed-and-breakfast is called *1871 Historic House.* John Lennon slept here!

Love, Marissa

Communication Practice

6 | LISTENING

🎧 *May and Dan are deciding on a hotel for their vacation in Toronto. Listen to their conversation. Then check the correct hotel for each superlative adjective.*

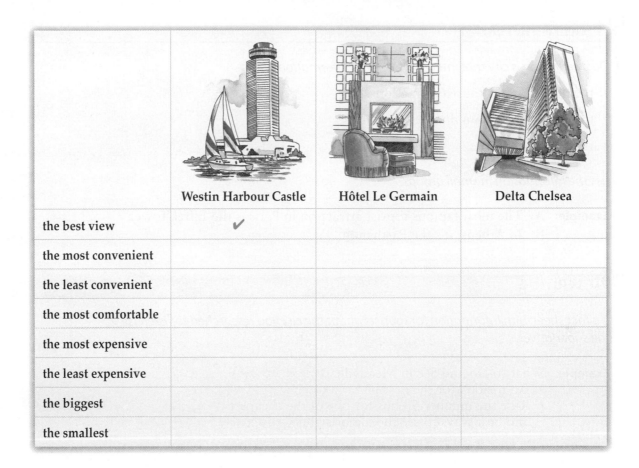

	Westin Harbour Castle	Hôtel Le Germain	Delta Chelsea
the best view	✔		
the most convenient			
the least convenient			
the most comfortable			
the most expensive			
the least expensive			
the biggest			
the smallest			

7 | IN YOUR COUNTRY

Work in small groups. Discuss cities in your country. You can use these adjectives:

beautiful	interesting
clean	international
crowded	modern
exciting	old
friendly	safe

Example: **A:** What's the most interesting city in Argentina?

B: I think Buenos Aires is the most interesting city in Argentina. There's so much to do—theater, sports, movies. It's also the most diverse city in the country. People from all over the world live there.

8 | IN THE WORLD

Work in small groups. Discuss your answers to Exercise 4.

> **Example:** **A:** What's the most interesting city you've ever visited?
> **B:** Barcelona. It has some of the most wonderful buildings in the world. It also has some of the best restaurants . . .

9 | ON THE INTERNET

Do a search on a city that interests you. Find information about:

- the most famous tourist attractions
- the most historic buildings and areas
- the best restaurants

Discuss the information in small groups.

> **Example:** **A:** The most famous tourist attraction in Paris is the Eiffel Tower.
> **B:** In Athens, it's the Parthenon.

10 | WRITING

Write a fact sheet with information for tourists about the city you researched for Exercise 9. Include superlatives.

> **Example:** What to Do and See in Meadville
> - Go to Joe's for the best pizza in town.
> - Ride the number 53 bus for one of the cheapest and best ways to see the major sights.

Adverbs: *As . . . as*, Comparatives, Superlatives

Grammar in Context

BEFORE YOU READ

🎧 *Look at the photo. What game are they playing? Which sports do you like to watch? Do you play any sports? Which ones? Why do you like them? Read the transcript of a TV sports program.*

The Halftime Report

Tamecka Dixon of the LA Sparks and Ruth Riley of the Detroit Shock

CINDY: What a game! Spero, have you ever seen two teams play **more aggressively**?

SPERO: No, I haven't, Cindy. Folks, we're watching the Detroit Shock battle the Los Angeles Sparks. It's halftime, and just listen to that Sparks crowd! I think they cheer **the loudest** of any fans in the game!

CINDY: Well, the court really belonged to the Sparks for the first few minutes of the game, Spero. But the Shock recovered quickly. They've scored almost **as frequently as** the Sparks in the first half. The score is now 30–28, Sparks, and no one can predict a winner at this point.

SPERO: I heard that Ruth Riley, the Shock's star player, injured her arm yesterday, but you can't tell from the way she's playing today. She's scored **the most** of her team so far.

CINDY: But Tamecka Dixon of the Sparks isn't far behind. She's playing **more and more intensely**. You can see that she really wants the ball, and she's getting it **more consistently** in every game.

SPERO: You're right, Cindy. **The harder** she plays, **the more** she scores.

CINDY: The Sparks have really been playing a great defense tonight. They've been blocking Riley **more effectively than** any other team this season. But can they stop her?

SPERO: We'll find out now! The second half is ready to begin. See you again after the game.

AFTER YOU READ

Read the statements. Check **True** *or* **False**.

	True	False
1. Both teams are playing aggressively.	☐	☐
2. The Sparks fans cheer louder than the Shock fans.	☐	☐
3. In the first half, the Shock scored as many points as the Sparks.	☐	☐
4. Tamecka Dixon is playing badly.	☐	☐
5. Other Shock players have scored more than Riley.	☐	☐
6. Other teams have blocked Ruth Riley better than the Sparks.	☐	☐

Grammar Presentation

ADVERBS: *AS . . . AS*, COMPARATIVES, SUPERLATIVES

As . . . as					
		As	Adverb	As	
The Huskies	played didn't play	as	hard well aggressively consistently	as	the Gophers.

Comparatives				
		Comparative Adverb Form	*Than*	
The Huskies	played	harder better	than	the Gophers.
		more aggressively less consistently		

Superlatives		
		Superlative Adverb Form	
The star player	played	the hardest the best	of anyone in the game.
		the most aggressively the least consistently	

GRAMMAR NOTES	EXAMPLES
1. Use (*not*) *as* + adverb + *as* to compare actions and show how they are (or aren't) **similar**.	
• Use *as* + adverb + *as* to show how actions are <u>the same or equal</u>. Use *just* to make the comparison stronger.	• Riley played *just* **as well as** most players. *(She and the other players played equally well.)*
• Use *not as* + adverb + *as* to show how actions are <u>not the same or equal</u>.	• Cash did**n't** play **as aggressively as** Ely. *(Cash and Ely didn't play the same. Cash played less aggressively.)*

2. Use **comparative adverbs** + *than* to show how the actions of two people or things are **different**.	• The Sparks played **better than** the Shock. • Riley played **more skillfully than** Nolan. • She played **less aggressively than** Nolan.

3. REMEMBER: It's not necessary to mention both parts of the comparison when the meaning is clear.	• He played hard. She played just **as hard** (as he did). • Beard shot **more consistently** (than King).

4. Use **superlative adverbs** to compare <u>one</u> action with the actions of other people or things in a <u>group</u>.	• All the players worked hard, but Robins worked **the hardest**.
We often use the superlative with **expressions** beginning with *of*.	• Villaneuva scored **the most frequently** *of any player* on the team.

5. There are several ways of **forming comparative and superlative adverbs**.

ADVERB	COMPARATIVE	SUPERLATIVE
fast	fast**er**	**the** fast**est**
hard	hard**er**	**the** hard**est**
well	**better**	**the best**
badly	**worse**	**the worst**
skillfully	**more / less** skillfully	**the most / the least** skillfully
quickly	**more** quickly quick**er**	**the most** quickly **the** quick**est**
slowly	**more** slowly slow**er**	**the most** slowly **the** slow**est**

a. For **short adverbs** (one syllable), use adverb + *-er* or *the* + adverb + *-est*.

Some adverbs have **irregular** comparative and superlative forms.

b. For **long adverbs** (two or more syllables), use *more / less* + adverb or *the most / the least* + adverb.

c. Note that **some adverbs of manner** have <u>two comparative</u> and <u>two superlative</u> forms.

USAGE NOTE: The *-er / -est* forms are <u>informal</u>. Do not use them in formal speech and writing.

(continued)

6. Comparatives with *than* and comparisons with *as . . . as* often express the <u>same meaning</u> in different ways.	• The Sparks played **more aggressively than** the Shock. • The Shock did**n't** play **as aggressively as** the Sparks. • The Shock played **less aggressively than** the Sparks.
USAGE NOTE: With <u>one-syllable adverbs</u>, *not as . . . as* is more common than *less . . . than*.	• The Shock did**n't** play **as hard as** the Sparks. NOT The Shock played ~~less hard than~~ the Sparks.

7. REMEMBER: Do not put an adverb of manner between the verb and the object.	verb object adverb • Davis handled *the ball* **more skillfully** than Adams. NOT Davis handled ~~more skillfully the ball~~ than Adams.

8. Repeat the comparative adverb to show how something is <u>increasing or decreasing</u>: **comparative adverb** + *and* + **comparative adverb** With long adverbs, repeat only *more* or *less*.	• Kukoc is playing **better and better** as the season continues. *(His performance keeps getting better.)* • He is playing **more and more aggressively**. • The Gophers play **less and less skillfully**.

9. Use **two comparative adverbs** to show <u>cause and effect</u>: *the* + **comparative adverb** + *the* + **comparative adverb**	• **The harder** he played, **the better** he got. *(When he played harder, he got better.)*

Reference Notes

For a list of **irregular comparative and superlative adverbs** see Appendix 10 on page A-6.
For more information about **adverbs**, see Unit 23 on page 270.

Focused Practice

1 | DISCOVER THE GRAMMAR

Read this story from the sports section of the newspaper. Underline all the comparisons with (not) as *+* adverb *+* as, *and all the comparative and superlative adverb forms.*

Comets Beat Lions!

In the first basketball game of the season, the Comets beat the Lions, 90 to 83. The Lions played a truly fantastic game, but their defense is still weak. The Comets defended the ball much more aggressively than the Lions did.

Of course, Ace Hernandez certainly helped win the game for the Comets. The Comets' star player was back on the court today to the delight of his many fans. He was hurt badly at the end of last season, but he has recovered quickly. Although he didn't play as well as people expected, he still handled the ball like the old Ace. He certainly handled it the most skillfully of anyone on the team. He controlled the ball the best, shot the ball the most accurately, and scored the most consistently of any of the players on either team. He played hard and helped the Comets look good. In fact, the harder he played, the better the Comets performed. Watch Ace this season.

And watch the Lions. They have a new coach, and they're training more seriously this year. I think we'll see them play better and better as the season progresses.

2 | PICKS OF THE KICKS

Grammar Notes 1, 6–7

Read this chart comparing several brands of basketball shoes. Complete the sentences. Use (not) as *+* adverb *+* as *and the words in parentheses. Change the adjectives to adverbs.*

SHOES	Better ◄———————► Worse			
	●	◐	○	
Brand	**Comfort**	**Support**	**Protection**	**Durability***
X	●	◐	●	◐
Y	●	○	●	○
Z	○	○	◐	◐

*how long the product lasts

1. X ___*fits as comfortably as*___ Y.
      (fit / comfortable)

2. Z _____ X or Y.
      (fit / comfortable)

3. Y _____ Z.
      (support / the ankles / good)

4. Y and Z _____ X.
      (support / the ankles / good)

5. Z _____ X or Y.
      (protect / the feet / effective)

6. X_____ Y.
      (protect / the feet / effective)

7. X _____ Z.
      (last / long)

8. Y _____ X or Z.
      (last / long)

3 | A WHOLE NEW BALL GAME

Grammar Notes 1–6, 8–9

◯ *Complete the conversation between sports commentator Carla Lobo and player Elena Bard. Use the words in parentheses with* **as . . . as** *or with the comparative or superlative forms. Add* **the** *or* **than**, *and choose between* **more** *or* **less** *where necessary.*

LOBO: Why do people still take female basketball players _____*less seriously than*_____
                                                             1. (seriously)

male players? Do women really play _____ men?
                                          2. (aggressively)

BARD: Absolutely not! We play just _____. And when we fall,
                                          3. (aggressively)

we hit the floor just _____ the guys do.
                              4. (hard)

LOBO: You could sure see that in tonight's game. Jackson played _____
                                                                      5. (fearlessly)

of any player I've seen, male or female.

BARD: Yes. And _____ women athletes compete,
                      6. (often)

_____ audiences are going to see that.
        7. (soon)

LOBO: Some people say women play _____ men.
                                        8. (cooperatively)

BARD: I agree. I think we have better teamwork—we play _____
                                                              9. (well)

on a team. We also play _____. Women players will
                              10. (patiently)

wait _____ for a good chance to shoot.
        11. (long)

LOBO: Tickets for women's basketball games cost _____ tickets
                                                        12. (little)

for men's games. Does that bother you?

BARD: Sure, but _____ women players attract fans,
                      13. (fast)

_____ the women's leagues will make money.
        14. (fast)

LOBO: So as time goes on you'll be paid _____ and
                                                15. (well)

_____.
        15. (well)

BARD: We certainly hope so.

4 | THE ALL-AROUND ATHLETE

Grammar Notes 2–5

Look at the chart on the next page. Then complete the sentences. Use the comparative or superlative form of the adverbs in the box. You will use some adverbs more than once.

badly	far	fast	well	high	slowly

	Broad Jump (distance)	**Pole Vaulting (height)**	**5-mile Run (speed)**
Nolan	14.3 feet	7 feet, 3 inches	24 minutes
Smith	14.1 feet	7 feet, 2 inches	28 minutes
Diaz	15.2 feet	7 feet, 8 inches	30 minutes
Wang	15.4 feet	8 feet, 2 inches	22 minutes

1. Nolan jumped _____*farther than*_____ Smith.

2. Wang vaulted _____*the highest*_____ of all.

3. Diaz ran _____.

4. Smith ran _____ Wang.

5. Wang jumped _____.

6. Nolan ran _____ Smith.

7. Wang vaulted _____ Smith.

8. All in all, Wang did _____.

9. All in all, Smith did _____.

5 | EDITING

Read this article in a student newspaper. There are nine mistakes in the use of adverbs. The first mistake is already corrected. Find and correct eight more.

Last night was the last game of the season, and the Lions played the ~~goodest~~ *best* they've played for months. Both the Cubs and Lions play a great offensive game, but this time the Lions really played defense much more effectively as the Cubs. Hernandez, the Cubs' star player, has been shooting more aggressively and more aggressively all season. But in last night's game, the more aggressive he played, the most closely the Lions guarded him. Then, in the last two minutes, "Tiny Tim" O'Connell made the winning shot for the Lions. "He's less than six feet tall, but he runs more fastly than anyone else on the court," the Cubs' coach said. "O'Connell doesn't shoot as often other players, but he's a lot more accurately than the bigger guys." The Cubs played a great game last night too, but they just didn't play as good as the Lions.

Communication Practice

6 | LISTENING

🎧 *Listen to the sportscaster describing a horse race. Then listen again and rank the horses from first place (1) to last place (5).*

_____ Exuberant King

__1__ Get Packin'

_____ Inspired Winner

_____ Señor Speedy

_____ Wild Whirl

7 | SPORTS AROUND THE WORLD

Work as a class. Name several famous athletes for one sport. Compare their abilities. Use the comparative and superlative forms of adverbs. Use your own ideas or the ideas in the box to help you.

Activities	Adverbs
catch	carefully
hit	defensively
kick	easily
play	powerfully
race	regularly
run	seriously
throw	straight
train	successfully

Example: Fatuma Roba is a runner from Ethiopia. She runs faster and more gracefully than most other runners.

8 | A QUESTIONNAIRE

Answer the questionnaire.

1. How many hours do you work every week? _____

2. How many books have you read this month? _____

3. When did you last watch a sports event? _____

4. How many hours a week do you participate in sports? _____

5. How many trips have you taken in the last year? _____

6. How many countries have you visited? _____

Now add your own questions.

7. _____

8. _____

9. _____

10. _____

Work in groups. Compare your answers to questions 1–6 with those of your classmates.
Ask the group your own questions (7–10) and compare the answers.

Find out:

1. Who works the hardest?

2. Who reads the most?

3. Who has watched a sports event the most recently?

4. Who participates in sports the most regularly?

5. Who has traveled the most frequently?

6. Who has traveled the most extensively?

Example: Sharif works the hardest. He works 45 hours every week.

9 | WRITING

Write a paragraph comparing two sports figures. Choose either two people that you know
or two famous athletes. You can use the ideas from the box in Exercise 7.

Example: My friends Paul and Nick are both good soccer players, but they have different
styles. Nick plays more aggressively than Paul, but Paul runs faster and passes more
frequently. Nick scores more often, but Paul plays more cooperatively . . .

10 | ON THE INTERNET

Work in teams. Do a search on **Olympics 2004 results** to find the answers to the questions in this Olympics quiz. The first team to get all the correct answers wins!

1. Who ran the fastest in the women's marathon?

    a. Deena Kastor   **b.** Mizuki Noguchi   **c.** Catherine Ndereba

2. In the men's 100-meter race, who ran faster than Francis Obikwelu?

    a. Justin Gatlin   **b.** Maurice Green

3. Did Italy score as high as Argentina in men's basketball in the championship game?

    a. Yes   **b.** No

4. Which woman jumped the highest in the women's high jump?

    a. Yelena Isinbayeva   **b.** Viktoriya Styopina   **c.** Hestrie Cloete

From **Grammar** to **Writing**
Using Descriptive Adjectives

Descriptive adjectives can help your reader better picture what you are writing about.

Example: I live in an apartment. ⟶
I live in a **small comfortable one-bedroom** apartment.

1 Read this paragraph. Circle all the adjectives that describe the writer's apartment.

> I live in a (small) comfortable one-bedroom apartment that is close to school. The living
>
> room is my favorite room. It's sunny, warm, and cheerful. There's an old brick fireplace,
>
> which I use on cold winter nights. In the corner there's a large soft green couch. I like
>
> to sit there and read. Next to it is a small wood table with a beautiful antique lamp from
>
> my favorite aunt. It's a cozy living room, and I enjoy spending time there.

2 Complete this word map with the circled words from Exercise 1.

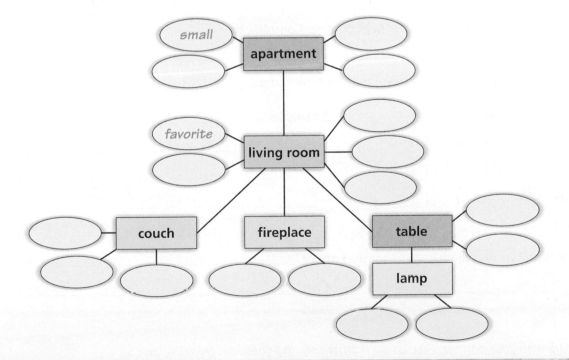

3 | *Before you write . . .*

1. Work in small groups. Put the adjectives from the box into the correct categories. Brainstorm other adjectives for each category. You can use a dictionary for help.

~~attractive~~	coarse	comfortable	cozy	cute	enormous
gorgeous	~~hard~~	hideous	huge	~~large~~	~~little~~
lovely	rough	run-down	~~soft~~	tiny	ugly

a. things that are big: _large,_____

b. things that are small: _little,_____

c. things that look good: _attractive,_____

d. things that look bad: _run-down,_____

e. things that feel good: _soft,_____

f. things that feel bad: _hard,_____

2. Think about a room you know. On a separate piece of paper, draw a word map like the one in Exercise 2. Use some of the adjectives in the box above.

3. Discuss your map with a partner. Do you want to add or change any adjectives?

Example: A: How small is the kitchen?
B: Oh, it's tiny.

4 | *Write a paragraph about the room from Exercise 3. Use your word map.*

5 | *Exchange paragraphs with a different partner. Complete the chart.*

Did the writer use adjectives that describe how things _____?			
	Yes	**No**	**Example(s)**
look	☐	☐	_____
feel	☐	☐	_____
smell	☐	☐	_____
sound	☐	☐	_____
What would you like more information about?			_____

6 | *Work with your partner. Discuss each other's editing questions from Exercise 5. Then rewrite your own paragraph. Answer any questions your partner asked.*

Review Test

I *Complete the advertisements by choosing the correct words in parentheses.*

1. FOR RENT. Live ___*comfortably*___ in this _____ studio
   a. (comfortable / comfortably)   b. (cozy / cozily)
   apartment. _____ rent makes it a _____
   c. (Cheap / Cheaply)   d. (perfect / perfectly)
   home for one student.

2. FOR SALE. Woman's bicycle. I'm asking the _____ low price of $65
   a. (incredible / incredibly)
   for this _____ five-speed bike. I've _____
   b. (new / newly)   c. (hard / hardly)
   used it at all. Don't miss this _____ bargain.
   d. (terrific / terrifically)

3. FREE to a _____ family. Skipper is a _____
   a. (good / well)   b. (beautiful / beautifully)
   and friendly puppy. He behaves _____ with children, and he is very
   c. (good / well)
   _____. We are moving very soon, so if you want Skipper, please act
   d. (obedient / obediently)
   _____.
   e. (quick / quickly)

II *Circle the letter of the correct answer to complete each sentence.*

1. I passed my driver's test. It seemed much _____ this time.   A (B) C D
   (**A**) easy   (**C**) easiest
   (**B**) easier   (**D**) easily

2. Our team didn't play _____ I expected. I was disappointed.   A B C D
   (**A**) as well as (**C**) as badly as
   (**B**) well   (**D**) better

3. The faster Tranh walks, _____.   A B C D
   (**A**) more tired   (**C**) the more tired he gets
   (**B**) he gets tired   (**D**) he gets more tired

(continued)

4. Could you talk _____? I'm trying to work.

   (**A**) more quietly   (**C**) more quiet

   (**B**) quieter   (**D**) quiet

                                          A B C D

5. Lisa is staying home. Her cold is a lot _____ today.

   (**A**) bad   (**C**) worst

   (**B**) worse   (**D**) the worst

                                          A B C D

6. Sorry we're late. Your house is much _____ than we thought.

   (**A**) far   (**C**) farther

   (**B**) the farthest   (**D**) the farther

                                          A B C D

7. The movie was so _____ that we couldn't sleep last night.

   (**A**) excitingly   (**C**) excite

   (**B**) excited   (**D**) exciting

                                          A B C D

8. Chris is working very _____ these days.

   (**A**) hardly   (**C**) harder

   (**B**) hard   (**D**) hardest

                                          A B C D

9. Write the report. It's more important _____ your other work.

   (**A**) than   (**C**) from

   (**B**) as   (**D**) then

                                          A B C D

10. The lunch menu is short. It's _____ than the dinner menu.

   (**A**) varied   (**C**) less varied

   (**B**) more varied   (**D**) the least varied

                                          A B C D

11. Thank you! That's _____ I've ever received.

   (**A**) the nicer gift   (**C**) nicest gift

   (**B**) a nice gift   (**D**) the nicest gift

                                          A B C D

12. It's getting more _____ to find a cheap apartment.

   (**A**) hardly   (**C**) the most difficult

   (**B**) and more difficult   (**D**) and very difficult

                                          A B C D

13. My history class is _____ my math class.

   (**A**) interesting than   (**C**) as interested as

   (**B**) more interesting   (**D**) more interesting than

                                          A B C D

III *Each sentence has four underlined words or phrases. The four underlined parts of the sentences are marked A, B, C, or D. Circle the letter of the one underlined word or phrase that is NOT CORRECT.*

1. My Spanish isn't <u>very</u> <u>good</u>, so I make <u>some</u> <u>embarrassed</u> mistakes.   **A B C (D)**
   A   B   C   D

2. <u>The harder</u> Sylvia <u>tries</u>, <u>less</u> she <u>succeeds</u>.   **A B C D**
  A   B   C   D

3. This <u>has</u> been <u>the</u> <u>best</u> day <u>than</u> my whole life!   **A B C D**
    A   B C   D

4. We're <u>always</u> <u>amazing</u> <u>by</u> John's <u>incredible</u> travel stories.   **A B C D**
      A   B   C   D

5. We took <u>a lot of</u> photos because she was <u>such</u> a <u>cutely</u> <u>little</u> baby.   **A B C D**
      A   B   C D

6. Our <u>new</u> car is <u>hard</u> to drive <u>than</u> our <u>old</u> one.   **A B C D**
    A   B   C   D

7. Patrick doesn't <u>run quickly</u> <u>as</u> Lee, <u>but</u> he can run <u>farther</u>.   **A B C D**
        A   B   C   D

8. You did <u>much</u> <u>more</u> <u>better</u> on the last test <u>than</u> on this one.   **A B C D**
    A   B   C   D

9. What's <u>the</u> <u>more</u> <u>popular</u> of all the <u>new</u> TV shows?   **A B C D**
    A   B   C   D

10. <u>The</u> <u>more</u> I practice my English, the <u>most</u> <u>fluent</u> I get.   **A B C D**
  A   B   C   D

11. The garbage in the street <u>is</u> <u>more</u> <u>disgusted</u> <u>than</u> the potholes.   **A B C D**
             A   B   C   D

12. Today seems <u>as</u> <u>hotter</u> <u>as</u> yesterday, but the humidity is <u>lower</u>.   **A B C D**
       A B   C   D

IV *Complete the sentences with the comparative form of the adjectives and adverbs. Use the information in parentheses to help you.*

1. Ann's criticism was very unfair. I was convinced of that.

   (I thought about it thoroughly. I became angry.)

   The ___*more thoroughly*___ I thought about it, the ___*angrier*___ I became.

2. My teacher tried to explain the lesson, but she talked very fast.

   (She talked fast. I felt confused.)

   The _____ she talked, the _____ I felt.

(continued)

3. Bruce gets really silly when he's tired. Last night he studied until midnight.

(It got late. He became silly.)

The _____ it got, the _____ he became.

4. Sylvia studied hard for her French course last semester.

(She studied hard. She spoke fluently.)

The _____ she studied, the _____ she spoke.

5. Greg takes good care of his garden.

(He often waters his tomatoes. They get big.)

The _____ he waters his tomatoes, the _____ they get.

6. My neighbors' dog always barks at me when I run near their house.

(He barks loud. I run fast.)

The _____ he barks, the _____ I run.

7. Eric is frequently late to basketball practice, so he performs badly in games.

(He frequently comes late. He performs badly.)

The _____ he comes late, the _____ he performs.

V | *Read the sentences. Complete the summary sentence with the word in parentheses and **as . . .as** or **not as . . .as**. Use an appropriate verb.*

1. The rent for Apartment 5-G is $550.

The rent for Apartment 22-G is $720.

(expensive) Apartment 5-G *isn't as expensive as Apartment 22-G.*

2. Apartment 5-G has five rooms.

Apartment 22-G has five rooms.

(large) Apartment 5-G _____

3. Tony's pizzeria is two blocks away.

Sal's pizzeria is around the corner.

(far) Sal's pizzeria _____

4. A slice of Tony's pizza costs $5.00.

A slice of Sal's pizza also costs $5.00.

(expensive) Sal's pizza _____

5. The Sparks have won six games. They've played very well.

The Shock have won six games too. They've played very well also.

(well) The Sparks _____

6. Amanda runs a six-minute mile.

Jennifer runs a five-and-a-half-minute mile.

(fast) Amanda _____

VI Complete each paragraph with the words from the box. Use each word once.

| best | hardest | longest | of | ~~successful~~ | the |

1. Pat's the most ____successful____ salesperson in her office, and she deserves to be. She works
   a.

the _____ hours. Sometimes she works until 10:00 at night. She also works the
      b.

_____. When she works with a client, she talks _____ most
      c.   d.

persuasively _____ all our people. She's really the _____.
                    e.   f.

| as | big | exciting | much | sooner | than |

2. Communications equipment used to be only for _____ companies, but today,
                                                          a.

even small offices have the latest equipment. Scanners are cheaper _____ they
                                                                            b.

used to be, so they're common in home offices now. Cell phones are everywhere, and they're

_____ more useful—many include e-mail, cameras, and personal planners. The
      c.

most _____ new development is the computer with wireless Internet connection.
          d.

_____ than you think, "Wi-Fi" (Wireless Fidelity) will be _____
      e.   f.

common as the cell phone.

VII *Read this diary entry. There are ten mistakes in the use of adjectives and adverbs. The first mistake is already corrected. Find and correct nine more.*

> Wednesday
>
>   worst
> I think today has been the ~~bad~~ day of my life. My car broke down on the
> expressway during rush hour this morning — a busiest time of day. I sat there
> for an hour waiting for a tow truck. The longer I waited, the nervous I
> became. I was a wreck when I got to work. Of course, this was the day we
> were closing biggest deal of the year. My boss called me five times about one
> letter. And more frequently he called, the worse I typed. My next worry is the
> repair bill for the car. I hope it isn't as high the last time.
>
> I'm going to try to relax now. There's an interested movie on cable TV
> tonight. Jan saw it last week and says it's the better film she's seen in a
> long time. After the movie, I'll take a hotter bath and go to bed. I'm looking
> forward to tomorrow. It can't be as badly as today!

▶ *To check your answers, go to the Answer Key on page RT-4.*

Gerunds and Infinitives

27 Gerunds: Subject and Object

Grammar in Context

BEFORE YOU READ

🎧 *Where can you find posters or signs like these? How do you feel about them?*

INTERDIT DE FUMER NO SMOKING

SMOKING POLLUTES
YOU AND EVERYTHING ELSE

Read the online bulletin board about smoking.

Re: Can't Stand Seeing Those Signs!

Posted by Grofumeur on February 16, 2005, at 15:30:03
I **can't stand seeing** all the new No Smoking signs. **Eating** in a restaurant or **having** an espresso in a café is no fun anymore! Junk food is worse than **smoking**. But I bet the government won't **prohibit ordering** burgers and fries for lunch!

Reply posted by Nuffsed on February 17, 12:15:22
Hey, Grofumeur—I don't get sick when my boyfriend has a Big Mac, but **sitting** in a room full of his cigarette smoke makes my hair and clothing stink.

Reply posted by Swissfriend on February 17, 20:53:11
Hi, Smokers! I am a member of Freunde der Tabak, a Swiss group of smokers and non-smokers. We **suggest practicing** courtesy to non-smokers and tolerance of smokers. I **enjoy smoking**, but I **understand not wanting** to inhale second-hand smoke.

Reply posted by Cleanaire on February 18, 9:53:11
Friend—Have you ever tried to **stop smoking**? If so, then you know you are addicted to nicotine. The younger you **start smoking**, the harder it is to quit.

AFTER YOU READ

Check the correct answer(s).

Who _____?	Grofumeur	Nuffsed	Swissfriend	Cleanaire
1. smokes	☐	☐	☐	☐
2. thinks it's difficult to quit smoking	☐	☐	☐	☐
3. doesn't want to see No Smoking signs	☐	☐	☐	☐
4. hates secondhand smoke	☐	☐	☐	☐
5. thinks smokers and non-smokers should be polite	☐	☐	☐	☐

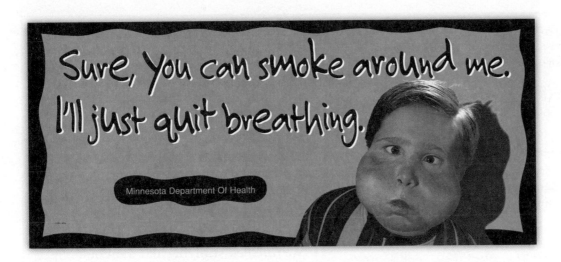

Sure, you can smoke around me. I'll just quit breathing.

Minnesota Department Of Health

Grammar Presentation

GERUNDS: AS SUBJECTS AND OBJECTS

Gerund as Subject		
Gerund (Subject)	**Verb**	
Smoking	causes	health problems.
Not smoking	is	healthier.

Gerund as Object		
Subject	**Verb**	**Gerund (Object)**
You	should quit	**smoking**.
We	suggest	**not smoking**.

GRAMMAR NOTES

EXAMPLES

1. A **gerund (base form of verb + -ing)** is a verb that we use like a <u>noun</u>.

- **Smoking** is bad for your health.
- **Swimming** is a good exercise.
- I enjoy **running** in the park.

BASE FORM	GERUND
smoke	smo**king**
swim	swim**ming**

▶ **BE CAREFUL!** There are often <u>spelling changes</u> when you add *-ing*.

Form the **negative** by placing *not* before the gerund.

- **Not exercising** is bad for you.
- The doctor suggested **not drinking** coffee for a while.

---

2. A gerund can be the **subject** of a sentence. It is always <u>singular</u>. Use the third-person-singular form of the verb after gerunds.

- **Eating** junk food *makes* me sick.
- **Inhaling** smoke *gives* me bronchitis.

▶ **BE CAREFUL!** Don't confuse a gerund with the progressive form of the verb.

- gerund
  Drinking a lot of coffee is unhealthy.
- progressive form
  He **is drinking** coffee right now.

---

3. A gerund can also be the **object** of certain verbs. Use a gerund **after these verbs**:

admit	*avoid*	*consider*	*deny*
dislike	*enjoy*	*finish*	*miss*
practice	*quit*	*suggest*	*understand*

- Jiang *avoids* **hanging out** with smokers.
- Have you ever *considered* **quitting**?
- I *dislike* **sitting** near smokers in cafés.
- We *finished* **studying** and went out.
- Did you *miss* **smoking** after you quit?
- Dr. Ho *suggested* **not staying up** late.

---

4. We often use *go + gerund* to describe <u>activities</u> such as shopping, fishing, skiing, swimming, and camping.

- Let's *go* **swimming** in the lake.
- I *went* **shopping** for running shoes yesterday.

Reference Notes

For a more complete list of **verbs** that can be **followed by gerunds,** see Appendix 13 on page A-7.
For **spelling rules for verb + -ing,** see Appendix 21 on page A-10.

Focused Practice

1 | DISCOVER THE GRAMMAR

Read part of an article from a health newsletter. Underline the gerunds.

YOUR HEALTH

SWIMMING is a great exercise. It's healthy, fun, and relaxing. Because swimming is a low-impact sport, people can enjoy participating in this activity without fear of injury to bones or muscles.

Jogging, a high-impact activity, can be harmful for some people. I know this from personal experience.

Last year while I was jogging, I injured my right knee. I don't go jogging anymore.

After a painful month of recovery, I stopped running and switched to water sports. I'm now considering joining the swimming team at my health club and competing in races. Staying fit should be fun!

2 | HEALTH ISSUES

Grammar Notes 1–3

Complete this article with gerunds. Use the verbs in the box. You will use one verb more than once. Choose between affirmative and negative.

eat	exercise	go	increase	~~pay~~	smoke	start	stay

_____*Not paying*_____ attention to their health is a mistake a lot of college students make.
1.

_____ healthy will help you do well in school and enjoy your college experience.
2.

Here are some tips:

- Smokers have more colds and less energy. Quit _____ now or don't start.
3.

- _____ regularly reduces stress and brings more oxygen to your brain. If you
4.

  don't exercise, consider _____ a program now.
  5.

- _____ breakfast is a common mistake. It's the most important meal of the day.
6.

- Avoid _____ foods with a lot of fat and sugar. Your brain will thank you!
7.

- Health experts advise _____ the fruits and vegetables in your diet. You need at
8.

  least four and a half cups a day, but more is better.

- _____ to the doctor when you're sick is another common mistake. Know where
9.

  your school Health Service is, and use it when you need it.

3 | A QUESTION OF HEALTH

Write a summary sentence for each conversation. Use the correct form of a verb from the box and the gerund form of the verb in parentheses.

admit	avoid	consider	~~deny~~	enjoy	go	mind	quit

1. **BRIAN:** Where are the cookies I bought? You ate them, didn't you?

   ELLEN: No, I didn't.

   SUMMARY: Ellen _____*denied eating*_____ the cookies.
   (eat)

2. **ANN:** Do you want to go running with me before work?

   TOM: Running? Are you kidding? I hate it!

   SUMMARY: Tom doesn't _____.
   (run)

3. **RALPH:** Would you like a cigarette?

   MARTA: Oh, no, thanks. I don't smoke anymore.

   SUMMARY: Marta _____.
   (smoke)

4. **CHEN:** What are you doing after work?

   AN-LING: I'm going to that new swimming pool. Would you like to go with me?

   SUMMARY: An-ling is going to _____.
   (swim)

5. **IRENE:** You're lazy. You really need to exercise more.

   MIKE: You're right. I *am* lazy.

   SUMMARY: Mike _____ lazy.
   (be)

6. **MONICA:** Would you like a piece of chocolate cake?

   PAULO: No, thanks. I try to stay away from sweets.

   SUMMARY: Paulo _____ sweets.
   (eat)

7. **CRAIG:** I know exercise is important, but I hate it. What about you?

   VILMA: Well, I don't *love* it, but it's OK.

   SUMMARY: Vilma doesn't _____.
   (exercise)

8. **ALICE:** We've been working too hard. Maybe we need a vacation.

   ERIK: A vacation? Hmmm. That's an interesting idea. Do you think we can afford it?

   SUMMARY: Erik and Alice _____ a vacation.
   (take)

4 | EDITING

Read part of an ex-smoker's journal. There are fourteen mistakes in the use of gerunds as subject and object. The first mistake is already corrected. Find and correct thirteen more. Remember to check for spelling mistakes.

> ***smoking***
> DAY 1   I quit ~~to smoke~~! This was the first day of the rest of my life as a non-smoker. Get
>
> through the day wasn't too difficult. I quit drinking coffee today too, and I think that helped.
>
> I used to enjoy had a cigarette with a cup of coffee in the morning.
>
> DAY 3   Today was harder. I called Dinah and admitted wanted to smoke. She advised takeing
>
> deep breaths and staying busy. That worked. I have to resist eat too much. Gaining five pounds
>
> aren't a big deal, but I don't want to gain more than that.
>
> DAY 5   I got through the workweek smoke free. My boss keeps tells me, "You can do it." I really
>
> appreciate to have her support. I miss smoking, but I <u>don't</u> miss to standing outside in the cold
>
> just to smoke. I also don't mind don't burning holes in my clothes!
>
> DAY 7   Dinah suggested to go out to dinner, but I can't risk be around smokers . . . Instead, we
>
> went shoping and I bought a shirt with the money I saved during my first week as a non-smoker.

Communication Practice

5 | LISTENING

🎧 *A doctor is giving advice to a patient. Some things are OK for this patient to do, but other things are not. Listen to the conversation. Then listen again and check the correct column.*

	OK to Do	Not OK to Do
1. smoking	☐	☑
2. drinking coffee	☐	☐
3. losing more weight	☐	☐
4. eating more complex carbohydrates	☐	☐
5. running every day	☐	☐
6. riding a bike every day	☐	☐
7. working eight hours a day	☐	☐

6 | AN OPINION SURVEY

Take a class survey. How many students agree with the statements below? Write the numbers in the appropriate column.

	Agree	Disagree	No Opinion or Don't Know
Seeing someone with a cigarette turns me off.*			
I'd rather hang out with** people who don't smoke.			
It's safe to smoke for only a year or two.			
Smoking can help you when you're bored.			
Smoking helps reduce stress.			
Smoking helps keep your weight down.			
I quit, but sometimes I miss smoking.			

turns me off = disgusts me
**hang out with* = spend a lot of time with

Discuss your survey results.

Example: Ten people say that seeing someone smoke turns them off.

7 | POSTER TALK

Work in small groups. Discuss this poster. Complete some of the sentences below to help you in the discussion.

MOST TEEN SMOKERS BELIEVE THEY CAN QUIT BUT AFTER **SIX YEARS** 75% STILL SMOKE*

*it's not like they're addicted or anything.

CDC

The message of this poster is . . .

The man wants / doesn't want to quit . . .

The camel enjoys . . .

The camel keeps . . .

Lighting up a cigarette . . .

After six years, most people can't resist . . .

I can't imagine . . .

I can't stand . . .

This poster makes me feel like . . .

Smoking is . . .

Example: The message of this poster is:
Smoking is an addiction.

8 | NO SMOKING?

Many people agree with laws that prohibit smoking in all public places. What is your opinion? Work in small groups. Think of arguments for and against allowing smoking in public places. Take notes.

Example: Going outside to smoke wastes a lot of time at work.

9 | ON THE INTERNET

Do a search on **how to quit smoking**. *Discuss the tips with the rest of the class.*

Example: **A:** Many websites advise setting a "quit" date.
B: Yes. Setting a date is important. Getting support from your friends and family is also very important.

10 | WRITING

Write a letter to a friend who wants to stop smoking. Give your friend tips on how to quit. Use gerunds.

Example: Avoid being around people who smoke.

UNIT

28 Gerunds after Prepositions

Grammar in Context

BEFORE YOU READ

🎧 *Look at the website. What does the Student Council do? Does your school have a Student Council? Is student government useful? Have you ever been a member of a student government? Read the information on the website.*

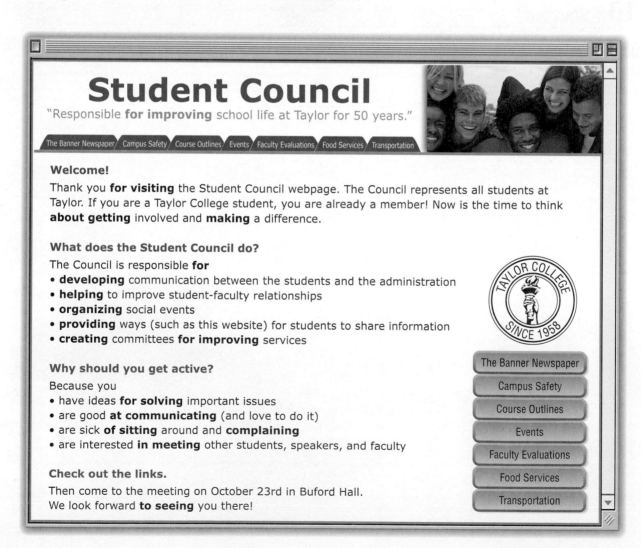

Student Council

"Responsible **for improving** school life at Taylor for 50 years."

| The Banner Newspaper | Campus Safety | Course Outlines | Events | Faculty Evaluations | Food Services | Transportation |

Welcome!

Thank you **for visiting** the Student Council webpage. The Council represents all students at Taylor. If you are a Taylor College student, you are already a member! Now is the time to think **about getting** involved and **making** a difference.

What does the Student Council do?

The Council is responsible **for**
- **developing** communication between the students and the administration
- **helping** to improve student-faculty relationships
- **organizing** social events
- **providing** ways (such as this website) for students to share information
- **creating** committees **for improving** services

Why should you get active?

Because you
- have ideas **for solving** important issues
- are good **at communicating** (and love to do it)
- are sick **of sitting** around and **complaining**
- are interested **in meeting** other students, speakers, and faculty

Check out the links.

Then come to the meeting on October 23rd in Buford Hall.
We look forward **to seeing** you there!

TAYLOR COLLEGE · SINCE 1958

The Banner Newspaper

Campus Safety

Course Outlines

Events

Faculty Evaluations

Food Services

Transportation

AFTER YOU READ

Check the things that Student Council members can do.

☐ **1.** plan a party for new students

☐ **2.** work on the Student Council website

☐ **3.** accept or reject tuition increases

☐ **4.** make new friends and meet teachers

☐ **5.** hire new employees for the school

☐ **6.** start a new committee

☐ **7.** talk to the administration

Grammar Presentation

GERUNDS AFTER PREPOSITIONS

Preposition + Gerund			
Do you have ideas	**about**	**improving**	life at school?
Are the teachers	**against**	**increasing**	tuition?
The students are	**for**	**having**	online courses.
My roommate left	**before**	**finishing**	the test.

Verb + Preposition + Gerund				
I	**plan**	**on**	**joining**	the Student Council.
We'll	**succeed**	**in**	**improving**	the school.
They	**object**	**to**	**paying**	higher fees.
Please	**think**	**about**	**voting**	for Latoya.

Adjective + Preposition + Gerund				
I'm	**interested**	**in**	**studying**	math.
Are you	**tired**	**of**	**hearing**	complaints?
They are	**happy**	**about**	**not missing**	the meeting.
She is	**used**	**to**	**organizing**	large groups.

GRAMMAR NOTES   **EXAMPLES**

---

1. Prepositions are words such as:

about	against	at	before
by	for	in	of
on	to	with	without

After prepositions, use <u>nouns</u> and <u>pronouns</u>.

Because **gerunds** (base form of verb + -*ing*) are nouns, they can also follow prepositions.

REMEMBER: Form the **negative** by placing *not* before the gerund.

- Sam is thinking *about* college.
- He's not *against* it.
- *Before* applying, he'll talk *to* a counselor.

- I thanked him *for the book*.
- I thanked him *for it*.
- I thanked him *for giving* me the book.

- She's happy *about* **not working** today.

---

2. Many common **expressions** have the forms:

- **verb + preposition**
  OR
- **adjective + preposition**

You can use a **gerund** after these expressions.

VERB + PREPOSITION	ADJECTIVE + PREPOSITION
advise *against*	be afraid *of*
believe *in*	be bored *with*
count *on*	be excited *about*

- She *believes in* **working** hard.
- He *is bored with* **working** in a store.

---

3. Do not confuse the **preposition** *to* with part of the infinitive (*to* + base form of verb).

Use a **gerund**, not an infinitive, <u>after</u> expressions with the preposition *to*.

▶ **BE CAREFUL!** Notice the difference in meanings:

a. Use *be / get used to* + gerund to mean *be / become accustomed to*.

b. Use *used to* + base form of verb for <u>past habits</u> or <u>past situations</u> that no longer exist in the present.

EXPRESSIONS WITH PREPOSITION *TO*

look forward *to*	be opposed *to*
object *to*	be used *to*
resort *to*	get used *to*

- I*'m looking forward to* **seeing** you.
  NOT I'm looking forward to ~~see~~ you.

- I*'m used to* **driving** to work because I drove to work for years.
- Now I have to *get used to* **taking** the train.
- I *used to* **drive** to work, but now I take the train.

Reference Notes

For a list of **adjectives followed by prepositions**, see Appendix 17 on page A-7.
For a list of **verbs followed by prepositions**, see Appendix 18 on page A-8.
For more on the meanings of *used to*, *be used to*, and *get used to*, see Unit 5 on page 46.

Focused Practice

1 | DISCOVER THE GRAMMAR

Read the Student Council petition to the president of Taylor College. Underline all the preposition + gerund combinations.

Student Council
Please sign this petition
TAYLOR COLLEGE NEEDS BETTER INTERNET ACCESS

To President Hacking:

We are concerned <u>about improving</u> Internet access at Taylor College. Times are changing. With Wi-Fi (for Wireless Fidelity, or a wireless Internet connection), students can get on the Internet anywhere on campus. Many schools have succeeded in making their campuses completely wireless. Taylor College has been slow at developing this technology, but it is becoming more necessary. Taylor College instructors are putting more and more course material online. With only a few Wi-Fi areas, busy students cannot count on finding a place to connect when they have the time to work on course material. By having more Wi-Fi areas, the college will make education more efficient. We are asking the administration to consider increasing the number of "hotspots" for wireless connections. We look forward to having a completely wireless campus in the next few years.

Sincerely,

The Undersigned

Print Name	Signature	Class
LEE RAND	Lee Rand	2010
ANTONIO RIVERA	Antonio Rivera	2008
MAGGIE CHANG	Maggie Chang	2009
RICARDO DA SILVA	Ricardo da Silva	2010

2 | **SPRING BREAK**   *Grammar Notes 2–3*

Complete the students' statements. Choose the appropriate preposition from the box.
(You will use some prepositions more than once.) Add the gerund form of the verb in
parentheses.

about	for	in	on	to

THE BANNER

Vol. 5, Issue 24   **March 1, 2006**

It's almost time for spring break! We asked students: *"What are your plans for spring break?"*
Here are some of their answers:

I'm always very interested

_____*in listening*_____ to jazz,
     1. (listen)

so I'm going to attend the

Spring Jazz Festival.

Lisa Suarez

We're driving to Quebec City

next weekend. It's famous

_____ great
     7. (have)

food.

Omar Sisane

Jim Hsu

I don't have any plans, but I'm

not concerned _____
     2. (get)

bored. I can always take a walk

or something.

Claire Kaplan

I'm really very worried

_____ well in my
     8. (not do)

Japanese class, so I'm studying

over the break.

My friends and I are driving to

New Orleans. I'm excited

_____ , but I'm
    3. (go)

nervous _____ .
     4. (drive)

Emilia Leale

My friends and I are going

camping, and, as usual, my

adorable little brother insists

_____ with us!
    9. (come)

Eun Ko

Don Pitt

I'm really looking forward

_____ at home
     5. (stay)

and _____ .
     6. (relax)

Tim Riley

My girlfriend plans

_____ to the
     10. (go)

movies a lot, so I guess I'll see

a lot of movies.

3 | SCHOOL ISSUES

Combine the following pairs of sentences to make statements about school life. Use the prepositions in parentheses.

1. You can't walk on campus late at night. You have to worry about your safety.

   You can't walk on campus late at night without worrying about your safety.
   (without)

2. We can make changes. We can tell the administration about our concerns.

   _____
   (by)

3. The administration can help. It can listen to our concerns.

   _____
   (by)

4. In some cases, students just complain. They don't make suggestions for improvements.

   _____
   (instead of)

5. Students get annoyed with some teachers. Some teachers don't come to class on time.

   _____
   (for)

6. You can improve your grades. Study regularly.

   _____
   (by)

7. We're proud of our school. It has the latest computer technology.

   _____
   (for)

8. Students should learn about issues. Then they'll vote for the next Student Council president.

   _____
   (before)

9. You have great ideas. Those ideas could solve some problems on campus.

   _____
   (for)

10. Our school has been slow. It hasn't improved food services.

    _____
    (at)

11. Latoya is happy. She's running for Student Council.

    _____
    (about)

4 | MAKING CHANGES

Larry Jones quit school after high school and had various jobs. Then he decided to go to college. That was a big change for him. Complete the sentences about Larry. Use the appropriate form of the verbs in parentheses.

1. Larry used to _____*be*_____ a student, but he quit after high school.
   (be)

2. He used to _____ a job.
   (have)

3. In fact, he used to _____ a lot of different jobs.
   (have)

4. When he went back to college, he had to get used to _____ a student again.
   (be)

5. He wasn't used to _____ to school every day and _____.
   (go)   (study)

6. He had to get used to _____ homework again.
   (do)

7. When Larry was working, he used to _____ quite a bit of money. He used to
   (earn)

   _____ everything too. Now he has to get used to _____ less.
   (spend)   (spend)

8. It hasn't been easy, but Larry has gotten used to _____ a student's life again.
   (live)

5 | EDITING

Read this post to a student council website. There are seven mistakes in the use of gerunds after prepositions. The first mistake is already corrected. Find and correct six more.

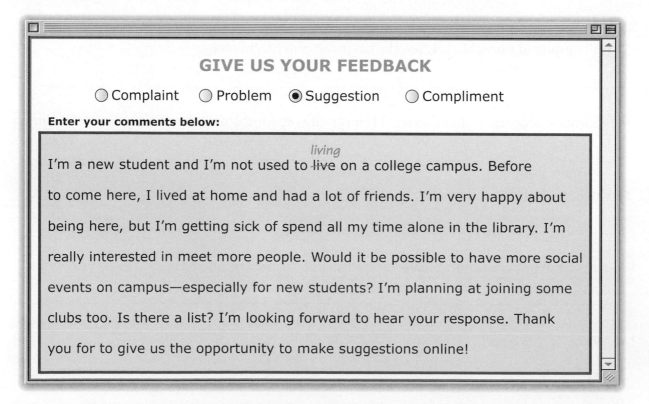

GIVE US YOUR FEEDBACK

○ Complaint   ○ Problem   ● Suggestion   ○ Compliment

Enter your comments below:

I'm a new student and I'm not used to ~~live~~ *living* on a college campus. Before

to come here, I lived at home and had a lot of friends. I'm very happy about

being here, but I'm getting sick of spend all my time alone in the library. I'm

really interested in meet more people. Would it be possible to have more social

events on campus—especially for new students? I'm planning at joining some

clubs too. Is there a list? I'm looking forward to hear your response. Thank

you for to give us the opportunity to make suggestions online!

Communication Practice

6 | LISTENING

🎧 *Listen to this speech by a candidate for the office of Student Council president. Then listen again and mark the following statements* **True (T)** *or* **False (F)**.

__T__ **1.** Latoya has experience in working for student government.

_____ **2.** She believes in raising student activity fees.

_____ **3.** There are only two kinds of food on campus.

_____ **4.** The computer labs and libraries close early.

_____ **5.** Students feel safe on the campus at night.

_____ **6.** Latoya is most interested in improving campus safety.

7 | VOTE FOR ME

Pretend you are running for president of the Student Council. Prepare your campaign speech and read it to the class. Answer some of these questions.

- What are you most interested in?
- What do you believe in?
- What will you insist on?

- What are you opposed to?
- What are you excited about?
- What are you good at?

Example: Vote for me. I'm interested in making our lives better by improving . . .

Now have an election.

8 | STRESS

*Below are some life events, both positive and negative, that can lead to stress. Work by yourself and rank them from most stressful (**1**) to least stressful (**8**). Then in small groups compare and discuss your lists. Use* **be used to** *and* **get used to** *to explain your choices.*

_____ starting college

_____ moving to a new city

_____ changing jobs or schools

_____ getting married

_____ getting divorced

_____ having or adopting a baby

_____ death of a close family member

_____ getting fired at work

Example: I think getting married is the third most stressful life event on the list. You have to get used to living with another person.

9 | WRITING

Read this letter to the editor of a school newspaper.

To the Editor . . .

I have been attending Longtree College for a year. I am an international student in the Chemistry Department. I am very happy about studying here. However, I have had some problems with academic advisers. The academic advisers are not used to talking to international students, so they get nervous about understanding us.

In addition, the school delays looking at the records of transfer students. I attended a university in Ukraine for two years, and I took several chemistry courses. The Chemistry Department has not yet looked at my records. My adviser recommends taking basic courses, but I am afraid of repeating courses and wasting my time.

I suggest giving a workshop for advisers. In the workshop they can practice talking clearly and organizing their information for international students. I also recommend looking at student records as soon as possible.

Respectfully,
Galina Terela

Now mark the following statements **True (T)** *or* **False (F).**

___F___ **1.** Galina is complaining about being a chemistry student.

_____ **2.** The advisers have a lot of experience in talking to international students.

_____ **3.** They feel confident about communicating with international students.

_____ **4.** Galina is a first-year college student.

_____ **5.** The Chemistry Department has been slow in reviewing Galina's records.

_____ **6.** Galina objects to taking basic chemistry courses.

_____ **7.** Galina thinks that advisers should learn about dealing with international students.

Write a letter to the editor of your school newspaper. Write about the things you like and dislike about your school. Use Galina's letter as a model.

10 | ON THE INTERNET

🌐 *Do a search on* **student council candidates**. *Take notes about one candidate's ideas and experience. Discuss your candidate with a small group. Which candidates do you think are the best? Why?*

Example: Natasha Gailes at Louisiana State University talks about a lot of issues. She's interested in improving communication between students and faculty.

Infinitives after Certain Verbs

BEFORE YOU READ

What kind of questions do you think Annie answers? Do you think this is a good place to get advice? Read the letter to the newspaper advice column, Ask Annie.

Lifestyles	Section 4

ASK ANNIE

Dear Annie,

I've just moved to Seattle and started going to a new school. I **try to meet** people but nothing **seems to work**. A few weeks ago, I **agreed to have** dinner with someone from my English class. Bad idea. Right after we got to the restaurant, he **asked to borrow** money from me for the check. And he also **wanted to correct** my pronunciation (I'm from Louisiana). Obviously, I **decided not to see** him again. Now my roommate **would like** me **to go out** with her boyfriend's brother. I **asked** her **not to arrange** anything because I really **don't want to date** anyone right now. First, I'd just **like to find** some friends to hang out with. Do you have any suggestions?

Lonely in Seattle

Dear Lonely,

You **seem to have** the right idea about making new friends. A lot of people **try to solve** the problem of loneliness by falling in love. I usually **advise** them **to make** friends first. Perhaps you just **need to relax** a bit. Don't **expect to develop** friendships overnight because that takes time. Instead, do things that you'**d like to do** anyway. Join a sports club. **Learn to dance**. **Try not to focus** so much on your problem, and just **remember to have** fun with your new activities. You'll come into contact with people who have similar interests. Even if you **fail to meet** your new best friends immediately, you will at least have a good time! Don't give up!

Annie

AFTER YOU READ

Read the statements. Check **True** *or* **False**.

	True	False
1. "Lonely" has been successful in meeting people.	☐	☐
2. She isn't asking for advice about dating.	☐	☐
3. Annie thinks making friends is a good idea.	☐	☐
4. She says that friendships develop quickly.	☐	☐
5. Annie thinks that "Lonely" ought to have some fun.	☐	☐

Grammar Presentation

INFINITIVES AFTER CERTAIN VERBS

Statements			
Subject	**Verb**	**(Object)**	**Infinitive**
I	**decided**		**(not) to write**	to Annie.
You	**urged**	John	**(not) to take**	her advice.
He	**wanted**	(her)	**to advise**	John.

GRAMMAR NOTES	EXAMPLES
1. An **infinitive** is *to* + base form of the verb. Form the **negative** by placing *not* before the infinitive.	• She asked me **to call** after 5:00 P.M. • She asked me **not to call** before 5:00 P.M.
2. Certain **verbs** can be **followed by an infinitive**.	• I *want* **to make** some new friends. • I *asked* Annie **to help** me. • She *advised* me **to relax**. • She *told* me **not to worry**.
3. Some verbs, like the ones below, can be **followed directly by an infinitive**. begin decide fail hope learn plan promise refuse try	verb + infinitive • He *decided* **to join** a health club. • He *hoped* **to meet** new people. • She *promised* **to go out** with him. • She *tried* **not to be** late.
4. Some verbs, like the ones below, need an **object** (noun or pronoun) **before the infinitive**. advise allow encourage force invite order remind tell warn	verb + object + infinitive • I *invited* Mary **to eat** with us. • I *reminded* her **to come**. • She *told* me **to call** her. • They *warned* us **not to forget**.
5. Some verbs, like the ones below, can be followed by: • **an infinitive** OR • **an object + infinitive** ask expect help need want would like	infinitive • I *asked* **to join** the club. object + infinitive • I *asked* them **to join** the club.

Reference Notes
For a list of **verbs** that are **followed by infinitives**, see Appendix 14 on page A-7.
For a more complete list of **verbs** that need an **object before the infinitive**, see Appendix 16 on page A-7.

Focused Practice

1 | DISCOVER THE GRAMMAR

Read this entry in a personal diary. Underline all the verb + infinitive and the verb + object + infinitive combinations.

Annie <u>advised me to join</u> a club or take a class, and I finally did it! I decided to join the school's Outdoor Adventure Club, and I went to my first meeting last night. I'm really excited about this. The club is planning a hiking trip next weekend. I definitely want to go. I hope it won't be too hard for my first adventure. Last night they also decided to go rafting in the spring. At first I didn't want to sign up, but the leader was so nice. He urged me not to miss this trip, so I put my name on the list. After the meeting, a group of people asked me to go out with them. We went to a coffee shop and talked for hours. Well, I hoped to make some new friends when I joined this club, but I didn't expect everyone to be so friendly. I'm glad Annie persuaded me not to give up.

2 | PLAN TO SUCCEED

Grammar Notes 1–5

Complete the article with the correct form of the verbs in parentheses. Use the simple present or the imperative form for the first verb.

Most people make careful plans when they _____*decide to take*_____ a vacation. Yet when
1. (decide / take)

they _____ a mate, they depend on luck.
2. (attempt / find)

Edward A. Dreyfus, Ph.D., _____ love to chance.
3. (warn / single people / not leave)

He _____ his relationship plan when they search for a life partner.
4. (urge / them / use)

Remember: when you _____, you _____.
5. (fail / plan)   6. (plan / fail)

STEP ONE: **Make a list.** What kind of person do you _____?
7. (wish / meet)

Someone intelligent? Someone who loves sports? List everything.

STEP TWO: **Make another list.** What kind of person are *you*? List all your characteristics.

_____ this list and comment on it.
8. (Ask / two friends / read)

_____ about hurting your feelings. The two lists should match.
9. (Tell / them / not worry)

STEP THREE: Increase your chances. _____ in activities you like.
10.(Choose / participate)

STEP FOUR: Ask for introductions. Dr. Dreyfus _____ embarrassed.
11.(advise / people / not feel)

Everyone _____ a matchmaker!
12.(want / be)

3 | IN OTHER WORDS

Grammar Notes 3–5

*For each conversation, use the correct form of a verb from the box followed by an infinitive
or an object + infinitive.*

| agree | encourage | forget | invite | need | remind | ~~would like~~ |

1. KAREN: (*yawn*) Don't you have a meeting tomorrow? Maybe you should go home now.

   TOM: It's only eleven o'clock. And *Star Wars* is on in five minutes!

   SUMMARY: Karen *would like Tom to go home.* _____

2. KURT: Hey, honey, did you get any stamps?

   LILY: Oh, I forgot. I'll stop at the post office on the way home.

   SUMMARY: Kurt _____

3. JOHN: We're going out for coffee. Would you like to join us?

   MARY: I'd love to.

   SUMMARY: John _____

4. DAD: I expect you to come home by 10:30. Do you understand? If you don't, I'm grounding you for two weeks.

   JASON: OK, OK. Take it easy, Dad.

   SUMMARY: Jason _____

5. DON: You didn't go to the staff meeting. We missed you.

   JEFF: Oh, no! The staff meeting!

   SUMMARY: Jeff _____

6. MOM: Don't be scared, sweetie. Just try once more. You'll love it.

   LISA: I hate to ice skate. I always fall down.

   SUMMARY: Lisa's mom _____

7. BRAD: Are you using the car tonight?

   TERRY: Well, I have a lot of shopping to do. And I promised Susan I'd give her a ride.

   SUMMARY: Terry _____

4 | EDITING

Read this magazine article. There are nine mistakes in the use of infinitives. The first mistake is already corrected. Find and correct eight more.

> make
> You'd like to ~~making~~ some new friends. Maybe you're at a new school or job, or, possibly, you have
>
> changed and the "new you" wants meet new people. First, I strongly advise to turn off the TV. Those
>
> people on *Friends* are not YOUR friends. You need go out with real people. Decide right now to don't
>
> refuse invitations. When a classmate or co-worker invites you for coffee, just say "Yes." Join a club
>
> and volunteer to doing something. That responsibility will force you to attend the meetings. By
>
> doing these things, you will manage meeting a lot of new people. But don't rush to become close
>
> friends with someone right away. Learn to listen. Encourage the person to talks by asking questions.
>
> Allow relationships develops naturally, and soon you'll have a group of people you're really
>
> comfortable with.

Communication Practice

5 | LISTENING

🎧 *Listen to a couple talk about their family. Then listen again and circle the letter of the sentences that you hear.*

1. **a.** I really wanted to discuss their problems.
   b. I really wanted them to discuss their problems.

2. **a.** I finally learned to argue with my stepdaughter.
   b. I finally learned not to argue with my stepdaughter.

3. **a.** I expected to have problems with my daughter.
   b. I expected you to have problems with my daughter.

4. **a.** Sometimes I just wanted to leave the house for a few hours.
   b. Sometimes I just wanted her to leave the house for a few hours.

5. **a.** After all, she didn't choose to live with us.
   b. After all, she chose not to live with us.

6. a. Then one day, she asked to go on a family vacation.

   b. Then one day, she asked me to go on a family vacation.

7. a. I didn't expect to have a good time.

   b. I didn't expect her to have a good time.

8. a. In fact, sometimes I'd like to stop talking for a few minutes.

   b. In fact, sometimes I'd like her to stop talking for a few minutes.

6 | DESCRIBE YOUR PARENTS

Work in pairs. Tell each other about your relationship with your parents.

- What did they encourage you to do?
- How did they encourage you to do that?
- What didn't they allow you to do?
- What did they force you to do?
- What would they like you to do?

- What did they advise you to do?
- Why did they advise you to do that?
- What do they expect you to do?
- What would you prefer to do?
- Why would you prefer to do that?

Example: My parents encouraged me to learn other languages.

Add your own questions.

_____

_____

_____

7 | SOCIALIZING AROUND THE WORLD

Discuss how people in your culture socialize. Do young men and women go out together? If so, do they go out in couples or in groups? What are some ways people meet their future husbands or wives?

Example: **A:** In Brazil, young people usually prefer to go out together in groups. They like to go to clubs or to the movies.

       B: In Germany, families allow young people to go out on dates.

8 | ON THE INTERNET

Do a search on **events** *in your town or city. Make a list of events that interest you. Include the date and time of each event. Discuss the events in a small group and plan to do something together.*

Example: **A:** I'd like to go to the outdoor concert in River Park on Sunday. It starts at 3:00 P.M.
B: That sounds great, but I promised to help my brother move on Sunday. How about . . .

9 | WRITING

Write e-mails to two or three friends and invite them to join you for the event your group chose for Exercise 8. Remember to use infinitives.

Example: Hi Ari,
Some classmates and I plan to see *Hero* at the Regis Cineplex on Saturday. Can you come with us? We want to go to the 7:00 P.M. show. After the movie, we'll probably go out for pizza. I hope to see you Saturday. It's going to be fun!
Liv

Infinitives of Purpose

Grammar in Context

BEFORE YOU READ

🎧 *What do you think* multi-use *means? What can you use a camera phone for?*
Read the magazine article.

Multi-Use Technology:
When 1 + 1 = more than 2

You can use it **to send** instant pictures home to your family. You can use it **to call** your friends. But a camera phone is so much more than just a camera plus phone! When the first model came out in 2000, some people (like me) thought, "Why do I need it?" Now, millions of people around the world ask, "How did I live without one?"

Megan uses hers **to get** instant advice on shopping trips. "If I'm shopping for a new sweater, and my friends aren't with me, I take a few pictures, send them, and ask, 'Which one?' "

Carlos, a student, uses his **to organize** everything in his busy life. "I use the calendar **to plan** my week, and I use

the address book **to store** phone numbers and e-mail addresses." In school he uses it **to take** pictures of the teacher's notes on the board.

Marie-Catherine is a TV journalist. "Sometimes I see something interesting, but I don't have a camera or video crew with me. But I

always have my camera phone. I can instantly send my story with a photo or video **in order to meet** my deadline—and **to get** the story before the competition, of course!"

Many people, like Omar, use the camera phone just **to have** fun. "I use it **to surf** the Internet, **e-mail** my friends, **listen** to music, **watch** videos, and **play** games."

For work or for play, camera phones have changed our lives. What will the newest technology bring? It's hard to predict. But one thing is certain: It will be faster and smaller. And, as always, people will find uses for it that are difficult to imagine today.

AFTER YOU READ

Complete the sentence. Check the correct answers.

According to the article, with a camera phone you can _____.

☐ **1.** pay bills   ☐ **3.** watch TV   ☐ **5.** make a weekly schedule

☐ **2.** listen to music   ☐ **4.** order clothes   ☐ **6.** have a good time

Grammar Presentation

INFINITIVES OF PURPOSE

Affirmative
I left at 9:00 **(in order) to be** on time.

Negative
I left at 9:00 **in order not to be** late.

GRAMMAR NOTES

EXAMPLES

1. Use an **infinitive** (*to* + **base form of verb**) to explain the **purpose** of an action. It often answers the question *Why?*

A: *Why* did you go to the mall?
B: I went there **to buy** a new camera phone.

USAGE NOTES:

a. In conversation, you can answer the question *Why?* with an incomplete sentence beginning with *to*.

A: *Why* did you go to the mall?
B: **To buy** a new camera phone.

b. We usually <u>do not repeat</u> *to* when we give more than one purpose.

- I went to the mall **to buy** a sweater, **eat** lunch, and **see** a movie.
  NOT I went to the mall to buy a sweater, ~~to~~ eat lunch, and ~~to~~ see a movie.

2. You can also use the longer form *in order to* + **base form of verb** to explain a purpose.

- I bought my first camera phone **in order to send** instant photos.

USAGE NOTE: *To* + **base form of verb** is much more common in <u>informal</u> speech and writing.

- I bought my first camera phone **to send** instant photos to friends.

3. Use *in order not to* + **base form of verb** to explain a <u>negative purpose</u>.

- Reporters use camera phones **in order not to miss** deadlines.

USAGE NOTE: *In order not to* is formal. In everyday <u>spoken English</u>, we often express a negative purpose with *because* + **a reason**.

- Reporters use camera phones *because they don't want to miss deadlines*.

Focused Practice

1 | DISCOVER THE GRAMMAR

Read more about camera phones. Underline all the infinitives that express a purpose.

No Camera Ph⊘nes Allowed!

New technology is great, but it often brings new problems. Most people use camera phones for good things, for example, <u>to take</u> pictures of their family and friends. But some people use them to play mean jokes on other people or even to steal. When camera phones first came out, some places had to prohibit their use. People were using them to take secret pictures in health clubs and other private places! Not very nice! And what about "digital shoplifting"? Here is an example: My friend Ned (not his real name) often goes to bookstores to look at magazines. Sometimes he sees an interesting article, but he doesn't want to buy the magazine. In order not to pay for the article, he secretly photographs it with his camera phone. Then he goes home to read it! Did Ned steal the article? Should stores ban camera phones in order to prevent digital shoplifting?

2 | THE REASON IS . . .   *Grammar Notes 1, 3*

Match each action with its purpose.

Action	Purpose
_b_ **1.** She bought a camera phone because she	**a.** didn't want to get calls.
_____ **2.** He took the bus because he	**b.** wanted to send instant photos.
_____ **3.** We turned our phone off because we	**c.** wanted to buy a new camera phone.
_____ **4.** She taped her favorite TV show because she	**d.** didn't want to be late.
_____ **5.** He enrolled in French 101 because he	**e.** didn't want to miss it.
_____ **6.** She went to the electronics store because she	**f.** wanted to learn the language.

Now combine the sentences. Use the infinitive of purpose.

1. *She bought a camera phone to send instant photos.* _____
2. _____
3. _____
4. _____
5. _____
6. _____

3 | PICTURE THIS!

On a moblog, you can post pictures, videos, and text from your camera phone directly to the Web for millions of people to see. Look at this moblog. Complete the sentences with the correct words from the box. Use the infinitive of purpose.

buy fruit and vegetables	communicate with her	drive to Montreal	exchange money
get more gas	have coffee	pass it	~~take my own picture~~

My Trip to Montreal

1. That's me! I used my camera phone

to take my own picture .

2. We rented this car _____

_____ .

3. This truck was in front of us. We had

to drive fast _____ .

4. We stopped here _____

_____ .

5. We went to the bank _____

_____ .

6. We came here _____

_____ .

7. We stopped here _____

_____ .

8. This is Fabienne. We had to speak

French _____ .

My Favorites
My Family
My Vacation
My Baby Pics
Home Page

4 | EDITING

Read this online bulletin board about camera phones. There are seven mistakes in the use of the infinitives of purpose. The first mistake is already corrected. Find and correct six more.

> *to tell*
> Click here ~~for telling~~ us how you've used your camera phone.

I was riding my bike when I saw an accident. A car hit a truck, but it didn't stop. I used my camera phone take a picture of the car and the license plate number. Then I used it to call the police. **Jason Harvey, England**

I was at a great concert in Mexico City. I wanted to share the experience with my best friend back home. I picked up my camera phone and used it to take a photo, record a little bit of a song, and writing a short message. Instantly my friend was "there" with me. Awesome! **Emilia Leale, Italy**

My brother needed a new part for his refrigerator. He called the supply store on his camera phone and tried to describe the broken part. They told him to use his phone to takes a picture. He did it, and the supply store was able to send him the correct part right away. **Min-Soo Kim, Korea**

I sell houses. I always use my camera phone in order no waste my customers' time. When I see an interesting house, I immediately send a photo. Then, if they are interested, I make an appointment for them. **Andrea Cook, USA**

While I was traveling, I got a terrible skin rash. I used my camera phone for calling my doctor and send her a photo of it. She was thousands of miles away, but she used the photo to give me instant advice! **Ana Diaz, Spain**

One of my classmates was sick and had to miss class. I used my camera phone to call him and taking a picture of the teacher's notes on the board. He heard the class fine, but had trouble reading the teacher's handwriting. But that's not the fault of the camera phone! **James Gordon, Australia**

Communication Practice

5 | LISTENING

🎧 *You are calling Lacy's Department Store to get information. Read the list below. Listen to Lacy's automatic telephone message. Then listen again and write the number of the telephone key that you should press for each of the following purposes.*

_____ **1.** place an order

_____ **2.** find out when the store opens

_____ **3.** report a lost or stolen credit card

_____ **4.** ask about a bill

_____ **5.** ask about a delivery

___1___ **6.** speak to a customer service representative

_____ **7.** listen to the message again

6 | WHAT'S IT FOR?

Work in groups. Think of uses for the following everyday objects. Use the infinitive of purpose and your imagination! Share your ideas with other groups.

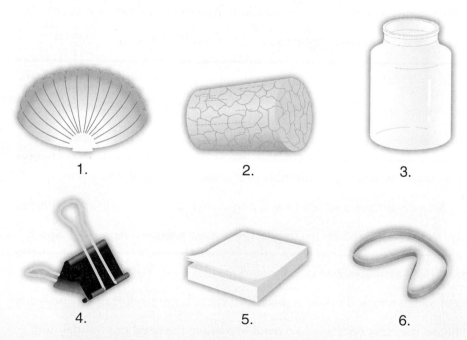

1.   2.   3.

4.   5.   6.

Example: You can use a shell to hold coins, keep soap in, or eat from.

Which item is the most useful? Why?

7 | THE CAMERA PHONE

You've won a camera phone in a contest. What will you use it for? What won't you use it for? Discuss your answers with a partner.

Example: A: I'll use it to send e-mails with photos.

B: I won't use it to copy magazine articles in a bookstore!

8 | REMOTE CONTROL

Read this ad for a remote control.

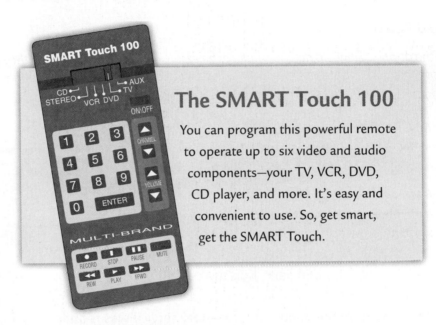

The SMART Touch 100

You can program this powerful remote to operate up to six video and audio components—your TV, VCR, DVD, CD player, and more. It's easy and convenient to use. So, get smart, get the SMART Touch.

Work in small groups. Imagine that in the future there will be a SMART Touch that will control everything in your house—not only electronic equipment. What will you use it for?

Example: A: I'll use it to turn on the shower.

B: I'll use it to open and close the windows.

9 | WRITING

Write an ad for a new electronic gadget. Describe a real item, or invent one. Use infinitives of purpose.

10 | ON THE INTERNET

*Do a search on **electronic gadgets**. Select one that interests you. What can you use it for? Tell your classmates.*

Example: You can use a Digi Pen to take pictures. It's smaller than a camera phone!

Grammar in Context

BEFORE YOU READ

 *Look at the photos. How old do you think each person is? In your opinion, are they old enough to vote? Read the transcript of a radio talk show about voting rights for people under age 18.*

VOICE OF THE PEOPLE

SMITH: Welcome to *Voice of the People*. I'm Ed Smith, and tonight our topic is youth voting rights. Kyle, you're only 16. For someone your age, is getting the vote **important enough to fight** for?

Kyle

KYLE: Sure. Without it, politicians won't take us **seriously enough to hear** our views.

SMITH: I don't get it. In the 1960s when military service was required, 18-year-olds had an argument: "If we're **old enough to fight** for our country, then we're **old enough to vote**." What's *your* argument?

Tina

TINA: Well, there are a lot of laws that discriminate against us. We want the vote so that politicians will listen to us and change those laws. We want the same rights adults have.

SMITH: Can you give examples of laws that discriminate against teens?

MICAH: Sure. My parents are divorced. I see my father every weekend. I'd really like to see him more often, but the law says I'm **too young to decide** for myself.

KYLE: My city has curfew laws. I'm **responsible enough to work** and **pay** taxes, but **too irresponsible to stay out** past 10:00. That's fair?

TINA: Women, ethnic minorities, and people with disabilities have won their civil rights. Now it's our turn.

Micah

AFTER YOU READ

Check the things Kyle can do.

☐ **1.** vote

☐ **2.** work

☐ **3.** pay taxes

☐ **4.** stay out past 10:00

Grammar Presentation

INFINITIVES WITH *TOO* AND *ENOUGH*

Infinitives with *Too*					
	Too	Adjective / Adverb	(*For* + Noun / Object Pronoun)	Infinitive	
We're (not)		**young**		**to vote**.	
They answered	**too**	**quickly**	for Kyle	**to understand**	the issues.
It's (not)		**hard**	(for us)	**to decide**.	

Infinitives with *Enough*					
	Adjective / Adverb	*Enough*	(*For* + Noun / Object Pronoun)	Infinitive	
We're (not)	**old**			**to vote**.	
They have(n't) answered	**clearly**	**enough**	for Kyle	**to understand**	the issues.
It's (not)	**easy**		(for us)	**to decide**.	

GRAMMAR NOTES	EXAMPLES
1. Use the following to give a <u>reason</u>: *too* + **adjective / adverb** + **infinitive**	adjective • I'm *too young* **to vote**. *(I can't vote.)* • She is**n't** *too young* **to vote**. *(She can vote.)* adverb • I arrived *too late* **to vote**. *(I couldn't vote.)* • She did**n't** arrive *too late* **to vote**. *(She could vote.)*
2. You can also use the following to give a <u>reason</u>: **adjective / adverb** + *enough* + **infinitive**	adjective • I'm *old enough* **to go** into the army. *(I can go into the army.)* • He is**n't** *old enough* **to go** into the army. *(He can't go into the army.)* adverb • I ran *fast enough* **to pass** the physical. *(I passed the physical.)* • She did**n't** run *fast enough* **to pass** the physical. *(She didn't pass the physical.)*
3. *Too* comes <u>before</u> the adjective or adverb. *Enough* comes <u>after</u> the adjective or adverb.	• She's *too* old to drive. • I'm not **old** *enough* to drive. NOT I'm not ~~enough old~~.
4. Sometimes we use *for* **+ noun / pronoun** <u>before</u> the infinitive.	• It's not too hard *for people* **to understand**. *(People understand.)* • It's easy enough *for them* **to understand**. *(They understand.)*
5. You **don't need the infinitive** when the meaning is clear.	**A:** Are you going to vote this year? **B:** No, I'm *too young* (to vote). OR No, I'm not *old enough* (to vote).

Focused Practice

1 | DISCOVER THE GRAMMAR

*People have different opinions about public issues. Read each statement of opinion. Then choose the sentence (**a** or **b**) that summarizes that opinion.*

1. Teenagers are responsible enough to stay out past 10:00 P.M.

   (a.) Teenagers should have permission to stay out past 10:00 P.M.

   b. Teenagers shouldn't have permission to stay out past 10:00 P.M.

2. Teenagers are too immature to vote.

   a. Teenagers should be able to vote.

   b. Teenagers shouldn't be able to vote.

3. Women are strong enough to be good soldiers.

   a. Women can be good soldiers.

   b. Women can't be good soldiers.

4. Children are mature enough to choose which parent to live with.

   a. Children can choose which parent to live with.

   b. Children can't choose which parent to live with.

5. Teenagers are responsible enough to use the Internet without censorship.

   a. Teenagers can use the Internet without censorship.

   b. Teenagers can't use the Internet without censorship.

6. Adults are too afraid of change to listen to children's ideas.

   a. Adults listen to children's ideas.

   b. Adults don't listen to children's ideas.

7. People with disabilities have worked too hard to give up the fight for equal rights.

   a. People with disabilities can give up the fight for equal rights.

   b. People with disabilities can't give up the fight for equal rights.

8. At age 70, we are not too old to work.

   a. At age 70, we can work.

   b. At age 70, we can't work.

9. Some children's movies are too violent for children to watch.

   a. Kids shouldn't watch some movies for children.

   b. Kids can watch all children's movies.

10. College is too expensive for a lot of people to afford.

    a. Everyone can afford to go to college.

    b. Some people can afford to go to college.

2 | CAN YOU GET BY?

Match the pictures with the sentences below.

1. e

2. ____

3. ____

4. ____

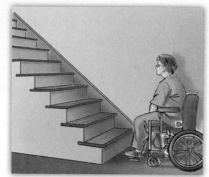

5. ____

6. ____

7. ____

8. ____

9. ____

a. The buttons are too high for him to reach.

b. The buttons are low enough.

c. The steps are too steep for him to get up.

d. The box is too heavy.

e. The street is too busy for them to cross.

f. The traffic is light enough for them to cross.

g. She's too old to join the army.

h. She is too young to vote.

i. She is old enough to vote.

3 | CURFEW!

Some teenagers are leaving a concert. Complete their conversations. Use the words in parentheses with the infinitive and **too** *or* **enough**.

1. **A:** Hologram is so cool! Did you catch the words in that last song?

   B: No. The guitar was _____*too loud for me to understand*_____ the words.
                                       (loud / me / understand)

2. **A:** They're playing in Hampton Stadium next month.

   B: Let's go. The tickets are _____.
                                       (cheap / us / afford)

3. **A:** I don't think the stadium has wheelchair access yet.

   B: We'll sit on the grass. This concert is going to be _____.
                                       (good / you / miss)

4. **A:** It's 9:30. Do we have time to get a slice of pizza?

   B: No. It's _____.
                                       (late / stop)

5. **A:** I hate this curfew!

   B: Me too! I think we're _____ out past 10:00!
                                       (old / stay)

6. **A:** Where's Kyle tonight?

   B: Working. He didn't get off _____.
                                       (early / come)

7. **A:** The new recreation center just opened. Do you want to play basketball tomorrow?

   B: Sure. But I'm still _____ you!
                                       (slow / beat)

4 | EDITING

Read this student's journal entry. There are six mistakes in the use of infinitives with **too** *or* **enough**. *The first mistake is already corrected. Find and correct five more.*

>   *to sleep*
> The Hologram concert was awesome! Now I'm too excited ~~for sleeping~~. That Eve
> Durkin can really sing. My voice isn't enough good to sing in the shower! After the
> concert we were really hungry, but it was to late to go for pizza. I HATE this stupid
> curfew! It's too weird understand. My friend Todd works and has to pay taxes, but
> the law says he's too young for staying out past 10:00 P.M.! That's really crazy!
> Well, I'd better try to get some sleep or I'll be too tired too get up in the morning.

Communication Practice

5 | LISTENING

🎧 *A new youth recreation center has been built so that people in wheelchairs can get around easily. Listen to the description of the center. Then listen again and circle the number of the picture that best fits the description.*

1.

2.

3.

4.

6 | YOUTH RIGHTS

Discuss one of these questions as a class. Then vote on your opinions.

- At what age should people start to vote?

- Should towns have curfews for people younger than age 18?

Example: **A:** I think 15 year olds are mature enough to vote. They can read newspapers and understand issues.

B: I disagree. I don't think 15 year olds are concerned enough about politics to vote.

7 | COMMON EXPRESSIONS

What do you think these expressions mean? When would you use them? Discuss your ideas in small groups.

- She's old enough to know better.
- Life is too short to worry about every little thing.
- You're never too old to try.
- It looks good enough to eat.
- It's too hot to handle.
- It's never too late!

8 | WHAT'S YOUR OPINION?

Complete the following sentences. In small groups, compare your opinions.

1. People over age 70 are too . . .

   Example: A: People over age 70 are too old to drive.
   B: Oh, I don't agree. Some elderly people drive better than young people.

2. The leaders of this country are powerful enough . . .

3. Teenagers are too crazy . . .

4. Guns are too dangerous . . .

5. Taxes aren't high enough . . .

6. Women are strong enough . . .

7. Radio and TV broadcasters speak (or don't speak) clearly enough . . .

8. Time goes by too quickly . . .

9 | WRITING

Write a letter to the editor of a newspaper. Choose a topic from Exercise 8.

   Example: To the Editor:
   I'm in favor of gun control. I believe that guns are too dangerous for ordinary people to own and use . . .

10 | ON THE INTERNET

🌐 *Do a search on* **teen voting rights**. *Make notes about some of the arguments for and against lowering the voting age to 16. Discuss the arguments in small groups.*

   Example: This article says that teenagers take courses in history, government, and current events. That means they are educated enough to vote.

Grammar in Context

BEFORE YOU READ

🎧 *Do you always find excuses not to do certain things? If you answered "yes," you are a procrastinator. What types of things do you put off doing? Why do you procrastinate? Read the excerpt from a magazine article about procrastinating.*

STOP PROCRASTINATING—NOW!

It's a beautiful day. Eva doesn't **feel like spending** it at the library. She goes to the park instead. She **keeps telling** herself she'll work better the next day.

Todd **planned to make** an appointment with the dentist, but he **decided to wait** another week, or maybe two.

Procrastinating—putting off until tomorrow things you **need to do** today—is a universal problem. College students are famous **for procrastinating**, but we all do it sometimes. What **causes** people **to put off** important tasks? Read what the experts say.

UNPLEASANT TASKS • It's not always fun **to do** a lot of the things on our To Do lists. Most people **prefer to do** enjoyable things.

POOR TIME MANAGEMENT • Having too little time for a task is discouraging. **It**'s hard **to get** started on a project when you feel that you can't finish it.

FEAR • An important test can make you feel so nervous that you **put off studying**.

PERFECTIONISM • The belief that you must do a perfect job can prevent you **from starting** or **finishing** a task.

As you can see, people often procrastinate because they **want to avoid** bad feelings. But procrastinators **end up feeling** even worse because of their procrastination. The only solution: **stop procrastinating**. Now!

Did you **finish writing** your paper on procrastination?

No. I'll do it tomorrow.

AFTER YOU READ

Check the reasons the article gives for procrastination.

☐ **1.** being lazy

☐ **2.** not enjoying the task

☐ **3.** feeling nervous about the task

☐ **4.** not having enough time

☐ **5.** not getting enough sleep

☐ **6.** feeling depressed

Grammar Presentation

GERUNDS AND INFINITIVES

Gerunds
Eva **enjoys going** to the park.
She **loves taking** long breaks.
She **stopped studying**.
Changing habits is hard.
She's worried **about finishing** her paper.

Infinitives
Eva **wants to go** to the park.
She **loves to take** long breaks.
She **stopped to study**.
It's hard **to change** habits.

GRAMMAR NOTES

1. Some **verbs**, like the ones below, are **followed by a gerund** (base form + *-ing*).

appreciate	*avoid*	*can't stand*
end up	*feel like*	*keep*
mind	*recall*	*regret*

2. Some **verbs**, like the ones below, are **followed by an infinitive** (*to* + base form).

afford	*agree*	*decide*
expect	*need*	*offer*
plan	*want*	*would like*

USAGE NOTE: We usually <u>do not repeat *to*</u> when there is more than one infinitive.

EXAMPLES

- Eva *avoids* **doing** her work.
- She *keeps* **making** excuses.
- She *regrets* **not studying** more.

- Todd doesn't *want* **to go** to the dentist.
- He'*d like* **to stay** home.
- He *decided* **not to keep** his appointment.

- He *plans* **to watch** TV, **read** the paper, and **call** his friends.
  NOT He plans to watch TV, ~~to~~ read the paper, and ~~to~~ call his friends.

(continued)

3. Some **verbs**, like the ones below, can be **followed by a gerund or an infinitive**. *begin continue hate* *like love prefer*	• Jeff *hates* studying. OR • Jeff *hates* **to study**.

4. **BE CAREFUL!** The verbs *stop*, *remember*, and *forget* can be followed by either the gerund or the infinitive, but they have very <u>different meanings</u>.	• Eva *stopped* **taking** breaks. *(She doesn't take breaks anymore.)* • Eva *stopped* **to take** a break. *(She stopped another activity in order to take a break.)* • Todd *remembered* **reading** the story. *(First he read the story. Then he remembered that he did it.)* • Todd *remembered* **to read** the story. *(First he remembered. Then he read the story. He didn't forget.)* • Jeff *forgot* **meeting** Dana. *(Jeff met Dana, but afterwards he didn't remember the event.)* • Jeff *forgot* **to meet** Dana. *(Jeff had plans to meet Dana, but he didn't meet her because he forgot about the plans.)*

5. The **gerund** is the only verb form that can **follow a preposition**.	preposition • Jeff is worried ***about*** **writing** his paper. preposition • He's looking forward ***to*** **finishing** it.

6. To make **general statements**, you can use:
 	
  • **gerund as subject**
 	
      OR
 	
  • *it* **+ infinitive**
	• **Writing** a paper is hard.
	
	      OR
	
	• *It*'s hard **to write** a paper.

Reference Notes

For a more complete list of **verbs followed by a gerund**, see Appendix 13 on page A-7.

For a more complete list of **verbs followed by an infinitive**, see Appendix 14 on page A-7.

For a more complete list of **verbs followed by a gerund or an infinitive**, see Appendix 15 on page A-7.

For more on **gerunds after prepositions**, see Unit 28 on page 326, and Appendices 17 and 18 on pages A-7 and A-8.

Focused Practice

1 | DISCOVER THE GRAMMAR

Read this paragraph. Circle the gerunds. Underline the infinitives.

Like many students, Eva is a procrastinator. She keeps (putting off) her school work. When she studies, she often stops <u>to go</u> for a walk in the park. She wants to improve her study habits, but she isn't sure how. Eva decided to make a list of things she needs to do every day. She always remembers to make her list, but she often forgets to read it. It's very frustrating. Last night Eva remembered reading an article in the school newspaper about a support group for procrastinators. She thinks being in a group is a good idea. She likes sharing ideas with other students.

Now read these sentences. Write **T (True)** *or* **F (False)**.

<u>F</u> 1. Eva never does her school work.

____ 2. She quit going for walks in the park.

____ 3. She'd like to be a better student.

____ 4. Eva makes a list every day.

____ 5. She always reads her list.

____ 6. She read about a support group.

____ 7. She thinks it's good to be in a group.

____ 8. She likes to share ideas with others.

2 | ARE YOU A PROCRASTINATOR? *Grammar Notes 1–3, 5*

Read this quiz. Circle the correct form of the verbs. In some cases, both forms are correct.

☐ When I don't feel like <u>to do</u> / (doing) something, I often put off <u>to start</u> / <u>starting</u> it.
   1.   **2.**

☐ I sometimes start <u>to study</u> / <u>studying</u> the night before a test.
   3.

☐ I sometimes start a job but then postpone <u>to finish</u> / <u>finishing</u> it.
   4.

☐ I often delay <u>to make</u> / <u>making</u> difficult decisions.
   5.

☐ I find excuses for not <u>to do</u> / <u>doing</u> things I dislike.
   6.

☐ When a task seems too difficult, I often avoid <u>to work</u> / <u>working</u> on it.
   7.

☐ I prefer <u>to do</u> / <u>doing</u> easy tasks first.
   8.

☐ I often promise myself <u>to work</u> / <u>working</u> on a project but then fail <u>to do</u> / <u>doing</u> it.
   9.   **10.**

☐ I worry about <u>to make</u> / <u>making</u> mistakes or about not <u>to be</u> / <u>being</u> perfect.
   11.   **12.**

☐ I often choose <u>to do</u> / <u>doing</u> other tasks instead of the most important one.
   13.

☐ I want <u>to improve</u> / <u>improving</u>, but I keep <u>to put</u> / <u>putting</u> it off!
   14.   **15.**

3 | FROM AN ADVICE COLUMN

Grammar Notes 1–2, 4–5

Complete these tips. Use the correct form of the verbs in parentheses.

Some Tips for _____Stopping_____ Procrastination
1. (stop)

🕐 If you have a large project to work on, break it into small tasks. Finish _____
2. (do)

one small task before _____ the next.
3. (start)

🕐 Choose _____ the hardest task first. You'll get it out of the way, and you'll feel
4. (do)

better about yourself.

🕐 Promise _____ at least 15 minutes on a task even if you don't really feel like
5. (spend)

_____ it. You'll be surprised. You can get a lot done in 15 minutes—and you'll
6. (do)

often keep _____ even longer.
7. (work)

🕐 Stop _____ *short* breaks—but no more than 10 minutes.
8. (take)

🕐 Arrange _____ yourself a reward when you succeed in _____
9. (give) **10. (finish)**

a task. Do something you enjoy _____.
11. (do)

🕐 Consider _____ a support group for procrastinators.
12. (join)

4 | SUPPORT GROUP

Grammar Notes 1–2, 4

Read these conversations that took place at a procrastinators' support group meeting.
Complete the summary statements. Use the gerund or the infinitive.

1.   **JEFF:** Hi, Todd. Did you bring the soda?

        TODD: Yes. Here it is.

   SUMMARY: Todd remembered _to bring the soda._____

2.   **LEE:** Eva, do you remember Todd?

        EVA: Oh, yes. We met last year.

   SUMMARY: Eva remembers _____

3.   **JEFF:** You take too many breaks.

        TODD: No, I don't!

   SUMMARY: Todd denied _____

4.   **Eva:** What do you do in your free time, Kay?

       Kay: I listen to music a lot.

   SUMMARY: Kay enjoys _____

5.   **Uta:** I'm tired. Let's go home.

       Kay: OK. Just five more minutes.

   SUMMARY: Uta wants _____

6.   **Uta:** Eva, can we give you a ride home?

       Eva: Thanks, but I think I'll stay a little longer.

   SUMMARY: Uta offered _____

              Eva decided _____

7.   **Pat:** Good night. Please drive carefully.

       Uta: Don't worry. I will.

   SUMMARY: Uta promised _____

5 | IN OTHER WORDS   *Grammar Note 6*

Eva and Todd are talking. They agree on everything. Read one person's opinion and write the other's. If the first person used the gerund, use the infinitive. If the first person used the infinitive, use the gerund.

1. **Eva:** It's hard to start a new project.

    Todd: I agree. *Starting a new project is hard.* _____

2. **Todd:** Taking short breaks is helpful.

    Eva: You're right. *It's helpful to take short breaks.* _____

3. **Eva:** It's difficult to work on a long project.

    Todd: That's true. _____

4. **Todd:** Completing a job on time feels great.

    Eva: You're right. _____

5. **Todd:** Rewarding yourself for finishing a project is a good idea.

    Eva: I agree. _____

6. **Eva:** Being in a support group is very helpful.

    Todd: Yes. _____

7. **Eva:** It's good to meet people with the same problem.

    Todd: I feel the same way. _____

6 | EDITING

Read Eva's journal entry. There are eight mistakes in the use of the gerund and infinitive.
The first mistake is already corrected. Find and correct seven more.

> *going*
> For months I was thinking about ~~to go~~ to a support group for procrastinators,
>
> but I kept putting it off! Last night I finally decided going, and I'm glad I did. I'm not
>
> alone! There were a lot of people there with the same problem as me. I expected
>
> being bored, but it was really quite interesting—and helpful. I even knew some of the
>
> other students there. I remembered to meet a few of them at a school party last
>
> year. I really enjoyed to talk to Todd, and before I left I promised coming again.
>
> I have a math test tomorrow, so I really should stop to write now and start
>
> studying. See, I've already learned something from to be in this group! I have to stop
>
> making excuses and start my work! Now!

Communication Practice

7 | LISTENING

🎧 *The school newspaper is interviewing Eva about her study habits. Read the list of*
activities. Listen to the interview. Then listen again and check the things Eva does and
doesn't do now when she is studying for a test.

	Things Eva Does	Things Eva Doesn't Do
1. clean her work area	✓	☐
2. start the night before the test	☐	☐
3. study the hardest thing first	☐	☐
4. make a To Do list	☐	☐
5. take long breaks	☐	☐
6. do relaxation exercises	☐	☐
7. reward herself for finishing	☐	☐

8 | TAKE A BREAK!

Taking short breaks can help you work more effectively. Work in groups. Brainstorm ideas for 10-minute work breaks. Share your ideas with the rest of your classmates.

> **Examples:** I enjoy . . .
> It's relaxing . . .
> You could consider . . .
> I recommend . . .
> I like . . .
> Try . . .

9 | STOP PUTTING THINGS OFF

Work in small groups. Discuss these questions:

1. Can you complete projects on time?

2. Do you follow any of the tips in Exercise 3?

> **Example:** A: I sometimes put off writing a paper.
> B: I always make a note on my calendar when the paper is due.

10 | QUOTABLE QUOTES

Read these quotes about procrastination. Discuss them with a partner. What do they mean? Do you agree with them?

Never put off till tomorrow what you can do today.

> —*Lord Chesterfield (British politician, 1694–1773)*

> **Example:** Lord Chesterfield advises doing things right away. I think that is not always possible because . . .

Procrastination is the art of keeping up with yesterday.

> —*Don Marquis (U.S. author, 1878–1937)*

Procrastination is the thief of time.

> —*Edward Young (British poet, 1683–1765)*

When there is a hill to climb, don't think that waiting will make it smaller.

> —*Anonymous*

Putting off an easy thing makes it hard, and putting off a hard one makes it impossible.

> —*George H. Lorimer (U.S. magazine editor, 1868–1937)*

Procrastination is like a credit card: It's a lot of fun until you get the bill.

> —*Christopher Parker*

11   INFORMATION GAP: AT THE SUPPORT GROUP

Work in pairs (A and B). Student A, follow the instructions on this page. Student B, turn to page 366 and follow the instructions there.

1. Look at the picture below. Ask your partner questions to complete what people said at the support group meeting.

   Example: A: What does Eva remember doing?
   B: She remembers meeting Todd.

2. Answer your partner's questions.

   Example: B: What does Todd hope to do?
   A: He hopes to see Eva again.

When you are done, compare your pictures. Are they the same?

12 | WRITING

Writing a goals worksheet is a good way to help prevent procrastination. First, complete this worksheet. List three goals for this month in order of importance (1 = the most important goal).

This Month's Goals		
Goal 1:		Complete by:
Goal 2:		Complete by:
Goal 3:		Complete by:

Now, write three paragraphs (one for each goal) on how you plan to accomplish your goals.

Example: I want to finish writing my English paper by March 28. First, I plan to . . .

13 | ON THE INTERNET

*Do a search on **procrastination quiz**. Take the quiz and discuss the results with your classmates.*

INFORMATION GAP FOR STUDENT B

1. Look at the picture below. Answer your partner's questions.

> **Example:** **A:** What does Eva remember doing?
> **B:** She remembers meeting Todd.

2. Ask you partner questions to complete what people said at the support group meeting.

> **Example:** **B:** What does Todd hope to do?
> **A:** He hopes to see Eva again.

When you are done, compare your pictures. Are they the same?

From **Grammar** to **Writing**
Combining Sentences with and, but, so, or

You can combine two sentences with *and*, *but*, *so*, and *or*. The resulting longer sentence is made up of two main clauses.

Example: Commuting to school is hard. I prefer to live in the dorm. $\longrightarrow$
main clause   main clause
Commuting to school is hard, **so** I prefer to live in the dorm.

The clause starting with *and*, *but*, *so*, or *or* always comes second. Note that a comma comes after the first clause.

1 Circle the correct words to complete this letter.

Dear Dania,

I have just a little time before my next class, (so) / but this will be a short letter. This
                                                    1.
semester has been difficult, but / or I'm enjoying it. I'm taking two English classes, and / so
                              2.   **3.**
I'm also on the Student Council. Being on the Council has taught me a lot, but / so it takes
                                                                            4.
up a lot of time.

I   Studying takes up most of my time, and / but I try to find time for sports too. I've got to
                                          5.
keep in shape! This weekend I'm going hiking with some classmates. Do you remember the
time we went hiking, and / so we couldn't find our way back?
                      6.
I   Your visit is in just two weeks! I'm really looking forward to seeing you, and / but I'm
                                                                              7.
sure we'll have a great time. You can stay in my dorm, and /or I can arrange for us both to
                                                         8.
stay with my parents. Which would you prefer to do? My parents don't live far from my dorm,
and / but I know they will want to see you.
9.
I   Let me know which train you're taking, so / but I can meet you at the station.
                                            10.
Love,

Monica

Note these different ways to close a personal letter:
• *Love*, for family and close friends
• *Warmly*, for friends
• *Best wishes*, for colleagues and acquaintances.

2 Complete these rules for using **and**, **but**, **so**, and **or**. Look at the letter in Exercise 1 for help.

1. Use ____*and*____ when the second sentence adds information.

2. Use _____ when the second sentence gives a choice.

3. Use _____ when the second sentence gives a contrasting idea.

4. Use _____ when the information in the second sentence is a result of the information in the first sentence.

3 Complete these sentences with your own ideas.

1. It has started to rain, but_____

2. I don't really want to study tonight, so_____

3. This weekend my friends and I will go to a movie, or_____

4. I'm reading a lot of books in English, and _____

5. After class I'm going shopping, so _____

6. I used to go dancing a lot, but_____

7. I'm looking forward to graduating, and _____

8. Ed is too young to vote, but_____

9. We can take a train, or_____

10. Dan is tired of staying home evenings, so _____

4 Before you write . . .

Talk to a partner about your life these days. Answer some of these questions.

- What are you doing these days?
- What do you enjoy doing?
- What can't you stand?
- What do you plan to do next semester?
- What are you looking forward to?

5 Write a letter to a friend describing your present life. Use the letter in Exercise 1 as a model. Include some of the ideas you spoke about in Exercise 4. Use **and**, **but**, **so**, and **or**.

6 Exchange letters with a new partner. Answer your partner's letter.

Review Test

I *Complete the conversation. Use the prepositions in the box and the gerund form of the verbs in parentheses.*

about	by	for	in	to	without

A: Carla, your English is just great. How did you learn so quickly?

B: _____*By using*_____ some special strategies.
     1. (use)

A: Like what?

B: Well, first I got used _____ my time. I scheduled time
                          2. (plan)

_____ television and writing letters in English to my pen pal.
3. (watch)

A: How did you practice speaking?

B: At first I was very nervous _____ English. I had to learn to talk
                                  4. (speak)

_____ about mistakes. I used deep breathing exercises and music to
5. (worry)

calm myself down.

A: What else helped you relax?

B: Jokes. I got interested _____ jokes in English. That way I always had
                              6. (learn)

something to say, and I also learned a lot about American culture.

II *Complete each conversation with the correct phrase in parentheses.*

1. A: Let's go running.

   B: No. You always run _____*too fast*_____ for me to keep up with you.
                           (too fast / fast enough)

   A: OK. Let's go swimming, then.

2. A: Why did you get an F on this paper?

   B: My handwriting was _____ for the teacher to read.
                           (messy enough / too messy)

   A: Then how did he know the answers were wrong?

(continued)

3. A: Have you tried the coffee?

B: I will in a minute. It's _____ to drink yet.

(too cool / not cool enough)

4. A: This steak is _____ to eat.

(too tough / tough enough)

B: Send it back and ask for something else.

5. A: John's a good player. Why didn't he make the soccer team?

B: He doesn't play _____ to win.

(too aggressively / aggressively enough)

6. A: What did the forecaster say about thunderstorms?

B: I'm not sure. The radio wasn't _____ for me to hear.

(loud enough / too loud)

III *Complete this text with the correct form of the verbs in the box. Choose between the gerund or the infinitive of purpose.*

drink	eat	feel	follow	give up	~~quit~~	read
reward	save	shop	smoke	take	tell	

Cigarettes. They're bad for your health. Your doctor recommends _____*quitting*_____.

1.
Your friends keep _____ you to stop. Even your dry cleaner suggests that you stop

2.
_____. (He says you burned holes in your suit jacket.) You want to stop, but

3.
_____ an old habit is difficult. _____ these suggestions can help.

4.   5.

- List your reasons for quitting. Are you quitting _____ better?

                                                     6.

  _____ money? Keep your list nearby _____ when you want

 7.   8.
  a cigarette.

- Stop _____ coffee and tea. Caffeine causes people to want a cigarette.

             9.

- When you feel the desire to light up, put it off for five minutes. Use the time

  _____ some deep breaths. The urge will pass quickly.

           10.

- Avoid _____ big meals for a few weeks.

           11.

- Save the money that you aren't spending on cigarettes. Go _____ for

                                                      12.

  something special _____ yourself for your success.

                           13.

If you follow these suggestions, it shouldn't be too hard to give up this unhealthy habit.

IV *Complete the conversation by writing the words and phrases in parentheses in the correct order.*

A: Why are so many people starting home-based businesses?

B: In offices, work hours are often _____*too long for people to spend*_____ time with their
1. (people / to spend / too long / for)

families.

A: What are some keys to home business success?

B: Networking is one. _____ organizations. After you
2. (necessary / to / It's / join)

join, you must _____ a lot of people. But don't get
3. (enough / meet / participate / to)

_____ people who sound interested in your product.
4. (too / to / busy / call)

A: Do business owners really work fewer hours?

B: No, they are most likely to work more. But they can arrange their time. Their hours are

_____ family time too.
5. (to have / enough / for them / flexible)

A: What do you warn new business owners about?

B: I _____ their privacy. Remember, the business phone is
6. (them / to think about / advise)

always going to ring right in the middle of the family dinner. Also,

_____ the loneliness of working alone, especially when
7. (important / it's / to know about)

you're used to a big office.

A: Anything else?

B: In my seminars, I teach strategies for getting paid on time. Home business owners often find

that they don't get paid _____ their own bills.
8. (for / enough / to pay / soon / them)

A: What kind of home businesses are people starting?

B: Well, as I said, a lot of working people are _____ care
9. (take / to / too / busy)

of things like shopping and planning parties. Many home-based businesses supply these

services.

A: You mean, someone will pay me for shopping?

B: Sure. In fact, I _____ planning your own shopping
10. (you / to start / encourage)

business. My class for new business owners starts next week.

V *Circle the letter of the correct answer to complete each sentence.*

1. Tom is late because he stopped _____ dinner.   A B C (D)

   (**A**) buying   (**C**) and buy

   (**B**) buy   (**D**) to buy

2. My key was in my pocket, but I don't remember _____ it there.   A B C D

   (**A**) to put   (**C**) I put

   (**B**) putting   (**D**) to put

3. Bob's 17 years old, so he's still _____ vote.   A B C D

   (**A**) too young to   (**C**) too old to

   (**B**) young enough to   (**D**) too young for

4. I bought a camera phone _____ photos to my friends.   A B C D

   (**A**) by sending   (**C**) to send

   (**B**) I sent   (**D**) send

5. Chris _____, so her grades are low this semester.   A B C D

   (**A**) stopped studying   (**C**) stopped to study

   (**B**) stopping to study   (**D**) was stopping to study

6. As firefighters, women work _____ the job done.   A B C D

   (**A**) hardly get   (**C**) not enough to get

   (**B**) too hard to get   (**D**) hard enough to get

7. He's used _____ a big breakfast.   A B C D

   (**A**) ate   (**C**) to eating

   (**B**) to eat   (**D**) eats

8. I used to be very nervous _____, but I'm not anymore.   A B C D

   (**A**) to drive   (**C**) to driving

   (**B**) for driving   (**D**) about driving

9. I didn't remember _____ my check, so I paid the rent twice!   A B C D

   (**A**) mailed   (**C**) mailing

   (**B**) to mail   (**D**) I mail

10. Sal enjoyed _____ in Texas.   A B C D

    (**A**) live   (**C**) living

    (**B**) to live   (**D**) lived

VI *Complete the interview with the gerund or infinitive form of the verbs in parentheses.*

INTERVIEWER: You're one of the best baseball players today, Anthony. Who taught you

_____*to play*_____?
　　　1. (play)

ANTHONY: I learned _____ a ball with my dad. We used to play together
　　　　　　　　　　2. (hit)

for hours on weekends.

INTERVIEWER: What was the most important thing he taught you?

ANTHONY: Dad believed in _____ fun. He always forgot about
　　　　　　　　　　3. (have)

_____ when he played. By _____ with him,
　　4. (win)　　　　　　　　　　　　**5. (play)**

I developed the same attitude.

INTERVIEWER: When did you decide _____ a professional?
　　　　　　　　　　　　　6. (become)

ANTHONY: Too early—in elementary school. That was a mistake. I was too young

_____ that decision.
　　7. (make)

INTERVIEWER: Why?

ANTHONY: My schoolwork suffered. I thought a lot about _____ a pro ball
　　　　　　　　　　　　　　　　　　　8. (become)

player, and I didn't think much about _____ homework.
　　　　　　　　　　　　　　　　9. (do)

INTERVIEWER: Did anything happen to change your mind about school?

ANTHONY: Yes, I planned _____ to City High School, which had a great team.
　　　　　　　　10. (go)

Then I found out that my grades were probably too low for the school

_____ me.
　　11. (accept)

INTERVIEWER: But you graduated from City High School. Right?

ANTHONY: Yes, I did. My parents urged me _____ harder. I followed their advice
　　　　　　　　　　　　　　　12. (study)

and I've never stopped _____.
　　　　　　　　　　13. (study)

INTERVIEWER: Well, thank you for _____ to this interview.
　　　　　　　　　　　　14. (agree)

ANTHONY: You're welcome. I enjoyed _____ your questions.
　　　　　　　　　　　　　15. (answer)

VII *Each sentence has four underlined words or phrases. The four underlined parts of the sentence are marked A, B, C, or D. Circle the letter of the <u>one</u> underlined word or phrase that is NOT CORRECT.*

1. It's <u>difficult</u> <u>study</u> in a foreign country, so students <u>need</u> <u>to prepare</u>
       A   B   C   D
   for the experience.   A Ⓑ C D

2. Students <u>look forward</u> <u>to traveling</u>, but they <u>worry about</u> <u>don't make</u>
              A   B   C   D
   a good impression.   A B C D

3. They're afraid <u>of</u> <u>not understanding</u> the culture, and they <u>don't want</u>
                     A   B   C
   <u>making</u> mistakes.   A B C D
   D

4. Counselors can <u>advise</u> them <u>against wear</u> the wrong <u>clothing</u> and
                       A   B   C
   <u>making</u> the wrong gestures.   A B C D
   D

5. It's <u>natural</u> <u>to have</u> some problems because no one can <u>get used to</u>
           A   B   C
   <u>live</u> in a new culture immediately.   A B C D
   D

6. No one escapes <u>from</u> <u>feeling</u> some culture shock, and <u>it's important</u>
                      A   B   C
   <u>realizing</u> this fact.   A B C D
   D

7. Jan <u>stopped</u> <u>to feel</u> uncomfortable after she <u>started</u> <u>to make</u> new
         A   B   C   D
   friends.   A B C D

8. Now she is <u>looking</u> <u>forward to</u> <u>stay</u> here and <u>getting</u> a job.   A B C D
                 A   B   C   D

▶ *To check your answers, go to the Answer Key on page RT-4.*

More Modals
and Similar Expressions

33 | Preferences: *Prefer, Would prefer, Would rather*

Grammar in Context

BEFORE YOU READ

🎧 *Look at the bar graph. What is leisure time? Which leisure-time activity is most popular? Read the online questionnaire about leisure-time preferences.*

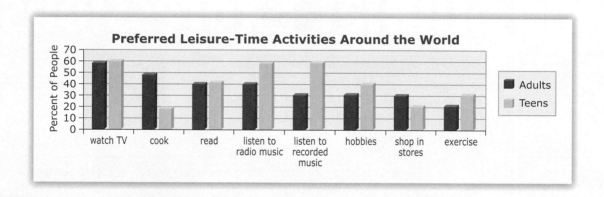

Preferred Leisure-Time Activities Around the World

Legend: ■ Adults ■ Teens

X-axis: watch TV, cook, read, listen to radio music, listen to recorded music, hobbies, shop in stores, exercise

Y-axis: Percent of People (0–70)

Leisure-Time Activities   **Market Survey, Inc.**

Click on the answer closest to your preference.

1 When you go to the movies, **would** you **rather see** a comedy or a thriller?
○ I **prefer seeing** a thriller.   ○ I'**d rather watch** a comedy.

2 When you choose a restaurant, do you look for interesting foods or big portions?
○ I **prefer** big portions.   ○ I'**d rather try** interesting foods.

3 Which **would** you **prefer**: tickets to a rock concert or tickets to a football game?
○ I'**d prefer to go** to the game.   ○ I'**d rather go** to the concert.

4 Which **do** you **prefer**—eating out or cooking at home?
○ I almost always **prefer eating out**.   ○ I'**d rather cook** at home.

5 How **do** you **prefer communicating** with friends?
○ I **prefer to e-mail**.   ○ I'**d rather talk** on the phone.

AFTER YOU READ

Look at the bar graph. Read the statements. Check **True** *or* **False**.

	True	False
1. Teens would rather watch TV than shop in stores.	☐	☐
2. Adults would rather listen to radio music than recorded music.	☐	☐
3. Adults and teens prefer hobbies to exercise.	☐	☐
4. Adults and teens prefer reading to watching TV.	☐	☐
5. Teens would prefer watching TV to all other activities.	☐	☐
6. Adults would rather shop than cook.	☐	☐

Grammar Presentation

PREFERENCES: *PREFER, WOULD PREFER*

Statements		
Subject	*Prefer / Would prefer**	Noun / Gerund / Infinitive
I You We They	**prefer** **would prefer**	**TV news** (to newspapers). **watching** the news (to reading newspapers). **(not) to watch** the news.
He She	**prefers** **would prefer**	

Contraction
would prefer = **'d prefer**

*Like modals, *would prefer* does not have *-s* in the third-person singular.

Yes / No Questions			
Do / Would	Subject	*Prefer*	Noun / Gerund / Infinitive
Do **Would**	I you we they	**prefer**	**TV news**? **watching** the news? **to watch** the news?
Does **Would**	he she		

Short Answers					
Affirmative			Negative		
Yes,	you I / we you they	**do.** **would.**	No,	you I / we you they	**don't.** **wouldn't.**
	he she	**does.** **would.**		he she	**doesn't.** **wouldn't.**

PREFERENCES: *WOULD RATHER*

Statements			
Subject	***Would rather****	**Base Form of Verb**	
I You He She We They	**would rather**	**watch**	the news (than read newspapers).
		not read	newspapers.

Contraction
would rather = **'d rather**

*Like modals, *would rather* does not have *-s* in the third-person singular.

Yes / No Questions			
Would	**Subject**	***Rather***	**Base Form of Verb**
Would	you she	**rather**	**read**?

Short Answers				
Affirmative			**Negative**	
Yes,	I she	**would.**	I'**d** She'**d**	**rather not.**

GRAMMAR NOTES

EXAMPLES

1. Use *prefer*, *would prefer*, and *would rather* to talk about things or activities that you <u>like better</u> than other things or activities.

- We usually **prefer** Italian food.
- I'**d prefer** to have Chinese food tonight.
- I'**d rather** cook at home.

USAGE NOTES:
a. We usually use the **contraction** for *would* in speech and <u>informal</u> writing.

- I'**d** rather go.
  NOT I ~~would rather~~ go.

b. We often use *prefer* to express a <u>general</u> preference.

- Which **do** you **prefer**—action movies or romantic comedies?

c. We use *would prefer* or *would rather* to talk about a preference in a <u>specific</u> situation.

- I usually **prefer** action movies, but tonight I'**d prefer** a romantic comedy.
- I'**d rather go** to the rock concert next weekend.
  NOT I ~~will rather go~~ to the rock concert next weekend.

▶ **BE CAREFUL!** Do not use *will* to talk about preferences.

2. *Prefer* and ***would prefer*** may be followed by a <u>noun</u>, a <u>gerund</u>, or an <u>infinitive</u>.	noun • Jeffrey usually **prefers** *comedies*. • Right now, he**'d prefer** *a thriller*. gerund • **Does** Kyle **prefer** *reading* magazines? • **Would** he **prefer** *watching* a movie?
USAGE NOTE: *Would prefer* + infinitive is more common than *would prefer* + gerund.	infinitive • Kathleen **prefers** *to read* magazines. • She **would prefer** *to watch* TV tonight.

3. ***Would rather*** can only be followed by the <u>base form</u> of the verb.	A: Would you like to eat out tonight? base form B: I**'d rather** *cook* dinner at home.
The <u>negative</u> of *I'd rather* is ***I'd rather not***.	• **I'd rather not** *have* dessert. NOT ~~I wouldn't rather~~ have dessert. NOT ~~I'd not rather~~.
USAGE NOTE: We often use ***I'd rather not***, by itself, <u>to refuse</u> an offer, suggestion, or invitation.	A: Let's see the movie at the Film House. B: I**'d rather not**. I hear it's terrible.

4. A **comparison with *to*** can follow *prefer / would prefer* + <u>noun</u>.	noun noun • Lani **prefers** comedies ***to*** thrillers. noun noun • She**'d prefer** *Life* **to** *Crash*.
A **comparison with *to*** can also follow *prefer / would prefer* + <u>gerund</u>.	gerund gerund • I **prefer** visiting friends ***to*** going to parties. gerund gerund • Tonight I**'d prefer** visiting Lani ***to*** going to the office party.

5. A **comparison with *than*** can follow *would rather* + <u>base form</u> of verb.	base form base form • They**'d rather** eat out ***than*** cook. base form base form • I**'d rather** watch football ***than*** play it.

Focused Practice

1 | DISCOVER THE GRAMMAR

🎧 *Terry and Grace are spending the afternoon at the mall. Underline the sentences that talk about preferences.*

TERRY: <u>Which would you rather do first, get stuff for your project or shop?</u>

GRACE: I think I'd rather get the things for my project first. There's ABC Crafts.

TERRY: Have you tried Franklin's? I really prefer them for science projects.

GRACE: So let's go there.

* * * *

GRACE: Do you want to look at computer games at Nerdly's?

TERRY: I'd prefer looking for DVDs at Goodly's. What about you?

GRACE: I'd rather do that too. Let's check out that group we saw at the concert last week.

* * * *

TERRY: There's Stella Blue. Do you want to buy new earrings for Sara's party?

GRACE: I've been thinking about it, and I'd rather not. I'll just wear some old ones.

* * * *

TERRY: Have you seen *The Racer* yet?

GRACE: No, but you know me. I always prefer romantic comedies to action movies.

TERRY: We can see *Breakfast in Bogotá* at 5:00. That's romantic.

GRACE: Sounds good. Are you hungry? Let's get a pizza.

TERRY: The line's awfully long.
I'd rather just get a taco.

GRACE: You're right. The movie
starts in about 10 minutes.

Now look at the Mall Directory. Check the places that Grace and Terry decide to go to.

MALL DIRECTORY

Computers & Electronics
- Nerdly's Software ☐
- Radio Hut ☐
- Goodly's Music ☐

Jewelry
- Gem Stones ☐
- Stella Blue ☐
- Dupree's Diamonds ☐

Fashions
- Fantastic Footwear ☐
- Jan Tyler Dresses ☐

Show Time Cinemas
- *The Racer* 4:30 ☐
- *Breakfast in Bogotá* 5:00 ☐

Food Court
- Candy Man ☐
- Taco Bill's ☐
- Viva Pizza! ☐

Toys and Hobbies
- ABC Crafts ☐
- Animal Farm Pets ☐
- Franklin's ☑

2 | MUSHROOMS OR PEPPERONI?

Grammar Notes 1, 3

Emma and Kyle are discussing their evening plans. Complete their conversation. Use
would rather (not) *with one of the verbs from the box. Use short answers.*

cook	have	see	~~stay~~

EMMA: Would you like to go to a movie tonight?

KYLE: _____*I'd rather stay*_____ home and watch TV.
　　　　　　　　1.

EMMA: Sounds good. Maybe we could make dinner later.

KYLE: _____ tonight. Let's order out for some pizza.
　　　　　　　　2.

EMMA: OK. Mushrooms or anchovies?

KYLE: I'm in the mood for pepperoni. Let's get a pepperoni pizza.

EMMA: _____. Pepperoni gives me heartburn.
　　　　　　　　3.

　　　　　_____ mushrooms than pepperoni, if that's OK.
　　　　　　　　4.

KYLE: Mushrooms it is! Now, what should we watch on TV? How about the new Stephen King

thriller?

EMMA: _____. His movies give me the creeps.
　　　　　　　　5.

KYLE: Well . . . there's a comedy on at 8:00 and a documentary at 8:30.

EMMA: _____ the comedy. I need a laugh.
　　　　　　　　6.

3 | DECISIONS

Complete the questions with **prefer**, **would prefer**, *or* **would rather**. *Use* **prefer** *to state general preferences.*

1. **A:** When we go to St. Louis next week, _____*would*_____ you _____*rather*_____ travel by train or by plane?

   B: Let's take the train. It's cheaper.

2. **A:** _____ Kyle usually _____ an aisle or a window seat?

   B: He always asks for an aisle seat. He says there's more room.

3. **A:** Look—we won the prize! We have two choices. _____ you _____ going to a World Series game or getting a new television set?

   B: Let's go to the baseball game. I've always wanted to go to a World Series game.

4. **A:** I'm looking for a movie.

   B: What do you like? _____ you _____ to watch comedies or thrillers?

5. **A:** Listen up, everyone! We're going on a field trip next week. You have a choice. _____ you _____ go to the museum or to the Capitol?

   B: The museum!

6. **A:** Waiter, this cigarette smoke is really bothering us.

   B: _____ you _____ a table in the non-smoking section?

4 | SPORTS PREFERENCES

Complete this report about sports preferences around the world. Use the words in parentheses plus **to** or **than** to make a comparison. If there is a verb, choose the correct form.

THE WIDE WORLD OF SPORTS

Soccer or Basketball?

You're going to play a sport today. Would you prefer _____*playing soccer to playing basketball*_____?

1. (play soccer / play basketball)

Your answer depends a lot on your age, your gender, and your nationality. Boys age 13 and older

prefer _____, but girls of the same age prefer

2. (soccer / basketball)

_____. Because of girls' preferences, teens as a group

3. (shoot hoops / make goals)

would rather _____. In this age group, basketball is
                    4. (play basketball / play soccer)
as popular in Colombia and Thailand as it is in the United States.

Play or Watch?

People of all ages prefer _____. Seventy percent of
                                      5. (watch / play)
Latin Americans prefer _____, but Filipinos would
                              6. (soccer / other TV sports)
rather see a basketball game (85 percent watch regularly). Worldwide, cricket is not a popular

sport on TV, but in India, 80 percent prefer _____.
                                                    7. (it / basketball or soccer)
In general, people like to watch the sports they love to play.

No, Thanks.

This is not true of car racing, figure skating, and wrestling. For these sports, almost everyone

would rather _____.
                    8. (watch a pro / participate)

5 | EDITING

Read Kyle's report. There are six mistakes in the use of **prefer** *and* **would rather**. *The first
mistake is already corrected. Find and correct five more.*

> For my study, I interviewed 50 men and women. There was no real
> difference in men's and women's preferences for television. I found that
>   *to*
> everyone prefers watching television ~~than~~ going to the movies.
>
>   Men and women both enjoy news programs and entertainment specials.
> However, men would rather watching adventure programs and science
> fiction, while women prefer soap operas. Men also like to watch all kinds
> of sports, but women would rather see game shows to sports events.
>
>   I found a big difference in reading preferences. Men prefer to reading
> newspapers while women would much rather read magazines and books.
> When men read books, they prefer read nonfiction and adventure stories.
> Women will prefer novels.

Communication Practice

6 | LISTENING

🎧 *Emma is ordering in a restaurant. Listen to her conversation with the server. Then listen again and circle the items on the menu that Emma wants.*

FISH DINNER
Comes with
- soup (tomato or onion) or salad
- rice or potatoes
- coffee, tea, or soda (diet or regular)
- apple pie or ice cream

STEAK DINNER
Comes with
- vegetables and potatoes
- coffee, tea, or soda (diet or regular)
- apple pie

7 | WHAT'S ON TV?

Work in small groups. Look at the TV schedule and try to agree on something to watch at 8:00 P.M. Use **would rather** *or* **would prefer** *to talk about your preferences.*

8:00	
2	**Hockey** Maple Leafs vs. Canucks
4	**Science Watch** Are we alone in the universe?
6	**Everybody Loves Raymond** The whole family goes to Italy.
CNN	**World News**
35	**Movie*** (2004) *Spiderman 2* Action film follows the adventures of the famous superhero. Entertaining and exciting. (127 min)
38	**Movie** (1999) *Life* Comedy starring Eddie Murphy. Two criminals discover the value of life after going to prison. Funny with serious message. (108 min)
40	**Movie**** (2003) *Love Actually* Romantic comedy follows the lives of eight couples in London. Very sweet "feel-good" movie. (134 min)

Example: **A:** Let's watch the hockey game at 8:00.
B: I don't really like hockey. I'd prefer to watch *Everybody Loves Raymond.*

8 | IF I HAD MY WAY

Read the choices below. In pairs, discuss your preferences. Give reasons for your choices.

- live in the city / live in the country
- work in an office / work at home
- be married / be single
- work for someone else / own your own business

Example: **A:** Would you rather live in the city or in the country?
B: I'd rather live in the city. There's a lot more to do.
A: Really? I'd prefer the country. It's quieter.

Now ask your partner about some other choices.

9 | INFORMATION GAP: PREFERRED SNACKS

Work in pairs (A and B). Student A, follow the instructions on this page. Student B, turn to page 387 and follow the instructions there.

1. Look at the bar graphs below. Ask your partner for the information you need to complete each graph. Draw the missing bar(s) on each graph.

   Example: **A:** In the overall favorites: What percentage of people would rather eat chips than any other snack?
   B: About 25 percent.

2. Answer your partner's questions.

   Example: **B:** What percentage prefer eating cheese?
   A: Fifteen percent prefer cheese to chips or popcorn.

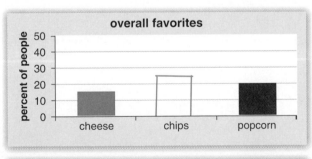

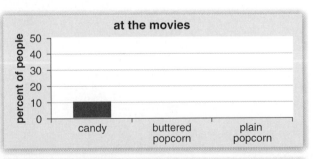

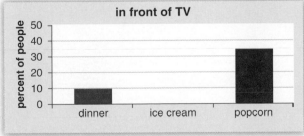

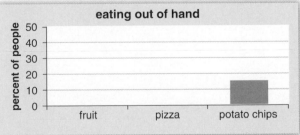

When you are finished, compare graphs. Are they the same?

10 | CHOICES

Complete the leisure-time activities questionnaire on page 376. Discuss your answers with a partner. Give reasons for your choices.

> **Example:** **A:** I prefer seeing thrillers. They're more exciting.
>
> **B:** Not me. I prefer comedies. I'd rather laugh than be frightened.

11 | WRITING

Write a paragraph about one of the choices you discussed in Exercise 8. Give reasons and examples for your choice.

> **Example:** I prefer living in the city to living in the country. There are a lot more choices of things to do in the city. For example . . .

12 | ON THE INTERNET

*Do a search on **movies** playing in your city or town (or a city of your choice). Discuss the choices with a partner and decide on a movie to see. Also choose a day and time.*

> **Example:** **A:** Would you rather see a comedy or a thriller?
>
> **B:** I always prefer comedies. *The Purple Cow* is playing at the Cineplex. How about that?
>
> **A:** Sure. We could go Monday night.
>
> **B:** I'd rather go on the weekend . . .

| INFORMATION GAP FOR STUDENT B |

1. Look at the bar graphs below. Answer your partner's questions.

   Example: **A:** In the overall favorites: What percentage of people would rather eat chips than any other snack?

   B: About 25 percent.

2. Ask your partner for the information you need to complete each bar graph. Draw the missing bar(s) on each graph.

   Example: **B:** What percentage prefer eating cheese?

   A: Fifteen percent prefer cheese to chips or popcorn.

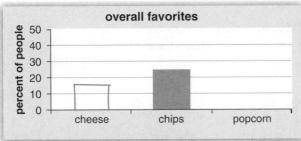

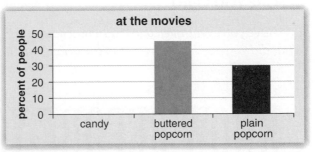

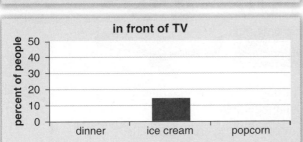

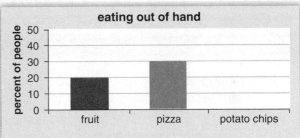

When you are finished, compare graphs. Are they the same?

34 Necessity: *Have (got) to, Must, Don't have to, Must not, Can't*

Grammar in Context

BEFORE YOU READ

🎧 *Have you ever traveled to a different country? How did you prepare for your trip? What did you need to know? Read the article about some rules for international travel.*

KNOW BEFORE YOU GO

What do international travelers **have to know** before they go? This week's column answers some questions from our readers.

Q: **Do** I **have to put** my computer and digital camera through the X-ray machine at airport security? I'm worried that the machine will damage them.

A: It probably won't, but you **don't have to put** them through the X-ray equipment. An agent **must inspect** them, though. Ask for an agent to inspect them by hand.

Q: My passport is going to expire in three months. Can I use it for a short trip to Asia next month?

A: For many countries, your passport **must be** valid for at least six months after you enter the country. Renew your passport before you leave, or you**'ll have to check** the rules of each country you plan to visit.

Q: I'm a French citizen. Last month I visited the U.S., and I brought some gifts for friends. Why did U.S. Customs take the cheese?

A: You **can't bring** most types of cheese into the U.S. without a special permit. Many governments have strict rules about bringing food into their countries. To avoid problems, don't bring gifts of fresh food and eat your snacks on the plane.

Q: I'm from Australia. My family and I are planning a trip to Europe and North America. We'd like to rent cars in a few places. **Do** I **have to get** an International Driver's Permit (IDP)?

A: Regulations differ: In Germany you **must not drive** without an IDP; in Canada you **don't have to have** one, but it's recommended. For an around-the-world tour, you really should get an IDP to avoid problems and disappointment.

KNOW BEFORE YOU GO

Q: I'm planning a trip from Toronto to New Delhi. There's a new nonstop flight, but it's more expensive, and it's about 14 hours long! What do you recommend?

A: Several airlines are now offering super-long flights. They provide more comfortable seats, wireless computers, and lots of entertainment. They cost a bit more, but you **won't have to make** as many connecting flights. That saves you time and hassles. But remember: To stay healthy on long flights you**'ve got to get up** and **move** around. You also **must drink** plenty of water. On a long flight these are "musts," not "shoulds"!

AFTER YOU READ

*Read the statements. Check **True** or **False**.*

	True	False
1. Passengers must put computers and cameras through security X-ray equipment.	☐	☐
2. An international visitor needs an IDP to drive in Germany.	☐	☐
3. Travelers are not permitted to bring cheese into the U.S.	☐	☐
4. Passengers are not permitted to move around on long flights.	☐	☐

Grammar Presentation

NECESSITY: *HAVE (GOT) TO, DON'T HAVE TO*

Affirmative Statements			
Subject	*Have to / Have got to*	Base Form of Verb	
I You We They	**have to** **have got to**	**leave**	now.
He She It	**has to** **has got to**		

Negative Statements				
Subject	*Do not*	*Have to*	Base Form of Verb	
I You We They	**don't**	**have to**	**leave**	now.
He She It	**doesn't**			

Contractions		
have got to	=	**'ve got to**
has got to	=	**'s got to**

Note: There are no contractions for *have to* and *has to*.

(continued)

Yes / No Questions				
Do	Subject	*Have to*	Base Form of Verb	
Do	I you we they	**have to**	**leave**	now?
Does	he she it			

Short Answers						
Affirmative			Negative			
Yes,	you I / we you they	**do**.	**No,**	you I / we you they	**don't**.	
	he she it	**does**.		he she it	**doesn't**.	

Wh- Questions				
Wh- Word	*Do*	Subject	*Have to*	Base Form of Verb
When	**do**	I you we they	**have to**	**leave**?
	does	he she it		

NECESSITY: *MUST, MUST NOT, CAN'T*

Must			
Subject	*Must** (*not*)	Base Form of Verb	
I You He She It We They	**must**	**leave**	early.
	must not	**arrive**	late.

Contraction
must not = **mustn't**

*Must is a modal. Modals have only one form.
They do not have *-s* in the third-person singular.

Can't			
Subject	*Can't*	Base Form of Verb	
You They	**can't**	**sit**	here.

GRAMMAR NOTES	**EXAMPLES**
1. Use *have to*, *have got to*, and *must* for **necessity**.	
a. *Have to* is the most common expression in <u>everyday speaking and writing</u>.	• You **have to carry** your passport for international travel.
b. *Have got to* is used in conversation and informal writing to express <u>strong feelings</u>.	• I**'ve got to apply** for a new passport right away!
c. *Must* is used in <u>writing</u>, including official forms, signs, and notices.	• Travelers **must show** their passports when they check in.
USAGE NOTE: *Must* is stronger than *have to*.	• Jess, you really **must pack** tonight.
2. Use the correct form of *have to* for **all tenses**.	• She **has to travel** a lot for her job.
	• He **had to travel** a lot last year.
	• We**'ll have to visit** them soon.
Use *have got to* and *must* only for the **present** and the **future**.	• You**'ve got to turn off** your cell phone on this flight.
	• Passengers **must arrive** one hour before the flight.
3. Use *have to* for most **questions**.	• **Did** you **have to get** an IDP?
	• **Do** you **have to leave** now?
USAGE NOTE: We almost never use *must* or *have got to* in questions.	
4. BE CAREFUL! *Have (got) to* and *must* have similar meanings. However, ***don't have to*** and ***must not*** have very <u>different meanings</u>.	
a. Use ***don't have to*** to show that something is <u>not necessary</u>. There is a choice.	• A tourist **doesn't have to have** an IDP in Canada.
b. Use ***must not*** for <u>prohibition</u>. There is no choice.	• Most tourists **must not drive** without an IDP in Spain.
USAGE NOTE: We often use ***can't*** instead of *must not* to express prohibition in <u>spoken English</u>.	• You **can't drive** without an IDP in Thailand.

Pronunciation Note
In informal speech, ***have to*** is often pronounced "hafta" and ***got to*** is often pronounced "gotta."

Reference Notes
For general information on **modals**, see Unit 11, Grammar Note 1, on page 126.
Have (got) to, *must*, and *can't* are also used to draw **conclusions** (see Unit 37).
Can't is also used to express **ability** (see Unit 11), refuse **permission** (see Unit 12) or **requests** (see Unit 13).
For a list of **modals and their functions**, see Appendix 19 on page A-8.

Focused Practice

1 DISCOVER THE GRAMMAR

🎧 *Read Ben Leonard's telephone conversation with a clerk from the Italian consulate. Underline the words in the conversation that express something **necessary**, **not necessary**, or **prohibited**.*

BEN: Hello. I'm Australian, and I'm planning to spend several weeks in Europe with my family. I have some questions. <u>First, do we have</u> to get visas to visit Italy?

CLERK: Not for a short visit. But you can't stay for longer than 90 days without a visa. Australians also need a Permit to Stay for visits in Italy longer than eight days. You must apply for the permit at a local police station within eight days of your arrival.

BEN: Can my wife and I use our Australian driver's licenses in Italy?

CLERK: You have to carry your Australian license, but you must also have an International Driver's Permit. And you've got to be at least 18 years old.

BEN: When do we have to get the IDPs? Is it possible to apply for them when we get to Europe?

CLERK: No, you must apply before you leave. The Australian Automobile Association can help you. You'll also have to get an International Insurance Certificate to show you have insurance. But you'll be able to get that at the car rental agency.

BEN: We'll be in Italy in January. We don't have a set schedule, so we haven't made any reservations.

CLERK: Oh, you've got to have reservations, even in January—especially in major cities like Rome, Florence, or Venice.

BEN: OK. Thanks a lot. You've been very helpful.

Now check the appropriate box for each instruction.

	Necessary	Not Necessary	Prohibited
1. Get a visa for a two-week visit.	☐	☑	☐
2. Get a Permit to Stay for visits longer than eight days.	☐	☐	☐
3. Apply for a Permit to Stay ten days after arrival.	☐	☐	☐
4. Get a visa for a one-month visit.	☐	☐	☐
5. Use only an Australian driver's license.	☐	☐	☐
6. Apply for an IDP in Europe.	☐	☐	☐
7. Make hotel reservations.	☐	☐	☐

2 | GETTING READY

Grammar Notes 1 and 4

*The Leonards have checked off the things they've already done to get ready for their trip. Read the lists and write sentences about what the Leonards still **have to do** and what they **don't have to do**.*

BEN
✔ make copies of passports and IDPs
buy euros
give the house keys to Nora

ANN
buy phone cards online
✔ call Pet Care
buy batteries for the digital camera
✔ stop the mail for two weeks

Sean and Maya
✔ pack clothes
choose DVDs and CDs for the trip
say good-bye to friends

Ben doesn't have to make copies of passports and IDPs.

He has to buy euros, and he has to give the house keys to Nora.

Ann . . .

3 | ARE WE THERE YET?

Grammar Notes 1–4

*Ben's family is traveling from Australia to Italy. Complete the conversations with the correct form of **have to**, **have got to**, or **can't** and the verbs in parentheses. Use short answers.*

1.   BEN: What time _____ do _____ we _____ have to leave _____ tomorrow?
                                                    a. (leave)

ANN: We _____ later than 5:30. We _____
              b. (start)   c. (check in)
with the airline by 7:00.

SEAN: _____ we really _____ there so early? Our flight leaves at
                              d. (get)
10:00. We've got plenty of time.

ANN: Yes, _____. It takes a long time to check in and get through
              e.
airport security these days.

MAYA: And Mom _____ the car. That takes some time too!
                     f. (park)

(continued)

2. **BEN:** Maya, this bag _____ over 70 pounds or we
    a.(weigh)

    _____ extra. _____ you _____
    b.(pay)   c.(bring)

    so many clothes?

    MAYA: Yes, _____ . I _____ all my stuff!
    d.   e.(have)

    We'll be gone for weeks.

    ANN: Put some in my bag. And hurry. We _____!
    f.(go)

3. **BEN:** We _____ never _____ this long to check in before.
    a.(wait)

    ANN: I know. But we _____ much longer. We're next.
    b.(wait)

4. **SEAN:** Look! They have computers and TV screens! I _____ Randy!
    a.(call)

    BEN: We _____ our cell phone on the plane. Send an e-mail.
    b.(use)

5. **ANN:** We _____ around again. Come on, everybody, let's go.
    a.(walk)

    SEAN: Why _____ we _____ up all the time?
    b.(get)

    BEN: Remember our rules? We _____ for more than three hours.
    c.(sit)

    It's unhealthy.

6. **MAYA:** Are we there yet? This flight is endless!

    ANN: We _____ in here much longer. We're landing in an hour.
    a.(not be)

4 | FOLLOWING THE RULES

Grammar Notes 1, 4

*Complete these rules for airline travel. Use **must** or **must not**.*

1. Passengers _____ *must* _____ arrive three hours before an international flight.

2. They _____ keep their bags with them at all times.

3. Carry-on bags _____ be bigger than 45 inches (115 cm).

4. They _____ fit under the seat or in the overhead compartment of the airplane.

5. They _____ contain knives, scissors, or other dangerous items.

6. Checked bags _____ have labels with the passenger's name.

7. They _____ weigh more than 70 pounds, or there will be additional charges.

8. Travelers _____ show identification when they check in with the airline.

9. Everyone _____ have a ticket in order to go through security.

10. On board, passengers _____ get up when the seat belt sign is on.

11. On many flights, passengers _____ use cell phones.

5 | AT THE POOL

Read the sign at the Casa Luciani swimming pool and complete each statement with
must not *or* **don't have to**.

Swimming Pool Rules and Regulations

Pool Hours 10:00 A.M. – 10:00 P.M.

Children under 12 years NOT ALLOWED

in pool without an adult.

Towels available at front desk.

- NO radio
- NO diving
- NO ball playing
- NO glass bottles
- NO alcoholic beverages

1. Children under age 12 ___must not swim___
   (swim)
   without an adult.

2. You _____ your own towel.
   (bring)

3. You _____ ball in or around
   (play)
   the pool.

4. You _____ into the pool.
   (dive)

5. Teenagers _____ swimming
   (go)
   with an adult.

6. You _____ the swimming
   (leave)
   pool at 8:00 P.M.

7. You _____ in the pool past
   (stay)
   10:00 P.M.

6 | EDITING

*Read Sean's e-mail to his friend. There are seven mistakes in expressing necessity. The first
mistake is already corrected. Find and correct six more.*

Hi Randy,

                    had
We're on our way back to Australia. We ~~have~~ to leave the hotel at 5:30 this morning, and then we

had got to wait in line at the airport for hours. This flight is great. There are computers and TVs

at every seat and hundreds of movies to watch. But we can't sit for more than three hours at a

time because it's unhealthy, and we must to drink water every hour when we're not sleeping. This

flight is 14 hours long, so we have to taking care of ourselves. Thanks for the camping knife.

I used it a lot in Italy, but before we left, I has to put it in my suitcase. You don't have to bring

knives in carry-on bags. Well, I got to get up and walk around again.

E-mail me. We'll be on this plane for 10 more hours! —Sean

Communication Practice

7 | LISTENING

🎧 *Listen to the conversations. Then listen again and write the number of each conversation next to the appropriate sign.*

a. _____

b. _____

c. _____

d. _____

e. _____

f. _1_

8 | READING THE SIGNS

Work in pairs. Where can you find these signs? What do they mean? What do you have to do when you see each one? What can't you do? What do you think of these rules?

9 | INVENT A SIGN

Draw your own sign to illustrate something people **have to do** *or* **must not do**. *Show it to a classmate. See if he or she can guess the meaning. Decide where the sign belongs.*

10 | TAKING CARE OF BUSINESS

Make a list of your most important tasks for this week. Check off the things you've already done. Tell a partner what you still **have to do** *and what you* **don't have to do**. *Report to a group.*

Examples: I don't have to do English homework. I've already done it.
Hamed has to wash the car. He doesn't have to go shopping because he went on Monday.

11 | WRITING

Write about the application procedure for getting a driver's license, a passport, a work permit, citizenship, school admission, or a new job. What do you have to do? What don't you have to do? Use **have to**, **don't have to**, **must**, *and* **must not**.

Example: To get a driver's license in my state, you must be at least 16 years and 3 months old. Drivers under the age of 19 also have to take a driver's education course. Then they have to . . .

12 | ON THE INTERNET

 Do a search on **driving rules** *in another country. Look for rules about some of the things below. Discuss the information in a group. Compare some of the rules.*

- cell phone use
- seat belts or air bags
- driver's license
- learner's permit
- speed limits

- side of the road
- car insurance
- helmets for motorcycle riders
- minimum and maximum age
- license plates

Example: In Japan, you have to drive on the left side of the road, but in Taiwan you can't drive on the left. You have to drive on the right.

Grammar in Context

BEFORE YOU READ

🎧 *What do you think the letter to Ms. Etiquette is about? What does* etiquette *mean? Read this page from Ms. Etiquette's book,* The Right Thing.

Wedding Wisdom

Dear Ms. Etiquette:

What **is** the maid of honor **supposed to do** in a wedding ceremony? My best friend is getting married soon. She has invited me to be her maid of honor. I was planning to buy a new dress to wear, but someone told me that the bride **is supposed to select** my dress. This surprised me. I'm new in this country, and I'm not sure what my friend expects of me.

Dear Reader:

First of all, you should be very proud. In the past, the bride's sister **was supposed to serve** as her maid of honor, and the groom's brother **was supposed to be** his best man. Today, however, the bride and groom can ask anyone they want. Your friend's invitation means that she values your friendship very highly.

The maid of honor is the bride's assistant, and the best man is the groom's. Before the wedding, these two **are supposed to help** the couple prepare for the ceremony. You might help the bride choose the bridesmaids' dresses and send the wedding invitations, for example. The day of the wedding, the best man **is supposed to drive** the groom to the ceremony. During the ceremony, the maid of honor holds the bride's flowers. After the wedding, the maid of honor and the best man **are** both **supposed to sign** the marriage certificate as witnesses.

AFTER YOU READ

Check the maid of honor's responsibilities.

She has to _____.

☐ **1.** choose her own dress for the wedding

☐ **2.** help send wedding invitations

☐ **3.** choose the best man

☐ **4.** drive the groom to the ceremony

☐ **5.** hold the bride's flowers during the ceremony

☐ **6.** sign the marriage certificate as a witness

Grammar Presentation

EXPECTATIONS: *BE SUPPOSED TO*

Statements					
Subject	*Be*	*(not)*	*Supposed to*	**Base Form of Verb**	
I	**am** **was**				
You We They	**are** **were**	**(not)**	**supposed to**	**sign**	the marriage certificate.
He She	**is** **was**				
It				**be**	a small wedding.

***Yes / No* Questions**			
Be	**Subject**	*Supposed to*	**Base Form of Verb**
Am **Was**	I		
Are **Were**	you	**supposed to**	**stand**?
Is **Was**	she		

Short Answers						
Affirmative			**Negative**			
Yes,	you	are. were.	**No,**	you	aren't. weren't.
	I	am. was.		I	'm not. wasn't.
	she	is. was.		she	isn't. wasn't.

(continued)

Wh- Questions				
Wh- Word	Be	Subject	Supposed to	Base Form of Verb
Where	am was	I	**supposed to**	**stand**?
	are were	you		
	is was	she		

GRAMMAR NOTES

EXAMPLES

1. Use *be supposed to* to talk about different kinds of <u>expectations</u>:

a. rules

b. customs (usual ways of doing things)

c. predictions

d. hearsay (what everyone says)

e. plans or **arrangements**

- You**'re not supposed to park** over here. There's a No Parking sign.
- The groom **is supposed to arrive** at the ceremony early. It's a custom.
- The weather forecast says it**'s supposed to rain** tomorrow.
- The beaches in Aruba **are supposed to be** beautiful. Everyone says so.
- Let's hurry. We**'re supposed to pick up** the Smiths at 6:00.

2. Use *be supposed to* only in the **simple present** or the **simple past**.

a. Use the **simple present** for the <u>present</u> or the <u>future</u>.

b. Use the **simple past** for <u>past</u> expectations.

USAGE NOTES:
Was / were supposed to and *was / were going to* can have similar meanings.

We often use *was / were supposed to* or *was / were going to* when something we expected to happen <u>did not happen</u>.

- The bride **is supposed to be** here *now*.
- I**'m supposed to be** at the wedding rehearsal *tomorrow*.
  NOT I ~~will be~~ supposed to be . . .

- They **were supposed to get** there by 6:00, so they took a taxi.

- The show **was supposed to start** at 8:00.
- The show **was going to start** at 8:00.

- Carl **was supposed to get** here at noon, *but* his train was late.
- Carl **was going to get** here at noon, *but* his train was late.

Focused Practice

1 | DISCOVER THE GRAMMAR

Read the article and underline the phrases that express expectations.

It wasn't supposed to be a big wedding.

BY MATT PEDDLER

PROVIDENCE, July 19—The Stricklands wanted a small, quiet wedding—that's why they eloped to Block Island, off the Atlantic Coast of the United States.

The ferry they took to their wedding site doesn't carry cars, so the Stricklands packed their bikes for the trip.

The couple found a lonely hill overlooking the ocean. The weather was supposed to be beautiful, so they asked the town mayor to marry them on the hill the next afternoon. They were going to have a small, private ceremony in this romantic setting.

"When we got there, we found a crowd of cyclists admiring the view," laughed Beth Strickland.

When Bill kissed his bride, the audience burst into loud applause and rang their bicycle bells. "We weren't supposed to have 50 wedding guests, but we love biking, and we're not sorry," Bill said.

When they packed to leave the island the next day, Beth left her wedding bouquet at the hotel. She remembered it minutes before the ferry was going to leave. Bill jumped on his bike, recovered the flowers, and made it back to the ferry before it departed.

"Cyclists are supposed to stay fast and fit," he said. "Now I know why."

Read the article again. Check **True** *or* **False** *for each statement.*

	True	False
1. The Stricklands planned a big wedding.	☐	☑
2. The weather forecaster predicted rain.	☐	☐
3. The Stricklands wanted an outdoor wedding.	☐	☐
4. They didn't expect 50 guests.	☐	☐
5. Beth remembered her bouquet after the ferry left.	☐	☐
6. People believe that cyclists are in good shape.	☐	☐

2 | GETTING READY

Complete the conversations with the verbs in parentheses and a form of **be supposed to**.

1. **A:** Netta, Gary called while you were out.

   B: ____Am____ I ____supposed to call____ him back?

          a. (call)

   A: No, he'll call you later in the afternoon.

2. **A:** The dress store called too. They delivered your wedding dress to your office this morning.

   _____ they _____ that?

       a. (do)

   B: No, they weren't! They _____ it here. That's why I

         b. (deliver)

   stayed home today.

3. **A:** Let's get in line. The rehearsal _____ in a few minutes.

            a. (start)

   B: We're bridesmaids. Where _____ we _____ ?

          b. (stand)

   A: Right here, behind Netta.

4. **A:** Hi. Where's Netta?

   B: Gary! You _____ here!

      a. (not be)

   A: Why not?

   B: The groom _____ the bride on the day of the wedding

        b. (not see)

   until the ceremony. It's bad luck.

5. **A:** Sophie, could I borrow your handkerchief, please?

   B: Sure, but why?

   A: I _____ something old, something new, something

      a. (wear)

   borrowed, and something blue. I don't have anything borrowed.

   B: It _____ this afternoon. Maybe I should lend you my

     b. (rain)

   umbrella instead.

6. **A:** Where are Gary and Netta going on their honeymoon?

   B: Aruba.

   A: Oh, that _____ a really nice island.

       a. (be)

7. **A:** How long are they going to be away?

   B: They _____ ten days, but they decided to stay two weeks.

    a. (stay)

3 | PLANS CHANGE

Grammar Note 2

Look at the list of wedding plans. There have been a lot of changes. Write sentences with
was / were going to.

TASK	WHO	COMPLETED
1. choose the bridesmaids' dresses	Netta *and Sophie*	☑
2. mail ~~180~~ *210* invitations	Netta's parents	☑
3. order a ~~vanilla~~ *chocolate!* cake	Netta	☑
4. hire a ~~rock~~ *jazz* band	Gary's parents	☑
5. give the bridal shower May ~~10~~ *20*	Sophie	☑
6. plan the rehearsal dinner	~~Gary~~ *Gary's parents*	☑
7. find a photographer	~~Netta~~ *Jack*	☑
8. rent a ~~limo~~ *red sports car*	Jack	☑
9. order flowers by ~~April 1~~ *April 15*	Sophie	☑
10. Buy ~~candles~~ *clocks* as bridesmaids' gifts	Netta's parents	☑
11. Send the wedding announcement to the newspaper	~~Gary~~ *Jack*	☑

1. *Netta was going to choose the bridesmaids' dresses, but Netta and Sophie chose them.*

2.

3.

4.

5.

6.

7.

8.

9.

10.

11.

4 | EDITING

*Read Jack's e-mail to a friend. There are eight mistakes in the use of **be supposed to** and* **was / were going to**. *The first mistake is already corrected. Find and correct seven more.*

Hi!

Remember my old college roommate Gary? He's getting married tomorrow, and I'm the best man!

He and his fiancée ~~supposed~~ *were* supposed to have a small wedding, but they ended up inviting more than 200

people! As best man, I have some important responsibilities. For one thing, I'm supposing to make

sure Gary gets to the wedding ceremony on time—not an easy job for me. At first we was going to

hire a limousine and driver, but I decided to drive him there myself in a rented red sports car. I'm

also supposed to hold the wedding rings during the ceremony. Then, at the end of the reception

party, I'm supposed to helping the newlyweds leave quickly for their honeymoon. They're going

straight to the airport (I'm also suppose to hold the plane tickets for them). They are going to go

to Hawaii, but they changed their minds and are going to Aruba instead. Oh! I just looked at the

clock. I'd better sign off now, or I'll be late for the rehearsal dinner. I going to leave five minutes

ago! By the way, Sophie, the maid of honor, will be there too. I've never met her, but she supposes

to be very nice. I'll let you know how it goes! —Jack

Communication Practice

5 | LISTENING

🎧 *It's the day of the wedding. Listen to the conversations. Then listen again and circle the correct words.*

1. Netta is / (isn't) supposed to be at the church by 2:00.

2. Netta <u>was / wasn't</u> going to walk to the wedding.

3. The photographer <u>is / isn't</u> supposed to take pictures during the ceremony.

4. Members of the bride's family <u>are / aren't</u> supposed to sit on the right.

5. The bridesmaids <u>were / weren't</u> going to wear pink.

6. The maid of honor <u>is / isn't</u> supposed to walk behind the bride.

7. Guests <u>are / aren't</u> supposed to say "congratulations" to the groom.

8. Guests <u>are / aren't</u> supposed to throw rice at the bride and groom.

6 | A CHANGE OF PLANS

Work with a partner. Discuss important plans that you had that changed.
Use **was / were supposed to** *and* **was / were going to.**

> **Example:** A: My family and I were supposed to move to Mexico City, but my mother got a
> better job in Guadalajara, so we moved there instead.
> B: When were you going to move to Mexico City?

7 | INTERNATIONAL CUSTOMS

Work in small groups. Discuss these important events. What are people in your culture
supposed to do and say at these times? Are people expected to give certain gifts? Report
to the class.

- a wedding
- an important birthday
- a graduation ceremony
- an engagement to be married
- an anniversary
- a birth
- a funeral

> **Example:** In traditional Japanese weddings,
> the bride and groom are supposed
> to wear kimonos.

8 | WRITING

Write a short essay about one of the events listed in Exercise 7. Use **be supposed to** *to*
describe customs.

9 | ON THE INTERNET

Do a search on **international etiquette***. Choose a country that interests you. Write*
about some things that you are supposed to do and some things you are not supposed to
do in that country.

> **Example:** In Turkey you're supposed to shake hands firmly when you meet someone.
> You're not supposed to show the bottom of your shoes when you're sitting.
> You're . . .

36 Future Possibility: May, Might, Could

Grammar in Context

BEFORE YOU READ

Look at the weather map. Are the temperatures in Celsius or Fahrenheit? How warm might it get in Ankara? How cool? What's the weather prediction for Madrid? Read this transcript of a weather report on British TV.

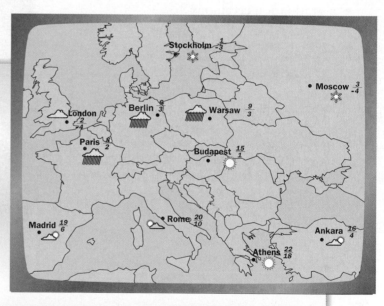

WEATHER WATCH

CAROL: Good morning. I'm Carol Johnson, and here's the local forecast. The cold front that has been affecting much of northern Europe is moving toward Great Britain. Temperatures **may drop** as much as 11 degrees by late tomorrow afternoon. In London, expect a high of only 2 and a low of –4 degrees. We **might** even **see** some snow flurries later on in the day. By evening, winds **could reach** 40 miles per hour. So, bundle up; it's going to be a cold one! And now it's time for our travelers' forecast with Ethan Harvey. Ethan?

ETHAN: Thanks, Carol. Take your umbrella if you're traveling to Paris. Stormy conditions **may move** into France by tomorrow morning. Rain **could turn** into snow by evening when temperatures fall to near or below freezing. On a warmer note— you **may not need** your coat at all if you plan to be in Rome. Expect to see partly cloudy skies with early morning highs around 10. Temperatures **could climb** to above 20 as skies clear up in the afternoon. It looks like it will turn out to be a beautiful, sunny day in central Italy.

CAROL: Italy sounds great! Will you join me on a Roman holiday?

ETHAN: I **might**!

AFTER YOU READ

Read the statements. Check **True** *or* **False**.

	True	False
1. Temperatures will definitely drop 11 degrees in Great Britain.	☐	☐
2. Snow is possible in London.	☐	☐
3. There will definitely be stormy weather in France.	☐	☐
4. Snow is possible in Paris.	☐	☐
5. Temperatures will definitely be above 20°C in Rome.	☐	☐

Grammar Presentation

FUTURE POSSIBILITY: *MAY, MIGHT, COULD*

Statements			
Subject	*May / Might / Could**	Base Form of Verb	
You It They	**may (not)** **might (not)** **could**	**get**	cold.

*May, *might*, and *could* are modals. Modals have only one form. They do not have -s in the third-person singular.

Yes / No Questions		
Are you going to fly to Paris? Are you leaving on Monday?		
Are you going to Will you Is it possible you'll	**be**	there long?

Short Answers		
I	**may (not).** **might (not).** **could.**	
We	**may** **might** **could**	**be.**

Note: *May not* and *might not* are not contracted.

Wh- Questions
When are you **going** to Paris?
How long are you going to **be** there?

Answers			
I We	**may** **might** **could**	**go** **be**	next week. there a week.

GRAMMAR NOTES   **EXAMPLES**

---

1. Use *may*, *might*, and *could* to talk about **future possibility**.

   ▶ BE CAREFUL! *May be* and *maybe* both express possibility. Notice these differences:

   - *May be* is a <u>modal + *be*</u>. It is always two words.

   - *Maybe* is not a modal. It is an <u>adverb</u>. It is always one word, and it comes at the beginning of the sentence.

   - It **may be** windy *later*.
   - It **might get** cold *tonight*.
   - It **could rain** *tomorrow*.

   - He **may be** late today.

   - *Maybe* he'll take the train.
     NOT He ~~maybe take~~ the train.

---

2. Use *may not* and *might not* to express the <u>possibility</u> that something <u>will not happen</u>.

   Use *couldn't* to express the idea that something is <u>impossible</u>.

   ▶ BE CAREFUL! We usually <u>do not contract</u> *might not*, and we never contract *may not*.

   - There are a lot of clouds, but it **might not rain**.

   A: Why don't you ask John for a ride?
   B: I **couldn't do** that. He's too busy.

   - You **may not** need a coat.
     NOT You ~~mayn't~~ need a coat.

---

3. **Questions** about possibility usually do not use *may*, *might*, or *could*. Instead, they use the future (*will*, *be going to*, the present progressive) or phrases such as *Do you think . . . ?* or *Is it possible that . . . ?*

   The **answers** to these questions often use *may*, *might*, or *could*.

   In **short answers** to *yes / no* questions, use *may*, *might*, or *could* alone.

   USAGE NOTE: If *be* is the main verb, it is common to include *be* in the short answer.

   A: When *will* it *start* snowing?
   B: It **might start** around lunchtime.

   A: *Are* you *going to drive* to work?
   B: I don't know. I **might take** the bus.

   A: When *are* you *leaving*?
   B: I **may leave** now.

   A: *Do you think* it'll snow tomorrow?
   B: It **could stop** tonight.

   A: Will your office close early?
   B: It **might**.

   A: Will our flight *be* on time?
   B: It **might be**.

Reference Notes

For general information on **modals**, see Unit 11, Grammar Note 1 on page 126.
May is also used to ask and give **permission** (see Unit 12).
Might is also used to draw **conclusions** (see Unit 37).
Could is also used to talk about **ability** (see Unit 11), ask and give **permission** (see Unit 12), make **requests** (see Unit 13), make **suggestions** (see Unit 15), and draw **conclusions** (see Unit 37).
For a list of **modals and their functions**, see Appendix 19 on page A-8.

Focused Practice

1 | DISCOVER THE GRAMMAR

🎧 *Anna is a college student who works part-time; Cody is her boyfriend. Read their conversation. Underline the words that express future possibility.*

ANNA: Are you going to drive to work tomorrow?

CODY: I <u>might</u>. Why?

ANNA: I just heard the weather report. It may snow tonight.

CODY: Then I might take the 7:30 train instead. I have a 9:00 meeting, and I don't want to miss it. Do you have a class tomorrow morning?

ANNA: No, but I'm going to the library to work on my paper. Maybe I'll take the train with you.

CODY: Could we have lunch together after you go to the library?

ANNA: Oh, I'm sorry. I have a class at noon every day this week.

CODY: Cut class tomorrow. One day won't make any difference.

ANNA: I couldn't do that. I'll meet you at 6:00 at the train station, OK? I'm going to take the 6:30 train home.

CODY: I might not catch the 6:30 train. My boss said something about working late tomorrow. I'll call you and let you know what I'm doing.

ANNA: OK. I'll get some takeout on the way home. Do you mind eating late?

CODY: No. I definitely want to have dinner together. Maybe I'll rent a movie.

ANNA: There might be something good on TV.

CODY: Let's decide tomorrow.

Read the conversation again. Check the appropriate box for each activity.

CODY'S SCHEDULE	Certain	Possible	Impossible
1. shovel snow	☐	✓	☐
2. take 7:30 A.M. train	☐	☐	☐
3. 9:00 A.M. meeting	☐	☐	☐
4. meet Anna for lunch	☐	☐	☐
5. call Anna	☐	☐	☐
6. work until 8:00 P.M.	☐	☐	☐
7. dinner with Anna	☐	☐	☐
8. rent a movie	☐	☐	☐

ANNA'S SCHEDULE	Certain	Possible	Impossible
1. ride train with Cody	☐	☐	☐
2. go to library	☐	☐	☐
3. go to class	☐	☐	☐
4. lunch with Cody	☐	☐	☐
5. 6:00 P.M.—meet Cody	☐	☐	☐
6. take 6:30 train home	☐	☐	☐
7. buy takeout for dinner	☐	☐	☐
8. dinner with Cody	☐	☐	☐

2 | MAKING PLANS

Anna is graduating from college with a degree in early childhood education. Complete this paragraph from her diary. Choose the appropriate words in parentheses.

I just got the notice from my school. I _____*'m going to*_____ graduate in June, but I still don't
1. (might not / 'm going to)

have plans. Some day-care centers hire students before they graduate, so I _____
2. (could / couldn't)

apply for a job now. On the other hand, I _____ apply to a graduate school and get
3. (might / might not)

my master's degree. I'm just not sure, though—these past two years have been really hard, and

I _____ be ready to study for two more years. At least I *am* sure about my career.
4. (may / may not)

I _____ work with children—that's certain. I made an appointment to discuss my
5. ('m going to / might)

grades with my teacher, Mrs. Humphrey, tomorrow. I _____ talk about my plans
6. (maybe / may)

with her. She _____ have an idea about what I should do.
7. (won't / might)

3 | I MIGHT

*Look at Anna's schedule for Monday. She put a question mark (?) next to each item she wasn't sure about. Write sentences about Anna's plans for Monday. Use **may** or **might** (for things that are possible) and **be going to** (for things that are certain).*

MONDAY
1. call Cody at 9:00
2. buy some notebooks before class ?
3. go to the meeting with Mrs. Humphrey at 11:00
4. have coffee with Sue after class ?
5. go to work at 1:00
6. go shopping after work ?
7. take the 7:00 train ?

1. ___Anna is going to call Cody at 9:00.___

2. _____

3. _____

4. _____

5. _____

6. _____

7. _____

4 | STORM WARNING *Grammar Notes 2-3*

For each question, write a short answer with **could** *or* **couldn't**. *Use* **be** *when necessary.*

1. **A:** Do you think the roads will be dangerous? It's snowing really hard.

   B: _____*They could be*_____. It's a big storm.

2. **A:** Will the schools stay open?

   B: Oh, no. _____. It's too dangerous for school buses in a storm as bad as this one.

3. **A:** Will it be very windy?

   B: _____. The winds are very strong already.

4. **A:** Will it get very cold?

   B: _____. The temperature in Centerville is below zero.

5. **A:** Is it possible that the storm will be over by Monday?

   B: _____. It's moving pretty quickly now.

6. **A:** Do you think it will be warmer on Tuesday?

   B: _____. It has stopped snowing in Centerville already.

5 | EDITING

Read this student's report about El Niño. There are seven mistakes in the use of **may**, **might**, *and* **could**. *The first mistake is already corrected. Find and correct six more.*

Every few years, the ocean near Peru becomes warmer. This change is called El Niño. An El Niño ~~maybe~~ *may* cause big weather changes all over the world. The west coasts of North and South America might have very heavy rains. On the other side of the Pacific, New Guinea might becomes very dry. Northern areas could have warmer, wetter winters, and southern areas maybe become much colder. These weather changes affect plants and animals. Some fish mayn't survive in warmer waters. They may die or swim to colder places. In addition, dry conditions could causing crops to die. When that happens, food may get very expensive. El Niño does not happen regularly. It may happen every two years, or it could not come for seven years. Will El Niños get worse in the future? They could be. Pollution might increase the effects of El Niño, but no one is sure yet.

Communication Practice

6 | LISTENING

🎧 *Listen to the weather forecast. Then listen again and check* **Certain** *or* **Possible** *for each forecast.*

Friday	Certain	Possible
Dry	☐	☑
Sunny	☐	☐
Low 50s	☐	☐

Saturday	Certain	Possible
Sunny	☐	☐
60°	☐	☐
Windy	☐	☐

Sunday	Certain	Possible
Cold	☐	☐
Windy	☐	☐
Snow flurries	☐	☐

7 | POSSIBILITIES

Look at these student profiles from a school newspaper. Work in a group. Talk about what these students might do in the future. Use the information in the box on the next page or your own ideas.

About Your Classmates

Name:	Anna Lane
Major:	Early Childhood Education
Activities:	Students' Association, school newspaper
Likes:	adventure, meeting new people
Dislikes:	snow, boring routines
Plans:	teach in a preschool
Dreams:	travel around the world

Name:	Nick Vanek
Major:	Information Systems
Activities:	Computer Club, Runners' Club
Likes:	learning something new
Dislikes:	crowded places
Plans:	go to a four-year college
Dreams:	become an inventor

FUTURE POSSIBILITIES		
Occupations	**Hobbies**	**Achievements**
• computer programmer	• dancing	• fly on space shuttle
• teacher	• skiing	• teach in Alaska
• manager, day-care center	• creative writing	• develop a computer program

Example: A: Anna is on the school newspaper. She might do creative writing as a hobby.

B: Nick hates crowded places. He couldn't work on the space shuttle.

Now write your own profile. Discuss your future possibilities with your group.

8 | WRITING

Write a paragraph about your future plans. Use **will** *and* **be going to** *for the things you are certain about. Use* **may**, **might**, *and* **could** *for the things you think are possible.*

Example: I'm going to graduate in a few months, and suddenly I'm facing a lot of choices. I might look for a job and work for a few years to get experience . . .

9 | ON THE INTERNET

Do a search on **weather** *in your area. Write about the weather for the next two days. Include modals of future possibility.*

Example: Monday will be warm and sunny in Miami, but there might be some thunderstorms in the afternoon . . .

Grammar in Context

BEFORE YOU READ

Who is Sherlock Holmes? What kind of a story is this? Read an excerpt from a Sherlock Holmes story called "The Red-Headed League."

When Dr. Watson arrived, Sherlock Holmes was with a visitor.

"Dr. Watson, this is Mr. Jabez Wilson," said Holmes. Watson shook hands with a fat, red-haired man.

"Mr. Wilson **must write** a lot," Dr. Watson said.

Holmes smiled. "You **could be** right. But why do you think so?"

"His right shirt cuff looks very old and worn. And he has a small hole in the left elbow of his jacket. He probably rests his left elbow on the desk when he writes."

Wilson looked amazed. "Dr. Watson is correct," he told Holmes. "Your methods **may be** useful after all."

"Please tell Dr. Watson your story," said Holmes.

"I have a small shop," began the red-haired man. "I don't have many customers, so I was very interested in this advertisement. My clerk, Vincent, showed it to me." He handed Watson a piece of newspaper:

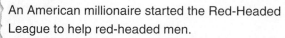
An American millionaire started the Red-Headed League to help red-headed men.

The League now has one position open. The salary is £4 per week for four hours of work every day. The job is to copy the encyclopedia in our offices.

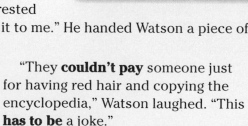
"They **couldn't pay** someone just for having red hair and copying the encyclopedia," Watson laughed. "This **has to be** a joke."

"It **might not be**," said Holmes. "Listen to Wilson tell the rest of his story."

"I got the job, and I worked at the League for two months. Then this morning I found a note on the door." Wilson gave Holmes the note . . .

AFTER YOU READ

Read the statements. Check **True** *or* **False**.

	True	False
1. Dr. Watson is almost certain that Mr. Wilson writes a lot.	☐	☐
2. Holmes thinks Dr. Watson is wrong about Mr. Wilson.	☐	☐
3. Mr. Wilson is certain that Holmes's methods will be useful.	☐	☐
4. Dr. Watson is sure that the newspaper job is a joke.	☐	☐
5. Holmes is sure that it isn't a joke.	☐	☐

Grammar Presentation

CONCLUSIONS: *MUST, HAVE (GOT) TO, MAY, MIGHT, COULD, CAN'T*

Affirmative Statements		
Subject	*Must / May / Might / Could**	**Base Form of Verb**
I You He She It We You They	**must** **may** **might** **could**	**be** wrong.

*Must, *may*, *might*, and *could* are modals. Modals have only one form. They do not have *-s* in the third-person singular.

Negative Statements				
Subject	*Must / May / Might / Could / Can*	*Not*	**Base Form of Verb**	
I You He She It We You They	**must** **may** **might** **could** **can**	**not**	**be**	right.

Contractions		
could not	=	**couldn't**
cannot OR can not	=	**can't**

Note: We usually do not contract *must not*, *may not*, and *might not* when we draw conclusions.

Affirmative Statements with *Have (got) to*

Subject	Have (got) to	Base Form	
I You We They	**have (got) to**	**be**	right.
He She It	**has (got) to**		

Yes / No Questions

Can / Could	Subject	Base Form	
Could **Can**	he	**know**	that?

Do	Subject	Base Form	
Does	he	**know**	that?

Short Answers

Subject	Modal
He	**must (not).** **may (not).** **might (not).** **could(n't).** **has (got) to.** **can't.**

Yes / No Questions with *Be*

Can / Could	Subject	Be	
Could **Can**	he	**be**	a detective?

Be	Subject	
Is	he	a detective?

Short Answers

Subject	Modal	Be
He	**must (not)** **may (not)** **might (not)** **could(n't)** **has (got) to** **can't**	**be.**

Wh- Questions with *Can* and *Could*

Wh- Word	Can / Could	Subject	Base Form
Who What	**can** **could**	it they	**be?** **want?**

GRAMMAR NOTES	**EXAMPLES**

1. We often make guesses and draw **conclusions** about present situations using the information we have.

We use **modals** to show <u>how certain or uncertain</u> we are about our conclusions.

100% certain

AFFIRMATIVE	NEGATIVE
must	**can't, couldn't**
have (got) to	**must not**
may	**may not**
might, could	**might not**

0% certain

---

2. When we are <u>almost 100 percent certain</u>, we use ***must***, ***have to***, or ***have got to*** to state **affirmative conclusions**.

USAGE NOTE: We often use ***have got to*** instead of *have to* in <u>informal</u> speech and writing. We usually contract *have* or *has*.

FACT	CONCLUSION
Wilson has only one clerk.	• His shop **must be** quite small.
Wilson applied for a job.	• He **has to need** money.
They pay men for having red hair.	• It**'s got to be** a joke.

Pronunciation Note
In informal speech, ***have to*** is usually pronounced "hafta" and ***got to*** is usually pronounced "gotta." Do not write "hafta" or "gotta."

---

3. When we are <u>less certain about our conclusion</u>, we use ***may***, ***might***, or ***could*** to express that something is **possible**.

FACT	CONCLUSION
Wilson has a hole in his sleeve.	• He **may write** a lot.
Watson knows a lot about medicine.	• He **might be** a doctor.
Vincent knows a lot about cameras.	• He **could be** a photographer.

---

4. To express **negative conclusions**, use the following modals:

- Use ***can't*** and ***couldn't*** when you are <u>almost 100 percent certain</u> that something is **impossible**.

- Use ***must not*** when you are <u>slightly less certain</u>.

- Use ***may not*** and ***might not*** when you are <u>even less certain</u>.

▶ **BE CAREFUL!** Do not use *have to* and *have got to* to draw negative conclusions.

- He **can't be** dead! I just saw him!
- Vincent **couldn't be** dishonest! I trust him completely!

- He **must not have** enough money. He never buys new clothes.

- He **may not know** about the plan. His boss doesn't tell him everything.

- It **can't be** true!
  NOT It ~~doesn't have to be~~ true!

(continued)

5. Use *can* and *could* in **questions**.	• Someone's coming. Who **can** it **be**? • **Could** Vincent **be** in the shop?

| **6.** In **short answers**, use a <u>modal alone</u>. | **A:** Does she still work at Wilson's?
B: She **may not**. I saw a new clerk there. |
| ▶ **BE CAREFUL!** Use *be* in short answers to questions that include *be*. | **A:** *Is* Ron still with City Bank?
B: I'm not sure. He **might not be**. |

Reference Notes
May, can, and *could* are also used to express **permission** (see Unit 12).
Must, have to, and *have got to* are also used to express **necessity** (see Unit 34).
May, might, and *could* are also used to express **future possibility** (see Unit 36).
For a list of **modals and their functions**, see Appendix 19 on page A-8.

Focused Practice

1 | DISCOVER THE GRAMMAR

🎧 *Read the next part of "The Red-Headed League." Underline the phrases that draw conclusions.*

Sherlock Holmes studied the note: *The Red-Headed League does not exist anymore.*
"This <u>could be serious</u>," Holmes told Wilson. "What can you tell us about your clerk Vincent?"

"Vincent couldn't be dishonest," replied Wilson. "In fact, he took this job for half-pay because he wanted to learn the business. His only fault is photography."

"Photography?" Holmes and Watson asked together.

"Yes," replied Wilson. "He's always running down to the basement to work with his cameras."

Wilson left soon after that.

"Wilson's clerk might be the key to this mystery," Holmes told Watson. "Let's go see him." An hour later, Holmes and Watson walked into Wilson's shop. The clerk was a man of about 30, with a scar on his forehead. Holmes asked him for directions. Then he and Watson left the shop.

"My dear Watson," Holmes began. "It's very unusual for a 30-year-old man to work for half-pay. This clerk has to have a very special reason for working here."

"Something to do with the Red-Headed League?" Watson asked.

"Yes. Perhaps the clerk placed that ad in the newspaper. He may want to be alone in the shop. Did you look at his legs?"

"No, I didn't."

"He has holes in his trouser knees. He must spend his time digging a tunnel from Wilson's basement. But where is it?"

Holmes hit the ground sharply with his walking stick. "The ground isn't hollow, so the tunnel must not be here in front of the shop. Let's walk to the street in back of Wilson's shop."

Read the second part of the story again. What does Holmes believe about each of the
*following statements? Check **Possible** or **Almost Certain** for each statement.*

	Possible	**Almost Certain**
1. Something serious is happening.	☑	☐
2. The clerk is the key to the mystery.	☐	☐
3. The clerk has a special reason for working in Wilson's shop.	☐	☐
4. He wants to be alone in the shop.	☐	☐
5. He's digging a tunnel from Wilson's basement.	☐	☐
6. The tunnel isn't in front of the shop.	☐	☐

2 | PICTURE THIS
Grammar Notes 1–4

Look at the picture. Think about it in connection to the story, "The Red-Headed League."
Draw conclusions and circle the appropriate words.

1. It (must)/ could be nighttime.

2. Number 27 <u>might / can't</u> be a bank.

3. The delivery <u>couldn't / might</u> be for the bank.

4. The box <u>could / must not</u> contain gold.

5. The two men on the sidewalk <u>must not / could</u> notice the delivery.

6. The manager <u>might not / must</u> want people to know about this delivery.

7. He <u>couldn't / may</u> worry about robbers.

3 | DRAWING CONCLUSIONS

Grammar Notes 1, 2, 4

Look at the poster and the map of Wilson's neighborhood. Use the evidence and the words in parentheses to write sentences with **must** *and* **must not**.

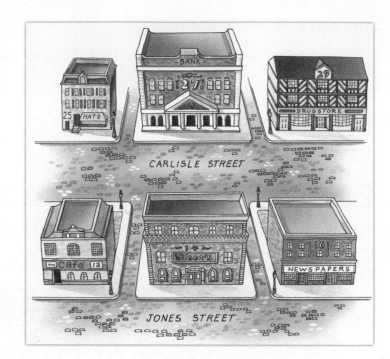

1. Wilson's clerk is the man on the poster.

   He must be a criminal.
   _____
   (He / be a criminal)

2. The man on the poster is named John Clay.

   _____
   (Vincent / be the clerk's real name)

3. Mr. Wilson trusts Vincent.

   _____
   (He / know about the poster)

4. John Clay has committed a lot of crimes, but the police haven't caught him.

   _____
   (He / be very clever)

5. The address of the bank on the map and the address in the picture for Exercise 2 are the same.

   _____
   (Number 27 Carlisle Street / be City Bank)

6. The hat shop and the drugstore don't make much money.

   _____
   (Vincent's tunnel / lead to those shops)

7. There's a lot of money in the bank, and it's very close to Wilson's shop.

   _____
   (Vincent's tunnel / lead to the bank)

8. The bank is expecting a shipment of gold.

   _____
   (The tunnel / be almost finished)

4 | IT'S GOT TO BE

Grammar Notes 1, 2, 4

Ann and Marie are buying hats in the shop on Carlisle Street. Read the conversation and rewrite the underlined sentences another way. Use **have got to** *or* **can't** *and the word in parentheses.*

ANN: Look at this hat, Marie. What do you think?

MARIE: Oh, come on. <u>That's got to be a joke.</u>

    You can't be serious.
    _____
                    1. (serious)

    Anyway, it's much too expensive. Look at the price tag.

ANN: It's $100! <u>That can't be right.</u>

    _____
                    2. (wrong)

MARIE: I know. <u>It can't cost more than $50.</u>

    _____
                    3. (less)

    Anyway, let's talk about it over lunch. I'm getting hungry.

ANN: It's too early for lunch. <u>It has to be before 11:00.</u>

    _____
                    4. (after)

MARIE: Look at my watch. It's already 12:30.

ANN: Then let's go to Café Au Lait. It's on Jones Street. <u>It can't be far.</u>

    _____
                    5. (nearby)

MARIE: Let's go home after lunch. I don't feel well.

ANN: Oh, come on. <u>You're fine.</u> You must be hungry.

    _____
                    6. (sick)

5 | BEST GUESSES

Grammar Note 6

Write a short answer to each question. Use **might (not)** *or* **must (not)** *and include* **be** *where necessary.*

A: You sound terrible. Are you sick?

B: I _____*must be*_____ . I have a headache and my throat is starting to hurt.
       1.

A: This bottle is empty. Are we all out of cough syrup?

B: We _____ . I think that was the last bottle.
       2.

(continued)

A: I'll go get you some cough medicine. Does that nighttime cough medicine work?

B: It _____. It's worth a try.
 _3._

A: I forgot to cash a check today. Do you have any money?

B: I _____. Look in my wallet. It's on the table downstairs.
 _4._

A: I found it. It's 9:30. Is Drake Drugstore still open?

B: It _____. Their advertisement says "Open 'til 11."
 _5._

A: Do you think they sell chicken soup? Some drugstores carry food.

B: They _____. It's a very small store.
 _6._

A: What about Quickshop? Do they have soup?

B: They _____. They've got everything.
 _7._

6 | MAYBE IT'S THE CAT
                                                                Grammar Notes 3–6

🎧 *Mr. and Mrs. Wilson are trying to get to sleep. Write questions and answers with*
could be, **couldn't be**, *or* **can't be**. *Choose between affirmative and negative forms.*

MRS. WILSON: Shh! I hear someone at the door. It's 9:30.

   Who _____*could*_____ it _____*be*_____ ?
                                          _1._

MR. WILSON: It _____ a late customer.
                         _2._

MRS. WILSON: No, it _____. It's much too late. Maybe it's the cat.
                           _3._

MR. WILSON: It _____. I put the cat out before we went to bed.
                        _4._

MRS. WILSON: _____ it _____ Vincent? He's always down in the
                                              _5._

   basement with his camera.

MR. WILSON: No, Vincent went out an hour ago. He _____ back this early.
                                                         _6._

   Wait a minute. It _____ Holmes and Dr. Watson. They said they
                           _7._

   wanted to talk to me.

MRS. WILSON: _____ they really _____ here so late?
                                                      _8._

MR. WILSON: No. You're right. It _____ them.
                                       _9._

MRS. WILSON: What _____ it _____ then?
                                               _10._

MR. WILSON: That door rattles whenever the wind blows. It _____ the wind.
                                                                 _11._

MRS. WILSON: That must be it. Let's go to sleep.

7 | EDITING

Read this student's reading journal for a mystery novel. There are six mistakes in the use of **must**, **have (got) to**, **may**, **might**, **could**, *and* **can't**. *The first mistake is already corrected. Find and correct five more.*

> The main character, Molly Smith, is a college ESL teacher. She is trying to
> find her dead grandparents' first home in the United States. It may ~~being~~ ^{be}
> in a nearby town. The townspeople there seem scared. They could be have a
> secret, or they must just hate strangers. Molly has some old letters that
> might lead her to the place. They are in Armenian, but one of her students
> mights translate them for her. They hafta be important because the
> author mentions them right away. The letters must contain family secrets.
> I'm sure of it. Who is the bad guy? It couldn't be the student because he
> wants to help. It might to be the newspaper editor in the town.

Communication Practice

8 | LISTENING

🎧 *Holmes, Dr. Watson, and a police captain meet in front of City Bank. Listen to their conversation. Then listen again and check* **Possible** *or* **Almost Certain** *for each statement.*

	Possible	Almost Certain
1. It's 10:00.	☐	☑
2. They have a long wait.	☐	☐
3. John Clay knows about the gold.	☐	☐
4. Clay's tunnel is finished.	☐	☐
5. The tunnel is under the bank floor.	☐	☐
6. John Clay is dangerous.	☐	☐
7. Clay is waiting for Wilson to go to sleep.	☐	☐
8. There's someone in the tunnel.	☐	☐
9. The man is John Clay.	☐	☐

9 | TELL-TALE SIGNS

Look at the pictures of Sandra Diaz and some things that she and her family own.
Make guesses about the Diaz family. Give reasons for your guesses.

> **Example:** **A:** Sandra might be a construction worker. She's wearing a hard hat.
> **B:** Or she could be an architect.

10 | POSSIBLE EXPLANATIONS

Read the following situations. In pairs, discuss possible explanations for each situation.
Then come to a conclusion. Discuss your explanations with the rest of the class. Use your
imagination!

1. You've been calling your sister on the phone for three days. No one has answered.

> **Example:** **A:** She might be at the library. She always studies hard for her exams.
> **B:** I don't think so. She's already finished her exams.
> **A:** You could have the wrong number.
> **B:** This is the number I always call. I think she's been on vacation this week.
> **A:** Then she must be away.

2. You are on the street. You have asked a woman three times for the time. She hasn't answered.

3. You go to dinner with a good friend. Your friend hardly says a word all evening.

4. You went on a picnic in the park. You ate strawberries and cheese. Now you are sneezing and your eyes are watering.

5. You're at a party, and no one is talking to you.

11 | WRITING

Agatha James, the mystery writer, starts a new novel by writing story outlines about each one of her characters. Read about the murder suspect's activities on the day of the crime.

MARCH 1	MURDER SUSPECT'S ACTIVITIES
7:00-8:00	gym-aerobics class—<u>talks</u> to exercise instructor!
9:30	calls Dr. Lorenzo
11:00-1:00	hairdresser—changes hair color
1:30	pharmacy—picks up prescription
2:00	bank—withdraws #10,000
3:00	Mr. Jordan
4:30	calls travel agency—vegetarian meal?

Work in small groups to speculate about the story and the characters. Consider questions like these:

- Is the murder suspect a man or a woman?
- Who is Dr. Lorenzo?
- Who is Mr. Jordan? What is his relationship with the suspect?
- Why does the suspect need $10,000?

Example: A: The suspect must be a woman. She's going to the hairdresser.
B: It could be a man. Men go to hairdressers too.

Now write possibilities and conclusions about the story and the characters.

12 | ON THE INTERNET

Do a search on **mystery pictures**. *Print out one picture. Then work in a group. Show your picture and discuss what it might be with your classmates. Do the same with your classmates' pictures.*

Example: A: It could be part of a plant.
B: I don't think so. It must be from outer space.

From **Grammar** to **Writing**
Combining Sentences with because, although, even though

You can combine two sentences with *because*, *although*, and *even though*. In the new sentence, the clause that begins with *because*, *although*, or *even though* is the dependent clause. The other clause is the main clause.

> **Example:** It was my mistake. I think the cashier was rude. ⟶
>
>   dependent clause   main clause
> **Even though** it was my mistake, I think the cashier was rude.

The dependent clause can come first or second. When it comes first, a comma separates the two clauses.

1 | *Circle the correct words to complete this business letter. Underline the main clauses once and the dependent clauses twice.*

---

                                            23 Creek Road
                                            Provo, UT 84001
                                            September 10, 2005

Customer Service Representative
Hardly's Restaurant
12345 Beafy Court
Provo, UT 84004

Dear Customer Service Representative:

   I am writing this letter of complaint although / (because) one of your cashiers treated me rudely.

Because / Even though I was sure I paid her with a $20 bill, I only received change for $10. I told her

that there was a mistake. She said, "You're wrong." Later the manager called. He said the cashier was

right although / because the money in the cash drawer was correct.

   Because / Even though the mistake was mine, I believe the cashier behaved extremely rudely.

Although / Because I like Hardly's, I also value polite service. I hope I won't have to change restaurants

although / because I can't get it there.

Sincerely,

Ken Nelson

Ken Nelson

---

2 Look at the letter in Exercise 1. Circle the correct words in the sentences below to complete these rules about dependent clauses and business letters.

1. Use *because* to (give a) reason / contrasting idea.

2. Use *although* or *even though* to give a reason / contrasting idea.

3. When you begin a sentence with a dependent clause, use a colon / comma after it.

4. When a sentence has a dependent clause, it must also / doesn't have to have a main clause.

5. When a sentence has a main clause, it must also / doesn't have to have a dependent clause.

6. In a business letter, the sender's / receiver's address comes first.

7. The date comes before / after the receiver's address.

8. Use a colon / comma after the receiver's name.

3 Before you write . . .

1. Work with a partner. Complete these complaints with dependent clauses and the correct punctuation. Use your own ideas.

   a. _____ I will not bring my car to your mechanic again.

   b. The server brought me a hamburger _____.

   c. _____ I missed my plane.

   d. My neighbor still won't turn down the TV _____.

2. Choose one of the above situations. Plan a role play about the conflict. Act out your role play for another pair of students.

3. Discuss what to write in a letter of complaint.

4 Write a letter of complaint. Use information from your role play in Exercise 3.

5 Exchange letters with a different partner. Complete the chart.

Did the writer _____?	Yes	No
1. use subordinate clauses correctly	☐	☐
2. use modals correctly	☐	☐
3. give enough information about the complaint	☐	☐
4. use correct business-letter form	☐	☐

6 Work with your partner. Discuss each other's editing questions from Exercise 5. Then rewrite your own letter and make any necessary corrections.

VIII Review Test

I *Circle the letter of the appropriate response to each question.*

1. Are we supposed to bring a gift?
(a.) Yes, we are.
b. Yes, we were.

2. Do you think Fred has the report?
a. Yes, he may. It's OK with me.
b. He might. Let's ask him.

3. Will the weather improve tomorrow?
a. It might.
b. It might be.

4. Do you have to practice every day?
a. Yes, I have.
b. Yes, I do.

5. Do we have any more orange juice?
a. We might.
b. We might have.

6. Would you prefer to go out or stay home?
a. Yes, I would.
b. Let's stay home.

7. Should I turn left at the corner?
a. You can't turn left. It says, Do Not Enter.
b. You don't have to turn left. It says, Do Not Enter.

8. Is it going to rain?
a. It might.
b. It can.

9. Was I supposed to call you?
a. No, you weren't.
b. Yes, I was.

10. There's someone at the door. Who can it be?

    a. It can be Melissa.

    b. It could be Melissa.

11. I'd rather stay home. What about you?

    a. So had I.

    b. So would I.

12. Lena isn't here yet. Was she going to take the 7:00 train?

    a. Yes. Maybe she missed it.

    b. Yes, she is.

13. Do I have to wear a suit to the wedding?

    a. Yes, you have.

    b. Yes, you do.

14. Would you rather walk or drive?

    a. I'd rather not.

    b. I'd rather walk.

II   *Read each sentence. Write its function. Use the words in the box. You will use some words more than once.*

conclusion	expectation	future possibility	necessity	preference	prohibition

1. She might arrive around noon. ___*future possibility*___

2. You must fill out the entire form. _____

3. I'd rather not see that movie. _____

4. He might be sick. _____

5. We're supposed to take the test on Friday. _____

6. You can't drive without a license. _____

7. Because of the cold front, the temperature could fall below freezing. _____

8. There is only one Maple Street, so this has to be the correct street. _____

9. That new restaurant is supposed to be very good. _____

10. She must be very happy about her promotion. _____

11. Please hurry. We've got to be home by 11:00. _____

12. You must not ride your bike without a helmet. _____

III *Circle the letter of the correct answer to complete each sentence.*

1. I'd rather _____ the movie. It's supposed to be good.   (Ⓐ) **B** **C** **D**

   (**A**) watch   (**C**) watching

   (**B**) to watch   (**D**) not watch

2. Take your umbrella. It _____ rain.   **A** **B** **C** **D**

   (**A**) might not   (**C**) 's supposed to

   (**B**) must   (**D**) going to

3. There are two umbrellas. This one is definitely mine, so the   **A** **B** **C** **D**

   other one _____ be yours.

   (**A**) must not   (**C**) might

   (**B**) might not   (**D**) must

4. Don't forget your sweater. The movie theater _____ be cold.   **A** **B** **C** **D**

   (**A**) might   (**C**) couldn't

   (**B**) has to   (**D**) must

5. We _____ bring a gift, but we can if we want to.   **A** **B** **C** **D**

   (**A**) have to   (**C**) must

   (**B**) don't have to   (**D**) must not

6. I _____ have dessert. I'm trying to lose some weight.   **A** **B** **C** **D**

   (**A**) 'd rather   (**C**) 'd prefer

   (**B**) 'd rather not   (**D**) 'd prefer not

7. That's a beautiful gold watch. It _____ be expensive.   **A** **B** **C** **D**

   (**A**) couldn't   (**C**) must

   (**B**) doesn't have to (**D**) maybe

8. Hurry up. We _____ be home by 11:00.   **A** **B** **C** **D**

   (**A**) have to   (**C**) must not

   (**B**) might   (**D**) prefer

9. We _____ be late, or we'll get into trouble.   **A** **B** **C** **D**

   (**A**) don't have to   (**C**) couldn't

   (**B**) can't   (**D**) might

10. We _____ to drive, but we took the train instead.   **A** **B** **C** **D**

   (**A**) were going   (**C**) might

   (**B**) are going   (**D**) 've got to

IV *Write a sentence about each situation. Use the negative or affirmative form of the modal and the words in parentheses.*

1. John gets headaches. At school, he can't see the board unless he sits in the front row.

   He might need glasses.
              (might / need glasses)

2. Your sister won't go see *Visitor from Another Planet* with you, and she turns off the TV when *Star Ship* starts.

   _____
              (prefer / watch science fiction)

3. Carmen is looking at some jewelry. It's beautiful and it's made of gold.

   _____
              (must / be expensive)

4. In Thai culture it's impolite to open a gift in front of the giver. Somchai felt embarrassed when Linda opened his birthday gift.

   _____
              (be supposed to / open it in front of him)

5. You've called your friend at work several times today. He doesn't answer, and he hasn't returned your messages.

   _____
              (must / be at work today)

6. You've invited some friends to dinner, and you've served curry. Everyone except Sue has had two servings. Sue hasn't even finished the first one.

   _____
              (might / like curry)

7. In the United States, international travelers must arrive at the airport three hours before their flight. Your flight from New York to Los Angeles leaves at 3:00 P.M.

   _____
              (have to / arrive at the airport by noon)

8. Marc invited his sister to his graduation. She accepted the invitation, but she got sick, so she didn't go.

   _____
              (be going to / go to his graduation)

9. Carl has just left for a trip to Hong Kong. You've seen him off at the airport. A few minutes after you get home, the doorbell rings.

   _____
              (could / be Carl)

10. You just bought a painting for $10 at a garage sale. Your friend Tim thinks it looks a lot like a Picasso. First you laughed, but then you looked at some art books.

    _____
               (could / be very valuable)

V Read this journal entry. There are eight mistakes in the use of modals and similar expressions. The first mistake is already corrected. Find and correct seven more.

Thursday

    I'm
    ~~I~~ supposed to take my road test tomorrow. I'm a little nervous because I heard that there might be a storm. I'd not rather drive in the rain! My instructor, John, is supposed to pick me up at 8:00 and drive me to the test area. Then he have to wait for me while I take the test. He doesn't have to be in the car with me during the test-it's not allowed. I like John. I don't know much about him. He says he's been driving for more than 40 years, so I guess he got to be at least 60. He maybe even older than that.

    Well, it's getting late, and I should go to bed. I'd rather watching some TV, but I hafta get up early tomorrow.

▶ *To check your answers, go to the Answer Key on page RT-5.*

APPENDICES

| **Irregular Verbs**

BASE FORM	SIMPLE PAST	PAST PARTICIPLE	BASE FORM	SIMPLE PAST	PAST PARTICIPLE
arise	arose	arisen	give	gave	given
awake	awoke	awoken	go	went	gone
be	was/were	been	grind	ground	ground
beat	beat	beaten/beat	grow	grew	grown
become	became	become	hang	hung	hung
begin	began	begun	have	had	had
bend	bent	bent	hear	heard	heard
bet	bet	bet	hide	hid	hidden
bite	bit	bitten	hit	hit	hit
bleed	bled	bled	hold	held	held
blow	blew	blown	hurt	hurt	hurt
break	broke	broken	keep	kept	kept
bring	brought	brought	kneel	knelt/kneeled	knelt/kneeled
build	built	built	knit	knit/knitted	knit/knitted
burn	burned/burnt	burned/burnt	know	knew	known
burst	burst	burst	lay	laid	laid
buy	bought	bought	lead	led	led
catch	caught	caught	leap	leaped/leapt	leaped/leapt
choose	chose	chosen	leave	left	left
cling	clung	clung	lend	lent	lent
come	came	come	let	let	let
cost	cost	cost	lie *(lie down)*	lay	lain
creep	crept	crept	light	lit/lighted	lit/lighted
cut	cut	cut	lose	lost	lost
deal	dealt	dealt	make	made	made
dig	dug	dug	mean	meant	meant
dive	dived/dove	dived	meet	met	met
do	did	done	pay	paid	paid
draw	drew	drawn	prove	proved	proved/proven
dream	dreamed/dreamt	dreamed/dreamt	put	put	put
drink	drank	drunk	quit	quit	quit
drive	drove	driven	read /rid/	read /rɛd/	read /rɛd/
eat	ate	eaten	ride	rode	ridden
fall	fell	fallen	ring	rang	rung
feed	fed	fed	rise	rose	risen
feel	felt	felt	run	ran	run
fight	fought	fought	say	said	said
find	found	found	see	saw	seen
fit	fit/fitted	fit	seek	sought	sought
flee	fled	fled	sell	sold	sold
fling	flung	flung	send	sent	sent
fly	flew	flown	set	set	set
forbid	forbade/forbid	forbidden	sew	sewed	sewn/sewed
forget	forgot	forgotten	shake	shook	shaken
forgive	forgave	forgiven	shave	shaved	shaved/shaven
freeze	froze	frozen	shine *(intransitive)*	shone/shined	shone/shined
get	got	gotten/got	shoot	shot	shot

(continued)

BASE FORM	SIMPLE PAST	PAST PARTICIPLE	BASE FORM	SIMPLE PAST	PAST PARTICIPLE
show	showed	shown	strike	struck	struck/stricken
shrink	shrank/shrunk	shrunk/shrunken	swear	swore	sworn
shut	shut	shut	sweep	swept	swept
sing	sang	sung	swim	swam	swum
sink	sank/sunk	sunk	swing	swung	swung
sit	sat	sat	take	took	taken
sleep	slept	slept	teach	taught	taught
slide	slid	slid	tear	tore	torn
speak	spoke	spoken	tell	told	told
speed	sped/speeded	sped/speeded	think	thought	thought
spend	spent	spent	throw	threw	thrown
spill	spilled/spilt	spilled/spilt	understand	understood	understood
spin	spun	spun	upset	upset	upset
spit	spit/spat	spat	wake	woke	woken
split	split	split	wear	wore	worn
spread	spread	spread	weave	wove/weaved	woven/weaved
spring	sprang	sprung	weep	wept	wept
stand	stood	stood	win	won	won
steal	stole	stolen	wind	wound	wound
stick	stuck	stuck	withdraw	withdrew	withdrawn
sting	stung	stung	wring	wrung	wrung
stink	stank/stunk	stunk	write	wrote	written

2 | Non-action Verbs

APPEARANCE
appear
be
look *(seem)*
represent
resemble
seem
signify

VALUE
cost
equal
weigh

EMOTIONS
admire
adore
appreciate
care
detest
dislike
doubt
envy
fear
hate
like
love
miss
regret
respect
trust

MENTAL STATES
agree
assume
believe
consider
disagree
disbelieve
estimate
expect
feel *(believe)*
find *(believe)*
guess
hesitate
hope
imagine
know
mean
mind
presume
realize
recognize
remember
see *(understand)*
suppose
suspect
think *(believe)*
understand
wonder

POSSESSION AND RELATIONSHIP
belong
contain
have
own
possess

SENSES AND PERCEPTIONS
feel
hear
notice
observe
perceive
see
smell
sound
taste

WANTS AND PREFERENCES
desire
hope
need
prefer
want
wish

3 | Verbs and Expressions Used Reflexively

allow yourself
amuse yourself
ask yourself
avail yourself of
be hard on yourself
be yourself
be pleased with yourself
be proud of yourself

behave yourself
believe in yourself
blame yourself
cut yourself
deprive yourself of
dry yourself
enjoy yourself
feel sorry for yourself

forgive yourself
help yourself
hurt yourself
imagine yourself
introduce yourself
kill yourself
look at yourself
prepare yourself

pride yourself on
push yourself
remind yourself
see yourself
take care of yourself
talk to yourself
teach yourself
tell yourself

(s.o. = someone   s.t. = something)

PHRASAL VERB	MEANING
ask s.o. **over**	*invite to one's home*
blow s.t. **out**	*stop burning by blowing air on it*
blow s.t. **up**	*make explode*
bring s.o. or s.t. **back**	*return*
bring s.o. **up**	*raise (a child)*
bring s.t. **up**	*bring attention to*
burn s.t. **down**	*burn completely*
call s.o. **back**	*return a phone call*
call s.t. **off**	*cancel*
call s.o. **up**	*contact by phone*
carry s.t. **out**	*complete (a plan)*
clean s.o. or s.t. **up**	*clean completely*
clear s.t. **up**	*explain*
close s.t. **down**	*close by force*
cover s.o. or s.t. **up**	*cover completely*
cross s.t. **out**	*draw a line through*
do s.t. **over**	*do again*
drink s.t. **up**	*drink completely*
drop s.o. or s.t. **off**	*take someplace in a car and leave there*
empty s.t. **out**	*empty completely*
figure s.o. **out**	*understand (the behavior)*
figure s.t. **out**	*solve, understand after thinking about it*
fill s.t. **in**	*complete with information*
fill s.t. **out**	*complete (a form)*
find s.t. **out**	*learn information*
give s.t. **back**	*return*
give s.t. **up**	*quit, abandon*
hand s.t. **in**	*give work (to a boss/teacher), submit*
hand s.t. **out**	*distribute*
hand s.t. **over**	*give*
help s.o. **out**	*assist*
keep s.o. or s.t. **away**	*cause to stay at a distance*
keep s.t. **on**	*not remove (a piece of clothing/ jewelry)*
keep s.o. or s.t. **out**	*not allow to enter*
lay s.o. **off**	*end employment*
leave s.t. **on**	*1. not turn off (a light/radio)*
	2. not remove (a piece of clothing/ jewelry)
leave s.t. **out**	*not include, omit*
let s.o. **down**	*disappoint*
let s.o. or s.t. **in**	*allow to enter*
let s.o. **off**	*allow to leave (from a bus/car)*
light s.t. **up**	*illuminate*
look s.o. or s.t. **over**	*examine*
look s.t. **up**	*try to find (in a book/on the Internet)*

PHRASAL VERB	MEANING
make s.t. **up**	*create*
pass s.t. **on**	*give to*
pass s.t. **out**	*distribute*
pass s.o. or s.t. **over**	*decide not to use*
pass s.o. or s.t. **up**	*decide not to use, reject*
pay s.o. or s.t. **back**	*repay*
pick s.o. or s.t. **out**	*choose*
pick s.o. or s.t. **up**	*1. lift*
	2. go get someone or something
pick s.t. **up**	*1. get (an idea/a new book)*
	2. answer the phone
point s.o. or s.t. **out**	*indicate*
put s.t. **away**	*put in an appropriate place*
put s.t. **back**	*return to its original place*
put s.o. or s.t. **down**	*stop holding*
put s.t. **off**	*delay*
put s.t. **on**	*cover the body (with clothes/lotion)*
put s.t. **together**	*assemble*
put s.t. **up**	*erect*
set s.t. **up**	*1. prepare for use*
	2. establish (a business)
shut s.t. **off**	*stop (a machine/light)*
straighten s.t. **up**	*make neat*
switch s.t. **on**	*start (a machine/light)*
take s.o. or s.t. **back**	*return*
take s.t. **off**	*remove*
talk s.o. **into**	*persuade*
talk s.t. **over**	*discuss*
tear s.t. **down**	*destroy*
tear s.t. **off**	*remove by tearing*
tear s.t. **up**	*tear into small pieces*
think s.t. **over**	*consider*
think s.t. **up**	*invent*
throw s.t. **away/out**	*put in the trash, discard*
try s.t. **on**	*put clothing on to see if it fits*
try s.t. **out**	*use to see if it works*
turn s.o. or s.t. **down**	*reject*
turn s.t. **down**	*lower the volume (a TV/radio)*
turn s.t. **in**	*give work (to a boss/teacher), submit*
turn s.o. or s.t. **into**	*change from one form to another*
turn s.o. **off**	*[slang] destroy interest in*
turn s.t. **off**	*stop (a machine/light), extinguish*
turn s.t. **on**	*start (a machine/light)*
turn s.t. **up**	*make louder (a TV/radio)*
use s.t. **up**	*use completely, consume*
wake s.o. **up**	*awaken*
work s.t. **out**	*solve, find a solution to a problem*
write s.t. **down**	*write on a piece of paper*
write s.t. **up**	*write in a finished form*

5 | Intransitive Phrasal Verbs

PHRASAL VERB	MEANING
blow up	*explode*
break down	*stop working (a machine)*
burn down	*burn completely*
call back	*return a phone call*
clear up	*become clear*
close down	*stop operating*
come about	*happen*
come along	*come with, accompany*
come back	*return*
come in	*enter*
come off	*become unattached*
come out	*appear*
come up	*arise*
dress up	*wear special clothes*
drop in	*visit by surprise*
drop out	*quit*
eat out	*eat in a restaurant*
empty out	*empty completely*
find out	*learn information*

PHRASAL VERB	MEANING
follow through	*complete*
fool around	*act playful*
get ahead	*make progress, succeed*
get along	*have a good relationship*
get back	*return*
get by	*survive*
get through	*finish*
get together	*meet*
get up	*get out of bed*
give up	*quit*
go on	*continue*
grow up	*become an adult*
hang up	*end a phone call*
keep away	*stay at a distance*
keep on	*continue*
keep out	*not enter*
keep up	*go as fast*
lie down	*recline*
light up	*illuminate*

PHRASAL VERB	MEANING
look out	*be careful*
make up	*end a disagreement, reconcile*
play around	*have fun*
run out	*not have enough*
set out	*begin a project*
show up	*appear*
sign up	*register*
sit down	*take a seat*
slip up	*make a mistake*
stand up	*rise*
start over	*start again*
stay up	*remain awake*
straighten up	*make neat*
take off	*depart (a plane)*
turn up	*appear*
wake up	*stop sleeping*
watch out	*be careful*
work out	*1. be resolved 2. exercise*

6 | Irregular Plural Nouns

SINGULAR	PLURAL
half	halves
knife	knives
leaf	leaves
life	lives
loaf	loaves
shelf	shelves
wife	wives

SINGULAR	PLURAL
man	men
woman	women
child	children
foot	feet
tooth	teeth
goose	geese
mouse	mice

SINGULAR	PLURAL
deer	deer
fish	fish
sheep	sheep
person	people

7 | Non-count Nouns

REMEMBER: Non-count nouns are singular.

ACTIVITIES	FOOD		IDEAS AND FEELINGS	LIQUIDS AND GASES	SCHOOL SUBJECTS	VERY SMALL THINGS
baseball	bread	ice cream	anger	air	art	dust
biking	butter	lettuce	beauty	gasoline	English	pepper
football	cake	meat	fear	milk	math	rice
golf	cheese	pasta	freedom	oil	music	salt
hiking	chicken	pizza	friendship	oxygen	photography	sand
running	chocolate	salad	happiness	water	science	sugar
sailing	coffee	soup	hate			
soccer	cream	spaghetti	hope	MATERIALS		WEATHER
swimming	fat	tea	loneliness	cotton		fog
tennis	fish	yogurt	love	glass		ice
				gold		rain
				leather		snow
				paper		wind
				wood		
				wool		

NAMES OF CATEGORIES

equipment	(BUT: computers, phones, TVs . . .)
food	(BUT: bananas, eggs, vegetables . . .)
furniture	(BUT: beds, chairs, lamps, tables . . .)
homework	(BUT: assignments, pages, problems . . .)
jewelry	(BUT: bracelets, earrings, necklaces . . .)
mail	(BUT: letters, packages, postcards . . .)
money	(BUT: dinars, dollars, euros, pounds . . .)
work	(BUT: jobs, projects, tasks . . .)

OTHER

(Some non-count nouns don't fit into any list. You must memorize these non-count nouns.)

advice
garbage/trash
information
traffic
news

8 | Proper Nouns

REMEMBER: Write proper nouns with a capital letter.

PEOPLE

• first names	Anne, Eduardo, Mehmet, Olga, Shao-fen
• family names	Chen, García, Haddad, Smith
• titles	Doctor, Grandma, Professor
• title + names	Mr. García, Professor Smith, Uncle Steve

PLACES

• continents	Africa, Asia, Australia, Europe, South America
• countries	Argentina, China, France, Nigeria, Turkey, the United States
• provinces/states	Brittany, Ontario, Szechwan, Texas
• cities	Beijing, Istanbul, Rio de Janeiro, Toronto
• streets	Adalbertstrasse, the Champs-Elysées, Fifth Avenue
• structures	Harrods, the Louvre, the Petronas Towers, the Golden Gate Bridge
• schools	Midwood High School, Oxford University
• parks	Central Park, the Tivoli Gardens
• mountains	the Andes, the Himalayas, the Pyrenees, the Rocky Mountains
• oceans	the Arctic, the Atlantic, the Indian Ocean, the Pacific
• rivers	the Amazon, the Ganges, the Seine
• lakes	Baikal, Erie, Tanganyika, Titicaca
• deserts	the Gobi, the Kalahari, the Sahara

LANGUAGES

Arabic, Chinese, Portuguese, Russian, Spanish

NATIONALITIES

Brazilian, Japanese, Mexican, Saudi, Turkish

RELIGIONS

Buddhism, Christianity, Hinduism, Islam, Judaism

COURSES

Introduction to Computer Sciences, Math 201

PRODUCT BRANDS

Adidas, Dell, Kleenex, Mercedes, Samsung

TIME

• months	January, March, December
• days	Monday, Wednesday, Saturday
• holidays	Bastille Day, Buddha Day, Christmas, Hanukah, New Year's Day, Ramadan

9 | Adjectives That Form the Comparative and Superlative in Two Ways

ADJECTIVE	COMPARATIVE	SUPERLATIVE
cruel	crueler/more cruel	cruelest/most cruel
deadly	deadlier/more deadly	deadliest/most deadly
friendly	friendlier/more friendly	friendliest/most friendly
handsome	handsomer/more handsome	handsomest/most handsome
happy	happier/more happy	happiest/most happy
likely	likelier/more likely	likeliest/most likely
lively	livelier/more lively	liveliest/most lively
lonely	lonelier/more lonely	loneliest/most lonely
lovely	lovelier/more lovely	loveliest/most lovely
narrow	narrower/more narrow	narrowest/most narrow
pleasant	pleasanter/more pleasant	pleasantest/most pleasant
polite	politer/more polite	politest/most polite
quiet	quieter/more quiet	quietest/most quiet
shallow	shallower/more shallow	shallowest/most shallow
sincere	sincerer/more sincere	sincerest/most sincere
stupid	stupider/more stupid	stupidest/most stupid
true	truer/more true	truest/most true

10 | Irregular Comparisons of Adjectives, Adverbs, and Quantifiers

ADJECTIVE	ADVERB	COMPARATIVE	SUPERLATIVE
bad	badly	worse	the worst
far	far	farther/further	the farthest/furthest
good	well	better	the best
little	little	less	the least
many/a lot of	—	more	the most
much*/a lot of	much*/a lot	more	the most

*Much is usually only used in questions and negative statements.

11 | Participial Adjectives

-ed	-ing	-ed	-ing	-ed	-ing
alarmed	alarming	disturbed	disturbing	moved	moving
amazed	amazing	embarrassed	embarrassing	paralyzed	paralyzing
amused	amusing	entertained	entertaining	pleased	pleasing
annoyed	annoying	excited	exciting	relaxed	relaxing
astonished	astonishing	exhausted	exhausting	satisfied	satisfying
bored	boring	fascinated	fascinating	shocked	shocking
charmed	charming	frightened	frightening	surprised	surprising
confused	confusing	horrified	horrifying	terrified	terrifying
depressed	depressing	inspired	inspiring	tired	tiring
disappointed	disappointing	interested	interesting	touched	touching
disgusted	disgusting	irritated	irritating	troubled	troubling

12 | Order of Adjectives before a Noun

REMEMBER: We do not usually use more than three adjectives before a noun.

1. **Order of Adjectives from Different Categories**

   Adjectives from different categories usually go in the following order. Do not use a comma between these adjectives.

Opinion	Size*	Age	Shape	Color	Origin	Material	Nouns used as Adjectives	
beautiful	enormous	antique	flat	blue	Asian	cotton	college	
comfortable	huge	modern	oval	gray	European	gold	flower	
cozy	little	new	rectangular	green	Greek	plastic	kitchen	+ NOUN
easy	tall	old	round	purple	Pacific	stone	mountain	
expensive	tiny	young	square	red	Southern	wooden	vacation	

   *EXCEPTION: Big and small usually go first in a series of adjectives: a **small** comfortable apartment

   EXAMPLES: I bought an **antique Greek flower** vase.   NOT a ~~Greek antique~~ flower vase
   She took some **easy college** courses.   NOT some ~~college-easy~~ courses
   We sat at an **enormous round wooden** table.   NOT a ~~wooden enormous~~ round table

2. **Order of Adjectives from the Same Category**

   Adjectives from the same category do not follow a specific order. Use a comma between these adjectives.

   EXAMPLES: We rented a **beautiful, comfortable, cozy** apartment. OR
   We rented a **cozy, comfortable, beautiful** apartment. OR
   We rented a **comfortable, cozy, beautiful** apartment.

13 | Verbs Followed by the Gerund (Base Form of Verb + -ing)

acknowledge	celebrate	dislike	finish	mind *(object to)*	quit	risk
admit	consider	endure	forgive	miss	recall	suggest
advise	delay	end up	give up *(stop)*	postpone	recommend	support
appreciate	deny	enjoy	imagine	practice	regret	tolerate
avoid	detest	escape	justify	prevent	report	understand
can't help	discontinue	explain	keep *(continue)*	prohibit	resent	
can't stand	discuss	feel like	mention	put off	resist	

14 | Verbs Followed by the Infinitive (*To* + Base Form of Verb)

agree	can't wait	fail	learn	pay	refuse	wait
appear	choose	help	manage	plan	request	want
arrange	consent	hesitate	mean *(intend)*	prepare	rush	wish
ask	decide	hope	need	pretend	seem	would like
attempt	deserve	hurry	neglect	promise	volunteer	
can't afford	expect	intend	offer			

15 | Verbs Followed by the Gerund or the Infinitive

begin	continue	hate	love	remember*	stop*
can't stand	forget*	like	prefer	start	try

*These verbs can be followed by either the gerund or the infinitive, but there is a big difference in meaning *(see Unit 32)*.

16 | Verbs Followed by Object + Infinitive

advise	convince	get	need*	persuade	require	want*
allow	encourage	help*	order	promise*	teach	warn
ask*	expect*	hire	pay*	remind	tell	wish
cause	forbid	invite	permit	request	urge	would like*
choose*	force					

*These verbs can also be followed by an infinitive without an object (example: *ask to leave* or *ask someone to leave*).

17 | Adjective + Preposition Combinations

accustomed to	bad at	different from	interested in	safe from	surprised
afraid of	bored with/by	excited about	nervous about	satisfied with	at/about/by
amazed at/by	capable of	famous for	opposed to	shocked at/by	terrible at
angry at	careful of	fond of	pleased about	sick of	tired of
ashamed of	concerned about	glad about	ready for	slow at/in	used to
aware of	content with	good at	responsible for	sorry for/about	worried about
awful at	curious about	happy about	sad about		

18 | Verb + Preposition Combinations

admit to	believe in	deal with	look forward to	rely on	thank someone for
advise against	choose between	dream about/of	object to	resort to	think about
apologize for	complain about	feel like	pay for	succeed in	wonder about
approve of	count on	insist on	plan on	talk about	

19 | Modals and Their Functions

FUNCTION	MODAL OR EXPRESSION	TIME	EXAMPLES
Ability	can can't	Present	• Sam **can swim**. • He **can't skate**.
	could couldn't	Past	• We **could swim** last year. • We **couldn't skate**.
	be able to* not be able to*	All verb forms	• Lea **is able to run** fast. • She **wasn't able to run** fast last year.
Permission	can	Present or Future	• **Can** I **sit** here? • **Can** I **call** tomorrow? • Yes, you **can**.
	can't		• No, you **can't**. Sorry.
	could		• **Could** he **leave** now?
	may		• **May** I **borrow** your pen? • Yes, you **may**.
	may not		• No, you **may not**. Sorry.
Requests	can	Present or Future	• **Can** you **close** the door, please? • Sure, I **can**.
	can't		• Sorry, I **can't**.
	could		• **Could** you please **answer** the phone?
	will		• **Will** you **wash** the dishes, please?
	would		• **Would** you please **mail** this letter?
Advice	should	Present or Future	• You **should study** more.
	shouldn't		• You **shouldn't miss** class.
	ought to**		• We **ought to leave**.
	had better**		• We**'d better go**.
	had better not**		• We**'d better not stay**.
Necessity	have to*	All verb forms	• He **has to go** now. • I **had to go** yesterday. • I **will have to go** soon.
	not have to*		• He **doesn't have to go** yet.
	have got to*	Present or Future	• He**'s got to leave**!
	must		• You **must use** a pen for the test.
Prohibition	must not	Present or Future	• You **must not drive** without a license.
	can't		• You **can't drive** without a license.

*The meaning of this expression is similar to the meaning of a modal. Unlike a modal, it has *-s* for third-person singular.
**The meaning of this expression is similar to the meaning of a modal. Like a modal, it has no *-s* for third-person singular.

FUNCTION	MODAL OR EXPRESSION	TIME	EXAMPLES
Possibility	must must not have to* have got to*	Present	• This **must be** her house. Her name is on the door. • She **must not be** home. I don't see her car. • She **has to know** him. They went to school together. • He's **got to be** guilty. We saw him do it.
	may may not might might not could	Present or Future	• She **may be** home now. • It **may not rain** tomorrow. • Lee **might be sick** today. • He **might not come** to class. • They **could be** at the library. • It **could rain** tomorrow.
Impossibility	can't couldn't	Present or Future	• That **can't be** Ana. She left for France yesterday. • It **can't snow** tomorrow. It's going to be too warm. • He **couldn't be** guilty. He wasn't in town when the crime occurred. • The teacher **couldn't give** the test tomorrow. Tomorrow's Saturday.

*The meaning of this expression is similar to the meaning of a modal. Unlike a modal, it has -*s* for third-person singular.

20 | Spelling Rules for the Simple Present: Third-Person Singular (*he, she, it*)

1. Add -*s* for most verbs.

work	work**s**
buy	buy**s**
ride	ride**s**
return	return**s**

2. Add -*es* for verbs that end in -*ch*, -*s*, -*sh*, -*x*, or -*z*.

watch	watch**es**
pass	pass**es**
rush	rush**es**
relax	relax**es**
buzz	buzz**es**

3. Change the *y* to *i* and add -*es* when the base form ends in **consonant** + *y*.

study	stud**ies**
hurry	hurr**ies**
dry	dr**ies**

   Do not change the *y* when the base form ends in **vowel** + *y*. Add -*s*.

play	play**s**
enjoy	enjoy**s**

4. A few verbs have **irregular forms**.

be	**is**
do	**does**
go	**goes**
have	**has**

21 | Spelling Rules for Base Form of Verb + -*ing* (Progressive and Gerund)

1. Add -*ing* to the base form of the verb.

read	read**ing**
stand	stand**ing**

2. If the verb ends in a **silent -e**, drop the final -*e* and add -*ing*.

leave	leav**ing**
take	tak**ing**

3. In **one-syllable** verbs, if the last three letters are a consonant-vowel-consonant combination (CVC), double the last consonant and add -*ing*.

   C V C
   ↓ ↓ ↓
   s i t   sit**ting**

   C V C
   ↓ ↓ ↓
   p l a n   plan**ning**

   Do not double the last consonant in verbs that end in -*w*, -*x*, or -*y*.

sew	sew**ing**
fix	fix**ing**
play	play**ing**

4. In verbs of **two or more syllables** that end in a consonant-vowel-consonant combination, double the last consonant only if the last syllable is stressed.

admít	admit**ting**	*(The last syllable is stressed.)*
whísper	whisper**ing**	*(The last syllable is not stressed, so don't double the -r.)*

5. If the verb ends in -*ie*, change the *ie* to *y* before adding -*ing*.

die	d**ying**

STRESS
´ shows main stress.

22 | Spelling Rules for Base Form of Verb + -*ed* (Simple Past and Past Participle of Regular Verbs)

1. If the verb ends in a **consonant**, add -*ed*.

return	return**ed**
help	help**ed**

2. If the verb ends in -*e*, add -*d*.

live	live**d**
create	create**d**
die	die**d**

3. In **one-syllable** verbs, if the last three letters are a consonant-vowel-consonant combination (CVC), double the last consonant and add -*ed*.

   C V C
   ↓ ↓ ↓
   h o p   hop**ped**

   C V C
   ↓ ↓ ↓
   g r a b   grab**bed**

   Do not double the last consonant in verbs that end in -*w*, -*x*, or -*y*.

bow	bow**ed**
mix	mix**ed**
play	play**ed**

4. In verbs of **two or more syllables** that end in a consonant-vowel-consonant combination, double the last consonant only if the last syllable is stressed.

prefér	prefer**red**	*(The last syllable is stressed.)*
vísit	visit**ed**	*(The last syllable is not stressed, so don't double the -t.)*

5. If the verb ends in **consonant + y**, change the *y* to *i* and add -*ed*.

worry	worr**ied**
carry	carr**ied**

6. If the verb ends in **vowel + y**, add -*ed*. (Do not change the *y* to *i*.)

play	play**ed**
annoy	annoy**ed**

   EXCEPTIONS:

lay	la**id**
pay	pa**id**
say	sa**id**

23 | Spelling Rules for the Comparative (-er) and Superlative (-est) of Adjectives

1. With **one-syllable** adjectives, add -er to form the comparative. Add -est to form the superlative.

cheap	cheap**er**	cheap**est**
bright	bright**er**	bright**est**

2. If the adjective ends in -e, add -r or -st.

nice	nice**r**	nice**st**

3. If the adjective ends in **consonant + y**, change y to i before you add -er or -est.

pretty	prett**ier**	prett**iest**

EXCEPTION:

shy	shy**er**	shy**est**

4. If a one-syllable adjective ends in a consonant-vowel-consonant combination (CVC), double the last consonant before adding -er or -est.

C V C
↓ ↓ ↓

b i g	big**ger**	big**gest**

Do not double the consonant in adjectives ending in -w or -y.

slow	slow**er**	slow**est**
gray	gray**er**	gray**est**

24 | Spelling Rules for Adverbs Ending in -ly

1. Add -ly to the corresponding adjective.

nice	nice**ly**
quiet	quiet**ly**
beautiful	beautiful**ly**

2. If the adjective ends in **consonant + y**, change the y to i before adding -ly.

easy	eas**ily**

3. If the adjective ends in -le, drop the e and add -y.

possible	possib**ly**

Do not drop the e for other adjectives ending in -e.

extreme	extreme**ly**

EXCEPTION:

true	tru**ly**

4. If the adjective ends in -ic, add -ally.

basic	basic**ally**
fantastic	fantastic**ally**

25 | Spelling Rules for Regular Plural Nouns

1. Add -s to most nouns.

book	book**s**
table	table**s**
cup	cup**s**

2. Add -es to nouns that end in -ch, -s, -sh, or -x.

watch	watch**es**
bus	bus**es**
dish	dish**es**
box	box**es**

3. Add -s to nouns that end in **vowel + y**.

day	day**s**
key	key**s**

4. Change the y to i and add -es to nouns that end in **consonant + y**.

baby	bab**ies**
city	cit**ies**
strawberry	strawberr**ies**

5. Add -s to nouns that end in **vowel + o**.

radio	radio**s**
video	video**s**
zoo	zoo**s**

6. Add -es to nouns that end in **consonant + o**.

potato	potato**es**
tomato	tomato**es**

EXCEPTIONS: kilo—kilos, photo—photos, piano—pianos

1. SIMPLE PRESENT, PRESENT PROGRESSIVE, AND IMPERATIVE

Contractions with *Be*

I am	=	I'm
you are	=	you're
he is	=	he's
she is	=	she's
it is	=	it's
we are	=	we're
you are	=	you're
they are	=	they're

I am not	=	I'm **not**		
you are not	=	you're **not**	OR	you **aren't**
he is not	=	he's **not**	OR	he **isn't**
she is not	=	she's **not**	OR	she **isn't**
it is not	=	it's **not**	OR	it **isn't**
we are not	=	we're **not**	OR	we **aren't**
you are not	=	you're **not**	OR	you **aren't**
they are not	=	they're **not**	OR	they **aren't**

Contractions with *Do*

do not	=	**don't**
does not	=	**doesn't**

2. SIMPLE PAST AND PAST PROGRESSIVE

Contractions with *Be*

was not	=	**wasn't**
were not	=	**weren't**

Contractions with *Do*

did not	=	**didn't**

3. FUTURE

Contractions with *Will*

I will	=	I'll
you will	=	you'll
he will	=	he'll
she will	=	she'll
it will	=	it'll
we will	=	we'll
you will	=	you'll
they will	=	they'll

will not	=	**won't**

Contractions with *Be going to*

I am going to	=	I'm going to
you are going to	=	you're going to
he is going to	=	he's going to
she is going to	=	she's going to
it is going to	=	it's going to
we are going to	=	we're going to
you are going to	=	you're going to
they are going to	=	they're going to

SIMPLE PRESENT	PRESENT PROGRESSIVE
I'm a student.	I'm **studying** here.
He's my teacher.	He's **teaching** verbs.
We're from Canada.	We're **living** here.

SIMPLE PRESENT	PRESENT PROGRESSIVE
She's **not** sick.	She's **not** reading.
He **isn't** late.	He **isn't** coming.
We **aren't** twins.	We **aren't** leaving.
They're **not** here.	They're **not** playing.

SIMPLE PRESENT	IMPERATIVE
They **don't live** here.	**Don't run!**
It **doesn't snow** much.	

SIMPLE PAST	PAST PROGRESSIVE
He **wasn't** a poet.	He **wasn't singing**.
They **weren't** twins.	They **weren't sleeping**.
We **didn't see** her.	

FUTURE WITH *WILL*
I'll **take** the train.
It'll **be** faster that way.
We'll **go** together.
He **won't come** with us.
They **won't miss** the train.

FUTURE WITH *BE GOING TO*
I'm **going to buy** tickets tomorrow.
She's **going to call** you.
It's **going to rain** soon.
We're **going to drive** to Boston.
They're **going to crash**!

4. PRESENT PERFECT AND PRESENT PERFECT PROGRESSIVE

Contractions with *Have*

I have	=	I**'ve**
you have	=	you**'ve**
he has	=	he**'s**
she has	=	she**'s**
it has	=	it**'s**
we have	=	we**'ve**
you have	=	you**'ve**
they have	=	they**'ve**
have not	=	**haven't**
has not	=	**hasn't**

You**'ve** already **read** that page.
We**'ve been writing** for an hour.
She**'s been** to Africa three times.
It**'s been raining** since yesterday.
We **haven't seen** any elephants yet.
They **haven't been living** here long.

5. MODALS AND SIMILAR EXPRESSIONS

cannot or can not	=	**can't**
could not	=	**couldn't**
should not	=	**shouldn't**
had better	=	**'d better**
would prefer	=	**'d prefer**
would rather	=	**'d rather**

She **can't dance**.
We **shouldn't go**.
They**'d better decide**.
I**'d prefer** coffee.
I**'d rather take** the bus.

27 | Capitalization and Punctuation Rules

	USE FOR . . .	EXAMPLES
capital letter	• the pronoun *I* • proper nouns • the first word of a sentence	• Tomorrow **I** will be here at 2:00. • His name is **Karl**. He lives in **Germany**. • **When** does the train leave? **At** 2:00.
apostrophe (')	• possessive nouns • contractions	• Is that **Marta's** coat? • **That's** not hers. **It's** mine.
comma (,)	• after items in a list • before sentence connectors *and*, *but*, *or*, and *so* • after the first part of a sentence that begins with *because* • after the first part of a sentence that begins with a preposition • after the first part of a sentence that begins with a time clause or an *if* clause	• He bought **apples, pears, oranges,** and **bananas**. • They watched TV, **and** she played video games. • *Because* **it's raining,** we're not walking to the office. • *Across from* **the post office,** there's a good restaurant. • *After* **he arrived,** we ate dinner. • *If* **it rains,** we won't go.
exclamation mark (!)	• at the end of a sentence to show surprise or a strong feeling	• You're here! That's great! • Stop! A car is coming!
period (.)	• at the end of a statement	• Today is Wednesday.
question mark (?)	• at the end of a question	• What day is today**?**

🎧 These are the pronunciation symbols used in this text. Listen to the pronunciation of the key words.

VOWELS				CONSONANTS			
Symbol	**Key Word**	**Symbol**	**Key Word**	**Symbol**	**Key Word**	**Symbol**	**Key Word**
i	beat, feed	ə	banana, among	p	pack, happy	ʃ	ship, machine, station, special, discussion
ɪ	bit, did	ɚ	shirt, murder	b	back, rubber		
eɪ	date, paid	aɪ	bite, cry, buy, eye	t	tie	ʒ	measure, vision
ɛ	bet, bed	aʊ	about, how	d	die	h	hot, who
æ	bat, bad	ɔɪ	voice, boy	k	came, key, quick	m	men
ɑ	box, odd, father	ɪr	beer	g	game, guest	n	sun, know, pneumonia
ɔ	bought, dog	ɛr	bare	tʃ	church, nature, watch	ŋ	sung, ringing
oʊ	boat, road	ɑr	bar	dʒ	judge, general, major	w	wet, white
ʊ	book, good	ɔr	door	f	fan, photograph	l	light, long
u	boot, food, student	ʊr	tour	v	van	r	right, wrong
ʌ	but, mud, mother			θ	thing, breath	y	yes, use, music
				ð	then, breathe	t̬	butter, bottle
				s	sip, city, psychology		
				z	zip, please, goes		

```
┌─────────────────────────────┐
│           STRESS            │
│   ′ shows main stress.      │
└─────────────────────────────┘
```

29 | Pronunciation Rules for the Simple Present: Third-Person Singular *(he, she, it)*

1. The third-person singular in the simple present always ends in the letter *-s*. There are, however, three different pronunciations for the final sound of the third-person singular.

/s/	/z/	/ɪz/
talks	loves	dances

2. The final sound is pronounced /s/ after the voiceless sounds /p/, /t/, /k/, and /f/.

top	tops
get	gets
take	takes
laugh	laughs

3. The final sound is pronounced /z/ after the voiced sounds /b/, /d/, /g/, /v/, /m/, /n/, /ŋ/, /l/, /r/, and /ð/.

describe	describes
spend	spends
hug	hugs
live	lives
seem	seems
remain	remains
sing	sings
tell	tells
lower	lowers
bathe	bathes

4. The final sound is pronounced /z/ after all **vowel sounds**.

agree	agrees
try	tries
stay	stays
know	knows

5. The final sound is pronounced /ɪz/ after the sounds /s/, /z/, /ʃ/, /ʒ/, /tʃ/, and /dʒ/. /ɪz/ adds a syllable to the verb.

miss	misses
freeze	freezes
rush	rushes
massage	massages
watch	watches
judge	judges

6. *Do* and *say* have a change in vowel sound.

do	/du/	does	/dʌz/
say	/seɪ/	says	/sɛz/

30 | Pronunciation Rules for the Simple Past and Past Participle of Regular Verbs

1. The regular simple past and past participle always end in the letter -*d*. There are three different pronunciations for the final sound of the regular simple past and past participle.

/t/	/d/	/ɪd/
raced	lived	attended

2. The final sound is pronounced /**t**/ after the voiceless sounds /**p**/, /**k**/, /**f**/, /**s**/, /**ʃ**/, and /**tʃ**/.

hop	hopped
work	worked
laugh	laughed
address	addressed
publish	published
watch	watched

3. The final sound is pronounced /**d**/ after the voiced sounds /**b**/, /**g**/, /**v**/, /**z**/, /**ʒ**/, /**dʒ**/, /**m**/, /**n**/, /**ŋ**/, /**l**/, /**r**/, and /**ð**/.

rub	rubbed
hug	hugged
live	lived
surprise	surprised
massage	massaged
change	changed
rhyme	rhymed
return	returned
bang	banged
enroll	enrolled
appear	appeared
bathe	bathed

4. The final sound is pronounced /**d**/ after all **vowel sounds**.

agree	agreed
die	died
play	played
enjoy	enjoyed
snow	snowed

5. The final sound is pronounced /**ɪd**/ after /**t**/ and /**d**/. /ɪd/ adds a syllable to the verb.

start	started
decide	decided

GLOSSARY OF GRAMMAR TERMS

action verb   a verb that describes an action.

- *Alicia **ran** home.*

adjective   a word that describes a noun or pronoun.

- *That's a **great** idea.*
- *It's **wonderful**.*

adverb   a word that describes a verb, an adjective, or another adverb.

- *She drives **carefully**.*
- *She's a **very** good driver.*
- *She drives **really** well.*

adverb of frequency   an adverb that describes how often something happens.

- *We **always** watch that program.*

adverb of manner   an adverb that describes how someone does something or how something happens. It usually ends in *-ly*.

- *He sings **beautifully**.*

adverb of time   an adverb that describes when something happens.

- *We'll see you **soon**.*

affirmative   a statement or answer meaning *Yes*.

- *He **works**.* (affirmative statement)
- ***Yes**, he **does**.* (affirmative short answer)

article   a word that goes before a noun. The indefinite articles are *a* and *an*.

- *I ate **a** sandwich and **an** apple.*

The definite article is *the*.

- *I didn't like **the** sandwich. **The** apple was good.*

auxiliary verb   (also called **helping verb**) a verb used with a main verb. *Be, do,* and *have* are often auxiliary verbs. Modals (*can, should, may . . .*) are also auxiliary verbs.

- *I **am** exercising right now.*
- ***Does** he exercise every day?*
- *She **should** exercise every day.*

base form   the simple form of a verb without any endings (*-s, -ed, -ing*) or other changes.

- ***be, have, go, drive***

capital letter   the large form of a letter. The capital letters are: *A, B, C, D, . . .*

- ***A**licia lives in the **U**nited **S**tates.*

clause   a group of words that has a subject and a verb. A sentence can have one or more clauses.

- ***We are leaving now.*** (one clause)
- ***When he calls, we'll leave.*** (two clauses)

common noun   a word for a person, place, or thing (but not the name of the person, place, or thing).

- *Teresa lives in a **house** near the **beach**.*

comparative   the form of an adjective or adverb that shows the difference between two people, places, or things.

- *Alain is **shorter** than Brendan.* (adjective)
- *Brendan runs **faster** than Alain.* (adverb)

comparison   a statement that shows the difference between two people, places, or things. A comparison can use comparative adjectives and comparative adverbs. It can also use *as . . . as*.

- *Alain is **shorter than** Brendan.*
- *Alain isn't **as tall as** Brendan.*
- *He runs **faster than** Brendan.*

consonant   a letter of the alphabet. The consonants are:

- ***b, c, d, f, g, h, j, k, l, m, n, p, q, r, s, t, v, w, x, y, z***

continuous   See **progressive**.

contraction   a short form of a word or words. An apostrophe (') replaces the missing letter or letters.

- ***she's** = she is*
- ***hasn't** = has not*
- ***can't** = cannot*
- ***won't** = will not*

count noun   a noun that you can count. It has a singular and a plural form.

- one **book**, two **books**

definite article   *the*.
This article goes before a noun that refers to a specific person, place, or thing.

- *Please bring me **the book** on the table. I'm almost finished reading it.*

dependent clause   (also called **subordinate clause**) a clause that needs a main clause for its meaning.

- ***When I get home**, I'll call you.*

direct object   a noun or pronoun that receives the action of a verb.

- *Marta kicked **the ball**. I saw **her**.*

formal   language used in business situations or with adults you do not know.

- *Good afternoon, Mr. Rivera. Please have a seat.*

gerund   a noun formed with verb + *-ing*.
It can be the subject or object of a sentence.

- ***Swimming** is great exercise.*
- *I enjoy **swimming**.*

helping verb   See **auxiliary verb**.

imperative   a sentence that gives a command or instructions.

- ***Hurry!***
- ***Don't touch that!***

indefinite article   *a* or *an*.
These articles go before a noun that does not refer to a specific person, place, or thing.

- *Can you bring me **a book**? I'm looking for something to read.*

indefinite past   past time, but not a specific time. It is often used with the present perfect.

- *I**'ve** already **seen** that movie.*

indefinite pronoun   a pronoun such as *someone, something, anyone, anything, anywhere, no one, nothing, everyone*, and *everything*. An indefinite pronoun does not refer to a specific person, place, or thing.

- ***Someone** called you last night.*
- *Did **anything** happen?*

indirect object   a noun or pronoun (often a person) that receives something as the result of the action of the verb.

- *I told **John** the story.*
- *He gave **me** some good advice.*

infinitive   *to* + base form of the verb.

- *I want **to leave** now.*

infinitive of purpose   *(in order) to* + base form.
This form gives the reason for an action.

- *I go to school **in order to learn** English.*

informal   language used with family, friends, and children.

- *Hi, Pete. Sit down.*

information question   See **wh- question**.

inseparable phrasal verb   a phrasal verb whose parts must stay together.

- *We **ran into** Tomás at the supermarket.*

intransitive verb   a verb that does not have an object.

- *We **fell**.*

irregular   a word that does not change its form in the usual way.

- ***good → well***
- ***bad → worse***

irregular verb   a verb that does not form its past with *-ed*.

- ***leave → left***

main clause   a clause that can stand alone as a sentence.

- *When I get home, **I'll call you**.*

main verb   a verb that describes an action or state. It is often used with an auxiliary verb.

- *Jared is **calling**.*
- *He'll **call** again later.*
- *Does he **call** every day?*

modal   a type of auxiliary verb. It goes before a main verb and expresses ideas such as ability, advice, obligation, permission, and possibility. *Can, could, will, would, may, might, should*, and *must* are modals.

- ***Can** you swim?*
- *You really **should** learn to swim.*

negative a statement or answer meaning *No*.
- *He **doesn't** work.* (negative statement)
- ***No**, he **doesn't**.* (negative short answer)

non-action verb (also called **stative verb**)
a verb that does not describe an action. It describes such things as thoughts, feelings, and senses.
- *I **remember** that word.*
- *Chris **loves** ice cream.*
- *It **tastes** great.*

non-count noun a noun that you usually do not count *(air, water, rice, love, . . .)*. It has only a singular form.
- *The **rice** is delicious.*

noun a word for a person, place, or thing.
- *My **sister**, **Anne**, works in an **office**.*
- *She uses a **computer**.*

object a noun or pronoun that receives the action of a verb. Sometimes a verb has two objects.
- *She wrote **a letter to Tom**.*
- *She wrote **him a letter**.*

object pronoun a pronoun *(me, you, him, her, it, us, them)* that receives the action of a verb.
- *I gave **her** a book.*
- *I gave **it** to **her**.*

paragraph a group of sentences, usually about one topic.

participial adjective an adjective that ends in *-ing* or *-ed*. It comes from a verb.
- *That's an **interesting** book.*
- *She's **interested** in the book.*

particle a word that looks like a preposition and combines with a main verb to form a phrasal verb. It often changes the meaning of the main verb.
- *He looked the word **up**.*
(He looked for the meaning in the dictionary.)
- *I ran **into** my teacher.*
(I met my teacher accidentally.)

past participle a verb form (verb + *-ed*).
It can also be irregular. It is used to form the present perfect. It can also be an adjective.
- *We've **lived** here since April.*
- *She's **interested** in math.*

phrasal verb (also called **two-word verb**)
a verb that has two parts (verb + particle). The meaning is often different from the meaning of its separate parts.
- *He **grew up** in Texas.* (became an adult)
- *His parents **brought** him **up** to be honest.* (raised)

phrase a group of words that forms a unit but does not have a main verb. Many phrases give information about time or place.
- ***Last year**, we were living **in Canada**.*

plural two or more.
- *There **are** three **people** in the restaurant.*
- ***They are** eating dinner.*
- ***We** saw **them**.*

possessive nouns, pronouns, or adjectives that show a relationship or show that someone owns something.
- *Zach is **Megan's** brother.* (possessive noun)
- *Is that car **his**?* (possessive pronoun)
- *That's **his** car.* (possessive adjective)

predicate the part of a sentence that has the main verb. It tells what the subject is doing or describes the subject.
- *My sister **works for a travel agency**.*

preposition a word that goes before a noun or a pronoun to show time, place, or direction.
- *I went **to** the bank **on** Monday. It's **next to** my office.*
Prepositions also go before nouns, pronouns, and gerunds in expressions with verbs and adjectives.
- *We rely **on** him.*
- *She's accustomed **to** getting up early.*

progressive (also called **continuous**)
the verb form *be* + verb + *-ing*. It focuses on the continuation (not the completion) of an action.
- *She**'s reading** the paper.*
- *We **were watching** TV when you called.*

pronoun a word used in place of a noun.
- *That's my brother. You met **him** at my party.*

proper noun a noun that is the name of a person, place, or thing. It begins with a capital letter.
- ***Maria** goes to **Central High School**.*
- *It's on **High Street**.*

punctuation marks used in writing (period, comma, . . .). They make the meaning clear. For example, a period (.) shows the end of a sentence. It also shows that the sentence is a statement, not a question.

quantifier a word or phrase that shows an amount (but not an exact amount). It often comes before a noun.

- *Josh bought **a lot of** books last year, but he only read **a few**.*
- *He doesn't have **much** time.*

question See *yes/no* **question** and *wh-* **question**.

question word See *wh-* **word**.

reciprocal pronoun a pronoun (*each other* or *one another*) that shows that the subject and object of a sentence refer to the same people and that these people have a two-way relationship.

- *Megan and Jason have known **each other** since high school.*
- *All the students worked with **one another** on the project.*

reflexive pronoun a pronoun (*myself, yourself, himself, herself, itself, ourselves, yourselves, themselves*) that shows that the subject and the object of the sentence refer to the same people or things.

- *He looked at **himself** in the mirror.*
- *They enjoyed **themselves** at the party.*

regular a word that changes its form in the usual way.

- ***play** → play**ed***
- ***fast** → fast**er***
- ***quick** → quick**ly***

sentence a group of words that has a subject and a main verb. It begins with a capital letter and ends with a period (.), question mark (?), or exclamation point (!).

- ***Computers are** very useful.*

EXCEPTION: In imperative sentences, the subject is *you*. We do not usually say or write the subject in imperative sentences.

- ***Call** her now!*

separable phrasal verb a phrasal verb whose parts can separate.

- *Tom **looked** the word **up** in a dictionary.*
- *He **looked** it **up**.*

short answer an answer to a *yes/no* question.

A: *Did you call me last night?*
B: ***No, I didn't.*** OR ***No.***

singular one.

- *They have **a sister**.*
- ***She** works in **a hospital**.*

statement a sentence that gives information. In writing, it ends in a period.

- *Today is Monday.*

stative verb See **non-action verb**.

subject the person, place, or thing that the sentence is about.

- ***Ms. Chen** teaches English.*
- ***Her class** is interesting.*

subject pronoun a pronoun that shows the person or thing (*I, you, he, she, it, we, they*) that the sentence is about.

- ***I** read a lot.*
- ***She** reads a lot too.*

subordinate clause See **dependent clause**.

superlative the form of an adjective or adverb that is used to compare a person, place, or thing to a group of people, places, or things.

- *Cindi is **the best** dancer in the group.* (adjective)
- *She dances **the most gracefully**.* (adverb)

tense the form of a verb that shows the time of the action.

- **simple present**: *Fabio **talks** to his friend every day.*
- **simple past**: *Fabio **talked** to his teacher yesterday.*

third-person singular the pronouns *he, she*, and *it* or a singular noun. In the simple present, the third-person-singular verb ends in *-s*.

- *Tomás **works** in an office.* (Tomás = he)

time clause a clause that begins with a time word such as *when, before, after, while*, or *as soon as*.

- *I'll call you **when I get home**.*

time expression a phrase that describes when something happened or will happen.

- *We saw Tomás **last week**.*
- *He'll graduate **next year**.*

transitive verb   a verb that has an object.

- She **paints** beautiful pictures.

two-word verb   See **phrasal verb**.

verb   a word that describes what the subject of the sentence does, thinks, feels, senses, or owns.

- They **run** two miles every day.
- She **loved** that movie.
- He **has** a new camera.

vowel   a letter of the alphabet. The vowels are:

- **a, e, i, o, u.**

wh- question   (also called **information question**) a question that begins with a *wh-* word. You answer a *wh-* question with information.

A: Where are you going?

B: To the store.

wh- word   (also called **question word**) a word such as *who, what, when, where, which, why, how,* and *how much.* It can begin a *wh-* question.

- **Who** is that?
- **What** did you see?
- **When** does the movie usually start?
- **How** long is it?

yes/no question   a question that begins with a form of *be* or an auxiliary verb. You can answer a *yes/no* question with *yes* or *no.*

A: Are you a student?

B: Yes, I am. OR **No,** I'm not.

A: Do you come here often?

B: Yes, I do. OR **No,** I don't.

REVIEW TESTS ANSWER KEY

Note: In this answer key, where the contracted verb form is given, it is the preferred form, though the full form is also acceptable. Where the full verb form is given, it is the preferred form, though the contracted form is also acceptable.

PART I

I (Unit 1)
2. breathe
3. 's going
4. goes
5. rains
6. 's raining
7. 're dancing
8. dance

II (Unit 1)
1. c. 'm brushing
   d. Is . . . getting
   e. think
   f. 's looking
2. a. smells
   b. are . . . cooking
   c. do . . . have
   d. don't
   e. Do . . . know
   f. 're keeping OR keep
   g. 'm standing
   h. don't see
3. a. tastes
   b. 'm packing
   c. Is
   d. don't want
   e. 'm not
   f. look
   g. Do . . . feel OR Are . . . feeling
   h. do OR am
   i. hear
   j. 're leaving

III (Unit 2)
2. don't walk
3. lock
4. don't forget
5. Don't put
6. Put
7. Call
8. don't call
9. Have . . . enjoy

IV (Unit 3)
2. moved
3. did . . . live
4. was
5. taught
6. Did . . . like
7. did
8. Did . . . appear
9. did

10. wasn't
11. didn't seem
12. was
13. went
14. Were
15. wasn't
16. began
17. Did . . . expect
18. didn't

V (Units 3 and 5)
2. cook
3. Were
4. used to
5. go
6. went
7. Did
8. didn't have

VI (Unit 4)
2. was mowing
3. rang
4. had
5. wasn't
6. wasn't driving
7. hit
8. did . . . do
9. was trying
10. wasn't paying
11. Did . . . call
12. happened
13. appeared
14. got
15. left
16. called

VII (Unit 6)
2. 'll be
3. 'll
4. does
5. 's going to
6. 'll have
7. 's going to
8. are we going to
9. Will
10. are

VIII (Unit 7)
2. a. get
   b. 'll see
3. a. 'll stay
   b. finish
4. a. graduates
   b. 'll live
5. a. 'll read
   b. eat
6. a. 'll buy
   b. save
7. a. will call
   b. leaves
8. a. turn
   b. 'll be

IX (Unit 8)
1. b. Who went
   c. What did you see
2. a. What happened
   b. What did you get
   c. Who(m) did you study

X (Units 1–8)

2. C	7. A	12. D
3. C	8. B	13. B
4. D	9. D	14. C
5. B	10. B	
6. A	11. A	

XI (Units 1–8)

2. D	5. B	8. D	11. B
3. C	6. A	9. B	12. D
4. B	7. B	10. D	13. A

PART II

I (Unit 9)

2. herself	9. them
3. their	10. yourself
4. themselves	11. yourself
5. yourself	12. you
6. themselves	13. them
7. them	14. each other's
8. one another	

II (Unit 10)

2. turned into	8. pass over
3. found out	9. get back
4. set up	10. went on
5. help out	11. get by
6. look up	12. hand . . . over
7. pick out	

III (Unit 10)

2. wrote it down	5. help him out
3. pick her up	6. picked it out
4. put it on	7. write them up

IV (Units 9 and 10)

2. B	5. A	8. A
3. A	6. C	9. A
4. D	7. C	10. A

V (Units 9 and 10)

I have three older brothers, but my role model is my next oldest brother, Orlando. Orlando was

me

always there for ~~myself~~ when we were growing up. I was very small, and he always kept the bullies

out

away. When I couldn't figure ~~up~~ homework

me out

problems by myself, he helped ~~out me~~. Orlando never gave up when he had problems. Once, in

me

high school, my baseball team passed ~~myself~~ up for pitcher. I wanted to quit the team, but he talked me

into   *up*

~~over~~ playing. In fact, he woke early every morning

up

∧ to practice with me. When they chose me for pitcher the following year, we were really

each other

proud of ~~ourselves~~—he was proud of me for

him

succeeding, and I was proud of ~~himself~~ for being such a great coach.

PART III

I (Units 11–15)

2. b	6. a
3. a	7. a
4. a	8. a
5. b	9. a

II (Units 11–15)

2. request	9. request
3. suggestion	10. request
4. permission	11. ability
5. ability	12. suggestion
6. permission	13. advice
7. suggestion	14. ability
8. advice	

III (Units 11–15)

1. b. should we	2. a. Let's
c. could	b. Could
d. Why not	c. be able to
e. 'd better	d. Do you mind if
f. How about	e. Not at all.
g. should	f. could
h. Let's	g. 'd better
i. We should	3. a. Why don't
	b. Could
	c. could
	d. Would you mind

IV (Units 11–15)

2. D	6. D	10. A
3. C	7. D	11. C
4. A	8. A	
5. D	9. B	

V (Units 11–15)

2. A: When you were a child, were you able to skate?

was able to

B: Yes. In fact, I once ~~could~~ win a competition in my school.

3. A: Could ~~please you~~ *you please* help me?
   OR *Could you help me, please?*

   B: Sure. What seems to be the problem?

4. A: Would you mind giving me a ride home?

   Not at all. OR *No, I wouldn't.*
   B: ~~Yes, I would~~. When would you like to leave?

5. A: You really ought ∧ *to* update your virus protection.

   B: OK. I'll do it today.

6. A: We ~~would~~ *'d* better hurry, or we'll be late.

   B: Don't worry. We can still get there on time.

7. A: Could I borrow the car tonight?

   B: Sorry, but you ~~couldn't~~ *can't*. I need it myself.

8. A: Do you mind if my friend ~~coming~~ *comes* to the party with me?

   B: Not at all. There's always room for one more!

PART IV

I (Unit 16)

2. have . . . been	7. have . . . won
3. has . . . gotten	8. haven't told
4. 've . . . paid	9. Has . . . come
5. Have . . . written	10. 've had
6. hasn't read	11. Have . . . chosen

II (Unit 16)

2. Since, for	6. Since
3. for	7. since
4. since	8. for
5. for	

III (Units 17 and 18)

2. C	5. B	8. A
3. D	6. C	9. A
4. A	7. B	10. A

IV (Unit 20)

2. D	6. B	10. C
3. A	7. C	11. D
4. D	8. A	
5. C	9. C	

V (Units 16–20)

1. b. saw
2. a. drank (OR 's drunk)
   b. haven't drunk
   c. 've been drinking
3. a. has written
   b. Did . . . write
   c. wrote
4. a. 've been cooking
   b. cooked (OR 've cooked)
   c. 've cooked
5. a. 've been having (OR 've had)
   b. haven't had
   c. 've had
   d. had
   e. didn't have
6. a. looked
   b. 's been looking
   c. Has . . . looked (OR Did . . . look)
   d. looked

VI (Units 16–20)

2. I have been working as a bookkeeper in this company ~~since~~ *for* OR *since four years ago.* four years.

3. I have ~~did~~ *done* a good job.

4. I have already ~~been getting~~ *gotten* a promotion.

5. I ~~has~~ *have* gained a lot of experience in retail sales.

6. In addition, I have ~~took~~ *taken* several accounting courses.

7. Since February my boss ~~like~~ *has liked* my work a lot.

8. She has ~~gave~~ *given* me more and more responsibility.

9. I have already ~~show~~ *shown* my accounting skills.

10. This has been ~~being~~ a very good experience for me.

PART V

I (Unit 21)

1. b. many letters
2. a. it doesn't
3. a. 's
   b. several
   c. computers
4. a. It's
5. a. too much salt
   b. It tastes
6. a. it
7. a. a lot of
   b. many bags
8. a. much
   b. some
9. a. it

II (Unit 21)

2. enough
3. a lot of
4. How much
5. a little
6. a few
7. some
8. How many
9. any
10. much
11. a lot of
12. a few

III (Unit 22)

2. a, a, an
3. the
4. The
5. the, the
6. the
7. an
8. a
9. the, an

IV (Unit 22)

3. the
4. Money
5. Travel, Staying
6. The
7. Vegetables

V (Unit 22)

1. b. some
   c. a
   d. an
   e. The
   f. The
2. a. some
   b. some
   c. the
   d. some
   e. The
   f. the

VI (Units 21 and 22)

2. B
3. C
4. A
5. A
6. C
7. A

PART VI

I (Unit 23)

1. b. cozy
   c. Cheap
   d. perfect
2. a. incredibly
   b. new
   c. hardly
   d. terrific
3. a. good
   b. beautiful
   c. well
   d. obedient
   e. quickly

II (Units 25 and 26)

2. A
3. C
4. A
5. B
6. C
7. D
8. B
9. A
10. C
11. D
12. B
13. D

III (Unit 23)

2. C
3. D
4. B
5. C
6. B
7. A
8. B
9. B
10. C
11. C
12. B

IV (Units 25 and 26)

2. faster, more confused
3. later, sillier
4. harder, more fluently
5. more often, bigger
6. louder, faster
7. more frequently, worse

V (Units 24 and 26)

2. is as large as Apartment 22-G.
3. isn't as far (away) as Tony's pizzeria.
4. is as expensive as Tony's pizza.
5. play (OR are playing OR have played) as well as the Shock.
6. doesn't run as fast as (OR isn't as fast as) Jennifer.

VI (Units 25 and 26)

1. b. longest
   c. hardest
   d. the
   e. of
   f. best
2. a. big
   b. than
   c. much
   d. exciting
   e. Sooner
   f. as

VII (Units 23–26)

I think today has been the ~~bad~~ *worst* day of my life. My car broke down on the expressway during rush hour this morning—~~a~~ *the* busiest time of day. I sat there for an hour waiting for a tow truck. The longer I waited, the ^*more* nervous I became. I was a wreck when I got to work. Of course, this was the day we were closing ^*the* biggest deal of the year. My boss called me five times about one letter. And ^*the* more frequently he called, the worse I typed. My next worry is the repair bill for the car. I hope it isn't as high ^*as* the last time.

I'm going to try to relax now. There's an ~~interested~~ *interesting* movie on cable TV tonight. Jan saw it last week and says it's the ~~better~~ *best* film she's seen in a long time. After the movie, I'll take a ~~hotter~~ *hot* bath and go to bed. I'm looking forward to tomorrow. It can't be as ~~badly~~ *bad* as today!

PART VII

I (Unit 28)
2. to planning
3. for watching
4. about speaking
5. without worrying
6. in learning

II (Unit 31)
2. too messy
3. not cool enough
4. too tough
5. aggressively enough
6. loud enough

III (Units 27 and 30)
2. telling
3. smoking
4. giving up
5. Following
6. to feel
7. To save
8. to read
9. drinking
10. to take
11. eating
12. shopping
13. to reward

IV (Unit 29)
2. It's necessary to join
3. participate enough to meet
4. too busy to call
5. flexible enough for them to have
6. advise them to think about
7. it's important to know about
8. soon enough for them to pay
9. too busy to take
10. encourage you to start

V (Units 27–32)
2. B
3. A
4. C
5. A
6. D
7. C
8. D
9. C
10. C

VI (Units 27–32)
2. to hit
3. having
4. winning
5. playing
6. to become
7. to make
8. becoming
9. doing
10. to go
11. to accept
12. to study
13. studying
14. agreeing
15. answering

VII (Units 27–32)
2. D
3. D
4. B
5. D
6. D
7. B
8. C

PART VIII

I (Units 33–37)
2. b
3. a
4. b
5. a
6. b
7. a
8. a
9. a
10. b
11. b
12. a
13. b
14. b

II (Units 33–37)
2. necessity
3. preference
4. conclusion
5. expectation
6. prohibition
7. future possibility
8. conclusion
9. expectation
10. conclusion
11. necessity
12. prohibition

III (Units 33–37)
2. C
3. D
4. A
5. B
6. B
7. C
8. A
9. B
10. A

IV (Units 33–37)
2. She prefers not to watch science fiction.
3. It must be expensive.
4. She (OR Linda) wasn't supposed to open it in front of him (OR Somchai).
5. He must not be at work today.
6. She (OR Sue) might not like curry.
7. You (OR I) have to arrive at the airport by noon.
8. She (OR His sister) was going to go to his graduation.
9. It couldn't be Carl.
10. It could be very valuable.

V (Units 33–37)

I *'m* supposed to take my road test tomorrow. I'm a little nervous because I heard that there might be a storm. I'd ~~not rather~~ *rather not* drive in the rain! My instructor, John, is supposed to pick me up at 8:00 and drive me to the test area. Then he ~~have~~ *has* to wait for me while I take the test. He ~~doesn't have to~~ *must not OR can't* be in the car with me during the test—it's not allowed. I like John. I don't know much about him. He says he's been driving for more than 40 years, so I guess he *'s* got to be at least 60. He ~~maybe~~ *may be* even older than that.

Well, it's getting late, and I should go to bed. I'd rather ~~watching~~ *watch* some TV, but I ~~hafta~~ *have to* get up early tomorrow.

INDEX

This Index is for the full and split editions. All entries are in the full book. Entries for Volume A of the split edition are in black. Entries for Volume B are in color.

Notes

Notes

Notes

Notes